Your Worldly
Possessions

Your Worldly Possessions

A Complete Guide to
Preserving, Passing On,
and Inheriting Property

Theodore L. Kubicek, J.D.

McGraw-Hill, Inc.

New York   St. Louis   San Francisco   Auckland   Bogotá
Caracas   Lisbon   London   Madrid   Mexico   Milan
Montreal   New Delhi   Paris   San Juan   São Paulo
Singapore   Sydney   Tokyo   Toronto

Library of Congress Cataloging-in-Publication Data

Kubicek, Theodore L., date.
    Your worldly possessions : a complete guide to preserving, passing
on, and inheriting property / Theodore L. Kubicek.
        p.   cm.
    Includes index.
    ISBN 0-07-035838-9 (cl).—ISBN 0-07-035835-4 (pbk.)
    1. Estate planning—United States—Popular works. 2. Inheritance
and succession—United States—Popular works. I. Title.
KF750.Z9K83 1992
346.7305'2—dc20
[347.30652]   92-6826
                                                                  CIP

1 2 3 4 5 6 7 8 9 0 DOC/DOC 9 8 7 6 5 4 3 2

ISBN 0-07-035838-9 {HC}
ISBN 0-07-035835-4 {PBK}

The sponsoring editor for this book was Caroline Carney, the editing supervisor
was Scott Amerman, and the production supervisor was Donald F. Schmidt.
It was set in Palatino by Carol Woolverton, Lexington, Mass.

Printed and bound by R. R. Donnelley & Sons Company.

To Becky and Margaret Kubicek
Two courageous women

Contents

Preface   xv

Part 1. Guide to Lifetime Estate Strategies

1. Benefiting from Proper Estate Planning   3

What Is Estate Planning?   4
The Importance of Developing an Estate Plan   5
The Process of Developing a Plan   5
  Your Own Private Inventory   8
  Why Develop a Plan?   9
  Updating Your Plan   9
The Effect of the Federal Estate Tax   9
Nontax Considerations   10
Use of Life Insurance   11
The Single Person and Estate Planning   11
The Goals of Estate Planning   12
Some Common Questions Answered   13

2. Taking Advantage of Lifetime Gifts   17

Reasons for Making a Lifetime Gift   17
  Using the Gift to Save Income Taxes   18
  Using the Gift to Save Death Taxes   19
  Giving for Reasons Other Than Tax Savings   19
The Federal Gift Tax   20

Gift Splitting   22
The Marriage of the Federal Gift and Estate Taxes   23
Charitable Gifts   24
Gifts to Minors   25
Gifts to Parents   26
State Gift Taxes   26
Summary   27
Some Common Questions Answered   27

3. The Risks and Rewards of Joint Tenancy   **29**

Forms of Co-Ownership   29
   Joint Tenancy   29
   Tenancy in Common   31
   Tenancy by the Entirety   33
   Community Property   34
Use of *Or* or Other Symbols   35
The Popularity of Joint Tenancy   35
Estate Proceedings Upon the Death of a Joint Tenant   36
The "Cheap" Will   37
Advantages of Joint Tenancy   37
Disadvantages of Joint Tenancy   38
"Convenience" Tenancies   40
Severing Joint Tenancy   40
The Uniform Simultaneous Death Statute   41
Summary   42
Some Common Questions Answered   42

4. Harnessing the Power of Attorney   **45**

Choosing Your Attorney   47
The Need for an Accounting   48
Choosing Your Form of Power   49
The Durable Power of Attorney   49
The Difficulties of the Standby Provision   50
The Effect of the Grantor's Death   51
Custodial or Agency Accounts   52
Some Common Questions Answered   54

5. Evaluating Conservatorship   **59**

Distinguishing Between Voluntary and Involuntary
   Conservatorships   60
Notice of the Proceeding   61
Which Conservatorship Is Preferable?   61

The Standby Conservatorship as an Alternative   62
Conservatorships for Minors   63
Effect on the Ward's Competency   63
Qualifications and Duties of a Conservator   64
Proposed Congressional Action   66
Protecting the Veteran   67
Some Common Questions Answered   67

6. **Opting for an Antenuptial Agreement**   **71**

Preservation of the Special Interests   72
What Is the Most Important Requirement?   73
What Are the Terms of the Agreement?   73
Some Provisions That May Fail   74
Postnuptial Agreements   76
Nonmarital Agreements   77
Some Common Questions Answered   77

7. **Everything You Should Know About Wills**   **81**

What Is a Will?   81
The Need for a Will   82
Misconceptions About Wills   83
Will Contests   85
Purposes of a Will   85
    Avoiding Laws of Inheritance   86
    Avoiding Bond Costs   87
    Avoiding Disputes Among Your Heirs   87
Advantages of a Will   87
    Listing Property   88
    Setting Up Testamentary Trusts   89
    Selling Real Property   89
    Avoiding Taxes   90
Form and Wording of Wills   90
What Should *Not* Be In Your Will   91
Considerations in Making Your Will   91
    The Residuary Clause   92
    Your Beneficiaries   94
The Antilapse Statute   96
Pretermitted Children   97
Ademption   98
Abatement   99
Parts of a Will   100
    The Introductory Clause   100
    The Debt Clause   100

Bequests   101
The Residuary Clause   102
Naming of Representative   102
Procedural Clauses   103
Witnessing a Will   103
Holographic Wills   105
Nuncupative Will   105
Effect of Marriage and Divorce (Annulment)   106
The "Simple" Will   106
The Marital Deduction Will   107
Joint, Reciprocal, and Mutual Wills   109
Trying to Protect the Children   112
The Pourover Will   115
Life Estates   116
Keeping Control After Death   117
Miscellaneous Will Clauses   119
Effect of Will on Nonprobate Property   120
The Alien as a Distributee   120
Postwill Treatment   121
Some Common Questions Answered   121

8. Using Trusts Wisely   **129**

What Is a Trust?   129
Reasons for Creating a Trust   130
Naming a Trustee   130
Two Types of Trusts   131
Rule Against Perpetuities   131
Living, or Inter Vivos, Trusts   132
    Revocability of the Trust   132
    Some Purposes of a Living Trust   133
    Charitable Remainder Trusts   133
    The Charitable Lead Trust   136
    The Irrevocable Life Insurance Trust   136
Testamentary Trusts   138
    The Marital Deduction Trust   139
    The Bypass Trust   139
    The QTIP Trust   142
Some Common Questions Answered   144

9. Providing for Disability   **147**

The Legal Pathways   148
    Doing Nothing   149
    Joint Tenancy   150
    Power of Attorney   152

Gifts   153
Trusts   154
Conservatorships   154
Deciding Which Pathway to Use   155
The Importance of Looking Ahead   157
Some Common Questions Answered   158

10. Choosing the Right Fiduciary   **161**

Investment Responsibilities   162
The Costs of a Fiduciary   163
The Special Liability of the Fiduciary   165
Choosing Your Fiduciary   165
The Requisite Qualities of a Fiduciary   167
Use of More Than One Fiduciary   168
Considerations in Requiring Bond   169
The Public Administrator   170
Some Common Questions Answered   170

11. Avoiding Probate   **175**

Understanding the Effect of Nonprobate Property   177
Revocable Living Trusts to Avoid Probate   179
    Kinds of Trusts   179
    Form of the Revocable Trust   180
    Final Steps in Preparation of the Trust   182
    Matters to Be Considered   183
    Advantages of the Trust   184
    Disadvantages of the Trust   185
    Alternatives to Using Trust to Avoid Probate   187
    Precautionary Measures to Take When Using
        the Trust   187
A Final Word About Avoiding Probate   190
Some Common Questions Answered   191

**12. Understanding Living Wills and Health Care
Powers of Attorney**   **195**

Living Wills   196
The Quinlan Case   196
The Cruzan Case   197
The Power of Attorney   197
Some Common Questions Answered   198

Part 2. Guide to Inheritance and Estate Proceedings

13. Dying Without a Will   203

Understanding the Laws of Descent   203
Application of the Inheritance Statutes   204
Escheat   208
Some Common Questions Answered   209

14. Salvaging the Rights of the Surviving Spouse   211

The Common Law Dower   211
Surviving Spouse's Rights When the Decedent Dies
    Testate   212
    Spousal Election   212
    Considerations in Making Election   216
Surviving Spouse's Rights When the Decedent Dies
    Intestate   217
    Interim Support Before the Estate Proceeding Is Closed
    219
    Salvaging the Estate of an Unscrupulous Spouse   221
Some Common Questions Answered   223

15. Minimizing Estate Proceedings   227

Preliminary Procedures   228
Probate Procedure Versus Administration   230
Probate Property Versus Nonprobate Property   230
Determining the Right Estate Proceeding to Use   231
Four Types of Proceedings   232
    The Affidavit   232
    The Short Form of Estate Proceeding   234
    Administration Proceedings   237
    Informal, Small-Estate Administration   249
Real Estate in Probate Administration   250
The Safe Deposit Box   251
Some Common Questions Answered   252

16. Understanding Death Taxes   257

State Death Taxes   257
    Kinds of Property Interests Taxed   258
    Deductions Allowable to Determine Taxable Estate   259
    The Pick-Up Tax   260
Federal Estate Tax   261
    The Spouse's Deduction   261

The Estate's Exemption   263
Determining the Gross Estate   263
The Importance of Elections   264
The Alternate Valuation Date   265
Special Use   265
The QTIP Trust and the Power-of-Appointment
   Trust   266
Generation Skipping Transfer Tax   267
Apportionment of Death Taxes   270
Some Common Questions Answered   271

17. Post-Mortem Estate Planning   275

Decedent's Planned Post-Mortem Opportunities   276
   Disclaimers   276
   The QTIP Trust   278
Decedent's Unplanned Post-Mortem Opportunities   279
   Income Tax Strategies   279
   Administration Expenses   281
   Fiduciary Fees   281
   Alternate Valuation Date   282
   Widow's or Widower's Allowance   282
   Choosing the Taxable Year   283
   Widow's or Widower's Election   285
   Will Contest   286
   Family Agreement   286
   Failure of Probate Property   286
   Special Use Valuation   287
   Estate Tax Payment Deferral   287
Some Common Questions Answered   289

18. Working With an Estate Attorney   293

Choosing Your Estate Attorney   294
Potential Conflicts of Interest   295
   Conflicts With the Married Couple   295
   Conflicts With the Estate Administration   296
   Conflicts With the Conservatorship   296

Glossary   297
Index   311

Preface

Everybody possesses an estate. All property that you own or have an interest in constitutes your estate. Your clothes, your car, your checking account, anything that you claim as yours—and which in fact is yours—is part of your estate. By using this book as a guide, you will realize that your estate, regardless of its size, requires your attention.

Why should you be concerned about your estate? Most likely your possessions have been accumulated by hard work. Presumably, then, you want to protect your property and be able to pass it on to whom you please. Except through pure luck, you can't do this unless you have some knowledge of the laws pertaining to your property.

This book gives you that knowledge. It discusses most of the estate situations you will experience. Use it to determine the legal aspects—the consequences and pitfalls—of owning and preserving your estate, whatever its size and content. You will then know what you must consider during your lifetime and what legally may have to be done upon your death or incompetency.

This book will alert you to possible legal problems with estates and will suggest how such problems can be avoided. Its goal is to keep you from inadvertently doing something, or failing to do something, that would adversely affect your estate. By referring to the book, you will gain knowledge about your property, understand what actions are needed to protect it, and realize when you should consult a lawyer.

You may want to either read this book from cover to cover or use it as a reference book in the event you have a particular estate problem. Begin by browsing through the book, paying attention to the table of contents, so that you have a clear understanding of the book's contents and benefits to you. Later, you can refer to either the table of contents or index to find information addressing an inquiry.

A note of caution: Exceptions abound in the law. What may be true in one state may not be true everywhere or in every situation. Even the so-called uniform acts are frequently dismantled by the states. So you should take the precaution of consulting your attorney with regard to important estate decisions.

I could not have written this book if I had not listened to many individuals over the years. Some were speakers at seminars and forums. Some were my students at Kirkwood Community College. And some were my clients who asked many of the questions and made some of the mistakes presented in this book. Each contributed in their own way, no doubt unwittingly so. My thanks to all of you.

I also thank the Cedar Rapids law firm of Simmons, Perrine, Albright & Ellwood, which kindly allowed me the use of its most respectable library. And, lastly, I thank Kathie Belgum, Executive Law Librarian of the great law library of the College of Law, University of Iowa, for her gracious help.

May this book benefit your understanding and protection of your estate.

Theodore L. Kubicek

PART 1

Guide to Lifetime Estate Strategies

1
Benefiting from Proper Estate Planning

Your estate consists of all property or interests in property that you own or hold at any particular time. Undoubtedly, you carefully guard this property from fire and theft. But have you considered what could happen to your estate without proper planning?

You cannot properly take care of your estate if you are not aware of what it is. Some people foolishly think that their wealth is measured by their income. While income is important in accumulating your estate, it is of no consequence unless it becomes a permanent part of your estate. Contrary to popular belief, your wealth is measured by your net worth, not by what you earn or spend. Appearances are of no importance in determining the extent of your estate.

In probate codes, that is, state statutes that deal with such things as wills, inheritance, conservatorships, and administration of estates, an estate is thought of as property administered by a third party. For example, one state probate code defines an estate as follows:

> The real and personal property of a decedent, a ward, or a trust, as from time to time changed in form by sale, reinvestment or otherwise, and augmented by any accretions or additions thereto and substitutions therefore, or diminished by any decreases and distributions therefrom.

This code defines your own estate, as well as the estate of a decedent, a conservatorship, or a trust. Your estate is like a pulsating heart: It expands (accrues) and contracts (diminishes) as property is received (additions) and paid out (distributions). Thus your estate is constantly changing. This normal ebb and flow of property should not concern you, if you have properly planned your estate affairs.

What Is Estate Planning?

One definition of estate planning is "the process of creating and implementing a program or plan for the protection and transfer of property." Notice that this definition covers your lifetime (protection) as well as the time of your death (transfer).

Estate planning is not only for the wealthy, despite what estate planners might think. Regardless of who you are, or what you own, your property should be important to you. You should try to protect what you own for your own benefit and for the benefit of your heirs and beneficiaries to whom the property can be passed on intact.

Estate planning can help almost anyone, regardless of marital status or wealth. In its broadest sense, "estate planning" refers to any legal procedure that will protect and distribute an individual's property. A good plan, to be modified from time to time, is concerned with the holding of the property during your lifetime, the managing of it during your incapacity, and the disposing of it at the time of your death.

Estate planning covers a broad area. How title to your property is held, powers of attorney, gifts, prenuptial agreements, conservatorships, wills, trusts, death taxes, and probate procedures, all have a bearing on your estate. One or more of these categories will apply to you for your entire lifetime.

Planning your estate is a never-ending endeavor. Even a good plan can end badly if you fail to constantly attend to your estate, particularly after your will is made.

You may dislike doing so, but you should attend to your estate from time to time, just as you periodically take stock of your health, your home, or your car. Here are some, but by no means all, of the things you should consider:

What is the nature of your property? Is it the kind of property that could cause difficulty for you as you grow older, or for your heirs and beneficiaries upon your death? Where is your property located? If your estate is located in more than one state, have you thought of the possible undesirable consequences of multistate ownership of property upon your death, especially if it has not been planned for?

Have you provided for the disposition of your property upon your death and, if so, are you keeping these provisions up to date? In other words, if you have a will, do you review it from time to time? Does your will cover all property you now and may later own? Does it include all and only those persons whom you wish to favor? Have you considered that changes in the law might adversely affect your will?

Will you always be in a position to properly manage your property? If not, have you provided for its management? Have you considered standby provisions in the event of your future physical or mental incapacity?

If you are contemplating remarriage, do you have children by a previous marriage or certain property that you wish to protect?

The above items may not necessarily apply to you right now. However, you should be aware of them when planning your own estate. A failure to do so could cause you or your heirs unnecessary grief.

The Importance of Developing an Estate Plan

There are many ways that you can improperly plan your estate; for example,

You might take title to your property in the wrong manner.

You might fail to plan for death taxes.

Your estate might be left unattended because of unforeseen incompetency or other disability.

You might even remarry without proper safeguards.

Or your estate might even decrease because of a catastrophic illness in the family.

To avoid such adversities, you should plan your estate with care. Your objectives should be to preserve your estate, make valid transfers both during your lifetime and at the time of your death, minimize taxes (primarily death taxes), designate and protect your successors in interest, and see that your estate is properly managed.

Interest in one's estate seems to increase in direct proportion to one's age. Many people do not consciously plan their estate until they marry, have children, accumulate a sizable estate, or start planning for their retirement. You will soon see why waiting for these events may be too late.

The Process of Developing a Plan

Estate planning probably will begin when you first consult a lawyer about your will. He or she will suggest that you take stock of your possessions.

This means making an inventory of your estate, listing and valuing your assets, and showing how title is held. Your attorney needs this information to make your will and give you other planning advice.

Even if your attorney knows you well, she or he will not begin to prepare your will until three kinds of information have been obtained from you:

1. *Your family and personal status.* Your attorney will want to know if there is a family problem or disability so that it can be accommodated in your will. For example, suppose an incompetency exists. If the disability were not provided for, upon your death a third party (a conservator) would have to be appointed for the incompetent person before the bequeathed property could be transferred by the personal representative to such beneficiary. Had you planned for this disability, a testamentary trust, a legal procedure considerably simpler and less costly than a conservatorship, could have been used. Or, perhaps, because of the eligibility rules for public benefits, you might have deemed it wiser to leave nothing to the beneficiary.

2. *Your objectives.* No plan is satisfactory unless it conforms as closely as possible to your desires. Yet, after discussing your objectives with your lawyer, you may be quite willing to modify your goals if something were to be gained by doing so. Two ways exist to obtain this information: (1) the client could state his or her objectives first, or (2) the lawyer could state first what would be best for the client. Lawyers disagree as to which is the most effective method. If your attorney does believe in making suggestions first, then a third kind of information, listed below, would have to be obtained first.

3. *An accurate listing of all the property interests that make up your total estate.* You should fully and frankly disclose everything you own or have an interest in. Why do you have to itemize? Without your doing so, your lawyer would be forced to talk to you in generalities, not being able to give you specific information about your estate, and not being able to provide you with the best estate plan possible. While a general discussion might be informative, it would not be particularly helpful.

Each of your assets must be listed separately, except household items, unless they are of extraordinary value. "Assets" covers everything having a monetary value such as life insurance (cash value, not face value) and pension plans. "Value" is the market value, not the value you may like it to be.

The list should properly include three things:

1. *Identification of each item of your property.* Some general categories are real estate, bank accounts, corporate stock, notes and bonds, cars, household items—especially valuable antiques and art work, life insur-

ance and, if you are a farmer or rancher, your livestock, grain, and machinery, or if you are a business proprietor, your business assets.

2. *The value of each listed item.* This value should be what the item is worth to others, not to you—in other words its "market value." The total value of your estate is needed to determine what taxes your estate may be subject to upon your death. If a federal estate tax might have to be paid, your lawyer should suggest the form and content of your will. By taking certain precautions, it is always possible to avoid or reduce the tax.

3. *The way in which title to each listed item is held.* Are you the sole title-holder or is the property owned jointly by you with someone else? If the property is co-owned, who is that co-owner? Is it your spouse or another person, or is it a combination of several persons—a "joint ownership"? Is the joint owner favored over others equally loved by you? It is important that you hold title to property consistent with the provisions of your will. Otherwise, your will might not be completely effective in accomplishing your objectives.

The manner in which you set up your inventory depends, in part, on the purpose for which you are making up a will. Your attorney needs to know the total value of your estate, including life insurance owned by you on your life (since it is considered an asset for federal estate tax purposes).

Your attorney will also want to know how title to all your property is held. Proof may be required. Be prepared to bring in your title documents, such as your deed to your home, for examination.

For the first estate planning conference, you may be asked to bring in a complete inventory on a form furnished by your attorney. In its simplest form it may look something like this:

List asset	Husband	Wife	Joint
Real estate	$	$	$
Home			
Farm			
Other			
Stocks and bonds			
Cash and savings			
Life insurance			
Household and personal			
Pension plans			
Miscellaneous			
Totals			

The net value of each asset would be placed under the appropriate column. If title to your home was held jointly by you and your spouse and it had a market value of $60,000 with $20,000 left on the mortgage, then under the column labeled "Joint" the figure $40,000 would be placed. By adding up the totals at the bottom, your net worth (total assets) could be determined.

A more detailed inventory might be desired by your attorney. But if the value of your estate is substantially less than $600,000, your attorney would be more interested in how you hold title to each asset, rather than in its particular value.

When all of this information has been gathered, your lawyer is ready to prepare your will.

Your Own Private Inventory

For your own purposes, you should keep a more detailed inventory than what you supply your attorney. For instance, for each category on the attorney's inventory form, you could make up a separate page listing all individual assets applying to it. Thus all real estate would be listed on one page, all stocks and bonds on another page, and so on. The inventory can be entered either on a computer program or on fourteen-column accounting paper. The first column should identify the asset, and each subsequent column should be used for the ensuing year. In setting up your inventory this way, the asset does not need to be relisted year after year. Under the year and opposite the listed asset would be shown the value at the end of that year. One sheet might look something like this:

Stocks, Bonds, and Notes				
Asset	1990	1991	1992	1993
ABC Co., RG1274	$1875	$1890		
U.S. Bond, M1234567HH	1000	1000		
John Smith Note	866	255		

Your inventory should be made annually on the same date. The end of the year is the preferred time since some of this information, such as for pension plans, is only available to you at this time. Consistency gives you continuity and informs you of your progress in accumulating an estate.

In doing this, you may be surprised at how much you are actually worth. And by doing this annually, you will realize that planning and maintaining your estate is of some importance after all.

Why Develop a Plan?

Without continuous, proper planning, your estate could decrease in value during your lifetime, in which event you might suffer adversity or your spouse, children, or other heirs could be deprived of the property you intend for them. And without giving this attention to your estate, you might have difficulty determining when additional planning is required.

Updating Your Plan

From time to time you may want to do certain anticipatory planning. But when you, your estate, or your intended beneficiaries change, then you should review your estate situation to determine whether such change affects your existing estate plan. If so, you should update your plan.

Whenever you do anything that affects your possessions, your actions should be consistent with your estate plan. Otherwise, you might end up with an estate that is a hodgepodge, which will not be to your best advantage.

The Effect of the Federal Estate Tax

Originally, estate planning was primarily limited to preparing one's will. When other needs for estate handling arose, they were dealt with as they occurred. But other considerations (such as the high federal estate tax rate) have compelled estate planners to broaden the concept of estate planning.

Because of the high federal estate tax rate, most professionals concentrate on how to avoid, or at least minimize, the tax through proper estate planning.

The federal estate tax is a death tax. It is assessed against the estate of a decedent if the decedent's net estate is large enough to exceed the exemption and all credits. Since the inception of the federal estate tax statute, every estate has had an exemption, which over the years has increased to its present amount of $600,000. If the taxable estate of the decedent is below the exemption, then there is no tax, even though a lengthy federal estate tax return (35 pages with 22 pages of instructions) may have to be filed to prove it. If the taxable estate exceeds the exemption, then a tax, starting for all practical purposes at a 37 percent rate, may result.

A married couple has an edge because each partner receives an exemption of $600,000, for a total exemption of $1,200,000 for the two. In order to protect this full amount from any federal estate tax, the couple's estates must be carefully planned as explained in Chapters 7 and 16.

Nontax Considerations

If you are single or never expect to have an estate of $600,000 or more, then you probably think, mistakenly, that estate planning would be fruitless. However, even if you own only a small amount of property, you must think in terms of where that property will go upon your death. If you have no will—an estate planning procedure—your state will determine where your property will go. Is this what you want?

You must consider how your estate is managed during your lifetime as well. How is title held to your bank account and car? Are other persons also joined with you in the titles? Who, if anybody, do you want to have some control over your property while you are competent to handle it yourself?

These are only some of the questions that your attorney might raise if you sought advice on estate planning. Some others are

Are you married?

Do you have children?

If not, who are your heirs?

Who do you want your property to go to?

What is your age and health?

Are you able to manage your property?

Do you want to manage it?

What are your possibilities of inheriting property?

Estate planning must take into account answers to all these, and other, questions.

Many factors affect the size, quality, value, and content of your estate: inflation and the economy, tax laws, the size and makeup of your family, marriage and divorce, employment, and lifestyle. Any of these factors may be reason for you to plan and maintain your estate.

Aside from the usual considerations when attending to one's estate (see pages 4–5), there may be special family situations to consider. Think about the following:

Concerning the children in your family, were they born to you, legally adopted by you, or are they your stepchildren?

Do the facts about your children apply to both you and your spouse or to only one of you?

Is this your first or a subsequent marriage?

If the latter, did you make any arrangements as to your property or as to your children prior to this latest marriage?

Is there, or could there be, discord among your family members?

Is this a situation that you should resolve prior to your death?

Is there any incompetency or lack of business acumen in your family?

Are these problems being resolved by you, now, before your death?

Use of Life Insurance

If your estate is small, you may not have to worry about defraying costs of a federal estate tax or a minimal state death tax through the purchase of life insurance.

Except for unusual circumstances, your incentive to purchase life insurance will be for the protection of close family members. Such protection may be for the payment of debts or for family support, or both. As your debts decrease, your estate size increases, and family members leave the nest, your incentive for such insurance protection probably decreases.

But if your estate begins to exceed the $600,000 federal estate tax exemption, or if the nature of your property poses certain liquidity problems, then you will need to think of obtaining life insurance. Now your incentive for the insurance may be to provide a means for payment of death taxes. Or perhaps business reasons provide the incentive or require such insurance, although in this situation the insurance may actually be held by a third party.

You may find that it is not advantageous to own life insurance on your own life, since upon your death the insurance proceeds would be included in your estate for federal estate tax purposes, and possibly for state death taxes as well. If the life insurance is considered an asset for taxing purposes, its presence in the estate actually increases the tax liability, a no-win situation, since the more insurance, the greater the liability.

If you as the insured are married,·a solution is for the ownership of the policy to be in the name of your spouse. But the Internal Revenue Code is clear that upon your death, you cannot have possessed any incidents of ownership. Such incidents include, among other things, the power to change the beneficiary and the paying of premiums.

The Single Person and Estate Planning

If you are single—here defined as "not presently married"—you still may not be convinced that estate planning is of much value for you. If you have an estate of over $600,000, then you are at a disadvantage compared with a married couple with a combined estate of between $600,000 and $1,200,000. Other than this discrepancy in monetary exemptions, both of your opportunities and problems are much the same; they are almost exactly the same if your estates are under $600,000.

As a single person, what might be your estate concerns?

You might wish to see that family members—parents, siblings, and children or other descendants—are provided for, either during your life or upon your death.

At some stage in your life you should be concerned not only about the disposition of your estate but also about the management of your estate in the event you are unable to care for it yourself. In other words, like married persons, you have or should have lifetime estate concerns as well as estate concerns upon your death.

The one thing that distinguishes you from the married couple with a $600,000 to $1,200,000 estate is that the couple in that bracket can take steps to totally eliminate the federal estate tax. You might feel frustrated because estate planning books stress the couple's situation and how they can avoid the tax. Thus, it may seem to you, the single person's situation is ignored or, even worse, that the single person has nothing to gain by estate planning.

The former may be true but not the latter. You will be able to do your own estate planning, if you can accept the fact that you do not have the same ability under the law to avoid the federal estate tax if your estate exceeds $600,000. Perhaps this will be easier for you to accept if you realize that with the married couple each partner is merely claiming his or her own $600,000 exemption, the same as you.

Except for the few estate concerns that affect only a married couple, your estate planning is much the same as the married couple's. You want control of your property while you are competent to manage it, you want to make your choice of agent if you are incapable of managing it, and you want to dictate how your property is to be distributed upon your death.

The Goals of Estate Planning

Estate planners usually concentrate on two goals: (1) the safeguarding of assets for the benefit of the individual, and (2) the preservation of assets for the benefit of the heirs and beneficiaries. A third goal ought to rank equally with the first two goals: doing what makes the client most comfortable.

Many professionals become fascinated with schemes to avoid death taxes and sometimes other estate procedures, such as probate. While their aims are noble, their clients often are left bewildered and uncertain as to what is happening, thus becoming uncomfortable with the recommended strategies.

Complicated estate planning may not be all that beneficial to you. The legal work in setting up an intricate plan often costs as much or more than what might be saved. Additionally, many such plans are somewhat risky, especially if created incorrectly or acted upon improperly or if not carefully maintained. And, what cannot be said often enough, your peace of mind is worth something.

You should remember this when taking any steps in relation to your estate. If you don't understand the legalities, then think twice before adopting a plan that makes you uncomfortable and is only nominally beneficial.

Some Common Questions Answered

Q. When lawyers and life insurance agents talk about estate planning, are they talking about the same thing?

A. Yes, to a certain extent. The insurance agent would be concerned chiefly with the investments and insurance sold to you, while the lawyer is more concerned with such things as prenuptial agreements, gifts, the manner in which you hold title to property, and so on.

Certainly the growth and protection of your estate through purchase of investments and insurance involves estate planning. Insurance, or something akin to it, is one method of protection. Lawyers cannot claim estate planning as their sole domain, but the lawyer's use of the term generally has a much broader meaning than an insurance agent's.

Q. If I plan to move to another state, should I wait to do my estate planning until after I move?

A. No, since death, for instance, could occur before you move. An untimely death without proper planning might result in unnecessary legal proceedings, possibly causing your property not to be distributed as you might have wished. If you consult a lawyer now, you might not need to duplicate your efforts later. A properly drawn will should carry over into your new state of residence. And your lawyer can recommend how you should hold your property, something that will apply in your new state.

Q. How often do I need to review my estate plan?

A. Few things remain constant. Wills become outmoded, families change, estate holdings change, and people have a tendency not to follow, or even remember, past instructions. A periodic review of your estate plan by your lawyer is the only safe procedure, unless you feel—and are competent—to do so yourself. A specified time period cannot be given. Five years, for instance, may be too long or too short a period.

Q. I would like to talk to a lawyer about my estate, but it costs money to talk to a lawyer. Is estate planning worth the cost?

A. If you take out fire insurance on your home, but never have a fire, are the annual insurance premiums worth it? By the same token, think of estate planning as insurance to protect your estate. In one way estate planning has an advantage over insurance. Unlike your annual insurance premiums, your estate planning costs are a one-shot expense, or at least sporadic and infrequent. Although it is difficult for some people to understand, it is as important to protect your estate through proper estate planning as it is to protect your house from loss by fire. Remember, your house is only part of your estate.

Perhaps one more comment is appropriate. You may never have a fire, but it is certain that at some point the matter of your estate and how well you handled it will become important. It may even become an issue before your death if you become incompetent.

Q. How can I keep my estate plan in shape if things constantly change?

A. Actually, unless you have a major change of circumstances, your will should not need changing, since it would already anticipate normal changes. Also, when you drew up your will, your lawyer should have given you instructions about taking and holding title. Following these instructions should not require further services of your attorney, especially if your attorney followed up your estate planning with an explanatory letter.

Q. What might be considered a major change of circumstances?

A. A drastic change in your net worth, or sudden incompetency of a beneficiary, or children telling you that they no longer want to take over the family property, or a remarriage—these would be changes that could not be anticipated.

Q. In estate planning, is one thing more important than another?

A. Not really. Estate plans can be formulated only after every element is considered. Can you imagine a lawyer developing your plan without knowing who your heirs are or the extent of your assets or what you want to accomplish?

Other things are important too. How is title to your property held and where is it located? Are your intended beneficiaries competent and can you trust them to manage their inheritance properly?

Would they be compatible if you leave them common property, such as a farm? Is this your first marriage? Do you have children born out of wedlock? Are any of your children adopted?

Q. Will a lawyer tell me how much it costs to do estate planning?

A. It is difficult for lawyers to set a price, although, if pressed, they will try to do so. But a lawyer will need to know something about you.

The lawyer will give you an hourly rate and, if pressed, may give you a maximum figure. But, human nature being what it is, that figure may well be what it ends up being.

The difficulty experienced by lawyers in estimating an amount is that the client frequently takes advantage of a "locked in" figure and asks for (and expects) more than what was bargained for. This is the other side of the human nature coin.

Q. How much time does it take to do estate planning?

A. The time varies because many things bear on the time. What is your estate size? Do certain beneficiaries need protection? What do you hope to accomplish? How well have you prepared for your initial meeting with your attorney?

Many commentators on estate planning dwell on large estates, making it sound as if months of hard work is involved. They talk about sending you several rough drafts of the proposed documents. They think in terms of team effort. You, the lawyer, an accountant, a financial advisor, and your life insurance agent make up the team. For most estate planning work, the team concept is unnecessary and could be financially disastrous.

2

Taking Advantage of Lifetime Gifts

One estate planning technique that may be beneficial to everyone is the gift. In general, two types of gifts exist: (1) a testamentary gift, which in a will is called a bequest, devise, or legacy, and (2) an inter vivos gift, usually called a lifetime or living gift, because it is made and takes effect during one's lifetime.

This chapter is concerned with the latter type: the typical, outright gift of money or other property made by one living person, known as the "donor," to another living person, known as the "donee." For estate planning purposes, a single gift may suffice or a program of many gifts to one or more individuals may be in order. There may be other reasons, discussed later, for giving lifetime gifts.

Later chapters discuss other types of gifts. Chapter 3 discusses joint tenancy, which oftentimes is one form of a gift. Chapter 7 discusses testamentary gifts, and Chapter 8, on trusts, deals with gifts but in an entirely different context.

Reasons for Making a Lifetime Gift

For estate planning purposes, a lifetime gift is made for any number of reasons. For instance, you may want to save income taxes by eliminating income-producing assets. Or you may want to save death taxes by reducing the size (value) of your estate. Or you may want to save administration expenses by shrinking your estate.

Using the Gift to Save
Income Taxes

For the purpose of saving income taxes you should carefully consider the kind of property you give away. Most property—including cash, since it can generate interest—is income-producing. But some property may be a better choice to give away than others.

For example, consider the type of property known as a capital asset. Because the Internal Revenue Code defines a capital asset in negative terms—what it isn't rather than what it is—it is impossible to define it. As a result, if you are contemplating giving property other than cash, then you should seek advice as to the nature of the property.

Capital assets have a basis, or value, which the property owner must use to determine capital gain or loss for income tax purposes at the time the property is sold. For instance, suppose that you purchased rental property for $50,000. If you ignore adjustments such as for improvements and depreciation, your basis is $50,000. If you sold this property for $70,000, again ignoring certain adjustments, your gain would be $20,000.

A donee of a living gift is required to keep the same basis that the donor had. Thus if you gave the rental property away during your lifetime, the basis of the property in the hands of the donee would also be $50,000. But if you waited to give the property to the donee at the time of your death (a testamentary gift), then the donee's basis would be the property's market value at the time of your death, a figure presumably higher. This is called the *stepped-up basis*, because the basis has increased (stepped-up) since the time the original owner bought it.

The caveat, then, is that rarely is it advisable to give appreciated property during your lifetime. Let it go at death, rather than during your lifetime. Another caveat is to not give away property that has a loss, since under the rules only a donor can take a loss. Suppose, for instance, that you gave away property that had a basis of $20,000, which at the time of the gift had a fair market value of $15,000. The basis of the property in the hands of the donee would be $15,000, not $20,000. If you had sold the property for $15,000, you could have taken a $5000 loss. Since you gave the property away, you have lost this opportunity. If the donee sells the property for $15,000, he or she has neither a gain nor a loss. But if the donee sells the property for $10,000, then the donee has a loss of $5000.

The ideal gift just may be cash. On the other hand, if you as a donor own property that is expected to appreciate in value later on, then you may want to consider giving it as a gift. By doing so, you will have reduced your gross estate at the time of your death by the value of the appreciated gift. Before you do so, you may want to consider the tax consequences that such a substantial gift may have on the part of the donee.

In summary, if property in the hands of a prospective donor has a low basis in relation to its present market value, then it usually is not a good idea for such donor to consider that particular property for a lifetime gift. A better alternative would be to give away property which is not a capital asset or at least which has a basis closer to its present market value.

The basis for the donee is either the donor's basis or the market value of the property at the time of the gift, whichever is lower. Thus, if you plan to make a gift of property other than cash, you should first seek the guidance of your lawyer or tax consultant. She or he can help you in filing the federal gift tax return, IRS form 709, which is required by the IRS for gifts totaling more than $10,000 in current market value (not basis) made to any one person in any one year.

Using the Gift to Save Death Taxes

The main estate tax concern of a married couple is that each spouse has sufficient property in his or her own name so that upon death the other partner can take full advantage of the lifetime $600,000 federal exemption. This may necessitate the transferring (giving) of property by one spouse to the other.

For example, suppose the total estate of a couple is $700,000, all of which is in the name of the husband. If the wife died first, no federal estate tax would be paid because she had no property. But upon the subsequent death of the husband, since his estate exceeded the $600,000 exemption by $100,000, his estate would pay a federal estate tax of $37,000. In other words, the $600,000 exemption which the wife also had (but couldn't use because she had no property) would be lost.

If the husband had given his wife at least $100,000 of his estate before she died, that property, upon her death, could have been sheltered by a trust from the federal estate tax. (See the discussion of testamentary trusts in Chapter 8.) If these two things—the gift and the trust—had been done, neither estate would have paid a tax.

The goal of couples having a combined estate of more than $600,000 should be for each spouse to utilize his or her individual lifetime exemptions so that the total federal estate tax is reduced to either zero or its lowest possible amount. To reach this goal, you and your spouse may be required to periodically transfer property to one another. Often the best plan is for each spouse to own roughly one-half of the total combined estate.

Giving for Reasons Other Than Tax Savings

Many reasons other than tax considerations can exist for making a gift. Among them are the following:

You may want to escape the management of the property, such as rental property.

A lifetime gift might provide more privacy than a testamentary gift, so you may not want to wait until your death to give certain property away.

You may want to avoid the possibility of creditors taking your property.

You may wish to favor one person over another, perhaps secretly, by making that person a gift.

Since administration costs upon your death are often based upon the size of your estate, you may wish to reduce the size of your estate by giving.

You may experience a certain satisfaction in making a gift.

You may be seeking political gain, such as acquiring a favor or advantage, in making a gift.

You may truly have an altruistic purpose in making a gift: "I don't need it as much as she (or he) does."

Lawyers often are concerned about a client's motive in wanting to make a particular gift, especially when good estate planning does not suggest such a gift or when the subsequent reduced size of the donor's estate could place the donor's comfort and support in jeopardy. Thus, it is advisable not to bring a "tag-along"—especially someone who may have a personal interest in a gift being made—to a session with your lawyer.

Whatever reason you may have for making a gift, you should make sure that it does not endanger your own welfare. If the gift is substantial in relation to the size of your estate, then before making the gift you should consult your lawyer. This precaution may save you from being overly generous, or from being influenced by others whose motives may be less than honorable or whose concerns may not be for your welfare.

The Federal Gift Tax

Under the Internal Revenue Code, you may give up to $10,000 annually to each of as many persons as you wish without incurring any gift tax liability. Only gifts of property are subject to the federal gift tax. Services are not considered property, and thus gifts of services are not subject to the tax.

To qualify for the annual $10,000 exclusion, the gift must be for present use, possession, or enjoyment ("present interest") and not of a future interest. Future interests—most commonly found in trusts—commence in use, possession, or enjoyment at some future time.

One example of a gift of a future interest occurs in the granting of a *remainder interest* in a life estate, which can be illustrated as follows: Suppose you grant a life estate in certain property to person A, with the remainder (or the full title) going to person B upon A's death. The gift to B is of a remainder interest, which is deemed a future interest. Thus the $10,000 exclusion does not apply to B. It would apply to A, as A's gift is of a present interest.

If the total value of gifts made to any one person in any one year exceeds $10,000, then you are required to file a gift tax return, form 709. This form must be filed with the IRS on or before April 15 of the year following the gift, even though no gift tax is due. Until your lifetime exemption of $600,000 is exhausted, these returns merely serve as an IRS record of your "excessive" gifts.

What has been said here about the $10,000 annual exclusion does not apply to gifts between spouses. If the donee spouse is a citizen of the United States, then there is no limit on the size or time of the gift. Each spouse has an unlimited marital deduction and thus can receive any amount at any time from the other spouse. For this reason, no gift tax return is required for interspousal gifts, regardless of the amount.

If the spouse is not a citizen of the United States, then the unlimited marital deduction does not apply. Instead, the noncitizen spouse may receive up to $100,000 per year. In other words, the sum of $100,000 is substituted for the normal $10,000 annual exclusion that applies to nonspouses and for the unlimited amount that applies to citizen spouses. To the extent that the gift exceeds $100,000, the normal rules apply regarding the gift tax filing requirements and the applicability of the $600,000 lifetime exemption.

Since 1981, at least, the timing of most—but not all—gifts is unimportant. Previously, all gifts made within three years of death were required to be added back to the deceased person's estate for purposes of determining federal estate tax liability. Under the present law, some incentive may exist for depleting one's estate by making so-called deathbed transfers as long as such gifts do not fall within certain limited exceptions.

This last-minute giving could enable you to hold onto those parts of your estate deemed necessary for your lifetime support until the last possible moment. However, the timing of your deathbed transfers may be tricky. You must use care not to adversely affect your will plans, unless you have time to change your will. In this latter instance, it may be better just to let your will do the giving. And, of course, last-minute giving often is suspect for a number of reasons.

The federal government is continually casting about for additional revenues. In recent years, for instance, the U.S. Treasury Department has suggested that no donor be allowed to give away a total of more than $30,000 in any one year, regardless of the number of donees. Presumably this limitation would be for the purpose of subjecting large estates to a greater federal estate tax upon the death of the donor. No doubt other changes in the gift tax law are continually under consideration. So if you are contemplating making gifts for the purpose of reducing the size of your estate, you may want to consult your lawyer. Perhaps she or he can help you to accelerate your present gift program.

Gift Splitting

If you are married and your spouse consents to giving specific gifts, then the annual amount that can be given to each person is $20,000, rather than $10,000. This is called gift splitting. IRS form 709 must be filed to show the consent.

Gift splitting doesn't mean that each of you, by consenting to the other's gift, can give $20,000 to the same individual in the same year. According to the IRS, the spouse consenting is charged with the $10,000 to which he or she gave consent. By giving two individual gifts of $20,000 annually, you would both have to file IRS form 709, since each of you would have exceeded the $10,000 limit for any one person in any one year.

In order to take advantage of gift splitting, both spouses at the time of the gift must be either citizens or residents of the United States. The spouses must be married to each other and they cannot remarry during the remainder of the calendar year. And, in order for the consent to be valid, the consent must be timely filed and it must show on the first return filed by either spouse.

To illustrate gift splitting, suppose that you and your spouse desire to give the maximum available amount annually to your four children, three of whom are married, and perhaps to the three in-laws as well.

If you limit the gifts to your four children, then the total maximum amount which the two of you can give annually is $80,000 ($20,000 to each child), split between your respective estates in any manner you wish. As long as proper consents are given, the full $80,000 can come out of one of your estates, or $40,000 can come out of each of your estates, or any combination in between, again with proper consents.

If you want to include the three in-laws, then add another $20,000 per in-law, or another $60,000, making a grand total of $140,000 that can be given annually.

But you may not want to give the maximum, if it means also giving to your in-laws, for two reasons, both of which could be important to you. First, this would result in some inequality in giving, because one of your children is not married. The single child would be receiving $20,000 while the married couples would each be receiving $40,000.

Secondly, possibly one of the in-laws may not be deserving or one of the marriages may be unstable. If a subsequent divorce occurred, you might want your child to claim all of the gifted property, which could not be done if part of the gift went to the in-law. And would you want to favor two of the in-laws and not the other? Family peace may be more important to you than saving some taxes by reducing your estate.

The Marriage of the Federal Gift and Estate Taxes

Earlier it was stated that a relationship exists between the federal estate tax and a lifetime gift. This is because the same lifetime exemption of $600,000 applies to both lifetime gifts and testamentary gifts. It does not apply to each of them separately. That part of the $600,000 exemption which you do not use during your lifetime to reduce or avoid a gift tax is available at the time of your death to avoid or at least reduce your federal estate tax.

That portion of your annual gifts to any one person which exceeds the annual exclusion of $10,000—or $20,000 if your spouse consents to the gift—is deducted from your lifetime federal estate tax exemption of $600,000. Until all of the $600,000 is used up, no gift tax is payable.

Your gift tax returns are used by the IRS to keep track of that portion of your $600,000 which remains at the time of your death. Whatever is left is available to offset any federal estate tax which you might otherwise owe. This, then, shows the close relationship between the lifetime gift tax and the federal estate tax. Because the same exemption is used to offset both taxes, the exemption is referred to in the law as the *unified credit*. The two gift taxes, the lifetime and the testamentary, are unified into one tax.

If during your lifetime you made no gift exceeding the $10,000 ceiling (or $20,000 if your spouse joins by consenting), then your lifetime exemption of $600,000 remains intact for your personal representative's use in reducing or eliminating any federal estate tax your estate might owe at the time of your death. But if you used $100,000 of the exemption during your lifetime (because you exceeded the $10,000 limit by a total of that amount one or more times), then $500,000 of the exemption would remain for offsetting the federal estate tax at the time of your death.

Because of the unified credit concept in the law, you probably will have little incentive to reduce the size of your estate by making annual gifts to any one person in excess of the annual $10,000-per-person (or $20,000-per-couple) exclusion. Prior to the inception of the unified credit, many wealthy persons used lifetime gifts as a means of reducing the size of their estate in order to lessen the impact of the federal estate tax. But with the advent of the unified credit, every gift exceeding the annual exclusion results in a penalty—the loss of the full exemption at time of death to the extent used during one's lifetime.

If your estate is large, however, a good estate plan would still consist of taking advantage of the annual exclusion, although there may be other, nontax reasons for you not to do so. If your estate is not large, you probably do not have a valid reason in terms of estate planning for making lifetime gifts.

In any event, you would be wise to consult your lawyer before making any substantial gift, regardless of the size of your estate. He or she, besides helping you to reduce taxes, will keep you from making gifts purely for emotional reasons or because someone has been pressuring you to make a gift.

Charitable Gifts

Charitable gifts are an entirely different matter. If a charity is qualified under the federal statute, then gifts made to it are free from all adverse federal tax consequences. The gifts may be of any size without affecting the lifetime exemption of $600,000, and the $10,000 annual exclusion is not relevant. Whether made during your lifetime or at time of death, these gifts reduce the size of your taxable estate. For these reasons, your lifetime exemption could actually be considered the sum of $600,000 plus the total of all eligible charitable gifts.

One precaution is in order, however. A few state statutes limit the amount that can be devised to charity at the time of one's death. These statutory restrictions are sometimes known as the Mortmain Acts. The original Mortmain Act was passed in England in 1736. It was repealed in 1888, a new act then being passed again in 1891. The purpose of the acts was to avoid property passing into the hands of a charity, primarily religious in nature, and remaining there forever.

The Mortmain statutes did not become part of the common law adopted in this country, but some state statutes reflect their influence. The amount going to charity may be limited or gifts devised to charity within a specified time prior to death may be prohibited, especially if the donor is married or has a child or other descendant. If you plan to leave a large amount to charity, then you should first ascertain whether your state restricts such gifts in any way.

The Internal Revenue Code defines what constitutes an eligible charity. Four categories are set out in the code: (1) any governmental body; (2) an organization organized for religious, charitable, scientific, literary, or educational purposes; (3) a fraternal (does not mean solely male) society that uses the gifts for such purposes; and (4) veteran organizations. For information about gifts to charitable remainder trusts, see Chapter 8.

Gifts to Minors

If you are contemplating making an outright, substantial gift to a minor, such as your minor child, then you should consider proceeding under your state's particular Minor's Act. It will be known as the Uniform Gifts to Minors Act (UGMA) or its later 1983 or 1986 equivalent, the Uniform Transfers to Minors Act (UTMA). Such transfers qualify for the $10,000 annual gift tax exclusion. The UTMA is generally deemed to be the more favorable. It allows more types of transferors to take advantage of the act and more types of property to be included.

The uniform statutes generally provide for a custodian to manage the property of the minor without court supervision. The uniform acts thus differ from the court-administered requirements of conservatorships and some trusts, but the provisions of the uniform statutes must be strictly followed.

In part due to possible adverse tax consequences, you should consult your attorney if you are contemplating utilizing your state's uniform statute. She or he can prevent you from acting unwisely. For instance, if you are contemplating acting as custodian of your child's property, your estate could be subject to a federal estate tax. Why? The IRS might include the child's property in your estate on the basis that such custodial property is in reality still yours.

The state statutes variously define a minor as a person who has not attained the age of 18 to 21. States vary as to whether marriage affects the minority of an individual. With a few unimportant exceptions, until a minor has reached the specified age or has married, if the particular statute so recognizes, the minor is considered legally incompetent to make contracts. Thus someone is required to be legally appointed to represent the minor. Rather than proceed with a guardianship or a conservatorship, the choice usually is to proceed under the state's existing uniform statute.

Uniform statutes set out certain requirements which generally must be followed in order to come under the particular act. By conforming to your state statute, you can avoid many difficulties and expenses, such as eliminating the necessity of opening a conservatorship.

Unlike a trust but like a conservatorship, under the uniform statutes title to the property remains in the minor. The custodianship is not a separate legal entity as is a trust. As in both a trust and a conservatorship, however, the possessor of the property is the custodian. Once the minor reaches the age specified in the custodianship statute or dies, whichever occurs first, the custodian must transfer the property either to the minor or to the minor's estate.

This is not to say that a minor cannot own property unless conforming to one of the uniform statutes. But the practical problems of a minor owning property must always be considered. Keep in mind that a minor may own property but cannot legally deal with it.

A minor may seem mature enough to manage certain property, but such a person might be frustrated by his or her legal disability. Without the representation by a custodian, a minor cannot enter into any arrangement considered contractual, such as leasing or selling real property or selling listed securities. This is because the law considers a minor legally incompetent, the same as a ward under conservatorship or a person of any age who has been determined mentally incompetent.

Some exceptions to a minor's legal inability to act exist. For example, the minor can own accounts in financial institutions or government savings bonds. Thus gifts of money placed in a financial institution or U.S. savings bonds do not ordinarily pose a problem for a minor. However, if the donor of a gifted bank account or savings bond does not want the minor to have control of the property, then the procedures under the existing uniform act, or some alternative procedure, must be utilized.

Some parents try to get around the problem of the minor's disability by creating various types of co-ownership with their children. But this procedure usually fails to remove the property from the estate of the parent for either administrative or income or death tax purposes. And various types of trust have the same difficulties. Depending on the reasons for making a gift to a minor, following one of the uniform acts is usually the best procedure.

Gifts to Parents

Perhaps it isn't your children you are thinking about. Possibly it is your parents whom you wish to protect, especially if something happens to you. You may want to be sure that they have sufficient support for the balance of their lives.

With this in mind, the National Conference of Commissioners on Uniform State Laws proposed the Uniform Custodial Trust Act in 1987. It was modeled after the Uniform Transfers to Minors Act.

The purpose of this proposed act is the same as the Minor's Act's: to avoid resort to a guardian or a conservator and to provide management of assets placed in a trust. Perhaps because it is a relatively new concept, only a few states have enacted the act.

State Gift Taxes

A few states also impose a tax on gifts, usually modeled after the federal gift tax. If they do, the donor is liable, as under the federal statute, for reporting the gift and paying any tax due.

Summary

If the value of your estate is under $600,000, it is doubtful you will be, or ought to be, considering substantial gifts, at least for estate planning purposes. And you do not have to be concerned about using up the exemption. But if your estate is substantial and you want to reduce it by annually giving through proper estate planning, then you must play by the rules of the IRS.

For instance, the gift tax may apply whether the transfer is in trust or otherwise, whether the gift is direct or indirect and whether the property is real or personal, tangible or intangible. In the case of a nonresident not a citizen of the United States, the tax applies to a transfer only if the property is situated within the United States. Additionally, gift tax liability could result from the exercise of a power of appointment. A disposition of a life estate may result in a tax liability.

Generation-skipping transfers, discussed in Chapter 7, can involve lifetime gifts as well as testamentary gifts.

Because of the many Internal Revenue Code provisions concerning gifts, if your proposed gift is substantial (more than $10,000), you should consult your lawyer and consider the gifts as part of your estate planning.

Some Common
Questions Answered

Q. Since I have an estate of about $700,000, should I begin to give $10,000 to my only heir each year to reduce the size of my estate to $600,000?

A. This kind of question always seems to need more information before answering. Does your heir need financial help? What is your life expectancy? Does your estate, for example, consist of a $300,000 home so that you actually have only $400,000 worth of income-producing property? What are your average monthly expenses?

Are you dipping into your principal or living entirely on your investment, with the help of pensions, social security, and so on? How is your health? Are you fully insured as to medical expenses? What is the nature of your property? Which is more important to you, saving your estate from death taxes, or living comfortably, carefree, for the rest of your life?

The last question may be the only important one. Unless a strong reason exists for doing otherwise, you should always consider your own well-being first. Too many people take risks of not living out their lives in comfortable fashion because they worry too much about paying death taxes.

Q. Since my only heir, a nephew, will be subject to state death taxes, should I begin making gifts to him now? I am single, age 60, crippled with arthritis, and have an estate of $100,000.

A. It would be surprising if any lawyer recommended lifetime gifts to your nephew under these circumstances. You may feel attached to him, especially if he has helped you. But you must think of your own welfare first. If he loves you, then he will feel the same way. Trying to avoid his death tax—which is probably minimal in any event—is commendable, but to jeopardize your future welfare in doing so is not wise. Your relatively young age, your physical condition and the size of your estate all dictate that you must try to preserve your estate for yourself.

Q. Every year I make gifts to each of my children and grandchildren for their birthdays, at Christmas time, and sometimes on other special occasions. Do I have to tell the IRS that I did so?

A. No, you do not have to file a gift tax return as long as the total of such gifts to each individual is not more than $10,000 for any one year. Since the law does not require you to report these gifts, the IRS is not interested in them.

Q. I was given a large amount of property by my father. He says he is not going to tell the IRS or pay any gift tax. What could happen?

A. Things could happen to both of you. In addition to criminal charges that could be filed against your father, he could be subject to penalties, which would accrue monthly. Any gift tax is a lien against the property given to you. And you would also be personally liable for such tax to the extent of the value of the gift.

Q. Do I have a gift tax problem if I sell my farm worth $110,000 to my son for $60,000?

A. Yes. Under the Internal Revenue Code the difference between the value of the property and the consideration paid for it, or $50,000, is deemed a gift. You must file a return.

Q. Will the IRS accept my estimation as to the value of a particular gift?

A. Not necessarily. You may be requested to back it up with an appraisal (valuation) by one or more qualified professional appraisers.

3

The Risks
and Rewards
of Joint Tenancy

The making of a lifetime gift is usually a conscious act, as opposed to an unconscious one. But in performing certain other acts you may not realize that they also may constitute the making of a gift.

One form of activity which you may not consciously think of as the making of a gift is the creation of joint ownership—sometimes referred to as co-ownership—in property. If you as a prospective owner of property cause another person's name to also be included in the title, then by such inclusion you may have made a gift of one-half of the value of that property to the other person.

Forms of Co-Ownership

Two or more persons, known as "joint tenants" herein, may jointly hold title to property as joint tenants with right of survivorship. This form of tenancy will be referred to as *joint tenancy*. Three other forms of co-ownership—tenancy in common, tenancy by the entirety, and community property—also exist. Each of these four forms will be described separately.

Joint Tenancy

This chapter is devoted primarily to joint tenancies, since they are a widely used method of holding both real and personal property. Most commonly, joint tenancy is used by a married couple. But joint tenancy is also used by other combinations of parties as well, such as between a parent and child. Unfortunately, these latter types of joint tenancies are usually not well thought out, seem to be used indiscriminately, and frequently result in unexpected grief.

Since many states require strict conformance to joint tenancy wording, especially as to real estate, the intent to create a joint tenancy should be clearly expressed. Otherwise the jointly held property may be construed as a tenancy in common. A few states, however, do not recognize the survivorship feature of joint tenancy, no matter how an instrument is worded.

To be distinguishable from the other forms of holding title, a joint tenancy should be clearly expressed. Specific wording should be used in documents to signify that the holding of title between the parties is as joint tenants. Unfortunately, this wording often varies from document to document and from state to state. This inconsistency often is caused by ignorance or just plain sloppiness in drafting.

If the complete phrase "as joint tenants and not as tenants in common, with full right of survivorship" is used, then no confusion can occur. An example would be, "John Doe and Mary Doe, husband and wife, as joint tenants and not as tenants in common, with full right of survivorship."

By using the full phrase, legal difficulties and possible misinterpretation of what the parties intended are avoided. But often a shorter version of the joint tenancy wording is used, especially when the property is not real estate.

If the property is personal property, such as bank accounts, corporate stock, and U.S. treasuries, then the designation of joint tenancy may be different. Financial institutions, stock transfer agents, and the federal government create their own rules and conditions for the manner in which their investors hold jointly owned property. As long as their specific rules and conditions are clearly explained and followed, no difficulty occurs.

It is not uncommon, however, to see a shorter version of the complete clause used even in real estate transactions. Such a shorter version may be "as joint tenants and not as tenants in common." Clearly, it is generally held, if the form of ownership is not a tenancy in common then it must be a joint tenancy. Another short version, generally acceptable, is "as joint tenants, with full right of survivorship." Still another—the one that causes the most difficulty—is merely, "as joint tenants." But good practice dictates that the complete phrase be used, especially in real estate documents, so that resort to the courts is not required to interpret the intention of the parties.

Unlike in a tenancy in common, in a joint tenancy, upon the death of the first joint tenant, title to the deceased tenant's interest passes to the surviving joint tenant(s) by operation of law. This passing occurs regardless of the tenants' relationship to each other and regardless of any contrary provision in the deceased tenant's will or any contrary laws of inheritance.

From one perspective, holding property in joint tenancy is a gamble in that the winner—the survivor—takes all. When a husband and wife hold property in joint tenancy, the matter of who dies first probably makes no difference to them. But the same is not necessarily true in other situations, especially as to a joint tenancy between parent and child. Undoubtedly, in these other situations the older tenant, or possibly the one in ill health, plans on dying first, but the result may be just the opposite.

Joint tenants almost always own their shares equally with each other, except in the rare instance when the document creating the joint tenancy specifically provides otherwise. If there are two joint tenants, each share is one-half. If there are three, each share is one-third. And so on. Several states allow the joint tenants to hold unequal shares in joint tenancy. But a few states hold that this inequality creates a tenancy in common, regardless of the joint tenancy wording.

Both the common law and many state statutes treat joint tenancy as a necessary evil. States are reluctant to recognize joint tenancy unless the formalities are strictly obeyed. For example, the Iowa Code provides that "conveyances to two or more in their own right create a tenancy in common, unless a contrary intent is expressed."

In relation to real property, if a document's wording following the names of the parties shows only the phrase "as joint tenants," and nothing more, slightly more than half of the states would hold this to be the creation of a good joint tenancy. Other states vary in their interpretation. Some hold that it creates a tenancy in common. Some—if the parties involved are husband and wife—hold that it creates a tenancy by the entirety. Other states haven't settled the issue.

If no wording as to the type of tenancy follows the names of the parties, then it is generally held that the property is held by the joint owners as tenants in common. An exception is in the community property states where it is generally held to be community property. However, if the parties are husband and wife, then those states recognizing tenancies by the entirety deem the holding to be that form of co-ownership.

Tenancy in Common

According to slightly more than half the states, a tenancy in common may be created when two (or more) parties receive property with no words of joint tenancy following their names. The instrument would merely name the parties as owners without additional designation or explanation, although their marital status might be shown. An example would be "John

Doe and Mary Doe." (Note that the conjunction *and* is—and should be—used between the names.)

Both parties in a tenancy in common normally hold an undivided one-half interest in the property, although the instrument may designate some other division. For example, you may specify in your will that one of your children receive two-thirds of your property and the other one-third. Upon your death, they would jointly hold the property as tenants in common, each with an undivided interest in the property, but their shares would not be equal.

If a document's wording is "John Doe and Mary Doe, husband and wife, as tenants in common," most states would describe the holding as a good tenancy in common. Only a few community property states would consider the property to be community property.

Difference Between Joint Tenancies and Tenancies in Common. It is important to understand the difference between joint tenancy and tenancy in common, especially as to how the ownership is affected upon the death of the first tenant. Although in both situations jointly owned property may be held by more than two persons, let's think in terms of the joint owners being two people rather than three or more.

Remember, under a joint tenancy the interest of the decedent automatically passes to the surviving joint tenant by operation of the law.

Under tenancy in common, however, the interest of the decedent is considered probate property, that is, property subject to a probate court's administration and to claims of the decedent's creditors. Upon the death of the first tenant in common, title to the deceased's interest in the property—which is normally an undivided one-half interest—passes only to the deceased's heirs (if there is no will), beneficiaries (if there is a will), or possibly the spouse. The surviving tenant has no rights to it unless he or she falls in one of the above categories.

Voluntary Versus Involuntary Tenancies in Common. A tenancy in common may be created voluntarily or involuntarily. For example, it is voluntary when you and another party take title to property with no words of survivorship in the title. By doing so, you each own an undivided (equal) one-half interest in the property.

It would be involuntary if you died intestate (without a will), leaving two children as your heirs. Involuntarily you would have created a tenancy in common between your two children. Each of them would own exactly one-half of your property—as tenants in common. You probably would have reached the same result if you had made a will, but then the creation of the tenancy in common would be considered voluntary upon your part.

Tenancy by the Entirety

Tenancy by the entirety (or by the entireties) is another form of joint ownership, once limited to real property but now broadened in some states to include personal property as well. This form of ownership is limited to husband and wife. It does not include other parties or relationships.

Under the common law, any transfer to a married couple, whether by gift, purchase, or will creates this type of tenancy. The couple is treated as a single person with right of survivorship. Except in the community property states, this form of tenancy is generally recognized by the states unless a statute exists to the contrary or a particular court believes the concept is against public policy.

Tenancy by the entirety differs from joint tenancy in that it only exists as between husband and wife and thus cannot be any number of persons. Another difference is that in tenancy by the entirety neither party can sever the tenancy by acting alone. The severance can occur only by joint action or consent of both.

In some states recognizing tenancy by the entirety, wording in titles to property following the husband and wife's names does not have to specify the form of tenancy. In other states, the words "tenancy by the entirety" must follow their names. In both instances, however, the survivorship feature prevails upon the death of the first spouse. The parties do not have to be described as husband and wife, but they do have to be married to each other at the time the ownership is established.

Upon the death of the first tenant in a tenancy by the entirety, title to the real property remains with the surviving spouse, regardless of the laws of inheritance or of stipulations to the contrary in the decedent's will. If tenants by the entirety die simultaneously, then the estate descends as if they held it as tenants in common. In other words, each tenant would die holding an undivided one-half interest in the property.

The most important distinction between joint tenancy and tenancy by the entirety is that in a joint tenancy either tenant can sever the joint tenancy by making a lifetime transfer. In fact, such transfer automatically severs the joint tenancy, creating a tenancy in common. When transferring the joint tenancy property, the joint tenant cannot pass the joint tenancy feature of the ownership on to another party. Whereas, a tenant holding by the entirety cannot, without the consent of the other tenant, transfer his or her interest in the property—which would be a half interest—to a third party.

This distinction exists because of the difference in the legal concept of the two joint ownerships. In a joint tenancy, the parties are each considered as owning an undivided interest in the property. In a tenancy by the entirety, the parties are considered as one. Neither can act without the other.

Because of this dissimilarity, various legal actions have different consequences. As a result, if you are contemplating any action that would affect the ownership of your property held in either tenancy, you should first consult your lawyer to determine what its legal effect would be.

Community Property

What has been said above may not apply at all to the eight community property states: Arizona, California, Idaho, Louisiana, Nevada, New Mexico, Texas, and Washington. By its adoption of a version of the Uniform Marital Property Act, the state of Wisconsin is now also considered a community property state, or at least similar to one.

In these states, property co-owned by the spouses may or may not go to the surviving spouse, regardless of the wording used. This issue becomes complicated because in many of the community property states the common law coexists with the community property law.

Like tenancy by the entirety, community property exists only between husband and wife. It applies to personal as well as real property, and consists of all property not held separately by the parties. Ordinarily, the state statutes describe what shall be considered separate property and then provide that all other property acquired by either spouse during the marriage shall be considered community property.

Separate property is generally acquired by one of the parties prior to the marriage, or separately received by gift or inheritance subsequent to the marriage. Otherwise, property acquired by either spouse during the marriage generally becomes community property. If the property becomes commingled, then its previous identity (as separate property) is lost and it becomes community property, as the interest of the couple—legally referred to as "the community"—is deemed paramount.

The concept of community property is founded on Spanish, Mexican and French law. Some community property states are said to have inherited the law, others to have adopted it. Community property law exists by reason of state statutes or by a state constitution, as in Texas, so the laws vary from state to state.

The community property states differ in their laws as to the right of a deceased party to leave his or her one-half share to anyone other than the surviving party. In no event can the decedent dispose of the half share owned by the surviving party without the consent of the surviving spouse.

If you are married, you should be aware that title and transfer problems might arise if you change your residence either to or from a community property state. As a general rule, however, property once acquired retains its original character even though you change your place of residence. If you and your spouse do change from one form of property state to another, you should consult a lawyer in your new state of residence. Be sure that your manner of holding property is still intact and consistent with your original estate planning.

If you live in, or have lived in, a community property state, you must be careful not to assume that what looks like joint tenancy property is in fact so. Perhaps no other state is as severe as Texas, which greatly restricts the conversion of community property to some other form of co-ownership.

Here, again, you may wish to consult a lawyer as to the status of your property. Lawyers in non–community property states, being mostly unfamiliar with the laws of community property, may not be able to give you a quick answer. Perhaps the reverse is true as well.

Use of *Or* or Other Symbols

As to personal property, some joint tenancies may be created in ways other than as described above. For instance, if you and another person jointly hold federal securities such as savings bonds, you may notice that the joint tenancy is created merely by the use of the word *or* between your two names. This is satisfactory since the federal government can make its own rules.

But the use of the word *or* is usually not considered good legal form in creating joint tenancy, as courts tend to give it various meanings. *Or* should never be used in real estate transactions, whether or not joint tenancy is desired. Nor should it be used in other transactions between individuals. In contracts and other documents, the word *and* should connect the names of the two joint owners. You should realize, though, that governments and corporations can make their own rules of interpretation as to the meaning of words such as *or* used by them.

Publicly held corporate stock is another type of property subject to specific interpretations of words describing the manner in which it is held by two or more persons. Transfer agents have their own definitions as to the various symbols and abbreviations used after—or between—the names of joint owners on stock certificates. Usually information as to the various meanings is contained on the reverse side of the stock certificate form. Because of this practice, no difficulty in determining the meaning is usually experienced.

The Popularity of
Joint Tenancy

Joint tenancy is a popular means of holding property for many people. You probably are in the minority if you hold none of your property in this manner. Laypersons often assume that since joint tenancy is beneficial in some cases, it should be utilized in all cases.

Apparently when something is as easily created as joint tenancy, it becomes popular, regardless of the consequences. With very little effort—and certainly with little thought—title to property can be placed in joint tenancy. As a result, many people create joint tenancy without regard to the possible adverse legal consequences.

A good psychological reason exists for the use of joint tenancy, especially as between husband and wife. The parties feel more comfortable with joint tenancy. It results in feelings of trust and security. And they usually realize that after one dies, the survivor will receive the jointly held property regardless of any will or law of descent.

Estate Proceedings Upon the Death of a Joint Tenant

Many people believe that if property is held in joint tenancy, no legal proceeding is necessary when the first joint tenant dies. Unfortunately, this belief is seldom correct, especially when real estate is involved.

Some correction in the record must always be made following the death of a joint owner, if for no other reason than to explain the absence of the deceased joint tenant. The deceased tenant's name must be cleared from the title records. Also, often a showing must be made in order to establish that the death did not result in liability for death taxes. Also, if a decedent owned other property that was not held in joint tenancy, a full administration of that decedent's estate might be necessary. Whatever the estate proceeding, the change in joint tenancy property must be reported and noted of record.

Unfortunately, laypersons often forge ahead with joint tenancy without regard to possible adverse consequences. Perhaps this is due to their zeal to avoid probate administration. Perhaps it is because they mistakenly believe that by so holding their property they have no liability for death taxes. Those with this attitude fail to realize that upon death of one tenant some form of proceeding still is required.

Joint tenancy is not always ideal, even though at first it may seem that way to you. Estate planning with your lawyer should precede any creation of joint tenancy, although in practice this is seldom done. Without planning, the presence of joint tenancy during your lifetime or at the time of your death could result in all kinds of difficulties.

Lawyers disagree amongst themselves as to when joint tenancy should be used. One reason for this is that what may be good for one person or family may not be good for another. Keep this in mind when you make up your estate plan, or you may end up with a poor one. In determining the benefits, if any, of joint tenancy to you, you must ignore what others do or say. Look only at your situation and do what is best for you.

The "Cheap" Will

Joint tenancy is sometimes referred to as a *cheap will* or a *will substitute*. Those people using this terminology assume that if all your property is held in joint tenancy, you do not need a will. Upon your death all your property will go to the surviving joint tenant. No estate proceeding will be required, so why have a will? You should be beginning to understand that some of this may be a myth.

It is true that when you die the property held by you in joint tenancy will go to the surviving joint tenant. It is also true that no administration of your estate would be necessary if all—not just some—of your property were held in joint tenancy. But some estate proceeding is normally required, regardless how your property is held. Because in this joint tenancy situation your will may not need to be probated, you might believe, erroneously, that therefore nothing at all needs to be done. This is the fiction referred to above as a myth.

Advantages of Joint Tenancy

In general, then, laypersons prefer holding property in joint tenancy for two principal reasons: (1) to avoid probate, or administration, of joint tenancy property upon death of the first joint tenant, and (2) to simplify and hence hasten the transfer of joint tenancy property upon death. But other advantages might exist, even though in some situations joint tenancy tends to thwart public policy.

Consider debts that you might owe at the time of your death. Upon your death, your creditors cannot reach your unsecured joint tenancy property, that is, joint property not specifically pledged as collateral for a debt. This assumes that no statute exists to the contrary. Should you die owing money, your unsecured creditors cannot make a claim against your jointly held property. It would go free and clear to the surviving joint tenant and your creditors would have to look to your other property, if any, for their money. This "advantage" has two disadvantages: (1) it nullifies public policy that tries to protect creditors; and (2) it may go against your wishes by preventing important obligations (such as your funeral expenses!) from being paid.

A few commentators claim another advantage of joint tenancy, one that has nothing to do with public policy: it avoids fragmented ownership. Upon your death, ownership of your jointly held property vests entirely in the surviving joint owner to the exclusion of third parties. Thus other heirs would be excluded from ownership.

Advocates of this viewpoint apparently are assuming that you would not have a will and that your heirs would be numerous, thus possibly causing considerable fragmentation. But with a will you can fragment, or not, as you wish. And certainly non–joint tenants who otherwise would inherit the property might consider such a tenancy as a disadvantage.

Married couples can benefit the most from joint tenancy. That is, they can if the marital relationship is a good one, the marriage is a first one with only one set of children, and there is at least a tacit agreement between the couple as to the ultimate disposition of their property. Ideally, the combined estates should also be small enough so that the arrangement is not adversely affected by death taxes. (For more on this subject, see Chapter 16.)

If these favorable conditions exist, then it usually is to the married couple's advantage to hold all their property in joint tenancy. By doing so, administration—but not all legal proceedings—of the first deceased's estate can be avoided. Any proceeding other than administration normally takes less time and is less costly.

Every married couple, however, should still have wills to ensure that each spouse is absolutely protected, if that is what they want. It is foolish for a married couple to rely merely on their joint tenancy to protect each other. The wills ensure that the surviving spouse will receive the deceased spouse's property; total reliance is thus not placed entirely on the various joint tenancy provisions. Chapter 7 on wills and Chapter 11 on avoiding probate discuss this situation further.

Disadvantages of Joint Tenancy

Holding property in joint tenancy with a person other than your spouse is the situation most likely to cause difficulties. All of the following examples have occurred many times, resulting in expensive, unhappy lessons for those involved.

Suppose you desire to leave all your property to your child who is your only heir. You name your child as a joint tenant on all your property, because then the child will receive all your property upon your death without need of your estate being administered.

But suppose the child dies before you do. Even though you may have always considered the property as yours, it would have to be listed in that child's estate proceeding, of whatever kind it may be. Although title to the property will come back to you as the surviving joint tenant, you could be subject to a state tax on your "inheritance"—the half coming back to you. If the estate is large enough, you could also be subject to a federal estate tax.

Or suppose your only child is a minor and the joint tenancy property is real estate that you now want to sell or mortgage. Your child's signature must also be on the deed, contract, or mortgage. But since the child, being a minor, is considered legally incompetent to sign a contract, his or her signature would be invalid. A conservatorship would have to be opened so that the signature of the conservator on behalf of the child could be affixed to the appropriate document. Although sometimes a necessity, a conservatorship is a legal proceeding which you should normally try to avoid. (See the discussion about conservatorships in Chapter 5.)

Or suppose your married child is a joint owner with you of certain real estate. You wish to sell or mortgage the real estate. Your child's spouse, as well as the child, must also sign the deed, contract or mortgage in order to legally complete the sale or loan. All the spouse's legal interests in the property have to be released, in writing on the document, before the transfer of property can occur. If the spouse refuses to join in the transaction, you would be unable to sell or borrow on the property.

Or suppose your married child, who is a joint owner with you of certain real or personal property, goes through divorce or dissolution proceedings. The court might grant to the child's spouse up to all of the child's half interest in that property, even though it originally belonged to you and you thought of it as being all yours until you died. In such instances, the court might reason—no matter what you might say or think—that you made a gift of one-half of the property to the child at the time you created the joint tenancy.

Other disadvantages in holding your property in joint tenancy may exist. You could possibly lose control of the property to the other joint tenant who legally has equal right to the property. For example, suppose the property is a bank account. First, you must be concerned with the integrity of the other joint tenant. What if, say as a result of pressure by others, the other joint tenant withdraws some or all of the bank account for his or her own use? Secondly, creditors of the other joint tenant can legally make a claim to, and levy upon, that account even though, again, you may think of that account as being all yours until you die.

And other problems exist. Any income received from certain jointly held property must be split equally between the joint tenants and reported on their respective income tax returns. And the creation of joint tenancy between persons other than husband and wife may result in a gift, thus resulting in a possible gift tax liability. Liability for any gift tax and the tax return would be yours if the property originally came from you. Of course, no gift would result if each of you contributed one-half to the cost of the property.

Many times a single parent having many children will create one or more joint bank accounts with one of the children, "in case something happens to me." In this instance, the parent trusts the child to share the account with the other children after the parent's death. In fact, this may be explicitly or implicitly agreed to. But can the parent be absolutely certain this will occur? Has the parent unintentionally disinherited other intended heirs or beneficiaries?

"Convenience" Tenancies

A situation similar to the above occurs when a parent is preparing for her or his incapacity. In this case, the parent wants the child to be available for the payment of bills. By naming the child as a joint owner of a bank account, the parent often feels that the child can take care of the bills in the event she is unable to do so.

Some courts refer to this joint tenancy as one "for convenience only." If so, upon the death of the parent the total amount in the bank account becomes a part of the probate estate of the deceased parent and is distributed according to the parent's will or the laws of inheritance, and no part goes to the child as a surviving joint tenant.

The difficulty with this kind of tenancy is that the taxing bodies may want it to be proven in court. Or worse yet, upon the death of the parent the child holding the joint interest may claim that the joint tenancy was not one of convenience. By making such a claim, the child is attempting to receive all of the joint property to the exclusion of the other heirs.

Even though after your death the money in the joint account may be shared by many heirs, the account often will be assessed for inheritance tax purposes to the one child named on the joint account. Without proof to the contrary, the account is considered to legally belong to the surviving joint tenant, regardless of what he thereafter does or intends to do with the money, and regardless of the intentions in setting up the account.

Some states try to avoid this result by making various presumptions, but you cannot be certain that they will. In this situation, the parent should consider the power of attorney as an alternative.

Severing Joint Tenancy

A severance can occur whether or not you are aware of the consequences of a particular action. The most obvious way to sever a joint tenancy is for both of you to agree to the severance. This may occur in several different ways. Suppose you and your spouse own real estate as joint tenants. You have several options of severance.

Both of you may convey your joint interests in the property to a third party.

One of you may convey your (half) interest to a third party. In certain states, however, because of your marriage to each other, the other partner may have to join in the conveyance to release any legal interests.

The two of you may create a tenancy in common by reconveying the real property to yourselves from yourselves (or, if required by local law, through another party).

One of you may convey all your interest in the property to the other one of you.

Some courts have held that the joint tenancy is destroyed and a tenancy in common has been created when any of the following situations occur:

When a joint, reciprocal, or mutual will (see Chapter 7) is made by the two joint tenants, if the will provisions are deemed inconsistent with the joint tenancy ownership of the property.

When a real estate sales contract is made in which the joint tenants agree to sell the property to a third party. Legally, this is sometimes referred to as an equitable conversion of the property. Such a conversion can usually be prevented if the contract provides that the joint tenants (the vendors) intend to preserve their joint tenancy.

When the couple divorces.

When a mortgage, sometimes referred to as a deed of trust, is made by the joint tenants. The deciding factor generally is whether the state thinks of the mortgage as a transfer of title, in which case the joint tenancy is severed by the lender, or merely the giving of a lien, in which case it is not.

The Uniform Simultaneous Death Statute

You should be aware of the Uniform Simultaneous Death Statute, some form of which is a part of the probate statutes of every state except Louisiana, Montana and Ohio. Under this statute, where there is not sufficient evidence that the joint tenants have died otherwise than simultaneously, the joint tenancy property is distributed in equal shares to the estates of each of the decedents. Since the effect of the statute is to change nonprobate property to probate property, a simultaneous death would necessitate a probate proceeding in each estate.

Even though simultaneous deaths are not likely, the possibility should be reason enough for married couples to have wills, even though all their property is held by them in joint tenancy. Otherwise, they may not be protecting their intended beneficiaries.

Summary

In conclusion, good judgment and knowledge of the consequences dictate when joint tenancy should be used. Because laws and court decisions affect this type of co-ownership, you would be wise to consult your lawyer concerning your use of joint tenancy, especially—but not necessarily—if it is intended to be with someone other than your spouse. Certainly, the use of joint tenancy should be discussed at the time you do any estate planning or make your will. This discussion should occur before, not after, you have entered into a joint tenancy arrangement, since joint tenancy once formed, unlike a will, can become rigid and inflexible.

Some Common Questions Answered

Q. Both when I opened a savings account and purchased an EE bond, a bank employee asked me what other name I wanted on the account. Does the law require two names to be on each?

A. No. It seems to be a common practice for employees of financial institutions to assume that all accounts and bonds should be in two names, generally in a joint tenancy arrangement. Since the manner of holding title cannot be determined without proper estate planning, it is obvious that such employees are not in a position to make such a determination.

The suggestive question is especially irritating to lawyers who have spent hours determining the correct estate plan, only to have it partially destroyed by inadvisable actions by the tenant as a result of such questions. You should know, before you enter the institution, how you want title to be held and not be influenced by such questions.

Q. If I use my own social security number on a joint account, won't that show whose money it actually is?

A. No. The institution is required by the IRS to obtain a number. But using your own number has no legal significance.

Q. I am a grandmother who wants to leave a small remembrance to each of my grandchildren at the time that I die. May I do this by setting up separate joint tenancy accounts with each of them without changing my will?

A. Yes, as long as it does not adversely affect your estate plan. But a better way would be to set up payable on death (POD) accounts, such as "Mary Jones, p.o.d. John Smith."

By setting up the accounts in this manner, you have not lost control of your property. You can change them periodically, if need be, and even close them out. If the money represented by these accounts were later needed for your support, it would be easily available to you. And the grandchildren would not need to sign the signature cards.

Q. I hold all my property in joint tenancy with my son, but my will gives $10,000 to my church. What happens when I die?

A. All of your property will go to your son to the exclusion of the church. Your question reveals a common error made by laypersons. Presumably, your will reflects what you desire at the time of your death. Yet by creating the joint tenancy you have circumvented your will, making the church gift a nullity.

Q. If I put all my property in joint tenancy, will my surviving joint tenants have to hire a lawyer?

A. Probably. At least two requirements may have to be met. First, all records must be cleared to show the death of the first joint tenant. This means land records, bank records, and so on. Secondly, legal proceedings may have to be undertaken to free your property from any death taxes. The land record correction and the death tax situation would require the services of a lawyer.

Q. If I hold all of my property in joint tenancy with another person and the other person dies before I do, do I need to hire a lawyer?

A. Yes, the same procedures are required as in the previous question. This does not mean that you would necessarily have to pay any death taxes, however. You may only have to prove that you do not owe any.

Q. If my bank account is held in joint tenancy with my two children when I die, how will the account be divided?

A. Your account will continue to be held by the two children in joint tenancy. But they should then immediately determine if they wish to keep on in that manner. Presumably, they would want to close out the account and divide the money so that upon their death their own families would receive their one-half share.

4

Harnessing the
Power of Attorney

Many reasons may exist for wanting to provide for your present or future incapacity. For example, you may be at an advanced age and unable to manage your financial affairs. Or you may want your business interests to be protected from liquidation. Or you may be unable to manage your estate and want to avoid a court-supervised proceeding such as a guardianship or conservatorship. Or perhaps you no longer want to handle your finances and may wish for someone else to take on the responsibility.

Whatever your reasons for having someone else manage your estate, you will probably have the same objectives in mind when choosing the legal form of control: to be able to make the initial decisions, to make sure that the person managing your finances is trustworthy, and to have minimal fuss and expenses.

Joint tenancy is one means of managing and preserving your estate. However, as has been shown in the last chapter, this form of co-ownership is not always utilized correctly.

There is another alternative to using joint tenancy. That is establishing the power of attorney. A *power of attorney* is a legal document in which one party authorizes another party to act as the first party's agent with respect to certain rights—generally property rights. The party granting the power is called the "grantor," or "principal." The party granted the power is called the "attorney in fact," sometimes referred to as a substitute, deputy, or agent.

The attorney in fact in this situation should not be confused with an attorney at law. For simplicity, the attorney in fact will hereafter be referred to merely as the attorney.

The attorney need not be a resident of the grantor's state. Few states place any limits on who can serve. The attorney may be an individual or some other party, such as a corporation (a bank, for instance). Multiple attorneys may be named, with the power to act individually or jointly. The powers must be contained in a document signed by the grantor. If the property designated in the document includes real estate, then some states require the document to be signed before a notary and the document made a matter of record. Some states also require witnessing or court approval of the document.

States vary as to whether the attorney is allowed compensation. Most estates do not require the attorney to give an accounting to the court or another party. However, the attorney should keep a record of his or her financial transactions for other reasons.

The extent of the powers given by the grantor to the attorney is specified in the document. To the extent of the given powers, the attorney acts on behalf of the grantor. The attorney's authority is limited only by the terms of the power, although a few states do place restrictions on the subject matter.

In general, the grantor may delegate to the attorney authority to do anything that the grantor could do himself. However, certain acts are exempt: those that are considered so personal to the principal that they would be invalid if performed by a delegate. For instance, the attorney generally is prohibited from making or remaking the grantor's will or contracting marriage. The attorney also cannot usually make a gift directly or indirectly (as by creating a joint tenancy), or transfer the grantor's property into a trust, or purchase life insurance on the grantor's life. If the latter were done, for example, who would be named as beneficiary? Some of these actions, however, may be possible if the authority to do so is specifically and carefully spelled out in the power.

The grantor also cannot delegate authority to the attorney to do something that the grantor could not legally do, such as commit a crime.

No matter what the extent of the given powers, however, the grantor retains—but no longer exclusively—all powers that were granted to the attorney. As you will find out in the next chapter, this retained power is quite different than if a conservatorship were created. In respect to the granted powers, the grantor and the attorney have equal authority to act individually. Each can operate independently of the other, actually without notifying the other as to such actions, although this is not necessarily recommended nor advisable.

Unlike a living trust (see Chapter 8), when a power of attorney is created, the grantor retains title and legal possession of the property. As a practical matter, however, in exercising the granted authority the attorney may end up with possession of certain of the grantor's property.

The attorney must never commingle the grantor's property with her own property. Such an action would be a violation of the attorney's responsibility as a fiduciary, even though it was done innocently. It could subject the attorney to civil or criminal liability or, at the least, raise doubts as to her integrity and motives.

So that an attorney can successfully perform his duties, he must have clear authority to act on behalf of the grantor as to the powers granted. If the provisions are ambiguous, then parties dealing with the attorney may be reluctant to proceed, since they would not want to be in the position of interpreting a poorly drafted instrument.

Even if the instrument is clearly drafted, the attorney may experience some difficulty in dealing with third parties. Unless overcome by statute, as has been done in Illinois, the common law rule of principal and agent applies. This provides that no party is required to deal with an agent. Thus, even if the third party would have dealt with the grantor on the same terms, he or she is not required to deal with the attorney. Fortunately, in the normal course of business this objection is rarely raised.

Choosing Your Attorney

When you think it would be a good idea to give someone a power of attorney, your first step should be to contact your lawyer. This should be long before you actually feel a need for help and it may actually be considered when you do your estate planning. You and your lawyer should discuss the pros and cons of the power, whether it is suitable for you under your circumstances, what the alternatives are, and who should be named as attorney.

Extreme care must be taken in choosing the attorney. He or she must be someone that can be relied upon, someone entirely trustworthy. In this sense, the attorney is no different than any other party having a fiduciary relationship, such as a personal representative, a conservator, or a trustee.

Unlike most other fiduciary relationships, the power of attorney is ordinarily created and maintained outside the jurisdiction of the court. Jurisdiction is not invoked unless some difficulty that cannot be resolved outside of the courts arises in the relationship between the grantor and the attorney.

Another reason exists for the careful choosing of the attorney. In effect, the attorney is administering the property of the grantor. This requires a demonstrable ability to manage and secure the property. Perhaps above all else, the attorney should have a feel for doing what the grantor would do under like circumstances.

Suppose you decide to execute a power of attorney. Who should you consider naming as your attorney? If you agree with the above requirements, probably you already have concluded that you should limit yourself to naming only a close member of your own family, such as one of your children.

Even then, the required existence of certain other qualifications should be evident. For instance, is your proposed attorney located conveniently to you and your property? If the proposed attorney lives many miles from you, would he or she be able to act on your behalf with promptness and with adequate knowledge of your affairs?

If your intended choice is one of your children, is the chosen child agreeable to the other children and their spouses? Even though it is conceded that the person to whom is granted power of attorney should be your choice and not someone else's, can you safely ignore possible family conflicts in a situation as important as this? In this respect, you must try to place yourself in the position of the proposed attorney. Do you want your attorney to be miserable in trying to fulfill his responsibility to you?

Would your attorney be free from the influence of others, such as his spouse? It is conceivable that as you become less competent, your attorney might wish to consult occasionally with others of your family for guidance and possible agreement as to what action should be taken on a particular matter. But he must be strong enough to avoid adverse influences and to act independently of others. In other words, your attorney must be able to act without always waiting for a consensus of family members.

You should be aware that the power places a great amount of responsibility on the attorney who ordinarily has no guidance from any court. Realize, too, that your attorney is not likely to seek further advice from your lawyer, even though that may be the proper forum to forestall subsequent problems.

If you decide to proceed with the power of attorney, then the one chosen to be the attorney should be brought into the discussion prior to the power's preparation. The proposed attorney should understand what the job entails and the two of you should be in agreement before the power is completed.

The Need for an Accounting

After your death, the attorney may be asked by interested parties to account for his or her actions during the period of the power. For this reason, a careful attorney, even though not usually required to do so by the power nor by a state statute, may wish to keep records of the financial transactions occurring during the period of the power. Some states, such as Illinois, require the attorney to do so.

A minimum record could be created by running all financial transactions in and out of the same checking account. Such transactions would include receipts, disbursements, and transfers of funds. This type of recordkeeping would minimize difficulties in disclosing—and proving—what occurred in the principal's estate while the power was being used.

Choosing Your Form of Power

There are two types of power of attorney: (1) the general or plenary power of attorney, and (2) the special or limited power of attorney. The general power usually grants to the attorney almost every conceivable power that the grantor has, with the possible exceptions stated above.

The special or limited power of attorney, sometimes also called a "short form" power of attorney, limits the authority of the attorney to one or more particular purposes, such as selling the grantor's home. In this situation, the grantor feels no need to give the attorney blanket power to do other things. When this form is used, the attorney must be careful not to exceed the limited granted powers. With this form also, more so than with the general form, the one dealing with the attorney must monitor the attorney's actions to see that he or she is not exceeding the granted powers. An examination of the power should be sufficient to determine the attorney's powers.

Having a power and using the power are two different things. The cautious attorney will not exercise a granted power that could be considered financially unsound, such as making certain high-return, but risky, investments. Nor will the cautious attorney do something that might cause a family squabble without previously clearing the proposed action with the other members of the family. If the grantor is still mentally competent to make a decision, the careful attorney should consult with the grantor before proceeding with any questionable action.

The Durable Power of Attorney

Prior to the early 1950s, most states followed the common law rule that a power of attorney automatically terminates, that is, becomes invalid, when the grantor of the power becomes incompetent. The theory behind the rule apparently is that upon incompetency the grantor no longer is able to revoke the power and therefore the law will do it for the grantor. Unfortunately, the event of incompetency is the very time that the grantor wants the power to be utilized and the very time that the power is most beneficial to the grantor. Who needs a power of attorney more than one who is incompetent?

About 1954, the various state legislatures began enacting the so-called durable or blockbuster power of attorney act. In substance, the so-called durable powers preserve the authority of the attorney to continue acting even though the grantor becomes incompetent. All 50 states now provide for some form of durable power.

Use of the durable power clause in the instrument generally is optional with the grantor. The old common law rule still applies for those powers of attorney not utilizing the newer durable power statutes. The durability of the power is generally established merely by inserting the statutory language of durability in the form.

These statutes provide that if the appropriate wording—usually the statutory language—is contained in the power of attorney, then the power survives the incompetency of the grantor. A common language form is "This power of attorney shall not be affected by disability of the principal (grantor)." In other words, incompetency of the grantor does not terminate the authority of the attorney, as would be the case prior to the enactment of the durable statute.

The ability of the power to survive the competency of the grantor is the reason that the provision is referred to as "durable." Regardless of the competency of the grantor the power of attorney remains in effect. No automatic revocation of the power—as under the common law—occurs when the grantor becomes incompetent.

The Difficulties of the Standby Provision

Most of the durable power statutes also provide that the exercise of the power of attorney may be contingent upon the incapacity of the grantor. In this instance, the statutory language may be "This power of attorney shall become effective upon the disability of the principal (grantor)." This provision is used when the grantor does not want the power to go into effect until she no longer is able to take care of her own affairs. Because this provision places the power in limbo until a specified event, this particular power sometimes is referred to as a "standby" power of attorney, or a "springing" power.

Specific instructions must be given as to when incapacity is deemed to have occurred. The condition of incapacity may be described as incompetency, disability, or some other term. It may be either a physical or mental breakdown or both. The directions in the instrument may require a determination of such incapacity by a court, a physician, one's lawyer, or by some other party or combination of parties. If a judicial decision is specified, the cost involved may be exactly what many powers of attorney attempt to avoid.

On the other hand, relying on your physician or some other party to make the determination of incompetency, although presumably not costly, places an undue amount of pressure on someone who may not be anxious to make the decision. And of course the possibility always exists that no one will be willing to take the initiative until you are totally incompetent so that no repercussions can possibly result. In the meantime, your estate may suffer considerable damage through the lack of proper management.

Some lawyers and laypersons favor the standby provision. But difficulties can arise in determining when a principal is so incapacitated that the attorney should begin using the power. Suppose you feel that you are still able to handle your own affairs but your son, whom you have named as your standby attorney, observes you doing things that seem to indicate otherwise. For instance, suppose he discovers that you are not paying your creditors. Unpaid bills are seen lying around your home. What does he do if you object to him starting to collect the bills for payment?

This illustrates one of the weaknesses of the standby power. If you trust your son to act responsibly after your incompetency, why don't you trust him to act according to your oral instructions before your incompetency?

It could be to your advantage to avoid, if at all possible, the standby durable clause that delays authority to act until you become incapacitated. This should not be difficult to do, since you should only name an attorney in whom you have total faith, one that will act only when you want him or her to do so. Your designated attorney will have enough responsibilities without you further burdening him or her with determinations as to your competency. Reliability of your attorney is important since any of his or her actions within the actual or apparent scope of the attorney's authority binds you as grantor.

The Effect of the Grantor's Death

Death of the grantor normally terminates the power of attorney, regardless of the existence of the durable clause. But if the attorney is unaware of the grantor's death or has no notice of the death, some states provide that the attorney may continue to act.

Custodial or Agency Accounts

A special kind of power of attorney, perhaps more properly described as a mini- or quasi-power of attorney, designates a bank to act as your custodian or agent. This alternate method should be considered when the conditions set out above for an attorney do not exist, especially when a qualified member of your own family is not readily available to serve as your attorney, and when your situation does not necessitate more general powers.

Suppose you are a single person with investment income and an estate sufficient to live on, but you feel inadequate to manage your financial affairs and nervous about making your own investment decisions. Or suppose you are elderly and want to minimize your responsibilities by having someone take over some of your affairs without a lot of legal complications. Or suppose your spouse who handled all of your financial affairs has just died. You now feel helpless and incapable of taking over your affairs. Maybe you no longer are able, or want, to write checks. Is there something similar, and yet an alternative, to the power of attorney?

Most banks provide a custodial or agency service which has various names such as agency account, investment management account, custodial management account, supervised investment management account, or discretionary investment management account. Regardless of how the service is labeled, it operates very much like a limited power of attorney. In fact, some of the agreements provide for a durable clause which continues the account arrangement in the event you become incapacitated.

The custodial account differs from the power of attorney in at least one respect. When the grantor creates a custodial account and transfers property to the custodial bank, the bank will take possession of such property until the arrangement is terminated. Banks must do so since they are responsible for the safekeeping and accounting of the property placed in trust with them. Such possession, however, would be subject to the specific instructions under the agreement. Conversely, an attorney may or may not take possession of the property, depending perhaps on the nature of the property and the convenience of doing so.

Title to the property, however, remains in the grantor in either case. Income from the custodial property, as well as from other assets for which the bank is not responsible, is reported on the grantor's income tax returns, which under the agreement the custodian may be responsible for.

The power is limited in that the bank only handles those assets that are delivered to it by the grantor. The agreement spells out the duties, responsibilities, and liabilities of the bank. It may be easily terminated by either party merely by written notice from one to the other. However, should the grantor later become incompetent, the agreement would become irrevocable, at least until the bank revokes the agreement or a conservatorship is opened.

The arrangement places the bank in a fiduciary capacity, similar to any other attorney in fact. In performing its services, the bank, like most attorneys in fact, is not subject to court supervision, although the courts may be used if necessary. Since courts and lawyers do not have to be used, the only costs involved in this type of arrangement are regular, periodic fees of the bank for serving as agent.

What are the pros and cons of using a bank agency account? The following are presumed disadvantages in using a bank:

1. Most agency accounts do not include all of the property of the principal, although no legal reason exists why they do not. In effect, then, they are limited powers of attorney. In the long run, a general power of attorney may be more desirable, since it can include powers that an agency account would not—for example, powers pertaining to life support systems.

2. Some people consider a bank to be too impersonal. Whether or not this is true would seem to depend upon the particular bank chosen as agent and the place where you live. A conscientious family member serving as attorney is believed to be more aware of the wants and comforts of the principal than a bank, since a family member presumably would spend more time with the principal than would a bank.

3. Unlike a family member, who normally would serve as attorney without compensation, the bank is a professional. As such, it performs services for which it charges a fee at least annually. The fee may seem expensive to some. The financial status of the principal should determine whether this is significantly important. Some states provide for a fee, regardless of the identity of the attorney.

The following are presumed advantages in using a bank:

1. A bank has more resources and experience in investing the principal's estate than would an individual family member. The bank employees are professionally trained to handle affairs of this kind.

2. If a family is somewhat divided or given to squabbling, a bank can serve as a compromise candidate for attorney.

3. Bank employees are bonded, whereas individual attorneys in fact are not, although they could be.

No doubt in specific situations other advantages or disadvantages also exist. You have to weigh each to determine what is most important to you and make your decision accordingly.

Some Common
Questions Answered

Q. Although I am elderly and somewhat crippled, I don't need the power of attorney yet. Can I wait until I need it?

A. Yes, you can even wait until the last minute—if you know when that last minute is. Since you apparently realize that at some point you will need someone to look after your affairs, you might be foolish to wait. By waiting, you may be putting an unfair burden on someone else to take action at a later date. It could then be much more expensive and otherwise less advantageous to implement.

Q. Is it better for me to name more than one attorney in fact?

A. Possibly, assuming that the attorney is an individual and not a bank. One way would be to name one individual to serve, with a provision for an alternate to serve under certain circumstances, such as death of the first named. The only problem would be to make the conditions for the second named so clear that no difficulty would arise when the second named took over under the power.

The other way would be to name two individuals to serve either jointly or severally, since multiple agents or attorneys are permissible. This may be done by one instrument or by separate instruments. If they serve jointly—in which event it would be one instrument— then both would have to join in all actions involving the power.

If they serve severally, then each could act independently of and separately from the other. The latter form would be preferable, although the two must have some understanding so that the accounts could be properly maintained and their actions synchronized. If the latter method were used, then most likely only one would use the power and the other would serve as a standby in the event the first were no longer able to serve as attorney.

Q. Since I don't want to choose between my four children, can I give a power of attorney to each of my children?

A. You can and you may, but think of the mess if all four attempted to exercise the power. Spreading out the responsibility would likely cause nothing but confusion and conflict. If you find it difficult to make a choice, then call the four together, explain your dilemma, and let them decide which one of them should have primary responsibility. One or more of the others can serve as alternates.

Q. Does any reason exist for giving more than a special or limited power of attorney?

A. It depends on what you have in mind, what you want accomplished. Limited powers are usually given for specific purposes and sometimes for a short period of time, such as to sell a tract of land or perhaps to manage a business, such as an apartment building, while you are out of the country. If you want the power to continue for the balance of your life, you could be making a mistake in limiting the powers of your attorney. Unless a good reason exists for only a limited power, then the general power is ordinarily best.

Q. What if after giving a power of attorney I feel I made a mistake?

A. Assuming that you are still competent, you can revoke the power at any time. No one can stop you. Your attorney at law can help you take the necessary steps and draw the necessary papers. One thing you must do is to notify all parties, such as your bank, that your attorney in fact no longer has any authority to act as your agent.

Q. Can I take any action if my attorney in fact turns out to be dishonest?

A. First of all, immediately revoke the power and notify all parties whom your attorney may have dealt with that you have done so. Your remedies would appear to be both civil and criminal. In other words, you can bring a civil suit against the attorney for return of your property and you can file a criminal complaint against the attorney with the local prosecutor. What steps you take may depend on who the attorney in fact is. Probably you should consult with your lawyer, whom you will need anyway to prepare the revocation.

Q. Why can't I name someone other than a close member of my family to serve as my attorney in fact? Is there anything wrong in doing so?

A. You can name any legal entity to serve as your attorney, such as an individual, a corporation, or a partnership. But this doesn't mean that you ought to. While it is not illegal to do so, it may be wrong in the sense that the party named may not be a good choice for serving as your attorney.

Your attorney serves in a fiduciary capacity, meaning that the position is one of special trust on your behalf. As your agent, the attorney must be in a position to know and react to your wants. The attorney must have the competency and time to administer your affairs in a proper manner.

The position of attorney can be time consuming. But unless the attorney is a bank and hence a professional entitled to payment for services rendered, ordinarily an individual serving as attorney does not expect compensation for serving, unless a statute so provides. If compensation is expected by the attorney or provided by statute, then it might be better to name a bank to serve as your agent.

Q. What if I want my attorney to serve only for a few weeks? Can I do so?

A. Yes. The power is an agreement between you and your agent. You can put in any provision limiting the period of the power that you want as long as it is not contrary to law. As a safeguard, however, this type of provision should be boldfaced and stand out so that anyone relying on the power can easily observe the limited time it is in effect.

Q. I have no child whom I want to serve as my attorney and I don't want a bank agency account. Is there anything wrong with naming a relative as my attorney?

A. "Wrong" is a difficult word to interpret. Presumably you have someone in mind whom you trust. No real distinction exists as between a relative and a friend, except that some may feel that a relative will be more caring and attentive to your wants.

You must be careful about the following when selecting an attorney: He or she should normally be younger than you, physically located conveniently near you, trustworthy, and capable of managing your affairs as well as or better than you do. The fact that individual attorneys usually do not charge may be a factor in your choice. If all factors are satisfactorily determined, then you might be quite comfortable with the relative, especially if you have a close relationship with each other.

Q. Is there any difference between a durable power of attorney and a blockbuster power of attorney?

A. No. The term "blockbuster" was used by a few commentators to describe the durable power soon after states began passing statutes authorizing its use. The term never seemed to catch on, probably because the word "durable" is so much more descriptive. It is doubtful that many lawyers now use the term in discussing durable powers of attorney.

Q. I am the attorney under a durable, general power of attorney of my incompetent mother. Do I have the authority under the power to make gifts to myself and my brothers and sisters?

A. In view of your question, it is assumed that the power of attorney makes no specific mention of gifts. Most powers do not, although the language of a general power usually is so broad that it may seem to indicate that the making of gifts is allowed. But courts generally hold otherwise. They consider the attorney's power to be limited to the normal, everyday business affairs of the grantor. Unspecified gifts are not deemed to fit in this category unless specifically provided for in the power.

5
Evaluating
Conservatorship

Many options are available to you in having someone share or take over the responsibilities of your property. Some of these, such as joint tenancy or power of attorney, have already been discussed.

Another option is a conservatorship, or guardianship. This option is considered not as desirable as the others because of the continuing costs, court supervision, and inflexibility involved. (For more about this, see Chapter 9.) In fact, many lawyers suggest that you use it only as a last resort.

A *conservatorship* is a court-supervised legal proceeding in which a party is appointed to protect, or conserve, your property interests. This legal option is much more formal than the power of attorney, which is normally an unsupervised arrangement. The proceeding is instigated by a petition to the court asking for the appointment of a fiduciary, the *conservator*.

At one time, most states referred to conservatorships as *guardianships*. Many still do. A guardianship can have two different purposes: (1) to take custody and control of a person's property, and (2) to take physical custody of a person. Over time, the following distinction has come to be made in many states such as Iowa: guardianships of estate property are referred to as conservatorships, and guardianships of the person are referred to as guardianships. This book will follow that distinction.

A few states refer to conservatorships by still other names. Louisiana, for instance, refers to the proceeding as a curatorship and the fiduciary as a curator when an adult is involved. Other variations in names occur, but for convenience the proceeding will be identified here as a conservator-ship, the fiduciary as a conservator, and the protected party as a *ward*.

Distinguishing Between Voluntary and Involuntary Conservatorships

If you are competent but believe you are no longer able to make or carry out important decisions concerning your financial affairs, or if you simply no longer wish to do so, then some states allow you to petition the court to have a conservator appointed over your estate. Sometimes no mental or physical impairment on your part need be shown or proved, although the court must be satisfied that the appointment is to your best interests. This situation is known as a *voluntary conservatorship*.

If someone else, such as one of your children, believes that you are unable to make or carry out important decisions concerning your financial affairs, or if some other statutory requirement exists, then that person may petition the court for the appointment of a conservator of your property. The appointment is made if the court is satisfied that the allegations of the petition are true and in conformance with the statute. This situation is known as an *involuntary conservatorship*.

States vary widely, however, as to what conditions are required to justify the appointment of a conservator. Most states set forth statutory requirements that are strictly interpreted. Courts believe that the liberty of the individual in controlling his or her own property is deemed paramount. Thus the reasons for the appointment must be urgent and justifiable. However, the courts do not generally hold that the individual must be insane in a technical sense, merely that he be incapable of handling his affairs.

Before an involuntary conservatorship is granted, courts generally require that the proposed ward be represented by a lawyer. This representative is charged with the duty of making certain that the proposed ward is a fit candidate for conservatorship. If necessary, the representative will litigate the issue in order to protect the interests of the proposed ward. The theory of the procedure is that no judgment should be entered without a proper defense.

In both the voluntary and involuntary situations, the petitioner usually chooses a specific party to serve as conservator, although in the involuntary conservatorship some state statutes provide a priority for those entitled to serve as conservator. Courts have the last word in deciding who shall serve as conservator, but if no objection is made to the party proposed in the petition, then the court will normally approve the proposed party.

Notice of the Proceeding

In a voluntary conservatorship, no notice is served upon anyone, since the only party in interest is the one petitioning the court. In the involuntary conservatorship, notice is served upon the proposed ward. If disputed by the proposed ward through her lawyer, an action is tried like any other lawsuit. A jury trial might even be demanded and granted.

What should you do if you are served with a notice that a petition for involuntary conservatorship has been filed against you? You have at least four options:

1. *Hire a lawyer to defend you and to prepare the necessary papers, if you want to resist the action.* You might do so for any number of reasons, such as because you do not believe that the statements made in the petition are true. Contact your lawyer immediately, as otherwise he or she may not have time to defend you.

In no event should you let the time mentioned in the notice expire before you file appropriate papers in the proceeding. If you do not legally take prompt action, you will be considered in default and whatever was requested in the petition, called a *prayer,* would be granted.

2. *With your lawyer, try to negotiate with the petitioner in an effort to determine whether some other course of action is possible.* Perhaps if you gave someone, not necessarily the petitioner, a power of attorney or transferred the management of your property into a trust, the action against you would be voluntarily dismissed.

Ordinarily, the filing of a petition indicates that the petitioner believes that you are no longer able to manage your own affairs. It is possible that the petitioner took this action as a last resort to force you to face up to some disability that you are believed to have.

3. *Allow the petition to go through and the involuntary conservatorship to occur.* In this event, the party suggested as conservator in the petition probably will be approved. If this does not suit you, then you must act accordingly through your attorney.

4. *File a voluntary petition for conservatorship* in which event you would have the opportunity to name the party you want to serve as your conservator. Your attorney presumably could then secure the dismissal of the other petition.

Which Conservatorship Is Preferable?

Obviously, of the two proceedings the voluntary proceeding is the more desirable. The involuntary proceeding is undesirable in that it places a strain on those who must make, and may have to prove, the statutory allegations. As a practical matter, other incompetency conditions may exist but the petitioner and other interested parties normally do not want to allege anything beyond what the statute requires.

Some statutory requirements for an involuntary conservatorship place the petitioner in an awkward position. Arkansas, for instance, requires the proposed ward to be evaluated by a professional with expertise appropriate for the respondent's alleged incapacity—for example, a physician, a psychologist, or a social worker—before a petition can be filed. New Mexico requires the proposed ward to be examined by a qualified health-care professional prior to the hearing. Some states, such as West Virginia, appoint a committee to adjudge whether a person deemed insane is legally competent.

If you are like most people, you will be reluctant to instigate a voluntary conservatorship action for yourself until you think you are no longer able to make decisions on your own. But waiting until the last minute often is too late, because at that point in your life you may be unable to perceive or admit that you need help. As a result, your family or friends then will be forced to start an involuntary action.

The Standby Conservatorship as an Alternative

A few state statutes try to anticipate the problem of when to instigate a voluntary conservatorship by providing for a standby conservatorship. The *standby* is similar to a voluntary proceeding in that the petition is voluntarily signed by an individual, but in this instance the petition is made ready only for possible future use.

In addition to nominating a conservator and specifying whether bond is waived, the petitioner asks that under certain specified conditions the petition be filed with the court. Until the prerequisites are met, the petition remains dormant. It "stands by" until the occurrence of the specified conditions that trigger its filing. The standby petition may be revoked at any time prior to its being filed with the court.

Usually the stated conditions in the standby petition refer to the ward's incapacity as determined by the ward's personal physician. Sometimes one condition may be that the petition is to be filed only if someone else files a petition for an involuntary conservatorship. The unfiled petition usually remains with the proposed ward's attorney for safekeeping until any one or more of the prescribed conditions are met.

The idea of a standby conservatorship has considerable appeal. However, in many instances the petition is not used because those designated in the standby petition to initiate action must determine that a prestated condition has been met. This places the parties in the same position as the parties filing an involuntary conservatorship: having to determine the competency of an individual before a petition can be filed. Few people, even the ward's doctor, are anxious to label someone as no longer competent and in need of a conservatorship.

Conservatorships for Minors

Conservatorships for minors may be treated differently. Minors who have not reached a certain age, usually 18, and who have never married are considered legally incompetent to make contracts. In the event a conservatorship for a minor is required, usually because of the minor's acquisition of property, either or both parents generally have first preference to serve as conservator(s).

If the minor has reached a certain age, a statute may give him preference in choosing the conservator. Both under the common law and the Uniform Probate Code the age almost always is 14 years. In such instances the minor's choice still must be approved by the court, which must find that the designated party is qualified and suitable to serve.

Under some state statutes no conservator need be appointed for a minor who is receiving or is entitled to receive property not exceeding a statutory limit, usually $10,000. The parent or one having custody of the minor may receipt for the property on behalf of the minor as long as certain statutory procedures are followed. See also Chapter 2 concerning the Uniform Transfers to Minors Act.

Effect on the Ward's Competency

As indicated earlier, a conservatorship ordinarily can be instigated before proving that a proposed ward is of unsound mind. And the appointment of a conservator does not necessarily mean that the court has judged the ward to be of unsound mind. But in some states once a ward is under conservatorship, regardless whether the proceeding is voluntary or involuntary, she loses all legal power to enter into contracts and is considered legally incompetent to perform most other acts.

In other states, the ward's powers may be merely limited. In Alaska and Florida, for instance, the ward retains all civil and legal rights unless limited by the court or granted to the conservator. In Minnesota the appointment of a conservator is not evidence of incompetency, although the appointment of a guardian is. In Utah, whenever possible the court must select a limited conservatorship rather than the full conservatorship.

In other states, the ward may still be able to make or change his will and perform certain other acts as long as he continues to possess the requisite testamentary capacity—the ability to make a will. In other states, the appointment of a conservator may be deemed evidence of the lack of the ward's testamentary capacity.

Qualifications and Duties of a Conservator

The qualifications needed for an individual conservator are not any different than the qualifications needed for a power of attorney or for any other fiduciary. The party serving should be reliable, trustworthy, capable of managing the property, conveniently located to the ward, and competent to keep proper records.

Preferably, an individual conservator should be closely related to and younger than the ward. If the proposed individual is not closely related to the ward, consider whether he or a bank would do a better job. The proposed individual will be required to be bonded, whereas the bank probably would not have to be. Both are entitled to a fee for serving. Which one would be more entitled to the fee? If no individual seems to qualify, then a bank should be seriously considered for the position.

Upon appointment, the conservator possesses substantially the same powers to manage the ward's property as did the ward prior to the conservatorship. In a few states, the appointment of a conservator automatically terminates a power of attorney. In most of the others, the conservator has the power to revoke any power of attorney given by the ward.

As with the power of attorney, however, the fiduciary in a conservatorship (the conservator) presumably has some limitations on her powers. For instance, she normally cannot make or remake the ward's will nor transfer property to a trust. The making of lifetime gifts to individuals may be possible if the conservator can show a long-standing history of certain gift making on the part of the ward, or if it can be shown that such gifts are good for estate planning purposes—such as to avoid death taxes—and not necessary for the support and care of the ward.

Charitable gifts may be made if it can be shown that the ward either would have done so if competent or had a habit of making such gifts, especially to a particular charity. Authority to do so, however, normally would have to be obtained from the court.

In Rhode Island the court is authorized to allow estate planning and gifts to charities, relatives, and friends, as its statute favors reduction of taxes by partial distribution of the estate. Texas also favors tax-motivated gifts. With the approval of the court, Wyoming allows the creation of, and transfer of property over to, a revocable inter vivos trust.

After a conservatorship is opened, for purposes of administration the conservator takes possession and control of the ward's property, subject always to statutory limitations and the supervision of the court. Title to the ward's property, however, remains in the ward, just as it does with a power of attorney. This differs from a trust in that a trustee not only has possession of, but also title to, the property held in trust.

Some state statutes provide that the will of the ward is to be presented to the court upon the opening of the conservatorship. Supposedly this is for the purpose of alerting the court to the provisions in the ward's will about disposition of property. The conservator, presumably, then could do nothing that would prevent the carrying out of the ward's wishes.

Because the conservatorship proceedings are a public record, after the will is examined by the court it is resealed and placed with a proper official of the court. But this makes the statutory requirement of presenting the will to the court somewhat of a farce, since the court itself is not situated so as to guard against contradictory actions of the conservator. What usually occurs is that a copy of the will is kept by the conservator and the conservator's attorney so that due respect can be paid to its provisions.

In those states that follow the Uniform Probate Code, statutes provide that the conservator and the court shall take into account any known estate plan of the ward, including his or her will. In order that this may be done, the conservator has the statutory right to examine any will of the ward that was previously deposited with the court.

Generally after the appointment, the conservator must determine the assets of the ward and file an inventory with the court. The period for filing varies from state to state, but it generally runs between 30 days and 3 months. Thereafter the conservator is accountable to the court for the use and management of these assets.

Periodically, but usually annually, the conservator is required to report to the court any change in assets and any other matters affecting the conservatorship and the ward which occurred since the last report. The Uniform Probate Code provides that these reports be done at such times as the court may direct.

Upon the death or ending of the disability of the ward, or upon the conservator's resignation or removal, the conservator must file a final accounting and report. Thereafter, except for his or her resignation or removal, the conservator must make a distribution of the conservatorship assets remaining after all debts and charges have been paid, and secure a discharge. At this time the conservatorship is closed and any conservator's bond is released.

In conclusion, because of its adverse nature, almost always involving family members, the involuntary proceeding is the least desirable method for managing the estate of an incapacitated person. (See Chapter 9.) Although the standby conservatorship may also have problems, it and the voluntary conservatorship are preferable to the involuntary conservatorship. But neither voluntary method is as preferable as a power of attorney, if that power is feasible to use.

Under either the voluntary or the involuntary conservatorship, the ward may subsequently petition the court for termination of the conservatorship. The ward's claim ordinarily would be that the reason for opening the conservatorship, such as the ward's original incapacity, no longer exists. But even in the voluntary situation the court will deny the request if the allegations of the ward are not proved. Of course, if the ward had been a minor and now has reached adulthood, either by reason of age or marriage, then the conservatorship would be terminated.

Proposed Congressional Action

Because of perceived abuses under state statutes pertaining to conservatorships, reform bills have been introduced in both houses of Congress. Compliance of the states would be secured in most instances by the withholding of certain federal benefits in the event the required state statutes were not enacted.

In brief, Congress wants to ensure that a party is a fit subject for conservatorship and that the party's rights are protected during the period of the conservatorship. Unlike under present state conservatorship laws, under Congressional proposals some wards would be subject to only a limited conservatorship. In other words, they would retain certain rights and not, as often occurs now, be stripped of all legal powers upon being placed under conservatorship. The reasoning behind this is that in many cases an individual is not entirely incompetent and therefore should not be denied all rights and responsibilities.

The Congressional bills would require parties to show more incapacity on the part of the ward before a conservatorship could be granted. At present, the lawyer representing the proposed ward at the time of the petition often serves mainly in a passive capacity. The lawyer merely tries to determine what is best for the individual. The proposed bills would require the lawyer to act as an advocate. The proceeding would be adversarial in nature.

The bills would also require the conservator to be trained in the duties and responsibilities of the position. For the most part this would tend to eliminate individuals, even family members, from serving as conservators. Whether this would always be an improvement is debatable. Although these bills may never be passed, they may have the effect of causing reform in the conservatorship laws.

Protecting the Veteran

Special rules apply to conservatorships for veterans. A Uniform Veterans' Guardianship Act was proposed in 1928 and subsequently amended in 1942. All but eight states have adopted at least some version of the act. Generally, it provides that a conservator shall be appointed to service payments to a veteran rated incompetent by the Veterans' Administration. Ordinarily a bond is required of the conservator, if not a bank or trust company.

Generally, the act is not exclusive of other conservatorship provisions. But the Veterans' Administration is a necessary party to any proceeding affecting the administration of a veteran's assets. And it is an interested party in the appointment or removal of a conservator or in the termination of the conservatorship.

Some Common Questions Answered

Q. I set up a voluntary conservatorship because I wanted someone to look after my affairs, but I am not happy with the party I chose as conservator. Is there anything I can do about it?

A. Although you as a ward are now considered legally incompetent, you should first try to get the conservator to resign. If the conservator refuses to resign, statutes usually provide a procedure for terminating a conservatorship, after which time you can start over.

You may have to prove to the court's satisfaction that you are still competent to handle your own affairs. Or you may have grounds to apply to the court for removal of the conservator. For the court appearance, your main concern is to make certain that the lawyer is loyal to you and not the conservator. This could preclude the lawyer presently representing the conservator, since that lawyer could be considered to have a conflict of interest.

Q. As a result of my minor son being in a car accident he is entitled to damages. The insurance carrier won't pay until a conservatorship is opened. Is this necessary?

A. The position taken by the insurance company is correct. In these situations both the liable party and the party's insurance carrier want to make certain that the matter is finally and totally settled. Thus securing a binding release from all further liability is important to them. Your son, being a minor, cannot enter into such a binding agreement. Only someone legally representing your son can do so. The only method for this purpose is a conservatorship. Parents in their individual capacity cannot legally represent him and neither can a custodian under the Uniform Transfers to Minors Act.

Q. My son, who is under conservatorship, is now 18 years old, but I don't believe he is mature enough to be entrusted with property. Does the conservatorship have to be closed?

A. Legally, you have no choice to do otherwise. Your only recourse is to try to convince your son that it would be for his benefit to voluntarily set up some system whereby his property would continue to be managed by someone else. Legally, your son can establish this system himself when he becomes 18, before you distribute the conservatorship property to him.

The system set up can take one of many forms. The conservatorship could continue but as a voluntary conservatorship. Your son could give you or someone else a power of attorney. He could create a trust, either revocable or irrevocable, or a bank agency account. All of these options are voluntary and therefore could be terminated by him at any time, unless he entered into an irrevocable trust, an unlikely action.

Q. My father is a spendthrift. We three children want to put him under conservatorship, but our father says that a power of attorney is all that is necessary. Is he right?

A. No. A power of attorney would give the attorney in fact a coexisting right to manage his affairs. It does not take away any power of your father to continue to act in his own right. Thus your father could keep on with his spending habits and his attorney in fact could do nothing to stop him.

If your father is under conservatorship, then the conservator would take control of all of his property so that he would have no means to spend foolishly. A conservatorship, then, unlike a power of attorney, would protect your father's estate from his spendthrift habits.

Q. My father is dying, his doctor giving him less than a year to live. He is incompetent and unable to take care of his bills. Is there anything I can do other than open a conservatorship?

A. Unfortunately, not. Since he is incompetent, alternatives are not available to him. This situation is not uncommon. Most people go through life feeling that this won't happen to them and therefore do not prepare for such a contingency. As a result, an involuntary conservatorship has to be opened, even though it has limited value for a limited time. This means that in a short space of time you must hire a lawyer to open up a conservatorship and then upon his death use the lawyer to close it.

Both the attorney and the conservator are entitled to compensation, and court costs are involved. This could have been easily avoided if your father, when he was still competent, had properly planned and anticipated a possible need for representation at a later stage of his life.

6

Opting for an Antenuptial Agreement

Sometimes a man and woman contemplating marriage, no matter how much they love and respect each other, want to protect their respective estates from the legal effect of their pending marriage. They are aware that each of their estates, after marriage, will become vulnerable to a claim of the other party, so one or both of them may want to keep their own estates separate from that of the other party.

The people most likely to have these feelings are marrying for the second time—in other words, divorced or widowed persons. They may have children by a previous marriage or they may have already accumulated a sizable estate. Or possibly they may even be marrying for the first time but have substantial family assets that they wish to retain in the same bloodline.

There may be many reasons for a betrothed to want to prevent commingling of estates. Perhaps a man about to be married wants to preserve his estate for the benefit of his heirs or beneficiaries to the exclusion of his prospective spouse. Or perhaps a woman may be somewhat skeptical of the success of her pending marriage because of a wide difference in the partners' ages. She may not want to gamble her already-accumulated estate on the outcome of the new marriage. Or perhaps the parties may have unequal estates so that one party may possibly be "jeopardizing" a much larger estate than the other party.

Many parents may see themselves as having a stake in a proposed marriage. Perhaps one set of parents has already passed down ancestral prop-

71

erty to one of the parties to be married. Or perhaps the same parents have already begun a gift program to that child. In either case, the parents are afraid that the gifted property could end up in the hands of the other party. They hope, by use of a legal agreement, to preclude that from happening.

All of the above people have good reasons for wanting the spouses' estates to remain identifiable as theirs, when and if the prospective marriage relationship ends. As will be seen, this may not be entirely possible in some states of residence, even with a legal agreement.

Preservation of the Special Interests

For a man and a woman to keep their estates separate, they must enter into what is called an *antenuptial agreement*, sometimes referred to as a *premarital agreement*—literally a contract entered into before marriage. This contract determines the property rights of the betrothed after their marriage. Such contracts, although not always upheld, are favored by public policy.

They are available in all common law and community property states, except that Louisiana limits the right of the parties to contract. Of the balance of the states, less than a third have adopted the Uniform Premarital Agreement Act.

Many people contemplating an antenuptial agreement have difficulty suggesting the agreement to their prospective partners. Somehow, they think, it indicates a lack of love or faith in the other party or in the arrangement about to be consummated. But as a New York lawyer once said, "They don't realize that prenuptial agreements don't kill romance. They just suspend it for a short time."

When the antenuptial agreement goes into effect, the enforcing party must be able to show that it was entered into prior to the marriage. If it is in writing and was recorded in the appropriate county office prior to the date of the marriage, then there is no difficulty in making this proof. If the agreement was not timely placed on record, it could be difficult for the enforcing party to prove its existence and its contents and the fact that it was entered into prior to the marriage.

To be enforceable, the agreement must be proven by the enforcing party to be fair and reasonable, and entered into freely, knowledgeably, and in good faith without exertion of duress or undue influence. Full disclosure of all the assets held and owned prior to the marriage must also be shown to have been made by each party to the other. A few courts, however, have held that mere knowledge of such assets is sufficient.

Other requirements of enforceability also exist. Many of these are not much different from the ordinary requirements for any contract to be upheld. There must be adequate consideration for the agreement. Each party must have the capacity to contract—in other words not be legally incompetent by reason of minority or otherwise. And the provisions of the contract must be sufficiently explicit. A few states also have certain statutory requirements, such as that the agreement be in writing and properly acknowledged and recorded.

What Is the Most Important Requirement?

Of all the requirements, that of disclosure probably creates the most controversy. According to at least one authority, this type of contractual relationship is distinguishable from ordinary business transactions in which people deal with each other at arm's length. With an antenuptial agreement, a special duty of full disclosure arises that has no place in other types of contractual relationships.

For that reason, both parties as well as their attorneys should insist upon a complete, itemized list of assets, each carefully valued. Such a list should be made a part of the agreement, either contained within the document or mentioned there by reference. Mere recitation of net worth may not be held sufficient.

If at the time of the agreement fraud existed—for example, if the enforcing party concealed the real value of his or her estate—then the agreement is unenforceable.

The courts want both parties to be fully aware of what they are doing and what they may be giving up by signing the agreement. As a result, lawyers generally require each party to be represented by his or her own attorney, so that neither party can later allege a conflict of interest or collusion. Each party's attorney also tries to ensure that the client does not conceal or misrepresent his or her assets, as that could also endanger the validity of the agreement.

What Are the Terms of the Agreement?

Antenuptial agreements contain several important basic provisions:

1. *All facts and circumstances of the parties, including the financial conditions and prospects of each, are to be disclosed.* These should be spelled out within the document.

2. *Neither party will make any claim to any part of the other's estate during the marriage or upon the other party's death.* Any exceptions to this provision must be stated in the agreement.

3. *No claim will be made upon the other party in the event of divorce.* This provision may or may not be legally recognized, depending upon the jurisdiction involved. When a particular court holds that this provision is against public policy, then the condition is generally held invalid and hence unenforceable. If not recognized, sometimes this stipulation voids the contract, and sometimes only the stipulation itself is voided.

The matter of spousal maintenance in the event of divorce creates a dilemma. Different decisions about maintenance have been reached by different courts, depending upon how the antenuptial agreements are worded, what statutes are, what public policy is deemed to be, and what social trends are.

Some courts may allow support even though it was not provided for in the agreement. Others may not have had to decide whether maintenance is necessary, even after deeming other divorce provisions valid. Still others may hold both maintenance and divorce provisions to be invalid.

4. *Each party waives dower, homestead, elective, or other statutory rights in the property of the other, regardless of any law to the contrary.* Some agreements go further and state that, by virtue of the marriage, neither party acquires *any* interest in the property of the other.

Besides these basic provisions, other miscellaneous provisions may exist. These may pertain to the filing of income tax returns and the payment of debts and household and living expenses.

All of these provisions seem simple enough. Unless otherwise stated, you may keep what you brought into the marriage. The other party keeps what he or she brought into the marriage. When the marriage terminates, by death or dissolution, the other party gets only what you want him or her to get. Unfortunately, it doesn't always work out this way. Some jurisdictions may not honor every provision of an antenuptial agreement, no matter how carefully it is drawn.

Some Provisions
That May Fail

Certain statutes provide for family members to be supported after the death of a spouse or the dissolution of a couple's marriage. This type of support is referred to as the "family allowance," or sometimes as a "widow's [or widower's] allowance" (see Chapter 17). This allowance can generally be waived by an antenuptial agreement, provided no minor or dependent children exist. But in a few states the survivor may be entitled to the statutory allowance regardless of the existence of an antenuptial agreement to the contrary.

In spite of the agreement, in a few jurisdictions a surviving spouse may ask the probate court for, and may receive, an allowance to provide support for a period of time following the spouse's death. The monies are to come out of the deceased spouse's estate, regardless of the comparative sizes of the estates—and regardless of the antenuptial agreement.

Such sidestepping of the agreement up to the amount of the allowance may occur because of the particular jurisdiction or because the wording of the agreement was not specific enough. In spite of the rule, courts generally hold that the allowance must be specifically referred to. It is not sufficient merely to waive dower, homestead, or inheritance, or to refer to rights, claims, or interests. The intention of the parties must be clear. Waiver cannot arise by presumption, assumption, or construction.

The rights of minor children to support cannot be barred by an agreement, even if it specifically states they can. Courts have stated this and some statutes so provide, including the Uniform Premarital Agreement Act. But the right of children of the marriage to inheritance—not support—may be barred by proper language in the agreement.

Some courts object to an agreement that specifically stipulates as to the division of property in event of dissolution of the marriage. Suppose that a marriage has not been harmonious and one estate is much larger than the other. In these jurisdictions, if the marriage is dissolved, the party with the smaller estate may be entitled to a property settlement out of the other spouse's estate even though the antenuptial agreement specifically provides otherwise. The basis for the holding is that the contract provision is contrary to public policy and thus void and unenforceable.

According to these courts, this policy rule is based upon two principles: (1) the contract provision facilitates or induces dissolution of the marriage, and (2) the interspousal support obligation is imposed by law and cannot be contracted away. The theory is that the state has an interest in ensuring that the divorced spouse receives adequate support so as not to become a ward of the state.

In the 1970s, courts began to take a different view of—the so-called modern approach to—divorce. These courts analyze cases individually, resulting in some dissolution provisions of an antenuptial agreement being held enforceable and not against public policy. Whether property rights or support rights or both are affected depends upon the jurisdiction involved.

There appear to be two reasons for the change in attitude of the courts: (1) evidence that such agreements facilitate divorce is lacking, and (2) the idea that marriage is to be preserved at all costs no longer is considered valid. And some believe that the advent of no-fault divorce and a change in society's view of divorce justifies the upholding of this provision by the courts.

A few other states have other concerns. Homestead rights—the statutory or constitutional rights to retain a person's place of residence under varying circumstances—are sometimes considered as nonnegotiable. In other words, the parties cannot agree to contract away their homestead rights. Louisiana does not honor any form of marriage agreement, made before or during marriage, that would renounce or alter the marital portion or the established order of succession.

Courts have refused to honor certain other provisions: to refrain from cohabitation, to govern sexual relations between the parties, and to forbid the children of the wife's prior marriage from living with the parties.

With these possible exceptions, an antenuptial agreement is valid and enforceable if it is fair, just, equitable, and conscionable. That is not the same as saying, however, that antenuptial agreements should be routinely utilized.

Although from time to time valid reasons may exist for such agreements, some commentators discourage their use for routine first marriages, especially by young couples. Fear is expressed that the agreement may act like a cancer, spreading its poison into the marriage and eventually destroying what began as a loving relationship.

Postnuptial Agreements

At one time postnuptial agreements—that is, marital agreements made during the period of a marriage—no matter how fairly entered into, were not considered valid and enforceable. They still are not in a few states. The courts' refusal to enforce was apparently a carryover from the common law, which did not allow contracts made between husband and wife. Now, however, the trend is for most states to allow postnuptial agreements, either by reason of court decisions or of statutes.

To be valid, contracts of any kind require adequate consideration. *Consideration* is something of value running from one party to a contract to the other party. It serves as an inducement to enter into the particular contract. It may be something of tangible value or merely a promise to do or not to do something.

The marriage is deemed sufficient consideration for an antenuptial agreement. But in a few states, the courts have been unable to find consideration. Not finding it, they hold the postnuptial agreement to be invalid.

In those states that recognize postnuptial agreements, the courts find that the consideration is the mutual release of valuable rights and future claims. Having found this consideration, the great majority of states hold postnuptial agreements valid.

The same requisites, however, must be present in a postnuptial agreement as in an antenuptial agreement. All the elements required of any contract must be present for the postnuptial agreement to be valid. The agreement can be entered into only after full disclosure and it must be done freely, knowledgeably, and in good faith without exertion of duress or undue influence.

Assuming all elements of a valid contract exist, a postnuptial agreement may waive the family allowance. As with the antenuptial agreement, the waiver must be expressly stated, although, again, courts differ as to the required terminology. And, again also, the parties may not waive the rights of minors.

The Uniform Premarital Agreement Act allows an antenuptial agreement to be amended or revoked after marriage, even without consideration, as long as it is in writing and signed by the parties. In effect, this constitutes the making of a contract after marriage.

Nonmarital Agreements

What about agreements made between two unmarried individuals—who may or may not be of the same sex—who live together? These are variously described as nonmarital agreements or cohabitation agreements. Are these agreements valid and thus enforceable?

Dating back to at least 1976, when a California court did so, several courts have held that nonmarital agreements are valid if not based upon sexual services. Such agreements may be based upon an implied contract as well as an express, written agreement. Because of the legal difficulties that can arise in the absence of an express agreement, at least one commentator has suggested that two parties cohabiting would be well advised to execute a nonmarital agreement, the terms of which would be similar to an antenuptial agreement.

Some Common Questions Answered

Q. I am getting married for the second time. Should I contact my attorney about an antenuptial agreement?

A. If you have any question concerning the protection of your estate or the protection of your children from the effect of this new marriage, certainly you should contact your attorney, discuss the proposed marriage frankly, and detail your concerns.

Q. Before I married my present husband, he and I orally agreed upon a division of our property in the event our marriage did not work out. But we never put it down in writing. If I file for divorce, will our agreement be upheld by the court?

A. Whether your agreement will be upheld by the court depends upon several things: the jurisdiction in which you reside, your husband's admissions, and your ability to prove the specific terms of the agreement.

Courts differ on the amount of proof required to prove an oral contract. In the situation you describe, it is assumed that it is to your advantage to prove the existence of the agreement. Presumably, you have the most to gain by doing so. By the same token, it is apparent that your husband has the most to lose. Thus it is doubtful that you will have an easy time of getting over the first hurdle, that of proving the existence of the agreement.

If you did succeed in proving the agreement, you still would have to prove the specific terms of the agreement. If your husband resists, you may not be able to prove to the court's satisfaction the provisions of your agreement. Although courts try to uphold contracts, they will not—in fact, they cannot—do so if a contract's terms are not clear.

Q. My husband and I executed an antenuptial agreement before our marriage but, although dated prior to our marriage, it was not placed of record until after our marriage. Is it valid and enforceable?

A. This question really is directed to those jurisdictions that require the marital agreement to be made prior to the marriage in order to be valid. Here, the purpose of the prior recording is merely to make the existence of the agreement prior to the marriage easily verifiable. When so recorded, it is impossible for the opposing party to deny that it was entered into. He or she also cannot claim that some provisions appearing in the instrument were not agreed upon. The recorded instrument speaks for itself.

When the agreement is not timely placed of record, then a dispute can arise as to whether, for instance, the agreement actually took place prior to the marriage. It would also be difficult to prove that the terms as shown in the written instrument were those agreed to prior to the marriage. In direct answer to your question as posed, the answer is yes, the contract is valid and enforceable unless a statute provides otherwise.

Q. My wife and I entered into an antenuptial agreement before we were married. But we now have some property in joint tenancy with each other and I would like to include my wife in my will. Will our pre-marital agreement take precedence over any will or joint tenancy provisions to the contrary?

A. No, most likely it will not. Any subsequent, voluntary act on your part that benefits your wife to a greater degree than agreed upon is permissible. In effect, such actions on your part amend the agreement. As long as it gives greater benefits to your wife, then no one can object to it. The joint tenancy provisions and the will provisions take precedence over the agreement.

The reverse may not be true. If you tried to avoid some or all of the terms of the antenuptial agreement by taking actions that would give your wife less than originally agreed upon, then presumably your wife could claim under the agreement.

A different result might occur if a court found that the changes more beneficial to your wife were the result of fraud or undue influence. For example, if the creation of the joint tenancies or the change in the will occurred when you were incompetent, then such events would be considered invalid.

Some courts are now beginning to recognize the rights of third parties to a contract, but it is doubtful that these courts would do so in these two situations. The rights of spouses are too strongly protected by our courts. In these situations "third parties" refer to those who would stand to lose benefits that they otherwise would be entitled to, such as your children.

Q. Does an antenuptial agreement have to provide that all property of each partner remain separate from the other? May the agreement, for instance, provide that all the property of the man goes to the woman but no property of the woman goes to the man?

A. The agreement may provide for any division of the property of each, as long as the agreement is deemed to be fair, just, equitable, and conscionable. At first glance, such an agreement as you describe does not seem to meet these requirements. But circumstances could be such that the terms would be considered entirely fair. As long as each party is competent and adequately represented by his or her own counsel and all the necessary information has been accurately presented by each to the other, the courts most likely would not interfere with the judgment of the parties. They would also not try to second-guess the reasons for the apparent disparity of the terms.

Q. At the time that my wife and I entered into an antenuptial agreement we used the same lawyer. Upon the death of the first one of us, will this cause any difficulty?

A. Probably not, unless the surviving one of you makes some contrary claims. However, it is advisable to hire separate attorneys to prevent possible conflicts of interest.

Nowadays estate lawyers are presumed to be like trial lawyers, who can only represent one litigant at a time. Apparently, the assumption is that all parties are potential litigants, even though the parties themselves may not feel that way.

7

Everything You Should Know About Wills

Much has been said and written about wills. Practically all writers and speakers, lawyers and laypersons alike, advocate everyone having a will. This position is meritorious. Unfortunately, in their eagerness to prove the value of a will, some advocates make statements that are either misleading or simply not true. And few people fully explain the various aspects of a will, thus causing more skepticism than understanding on the part of the general public.

This chapter discusses wills in considerable detail, with the hope that you will have a greater understanding and appreciation of them. It should also clear up any misunderstandings or misapprehensions you may have acquired about wills.

What Is a Will?

A *will*, or testament, is a legal declaration—based upon guidelines enunciated by statutes and court decisions—of what you want done with your estate upon your death. For now, this simplified definition should suffice, but later, when probate and nonprobate property is discussed, it may have to be modified somewhat so that no misunderstanding occurs.

One who makes a will is called a *testator.* The testator is said to have died *testate.* One who dies without a will is said to have died *intestate.* The ones to whom property is given in the will are called *beneficiaries.* Beneficiaries are also sometimes called *legatees* or *devisees* or even *distributees.* If you die intestate, the recipients of your property are called *heirs.*

Gifts made in a will are sometimes known as *bequests* or *devises.* To give, devise, or bequeath all mean the same thing. The one named in a will and who administers the estate upon the testator's death is called an *executor* or personal representative. The one administering an intestate estate is also called a *personal representative* or sometimes an *administrator.*

What if you change your mind about your will? If the change is sufficiently minor so that both the original will and the changed provision when read together do not cause confusion, you can make an amendment to the will, called a *codicil.* Like the will, a codicil must be executed according to statute, but the same witnesses need not be on both instruments.

In effect, the codicil amends your will to the extent specified in the codicil. Upon your death, both documents constitute your will and both are presented for probate. The two instruments are taken together and are treated as one instrument.

Suppose, however, that you intend to change your beneficiaries and do not want someone to find out what was stated in the old will. Then it would be advisable for you to make a totally new will, not a codicil, and destroy your old will. This precludes others from knowing what your original will contained.

Public policy favors wills. Statutes are clear on who can make a will, how they are to be executed and witnessed, and, to some extent, what they may contain.

The Need for a Will

For various reasons, many individuals believe they do not need a will. If you are one of them, one hopes you will change your mind as you read this chapter.

Because of its popularity, joint tenancy—one of the main reasons for not having a will—should be examined in more detail. Joint tenants say they don't need a will because when they die the surviving tenant will get all the property anyway. This is the "cheap will" referred to in Chapter 3. That surmise may or may not happen.

Suppose that your wife has a will but you do not. You don't think you need a will since all of your combined property is held in joint tenancy with each other. You believe that if you die first, she will get it all anyway. Is this necessarily true?

First, you believe that all of your property is held in joint tenancy with each other. By whose word are you accepting that this is true? Sometimes, in spite of the care taken, all your property may not be so held. Mistakes and oversights can and do happen.

Suppose a deed was not properly drawn, or the proper bank signature card was not used, or anyone handling the property misunderstood your instructions and created a tenancy in common instead of a joint tenancy. Would you always be able to recognize the difference or be able to recognize someone else's mistake? In many instances, you must accept someone else's word as to how your title is held.

Secondly, even though all your property is presently held in joint tenancy, suppose you receive an inheritance. Or suppose some joint tenancy property matured, had to be reinvested, and some of it was not put in joint tenancy. Or suppose you died an accidental death, which gave rise to a claim for damages against a third party. Such damages, if received by your estate, could not be held in joint tenancy and thus in the absence of a will would go according to the laws of descent and distribution, meaning according to the laws of inheritance. In any of these situations, your wife would only receive what the statutes gave to her.

Or suppose you both died simultaneously as a result of a car accident. Under the Uniform Simultaneous Death Act, which most states have, all of your joint property would be considered to be held by the two of you as tenants in common, one-half by you and one-half by your wife. Without wills, each of your halves would pass to others according to the same laws of inheritance.

Finally, one more consideration. What do you want to happen to your property upon the death of both of you? You may think that when your wife dies you can then make a will or set up some new joint tenancies. But what if at that time you are no longer competent to do so?

For the peace of mind and satisfaction that it gives, both of you should make your wills at the same time.

Misconceptions About Wills

A common misunderstanding is that if you don't leave a will, the state might get all of your property upon your death. This refers to what is known as *escheat*, which provides that if no legal heirs or claimants exist or can be found at the time of your death, your property will revert to the state.

It has been said that escheat occurs if the surviving heirs are not closely related to you. This is bunk. If you die leaving no will, statutes work very hard at finding and defining your heirs before your estate escheats to the state. But despite this fact, you should still make a will, for reasons that will be explained later in the chapter.

Possibly the next most common misunderstanding about wills is that by having a will you minimize death taxes. But the size of most estates does not warrant this concern. The federal tax can be, and is, substantial and a worry for the wealthy, that is, those individuals with gross estates of $600,000 or more. But state taxes are normally nominal or nonexistent.

Because state taxes are generally low and have fairly generous exemptions, most testators should be more interested in leaving their property to those they favor, rather than in trying to save any state tax. Fortunately, the heirs most likely to be favored are the ones most likely to have the highest tax exemptions and the lowest tax rates.

In any event, the presence or lack of a will, in and of itself, does not save death taxes. Death taxes apply whether or not a party receives an inheritance as an heir under the laws of inheritance or as a beneficiary under the terms of a will.

Some commentators have stated that a will speeds up administration and provides interim relief for the surviving spouse and minor children. The first part of that statement is doubtful and the second part is basically not true. Whether or not the decedent leaves a will, the estate proceedings are similar and normally proceed at the same pace. The same general probate procedures must be followed in both instances. And the benefits provided by statute for the surviving spouse and minor children are the same regardless of the type of estate administration.

One writer extolled the virtues of being able to specify burial arrangements in a will. However, the usual experience with decedents' estates and probate administration is to not open the will until after the funeral, or at least until after funeral arrangements have been made. Thus a will provision specifying burial arrangements could be worthless, or possibly even unnerving to those survivors who had made other arrangements.

This does not mean that you should forgo making such arrangements in the event you wish to do so. But specifying your desires to a family member in advance, either orally or in writing, should work out more to your advantage.

You may believe that if you die leaving a will, then no probate proceeding is necessary. As stated above, estate proceedings are similar whether or not there is a will.

Your will has no force or effect until it is admitted to probate through a proceeding in court. In other words, if your will leaves everything to your husband and you die, he cannot merely show the will around and say, "see, she left everything to me." Only when your will is admitted to probate is its validity then proved and its contents then enforced. But under some circumstances, your will may not be probated. See the discussion about this in Chapters 11 and 15.

The above recitation is not intended to belittle wills. To the contrary, wills can be, and usually are, extremely important, but they should be made for the right reasons.

Will Contests

For some mysterious reason, a number of persons believe that wills are frequently contested. Sometimes this is their excuse for not making a will. But how often are wills ever contested?

Any person who might gain from contesting your will has a potential right to do so. No one can guarantee that your will won't be contested for one reason or another. But contesting a person's will and proving the allegations are not the same thing. The charges of the contestant must be based upon facts which must be proven in court. As a result, will contests are rare and seldom successful.

Only one study of any consequence concerning will contests is known to have been made, that in Davidson County, Tennessee, for the years 1976 through 1984. Of all wills offered for probate in that county during that period, less than 1 percent were contested. Of these, less than half went to trial, and of these less than one-third of the contestants were successful in court. Results of this study would seem to imply that will contests shouldn't be of much concern, especially if your will is drawn by a lawyer.

The two predominant bases for contest, of equal importance, were found in the study to be undue influence and lack of testamentary capacity. While your attorney will be on the lookout for evidence of either of these possibilities and act accordingly, you yourself should be able to determine whether someone is trying to influence you. Be aware, however, that someone—your children, for instance—urging you to make a will is not the same as that person trying to influence you as to how to make it. Telling someone to make a will and telling someone how to make it are two entirely different things.

As to lack of testamentary capacity, incompetence of course can occur at any age. But as you grow older, the more likely you might be to lack such capacity. In other words, it is not a good idea to wait to make your will until you are on your deathbed.

Purposes of a Will

Why don't some persons have a will? If you don't have a will, perhaps you can answer this question. Procrastination is probably the chief culprit, although few people like to spend money on essentials before they are deemed necessary. Some people don't make a will because they don't like to think about their own mortality. Other people have a difficult time making up their mind, and still others are willing to let the laws of inheritance apply. If you do not have a will, this indicates that you have not yet done any estate planning, a situation that some day you and possibly your heirs will regret.

Common sense should tell you that you should have a will, regardless of your age, family status, sex, race, or station in life. But you may have difficulty in coming up with specific reasons for having one. This section will outline some valid reasons for having a will, although probably not all of them will apply to you.

As stated in Chapter 1, your will should be thought of as an insurance policy. An insurance policy protects you or your property and possibly other persons as well. So does a will. An insurance policy provides protection in the event you suffer a loss. A will also protects in the event of a loss—your death. You might be able to get by without insurance and you or your estate might be able to get by without a will, but those are not risks you should take.

Many people dislike paying legal fees for preparation of a will. This is foolish because the entire cost of will preparation and the accompanying estate planning are likely to be less than the total costs of the annual premiums for your various insurance coverages. Only in unusual instances would they not be.

Avoiding Laws of Inheritance

You may dislike laws that exist allegedly to protect you, such as helmet, seat belt, or smoking laws. But there exists a whole set of state inheritance laws, sometimes referred to as the laws of descent and distribution, to protect you, your estate, and your survivors if you die without leaving a will. See the discussion about these in Chapter 13.

These laws of inheritance, which mostly apply only if you die without a will, may not please you or your next of kin. But if you die without leaving a will, then your estate passes according to these laws of inheritance whether or not that would have been your wish and whether or not you like being "protected" by your government.

If you want to avoid the laws of inheritance, you must make your own death transfer arrangements, which is primarily done by making a testamentary disposition of your property. Chances are you do not know for sure how your state laws of inheritance affect you. Without a will, you are taking a risk as to who would receive your property upon your death. In addition, the laws of inheritance, although relatively stable, can change or may be different in another state to which you move. Thus while you may be able to tolerate your present state laws of inheritance, at the time of your death they may be different than you anticipated.

Before you decide whether or not to make a will, you should at least determine whether the laws of inheritance in your state will distribute your estate in a manner agreeable to you. And you will have to keep doing so for the rest of your life. In checking your laws, you will find that in limited instances you still cannot fully overcome certain laws of inheritance by making a will. See Chapters 13 and 14.

Avoiding Bond Costs

One cost can be saved by making a will—that of a bond. A *bond* is a device that guarantees the personal representative's performance according to law. (For a detailed discussion of bonds, see Chapter 10.) If you die intestate, your personal representative will usually be required to put up bond. Bond costs, which ordinarily are based on the size of the estate, can be expensive and usually should be avoided.

If you die testate and your will so specifies, your estate's personal representative will not have to put up bond. Most wills specify that the executor shall serve without bond.

Avoiding Disputes Among Your Heirs

If you leave no will, the possibility exists that upon your death your heirs may race to the courthouse in order to be named administrator of your estate. The ensuing dispute could cause hard feelings and could result in added expense. But even if your survivors are agreeable, it may take them a bit more time to agree upon a personal representative than if you yourself had taken care of this by making a will.

Advantages of a Will

Having a will can be very advantageous because you can set up certain provisions for the benefit of you and your heirs. Without a will, none of these advantages is possible. Of course, few wills contain all the provisions mentioned below, and you would want considerable guidance from your lawyer as to what items you should consider.

Unlike in an intestate situation, in a testate situation you have the right to choose your personal representative. The party you name in your will can be almost any competent adult or a qualified bank. Think twice, though, if you are considering an individual other than a family member or close relative. You should not be grasping to find any available and qualified individual. If you are, then you should seriously consider naming your bank as executor.

A will also gives you the opportunity to choose your beneficiaries, although there are other, perhaps less desirable, ways to do so. Choosing your heirs, so to speak, by making a will allows you to give preference to individuals of your choice, regardless of the laws of inheritance. And you can name alternate "heirs" in the event any of those first named die, either prior to your death or within a stated time after your death. This is not possible if you don't leave a will. Regardless of this fact, however, state statutes generally protect a surviving spouse from being entirely disinherited. See the discussion about this in Chapters 13 and 14.

Listing Property

You may have keepsakes, antiques, or heirlooms that you wish to distribute among several individuals. Many states allow you to make a list, separate from your will, of most tangible—as distinguished from intangible—personal property, designating to whom you want various items to go. You may change this list from time to time without changing your will, although some state statutes require the list to be in writing and in existence prior to the making of the will.

Some state statutes are specific as to how this separate identification of bequests can be accomplished. For instance, reference to this list may have to be made in your will. You should only attempt this list with the help of your lawyer, as otherwise your list may not be valid or binding. And your lawyer should be consulted as to whether the list is provided for in your state.

What are your alternatives if your state does not allow you to make a list separate from your will? First, of course, you can list the property in your will. But this places an almost impossible burden upon you: you may have to frequently change your will as your possessions and desires change from time to time.

Some individuals with this dilemma place a mark on each item, identifying its future owner, such as initials on the bottom of a chair. Or they may make a list, naming a beneficiary for each item, even though no statute exists to give the list any legal status. In neither case would the procedure be legally binding. But a close, amicable family may honor the "system" used by the decedent, even though it is doubtful that your lawyer would give wholehearted support for this procedure, since family arguments could result. And a testator can never be absolutely sure that promises by children or anyone else will be kept after death occurs.

If you are thinking of making a list, you should realize that many things you treasure may not have the same value to your next of kin. Thus the importance you place upon the gifts may not actually exist. On the other hand, chances are that if one of your children wants something of yours, then one or more of your other children will also want it.

To avoid some of this difficulty, many wills provide that the tangible personal property be divided equally between the children. These wills further provide that if the children cannot agree on the division, which of necessity cannot be exactly equal, then the executor shall dispose of this property by sale to the highest bidder.

In this instance, then, the children can bid on the property and divide the net sale proceeds equally between them. This generally works best, unless the executor is one of the children rather than a disinterested party such as a bank. In that event the individual executor may find him- or herself with an alleged conflict of interest.

If your state does allow the list and you want to make the distribution, then make up a separate list rather than list all items in the will. It will save a lot of clutter in your will and be much more flexible and inexpensive. If you use the list, be careful when making it up and avoid unintelligible markings and corrections on it.

Setting Up Testamentary Trusts

In a will, you can set up testamentary trusts for the benefit of such persons as your spouse, minor children, aged parents, incompetents, or spendthrifts. The trust provisions spell out the terms of the trust, including the designation of a trustee, under what conditions the trust property is to be used, and under what conditions the trust terminates.

Testamentary trusts are also used in larger estates involving a married couple to avoid the same property being subject to death taxes twice—once in the estate of the husband and once in the estate of the wife. A detailed discussion of trusts can be found in Chapter 8.

Selling Real Property

Finally, if the testator owns real estate, the testator may authorize its sale in order to simplify distribution of the estate. Such a will provision can avoid prolonged, and probably more costly, sale proceedings in the event the property is sold during the estate period.

The sales provisions can provide either that the personal representative has a discretionary power of sale of the decedent's property or that the sale is mandatory. The discretionary clause allows the personal representative to make the decision, whereas with the mandatory provision the testator makes the decision. The mandatory clause is more likely to be utilized by a testator for one of three reasons: (1) if there are no closely related beneficiaries, (2) if there are too many beneficiaries, whether or not closely related, or (3) if the estate needs to be liquidated in order to fulfill the bequests. If none of these situations exist, the discretionary clause would be the better one to have, since the decision of whether or when to sell can be made when the circumstances—such as market conditions—are better known.

In either case, a distribution of cash realized from the sale of the real property may be preferable to a distribution of the property itself. Without either a discretionary or a mandatory sale clause in the will, most statutes allow court-approved sales. Be advised, however, conforming to statutory sale provisions can be tedious and expensive.

Avoiding Taxes

For people with larger estates, having a will may enable the heirs to avoid certain death taxes. For more about these tax advantages relating to wills, see Chapter 16, which discusses death taxes, and Chapter 8, which discusses trusts.

Form and Wording of Wills

What should your will contain—and what should it leave out?

It is no accident that wills tend to look a lot alike. But don't let this fool you into thinking that you can make your own will. Both the form of a will and certain words contained therein are dictated by statute and court decisions. Only the substance is different in each case, although even then a similarity exists, since most people have somewhat similar views as to who is entitled to their property after their death.

Legal documents in plain English, helped along by statutes, fortunately are being used more frequently, but wills seem to continue to have a language all their own. Because of statutory definitions and numerous court interpretations of will language, not too many lawyers want to try to modernize the language in a will at the possible risk of loss to their clients.

Here are just a few examples of the kind of risks involved. Sometimes the word *child* refers to any descendant, not just the person born to the testator. The same interpretation might apply to the word *issue*. The word *heir* generally does not include a spouse, although many exceptions appear in statutes when a spouse is either considered to be or treated as an heir.

Your will should contain consistent language for clarity and understanding. If you first refer to your daughter as your child, then keep referring to her as your child. Don't suddenly begin referring to her as your issue. If you first use the word *give*, then continue to use that verb. Don't suddenly change to *bequeath* or *devise*.

Changing your terminology may only momentarily confuse those that read your will. But don't jeopardize the interpretation of your will by trying to be creative. You should want your will to have the same meaning for everyone, even though it may not be interesting to read.

Thus care must be taken in drawing a will. Carelessness or lack of know-how in the will draftsmanship can result in conflicts, misconstruction, lawsuits, confusion, or family squabbling. This does not mean that problems arise only with improper language. Disgruntled and disappointed heirs always can try to make trouble.

What Should *Not* Be in Your Will

If you think of your will as a business document that contains instructions effective upon your death, perhaps you will understand why certain matters are best omitted from your will. Surplus, redundant language should always be omitted. Some words or phrases that once were commonly used are no longer deemed appropriate, such as "beloved" or "believing in a supreme being" or "realizing the frailties of life."

As briefly indicated earlier, your will is not the best place to designate your funeral arrangements, nor is it the best place to direct disposition of your body, eyes, or organs. If you reflect on how and when your will is handled after your death, you will realize that these directions should be handled outside of your will, although because of many states' Uniform Anatomical Gift Laws you may wish to confirm in your will the arrangements you made outside of your will.

Considerations in Making Your Will

The two most important considerations in making your will are your present estate and your present, intended beneficiaries. In other words, your will must be made on the basis of the facts as they exist at the time of its making, not as you may hope they exist at the time of your death. When making your will, you cannot assume that it won't be used for years to come and that at a later time the facts will be different than at present.

Nevertheless as you begin preparation of your will, you should try to project what your estate may some day be worth. At the same time you should keep in mind that you may outlive one or more of your beneficiaries or that you may later have additional parties whom you may want to favor. If you do these things, you may never have to redo your will or, if you must, a codicil may be sufficient.

This doesn't mean that if you are careful you never again need to review your will. Whenever a change in your circumstances occurs, you should review your will to determine whether the new situation requires you to redraw it or at least to amend it. The change of circumstances involves the same considerations you had when you initially made your will—the status of your estate and the status of your beneficiaries.

For instance, if after your will is drawn you or your spouse inherit a substantial amount of property, or if any of your beneficiaries die, then you should make certain that your will has anticipated that possibility. If you failed, or were unable, to do so, then you will have to redraw or at least amend your will so that it takes into account the changed situation.

You may be concerned because the property interests you now have are entirely different than what they were at the time you drew your will. You may be wondering whether you should change your will to reflect what you now own. Under most conditions, this should cause you no concern whatsoever, unless the value or nature of your estate is so changed that a different type of will is desirable for tax or other reasons.

A will speaks only as to that property which you own at death, not as to that property you might have owned at the time of making your will. You need to be sure that your will distributes all the probate property which you own at the time of your death. As long as your will has a special clause, known as a residuary clause, this will be accomplished.

The Residuary Clause

A *residuary clause* is one that disposes of all of your property remaining after any specific bequests. A *specific bequest* is one that specifically identifies and describes a particular item of property—such as a piano, a bank account, or a farm—or a sum of money.

Some occurrences cannot be foreseen, but usually a carefully drawn will anticipates certain changing circumstances so that little or no redrafting is required if and when they occur.

If your will contains a residuary clause, then the size of your estate is irrelevant, except possibly for tax reasons. This is because your will under such circumstances will state where all your residuary property goes—

say, to A, or to A and B equally. In this situation, "all" can be small or large. A, or A and B, will receive all the balance of your estate, either alone or in equal shares, as the case may be.

But if you try to give all your property away, piece by piece, bequest by bequest, without a catch-all provision (the residuary clause), then any change in the nature of your property will require a modification of your will. Needless to say, this kind of will is rare and should remain so.

If you make specific gifts of money to one or more persons, presumably the amounts are based somewhat on the size of your estate. Thus if your estate size changes and you want the money bequests to represent approximately the same percentage of your estate, you will have to periodically amend your will in order to update the amount of money to be distributed.

If you want to avoid the possibility of such frequent amendments, you can do so simply by speaking in terms of percentages rather than in dollar amounts. As long as the percentages add up to exactly 100, no difficulty will occur.

Some wills use fractions, rather than percentages, but because fractions need a common denominator, sometimes they can cause all kinds of odd results—and difficulties. Even fractions of equal value can sometimes cause trouble, since the original fraction may be further divided if a prior death of one or more of the beneficiaries occurs. Thus fractions normally should be avoided, since speaking in terms of percentages is always available and understandable.

To illustrate, you should state "2 percent of my estate," not "2/100 (or 1/50) of my estate." Even mathematicians, presumably, would prefer to work with percentages.

Suppose you make a cash bequest in a certain amount instead of specifying a percentage. You run the danger of overgiving to one beneficiary to the detriment of other beneficiaries. Let's say you make a $15,000 cash bequest that at the time represents only a small fraction of your estate. If later you were confined to a nursing home and your estate was greatly reduced as a result, that amount would represent a much larger fraction of the total estate. Would you still want that bequest to remain in the same amount? Possibly not, but perhaps now you are unable to change your will because of incompetency. If you had originally specified the amount of the cash bequest in terms of the percentage of your estate, that amount would have remained constant in relation to the rest of your estate.

This discussion is not meant to apply to the nominal cash bequest that many testators like to make—to their grandchildren for instance. In these situations, the amounts generally are so small in relation to the balance of their estate that no harm is likely to occur in doing so.

Your Beneficiaries

Now consider your beneficiaries. The possibility that you may outlive one or more of your named beneficiaries should always be anticipated by naming alternate or contingent beneficiaries. If the first designated individual is not living at the time of your death, then by naming a successor beneficiary you have someone to take his or her place without your having to change your will.

Your will should identify each beneficiary not only by name but also by your relationship, by address (at least by city and state), and by whatever else it takes to pinpoint the identity of the beneficiary. But beneficiaries do not have to be named as long as they are specifically designated and identified, although it usually is best to do both.

Sometimes designating a particular group of beneficiaries may be preferable to naming individual ones. No chosen individual of a particular group can then be forgotten or omitted. Even a group, however, should be specified carefully. For instance, the mere word *cousin* could cause difficulties if the degree of kinship, such as *first cousin*, were not also stated.

But even in this situation you should be careful in your designation. For instance, "first cousin once removed" can be either a child of your first cousin or a child of your great uncle or aunt. See the chart in Chapter 13.

Even with these precautions for naming beneficiaries, difficulties can still sometimes arise. In one will a beneficiary was identified by name, relationship (cousin), and the city in which he was last known to have lived. Yet, apparently unknown to the testator and certainly not to the lawyer who prepared the will, two cousins exactly matched this identity. Fortunately, the bequest was small and the two individuals who matched the description agreed to split it, thereby avoiding a difficult, perhaps impossible, solution.

But this difficulty might not have occurred if the testator had not been "reaching" for someone to leave her property to. In this instance, she had only collateral heirs—no direct descendants. She did not know the one cousin, whichever one it was, well and apparently did not know, or barely knew, the other one at all. Although the situation escaped a major problem, it might have been better in this situation if the testator had considered leaving her property to charity.

Now think of your beneficiaries in a different sense. Are they minors or otherwise mentally or legally incompetent? Does their inheritance need to be protected in some manner by reason of their incapacity? Should you provide for someone to watch over their inheritance so that other legal proceedings, such as a conservatorship, are not necessary in order to make the distribution to them? If the answer to any of these questions is "yes," then you should consider testamentary trusts for such beneficiaries. Trusts are discussed in Chapter 8.

You can help beneficiaries by considering the effect of death taxes on any bequests you make to them. (See the discussion of death taxes in Chapter 16.) Unless otherwise stipulated in the will, in some states death taxes are assessed to the beneficiaries to whom property is bequeathed. Under other state statutes, death taxes are apportioned among all the beneficiaries. These statutes can normally be avoided by your will stipulating who shall bear the tax. Always consider whom you want to bear the burden of the taxes and state this in your will.

Sometimes gifts of tangible personal property, such as a piano, are made as a goodwill gesture, to let the beneficiary know, for instance, that her friendship or past help was appreciated. If the gift is the only bequest given to an individual who has no exemption, she might then have to dig into her own pocket to pay any tax resulting from the inheritance.

As you can see, by making a beneficiary pay a tax on a gift, especially a small gift, you tend to destroy whatever it was that you were originally trying to accomplish. This can be avoided by the will providing that any tax resulting from the gift is to be paid out of the residuary estate.

A will ordinarily stipulates that a beneficiary must be living when the testator dies or for some short period following the testator's death. This postdeath period often is based upon the period required by statute to keep an estate open, a time primarily given to claimants for filing claims. If a beneficiary dies during the early period of the estate administration, the testator is able to keep control of the bequest by providing for an alternate beneficiary. This could possibly save double taxation, or at least double handling, of the same property—once in the estate of the first to die and once again in the estate of the second to die.

Any gift in your will should specify that the named beneficiary must live a specified time beyond your death in order to qualify for the bequest. If not, then the bequest would go to an alternate beneficiary. The will clause should read like this: "to Mary Doe, provided she is living four months after my death. If she is not then living, then the same shall go to. . . . "

By providing for a time limit you are able to control the disposition of your property beyond the time of your death. It ordinarily would make little sense for your property to be given to someone who outlived you for only a short time. However the time frame does have limitations. In part, this can be due to statutory limitations. Or it may be tied in with how long you would want to keep the administration proceeding open in order to determine who is entitled to the property.

You may not want any time limitations because of the nature of the gift. But almost always you would want at least a clause following the name, such as "providing she is living at the time of my death. If not, then. . . . "

If an estate of $600,000 or more is liable for federal estate taxes, however, then the time period specified probably would be six months. This is the maximum time permitted under federal statute for certain purposes. Since a decedent's estate will be open much longer if it is subject to a federal estate tax, the time period will ordinarily be determined by the federal statute—six months—rather than by any state statute, which may be a shorter period.

Occasionally, it may not be wise to require any time period to elapse before the beneficiary is entitled to the bequest. It may be sufficient just to stipulate that the beneficiary be living at the time of the testator's death. For example, if the bequest is a business, it may not be wise to leave the bequest held in reserve—in *abeyance*—for any period of time. Loans and other business decisions might have to be resolved soon after the decedent's death, in which case the party entitled to the property must be identified quickly so that the business can continue operating without interruption.

As an example, suppose that a farm was bequeathed to the decedent's spouse. The death occurred just before a short-term loan for buying seed for the next crop year was to be negotiated at the local bank. The decedent's will further stipulated that the bequest of the farm to the spouse would only occur if the spouse was living six months after the decedent's death. Because of this time stipulation, the bank could not immediately make the loan to the surviving spouse if the farm or the crop were required as collateral. The bank could not be certain that the spouse would live six months thereafter—and thus be entitled to the farm. In other words, the collateral could be worthless. If she died within that six-month period, she would never have been the owner of the property and therefore would have had no legal right to put up such collateral.

Years ago, time-requirement clauses replaced the ancient practice of stipulating that a beneficiary would receive the bequest only if the testator and the beneficiary did not die as a result of a common accident. Over time it was realized that it was not the cause of the beneficiary's death that was important but rather the time of death. Perhaps this realization was prompted by the multitude of lawsuits that arose to determine the exact cause of death of the beneficiary—whether the two deaths were the result of a common accident.

The Antilapse Statute

To carry the discussion further, suppose you leave a piano to Mary Doe but she dies before you do and you failed to provide for any time limitation. The bequest merely was "to Mary Doe." In this event, who is entitled to the piano depends upon the particular state antilapse statute. All states have a statute that applies to this situation, but the statutes vary widely.

An *antilapse statute* provides that a bequest will not lapse, in the absence of a stated time period in the will, even though the beneficiary dies prior to the testator (and sometimes even before the execution of the will). Most of these statutes, however, limit who may succeed to the bequest under such circumstances. In the event no one qualifies to succeed, then the bequest lapses and becomes a part of the residuary estate.

Because of these variances and limitations, you should never rely on your state's antilapse statute. Instead you should always provide for alternative distributees in your will.

Pretermitted Children

To a limited degree, children born to or adopted by the testator are protected by most states. When these children are in existence at the time the will is made, many states are not concerned about their possible disinheritance, apparently believing that such children's omission was intentional. And some states make no distinction as to the timing of the will, whether before or after the occurrence of children.

Most states, however, are protective of children born to or adopted by a testator subsequent to the testator's will. These afterborn or afteradopted children are sometimes referred to as *pretermitted children*. The following discussion applies to the prevailing rule as to pretermitted children.

If you are married and still able to have children or the possibility exists that you may adopt a child, you must provide for such a contingency in your will. Ordinarily, this does not mean you have to leave them anything, only that you must state what you want them to receive, if anything. If you fail to do so and such children thereafter come into being, then they will be entitled to a share of your estate upon your death. This share ordinarily is what they would have received if you had died intestate.

Many people believe that they *must* leave something to their children born or adopted before or after the making of their will. This usually is not true. Except in those states that require something more than a stated intention of the testator, no law requires a testator to leave anything to anybody, although a surviving spouse has certain rights which are not available to others.

Sometimes, due to a peculiar family situation, a desire of the testator to set out something concerning disinherited children in the will, or a statute so requiring, a lawyer will insert a provision in a will to the effect that the testator intentionally leaves nothing to a certain individual. That person may or may not be the testator's child.

In this regard, the worst kind of will provision states that an individual is to receive just one dollar. When such a will provision exists, the personal representative is given the difficult task of trying to distribute the one-dollar bequest to a person who is not, understandably, very cooperative.

Ademption

If you bequeath a specific item of property that you don't own at your death, then the designated beneficiary may or may not receive something in its place. This problem refers to the legal situation known as *ademption.* Whether the property was owned by the testator at the time the will was made is irrelevant. Ademption only applies to a testate estate.

The reason for the property not being owned by the testator at the time of death usually is immaterial. It may have been consumed, lost, previously given away or sold, or even taken by condemnation. In any event, the specified distributee does not have to receive anything in its place. Put succinctly, ademption involves a taking away, not a giving to. The general rule is that nothing else may be substituted for that which originally was given, and the gift then is said to have *adeemed.*

There is a split of authority among the states over the part that intent plays in resolving ademption problems. The minority view adheres to a rigid "identity" theory, concerning itself solely with the presence of the property in the estate at the time of death. The majority rule gives consideration and effect to circumstances that explain why the property is not among the decedent's assets at the time of death. Some states following the majority rule refer to it as the "modified intention theory." Under this theory, when the property is missing from the estate because of some act or event not carried out voluntarily by the decedent, no ademption occurs.

Suppose, for instance, that a testator, Consuela, bequeaths a boat and motor to John. Under the modified intention theory, if a storm takes the life of the testator and also sinks the boat, no ademption would apply to Consuela's gift, since the act (the loss of the boat and motor) was not voluntary upon the part of the testator. John would thus be entitled to something of equal value from Consuela's estate.

But relying on the court to find intent, one way or another, is risky. Rather, the testator should show his or her own intentions in the will. If the testator wants to avoid ademption, an appropriate clause can be inserted in the will to prevent its operation. The intent of the testator then is clearly shown in the will itself and no ademption would result, nor would there be a need for a court interpretation of the testator's intention.

On the other hand, what if the testator wants ademption to apply—the beneficiary to receive specific property only if the testator still owns it at the time of death? A proper clause in the will should appear, following the provision making the gift, which should read: "providing I still own it at the time of my death."

Abatement

Suppose that you once thought your total net estate would amount to $10,000 at your death, so you left $5000 to each of two nephews, but at the time of your death your net estate amounted to only $8000. Would each nephew then receive $4000, or would one nephew receive $5000 and the other $3000? The answer may depend upon who was named first, how your will was worded, or what your statute provides. This situation refers to the condition known as abatement.

Abatement is the order established for setting aside or reducing bequests when the net assets of a testate estate are insufficient to pay all the bequests provided for in a will. *Net assets* are those assets of the estate remaining after the payment of all debts of the decedent and the payment of all charges against the estate. *Charges* consist of such items as death taxes and costs of administration.

Abatement only applies to a testate estate. And the term only applies to the bequests. It does not apply to the debts of the decedent or to the costs of administration. State statutes, however, usually provide for the order of priority of debts and charges in the event the assets of the estate are insufficient to pay all of them in full.

The debts and charges always have priority and must be paid before any distribution of the assets to the beneficiaries is undertaken. In the event that the gross estate is not sufficient to take care of all the estate's debts and charges, then some proration of the debts might occur, but this would not be considered abatement.

If the net estate is not sufficient to pay all of the specific bequests, which the distributee or distributees would suffer, or would they all lose out equally? Before this question is answered, keep in mind that abatement applies only to those wills which leave different amounts to different people. If the will leaves all property equally to various persons, no reason would exist for applying abatement—the reduction of someone's share.

Under abatement, which results from an unexpected shortage of assets, the specific beneficiaries do not lose out equally. They either lose out according to the terms of the will or according to the order provided by the abatement statute. Thus, if a will does not specify the order of priority—in other words, does not provide for the order of abatement—then the order will occur as provided by statute.

Going back to the above example, say you left $10,000 equally to the two nephews. Is there any doubt that with your estate actually being $8000 each nephew would receive something other than $4000?

But suppose you felt so confident of your estate that you gave $5000 to the first nephew and the balance of your estate to the second nephew, thinking that each would receive $5000. Again, is there any doubt that the first nephew would receive $5000 and the second nephew only $3000?

Other situations might not be as easily determined, which might result in possible disputes or even lawsuits. At least an appeal would be made by the personal representative to the probate court to determine the order of abatement.

Because many conflicts can arise under the statutory order of abatement, you should not leave abatement to be decided by others. Since you cannot be certain of the statutory provisions in effect at the time of your death, nor even what your estate might consist of, your will should clearly indicate the order that bequests should be paid.

If any possibility of abatement exists, consider bequests of cash in terms of percentages of the total net estate rather than in terms of specific amounts. By using percentages, it makes no difference what the size of your estate will be. Each beneficiary will receive a percentage of your net estate, perhaps in a lesser amount than you had hoped for, but at least without having to have gone through abatement procedures.

There is one other thing you should keep in mind. Your estate may be sufficient to pay all specific bequests so that no specific distributee's bequest is abated. But if at the time of your death your estate is smaller than anticipated, then the residuary beneficiaries will suffer. In a sense, it is the bequest to the residuary beneficiaries that is abated.

Specific bequests would be paid in full, but since you left a smaller estate than anticipated, the residuary beneficiaries—whom you might actually have intended to receive the lion's share—might receive even less than the others. This is another reason for describing cash bequests in terms of percentages. In so doing, the residuary beneficiaries always receive the same percentage that you contemplated when you made your will.

Parts of a Will

You will better understand the various parts that make up a will after reading this section. Once you know this information, you should be in a better position to discuss your will with your attorney.

These parts are stated in the order they normally would appear in your will. Thus your preparation in meeting with your attorney can be organized accordingly. Provisions specific to your situation may not be mentioned, nor will those applying to procedural aspects, which should be the concern of your attorney.

What are the usual parts to any will?

The Introductory Clause

First is the introductory clause. This clause identifies you by name and at least by a partial address, such as your county and state of residence. It is best to use your name as it appears on your title documents—primarily that of your home—to avoid later identification problems. And remember that you never use titles, such as Dr., Mr., Mrs., Miss, or Ms., in legal documents. In addition, the clause should declare the document as being your will.

Many lawyers also state that the will revokes all prior wills, even though no prior wills are known to exist. This statement probably seems redundant and unnecessary since your latest will, if properly drawn, always has the legal effect of revoking all prior wills. However, it should be stated for precautionary purposes.

In spite of the legal effect of a new will, it is advisable to physically destroy any previous will once the new one has been executed. This prevents the curious from knowing what you previously provided and also precludes the possibility that the wrong will may be found and used.

The Debt Clause

The first numbered paragraph of a will probably will recite that you want all your debts, funeral expenses, and costs of administration paid first, that is, before any bequests are made. In most instances this could be considered a redundant statement, since statutes require such payments to be made first whether or not that is your stated wish. But the statement does indicate what your intentions are and, perhaps, that you are aware of the statutory requirements.

Because of a special situation that you may have, your lawyer may have to take particular care in wording this clause concerning your debts. If you have or might sometime have an outstanding secured debt, such as a mortgage, you may or may not want to have your secured property go free of debt to a distributee. Using this clause, without additional specifications, might cause confusion as to your intentions. Which person is to suffer the payment of the particular debt—the party receiving the encumbered property or your residuary beneficiaries—might not be clear.

Bequests

Specific bequests usually appear next. The most common are gifts of personal property, such as heirlooms (being gifts of tangible property) or cash (being gifts of intangible property). Not as common are specific gifts of real property, such as farms. When describing personal property, it is best not to use terms such as "personal effects" or "household effects." Too many disputes arise as to the meaning of these terms.

If you are referring to *all* of your tangible personal property, then say so. If you are referring to all of your tangible personal property except, for example, your automobile and your boat, then say so. If your state allows a list of tangible personal property separate from your will, then take advantage of this convenience, but be sure to follow the statute.

If your will names only one beneficiary, or only a group of beneficiaries sharing equally in your estate, then there would be no need for a will clause providing for specific gifts. The specific clause would be superfluous.

The Residuary Clause

Some wills repeat themselves for no apparent good reason. For instance, a will may leave certain specific personal property to three individuals. Then, in the next paragraph, the same will leaves all the balance of the property to the same three individuals. What is the purpose of the first paragraph, which surely is redundant and certainly confusing?

Every will must have a residuary clause. This clause provides that any estate property remaining after the specific bequests have been distributed, and of course after all debts and administration expenses have been paid, goes to the residuary beneficiaries, either in equal or unequal amounts. It is a pick-up clause. It gets rid of anything that is left. Without this clause, your will could fail to dispose of all of your property, and such unbequeathed property would then go intestate, as if there were no will.

Even though you leave a will, property not disposed of by your will is considered intestate property. The intestate property would then descend according to the statutory laws of inheritance, sometimes referred to as the laws of descent and distribution, rather than according to the terms of your will. It is irrelevant who is named in the will. Presumably you would not want this to happen.

If you own real estate, your will should contain either a discretionary or mandatory provision for the sale of such real property. This assumes that you have sufficient faith in your personal representative handling the sale fairly and competently without following the statutory sale provisions. And you ought to have such trust. Otherwise you should not name the party in the first place.

A great amount of red tape is eliminated if this clause is included in your will. Without this clause, the statutory procedure for sale of real estate must be followed. (See the previous discussion about this under the heading "Purposes of a Will.")

Naming of Representative

Finally, a will names the party (the executor or the personal representative) chosen to probate the will and administer the estate of the testator.

The selection of the executor, who functions in a fiduciary capacity, must be made with care. The executor should possess qualifications similar to those required of an attorney in fact or a conservator.

If these qualifications cannot be met by a close family member, or if good reasons exist for not naming a family member to serve as the personal representative, then serious consideration should be given to naming a bank as executor.

Procedural Clauses

The balance of the will consists of the dating, testimonium clause, execution, attestation clause, and witnessing of the document. Don't worry about the testimonium and attestation clauses. These are procedural and will be taken care of by your attorney.

State statutes, quite similar to each other, are specific as to how these procedural acts are to be done. No variance with these rules of formality are allowed, although most states provide that a will is valid if at the time of execution it was done in accordance with the law either of the testator's place of residence or the will's place of execution. Thus if you move to another state after you have made your will, your will should still be valid in your new place of residence.

Because of a slight chance that your will was not executed properly according to the laws of your new jurisdiction, or because certain provisions may now be either undesirable or unenforceable in your new state, you might prefer to engage a lawyer in your new place of residence to review your will with you.

One common problem with relocating your residence, even to another part of the same state, is that your designated personal representative or alternate may no longer be able to serve your estate, either legally or practically. Many statutes prohibit a nonresident executor from serving alone. In such instances, a resident party must be named to serve as a co-executor. And sometimes the mere physical inability of the personal representative to serve from a far distance is reason enough to change executors.

Witnessing a Will

The purpose of the witnesses to your will is to prove the will upon your death, unless the will is what is termed "self-proved" at the time of execution, a procedure now provided for by most states. When your will is executed in conformance with a self-proving statute, your witnesses in effect prove your will at the time of execution rather than at the time you die. This saves the necessity, and sometimes the difficulty, of locating your witnesses, possibly years later, for the purpose of proving your will. The self-proving procedure is valid only if statutory authority exists for doing so.

Since the self-proving statute is of rather recent origin, many wills and codicils exist which are not self-proving. The new, self-proving statutes do not make these old wills or codicils obsolete. They only make the old procedure—which is still legal—obsolete. The non-self-proved wills and codicils still must be proved in the old-fashioned way, by taking testimony of at least one of the witnesses at the time of the testator's death.

Under the new statutes, if a subsequent codicil is self-proving, the old method of proving a will is usually not necessary. Many state statutes provide that a defectively executed will is cured by a properly executed codicil. In effect, the will, whether or not defective, is incorporated into and becomes a part of the codicil. Even though the will and the codicil constitute two documents, the two together are deemed to constitute one instrument: the will of the testator. Thus proving the codicil either at the time of making—by the self-proved method—or by a witness at the time of death also proves the will.

Some of the usual purposes of witnesses to a will are to state the following:

1. That the instrument is the testator's will

2. That the testator willingly signed and executed such instrument (or expressly directed another to sign the same in the presence of the witnesses)

3. That the signing was done as the free and voluntary act for the purposes expressed within the document

4. That the testator declared the instrument to be his or her will in the presence of witnesses

5. That the testator at the time of the execution of the will was of full age and of sound mind

6. That the witnesses were at least of the age provided for by statute and otherwise competent to be witnesses

7. That the witnesses in each other's presence did sign their names as attesting witnesses on the date of the will

You should take some precautions about your witnesses. All states require only two witnesses except Vermont, which requires three. You should not use an incompetent person to witness your will. "Incompetency" usually, but not always, includes minors, although a few states do not specify a minimum age. This "age" may be somewhat less than that establishing adulthood, but to be on the safe side you should avoid using minors.

A beneficiary in your will is not a proper or at times a legal witness. A bequest to such witness may be invalidated.

If you are not using a self-proved will, then your witnesses should have some probability of outliving you, since upon your death at least one of them may have to be produced to prove your will.

As a testator you may be wary about who witnesses your will. But no difficulty arises when your will is executed and witnessed in your attorney's office. Sometimes, however, circumstances are such that your will must be signed elsewhere, such as in a hospital.

In these unusual circumstances you may want to use a member of your family as one of the witnesses. But if the will names the proposed witness as either a beneficiary or the personal representative, many states do not permit such an individual to act as a witness. Because in those states such an improperly executed will would be considered invalid, it is not wise to take the chance in any case.

You should not concern yourself with the witnesses. Since this is a procedural matter, let your attorney do the worrying. Witnesses have no right to read or know the contents of your will. They only need to know that it is your declared will. Let your attorney provide the witnesses.

Holographic Wills

If a will is handwritten (rather than typed) but follows all the rules concerning execution and witnessing, it is legal. But what about the will that is in the handwriting of the testator, signed by the testator, but not properly attested to (witnessed)? Such a document is known as a *holographic* (in Louisiana, an olographic) will. Is the document legally recognized as the testator's last will? Slightly more than half the states consider such documents as valid, with varying degrees of requirements.

Several others recognize the validity of the will if it has met all the requirements in the state of execution or where the testator lived. Maryland, New York, and Rhode Island recognize holographic wills of military personnel under certain exceptional circumstances. Missouri has no provision for this type of will. Needless to say, holographic wills should be avoided.

Nuncupative Will

You may wonder about the validity of an oral will, legally known as a *nuncupative* will. Few states recognize nuncupative wills. Of those that do, most recognize them only as to certain limited amounts of property or only under certain limited circumstances, such as deathbed statements or statements made by military personnel or sailors. Some of these states also have some requirements concerning witnesses or notaries. Nuncupative wills often must be proved in a relatively short time. As you might surmise, nuncupative wills, even where valid, have only limited value and, like holographic wills, should be avoided.

Effect of Marriage and Divorce (Annulment)

States vary as to the effect of a marriage or divorce on a preexisting will.

In many states a subsequent marriage does not revoke a will, but the terms of that will may be effectively changed. Suppose a testator dies without changing his or her will. Some states provide that the surviving spouse receives the statutory share as if no will existed. In effect, it would be as if the deceased testator died intestate. Only if the omission of the second spouse appeared to be intentional would the terms *not* be changed. Other states merely provide that the surviving spouse, as in any marriage, is entitled to the elective (forced) share. If an antenuptial agreement has been entered into, then a subsequent marriage does not affect the validity or terms of a prior will.

If the parties divorce subsequent to the date of the will, most states provide that the former spouse is entitled to no part of testator's estate, unless the testator's will provides otherwise. A few states provide that the preexisting will is void. Most other states provide that only those terms of the will pertaining to the former spouse are void. And some states provide that a remarriage to the same spouse revives the provisions so revoked.

If you have a will in existence at the time of your remarriage or divorce, you should contact your attorney to determine the effect of that event on your will and on your spouse or former spouse. Presumably on either of these occasions you would have strong feelings one way or another. Regardless of your state's laws, you should strongly consider redoing your will to fit your new situation. This could save complications later.

The "Simple" Will

When a married couple first contacts their attorney they often specify that they want "simple" wills. The couple probably are thinking in terms of everything going to each other. Upon the death of the last one, everything would go to their children equally.

In wanting simple wills, they probably are also thinking of two other things: (1) the cost and (2) having something they can easily understand. While both objectives are important, the couple's attorney is more likely to be concerned about what is best for them under their circumstances.

To determine this, the attorney will need to review with the couple their entire estate plan, including their assets, goals, and heirs, the status of their marriage, and the relationship of their children to each other and to them. Without this background, the attorney—and the will—would be quite useless.

Many reasons exist for first securing this information. Here are three important ones:

1. If the couple's gross estate is greater than $600,000 (the federal estate exemption), then it is not likely that they should have, or even want, a simple will.

2. Drawing the will is only part of the process. Titles to property, for instance, must match what is desired in the will.

3. If the couple have minor children or other intended beneficiaries who are incompetent, then their wills are not likely to be as simple as they had hoped for, because a testamentary trust should be set up for the benefit of such parties.

Should a "simple" will be deemed best for the married couple, other things need to be done at the same time that it is drawn up. Consistent with a couple's will, consideration should be given to placing all of their property, both real and personal, into joint tenancy with each other. This eliminates the necessity of a full administration proceeding upon the first death.

Life insurance policies and pension plans should be checked to make certain that the beneficiaries are consistent with the will. And consideration should be given to the preparation of powers of attorney for both property and health care, as well as a living will.

What has been said here about married couples also applies to a great extent to the single person. Being single does not necessarily mean that your will can be simple, although if you are single, you are more likely to have a simple will.

The Marital Deduction Will

For a married couple having a total taxable estate, including life insurance, exceeding $600,000, a marital deduction will is advantageous, at least for federal death tax purposes. A *marital deduction will* conceivably could be any will that passes a decedent's property to a surviving spouse. However, the term usually is applied to a will that, by use of a trust, shelters up to $600,000 of the testator's property from taxes upon the death of the surviving spouse.

When an individual dies, that part of his or her estate that exceeds the $600,000 exemption and that does *not* pass to a surviving spouse is subject to the federal estate tax. Remember, all of the decedent's estate that passes outright to a surviving spouse is free from the federal estate tax. But in the larger estates an outright transfer from spouse to spouse rarely is wise.

To take advantage of the exemption, property having a value of $600,000 is placed in a trust, best referred to as a *bypass trust*. Some people call it a *credit shelter trust* because the trust shelters property up to the amount of the $600,000 exemption. Others call it a *nonmarital trust* because the trust property does not go directly to the spouse nor is it under the unlimited control of the spouse, although the spouse may be the trustee.

All property placed in the trust bypasses the second estate. The property sheltered in the trust is not included in the estate of the surviving spouse upon the second spouse's death. Thus the trust property, being no part of the second spouse's estate, is not subject to the federal estate tax (nor any state death tax) upon the death of the second spouse. And that property is not subject to the federal tax in the estate of the first spouse to die, as long as it does not exceed the amount of the $600,000 exemption.

Any estate property subject to the federal tax is taxed at a beginning rate of 37 percent and a top rate of 55 percent, although the top rate drops to 50 percent for those persons dying in 1993 and thereafter. (However, Congress may repeal the 1993 drop.) Because of the high tax rate, married couples have great incentive to enter into a marital deduction will.

Benefits other than tax savings can accrue by use of the marital deduction will. Since property in the bypass trust is not a part of the surviving spouse's estate, it is also not used to determine costs of administration, such as attorney and fiduciary fees and court costs. This can also constitute a substantial saving.

Not being part of the estate, the trust property is exempt from claims of the spouse's creditors for alimony, allowances, and inheritances. The trust, being a separate taxable entity, could result in some income tax benefits. And, finally, the trust property can be sheltered from the surviving spouse's temptations and bad management decisions, and from pleas by the spouse's heirs or others for handouts.

Although deemed desirable for most purposes by all estate planners, the marital deduction will does have some disadvantages. The cost of preparation obviously will be higher than a less-complicated will, although this cost is insignificant compared to the savings. And when the testator dies and the bypass trust comes into being, an annual administration cost may exist, although here again this cost can be avoided if the spouse—as is often the case—is the trustee.

If you are a candidate for a marital deduction will, you and your attorney will want to weigh and compare the advantages and disadvantages. For example, if your total combined estate is only slightly above $600,000 and there seems to be little chance of your estate greatly increasing in size, especially if you have established a gift program, then you may not want nor even need a marital deduction will. But if your combined estate is substantially over the exemption, then it would be foolhardy for you to ignore the available benefits.

Joint, Reciprocal, and Mutual Wills

Joint, reciprocal, and mutual wills normally concern only a married couple, although these wills can be used by other types of couples and by more than a twosome, such as by a married couple and their child. You are more likely to understand this discussion, however, if you think in terms of a situation involving a husband and wife.

The following discussion is considered the more enlightened view of joint, reciprocal, and mutual wills. This does not mean that your particular jurisdiction defines such wills in exactly the same way. But by following this discussion you should be able to distinguish between the three forms of wills.

Some courts create confusion—or are confused—as to the distinction between the three forms of wills. For instance, some courts call both a joint and a reciprocal will *double* or *counter* wills. Some courts also refer to both reciprocal wills and mutual wills as being "mutual." Such terminology, however, is better left unused.

After reading the following discussion, you and your spouse should be able to talk intelligently about these types of wills with your attorney. In almost all instances, however, you, as a married couple, should have little reason to want other than the reciprocal will. And your attorney no doubt will agree.

If you are married and thinking about making a will, you and your spouse probably have agreed between yourselves as to how your combined property should be distributed when each of you die. But you may not know whether you should both join in the same will document or each make your own separate will.

In a sense, this is a drafting problem that only your lawyer should worry about. Yet you as a married couple should understand the types of wills available to you so that you can make a choice most agreeable to both of you and most suitable to your situation.

A *joint will* is a single testamentary instrument, constituting the wills of two or more persons, jointly executed. The term refers to form rather than substance. It is in effect the separate will of each maker, and generally may be separately probated on the death of each. Sometimes, however, courts tend to disagree as to the effect of the first death. Occasionally they disagree as to the effect of the second death if the will was not probated upon the first death.

Usually a joint will may also be revoked or changed unilaterally by either of the parties at any time. Some courts, however, have stated that upon the first death the will becomes irrevocable as to the remaining party. You may think it cheaper for only one instrument to be prepared between the two of you, but for practical reasons and because courts have difficulty knowing what the testators intended, it is doubtful that your lawyer would recommend one instrument for you and your spouse.

Reciprocal wills are those in which two or more testators make testamentary dispositions in favor of each other. This may be done by one will, in which case it is both reciprocal and joint, or it may be done by separate wills, in which case each will is reciprocal but not joint.

Reciprocal wills ordinarily may be revoked or amended at any time without the consent of the other party. But some courts, apparently confusing a reciprocal will with a mutual will, deny that a reciprocal will may be unilaterally revoked. Again, for practical reasons, your lawyer will likely recommend two instruments—one will for each of you—even though the provisions of the two wills may be similar or identical.

Actually, your lawyer will be happy that you are considering reciprocal provisions, as this indicates an agreeable marriage. Most likely this means that you will agree on the terms of the wills. This does not mean that you tell your attorney that you want reciprocal wills. It only means that you agree on similar provisions for your own wills.

A *mutual will* is made when two or more individuals agree to dispose of their property in a special way. Such a will is contractual, being an agreement between the parties. Use of the term *mutual* as applied to wills has caused the greatest confusion.

The term *mutual* should be applied and confined to wills executed in pursuance of a compact or agreement between two or more persons to dispose of their property, either to each other or to third persons, in a particular mode or manner, each in consideration of the other. If there isn't sufficient evidence to show this binding agreement between the testators, the wills may be reciprocal or joint (or both), but they cannot be mutual.

In some states, whether you have a mutual will depends upon whether the terms of your state statute have been followed. At least half the states either follow the Uniform Probate Code, which limits the opportunity to prove a mutual will, or require the mutuality to be expressly stated. Louisiana does not recognize mutual wills as the term is used here.

To rephrase, both joint wills and separate wills may be reciprocal without being mutual, although they may be both reciprocal and mutual. For that matter, wills may be joint and reciprocal and mutual, but they are not necessarily so. A will is joint if it is the will of two or more persons in one instrument, reciprocal if it contains reciprocal gifts or property between two or more makers, and mutual—in most states—only if it is executed after an agreement has been made. Be aware of these distinctions, as lawyers seldom bother to inform you as to whether your wills are joint, reciprocal, or mutual.

Laypersons—married couples in particular, and, unfortunately, some lawyers and courts as well—often use the three terms interchangeably, without really giving much thought to their legal significance.

If you are married, you and your spouse probably will think that reciprocal wills would be best for you. Before your first appointment with your attorney you usually would have discussed the proposed terms between yourselves. You would want to be sure that you have reached some tentative agreement as to what you consider key provisions. Being in agreement probably means only that your wills will be similar, thus reciprocal.

You and your spouse may agree to have reciprocal wills, but you may be uncertain as to whether the two of you should have a joint will—a single instrument. Probably you have little or no knowledge of a mutual will or its effects. You may believe that it would be nice if your spouse were bound to the terms of your reciprocal wills forever, especially if you died first and your spouse remarried. But if you have gone through this process, you undoubtedly have found that your lawyer has discouraged use of a joint will. Most lawyers consider this type of will to be impractical and limiting.

And your lawyer might undoubtedly discourage you from considering a mutual will. Lawyers usually deem this type of will to be undesirable, as it ties parties together in a contractual manner. Thus they may not be able to deal with changed circumstances after the death of the first of them.

Even though you might think that you have a perfect will (if there is such a thing), and even though you might think that it will last for the remainder of your life, it may need changing for any number of reasons prior to your death. With the mutual will this may not be easy to do. During the lifetime of both testators in a mutual will, either party may revoke or change the will only if notice of that intention is given to the other party. Actual notice of the execution of a codicil or new will is not required.

However, after the death of the first testator to a mutual will, the second testator may be able to change the will only at risk of violating the contract. This could give cause for a lawsuit. Some courts, however, might hold that only the contractual portion of the will is irrevocable, not the entire will.

Generally with other types of wills the mere execution of the document creates no vested right in a beneficiary until the death of the testator. But with a mutual will a third-party beneficiary is usually entitled to enforce the will, even though not a party to it.

If, after knowing these risks, you still believe that you want a mutual will, you should discuss possible tax consequences with your attorney. He or she, though, might be unwilling and unable to give you any clear-cut answers. Part of the problem arises because no clear agreement exists among lawyers and courts as to whether mutual wills are irrevocable.

It is uncertain as to whether the making of a mutual will creates some gift tax consequences, either upon the execution of the will or upon the death of the first testator. And disagreement exists as to the federal estate tax consequences. For instance, is the marital deduction affected by the mutual will?

Some married couples are attracted to certain kinds of wills because they believe they will be cheaper. They might believe that a joint will, because it is one instrument, ought to be cheaper than two wills, and that a reciprocal or mutual will should also be cheaper because the terms are fairly similar. This is not necessarily the case.

Because of the unpredictability of the mutual will, you should never plan to use it based on the cost factor alone. Doing it correctly is much more important than doing it cheaply.

Trying to Protect
the Children

Even after knowing the above concerns and risks concerning wills, you still may be one of those people who is likely to tell your attorney, "I want to be sure that if I die first and my husband remarries our children will be protected."

Be advised, wills rarely can be used to guarantee that protection. In part this is true because other considerations must be taken into account.

Because most marital couples have an estate of less than $600,000, they are likely to own all of their property together in joint tenancy with the right of survivorship. With this type of ownership, most estate proceedings are eliminated at the time of the first death, since title to the couple's joint property will automatically vest in the surviving partner. See Chapter 15 for a more detailed discussion.

In using the joint tenancy, however, the will of the first one to die is not used, since the property goes according to the joint tenancy and not according to the will. No probate property would exist. Thus whatever the first will might say about the property going to the children could be irrelevant. Bear in mind that trying to keep a surviving spouse in line with your wishes after your death is almost an impossibility.

But, you say, even with joint tenancy a mutual will would protect the children. True, if your spouse didn't go to another lawyer—who was unaware of the mutual will—and have a new will made. But let's assume that this didn't happen.

State laws generally favor the existing spouse—whether the first, second, or whatever—over existing children. For example, suppose that you, the wife, enter into a mutual will with your husband. When the first one of you dies, all the estate goes to the survivor. When the second one of you dies, all goes to the children. You thereafter die and later your husband remarries. Then he dies, leaving his second wife surviving. Who gets his property, your children or his second wife?

Upon your husband's death, his second wife would have the right to elect not to take under that mutual will. And why should she? It leaves all the property to the children, nothing to her. Instead, she would have a right to take her distributive share set up by statute, which could be about one-third of your husband's estate.

The children would then receive two-thirds of the estate, right? But hold on! Should *you* die first, your husband would end up with all of the combined property. During his lifetime he could do anything he wanted with that property, although some courts may disagree. The worst possible scenario for you and your children would be for the husband to give it all to his new wife or to put it all in joint tenancy with her. The second wife would then end up with all of the property if the husband died before she did.

Joint tenancy with your spouse may not look so good after all. Is there an alternative? Suppose you and your spouse want none of your property to be held in joint tenancy. You could then divide the property up equally among you, each owning an undivided one-half interest. If you die first, your spouse could elect her or his distributive share, which might amount to one-third of your half. Your spouse thus could end up with two-thirds of your total estate (one-half plus one-third of one-half equals two-thirds).

If your total estate is not large to begin with, then your maneuvering might not be worth the difficulties and costs that could be incurred. For instance, if joint tenancy were not used, then both estates would have to be administered because both wills would have to be probated.

One way to make the children's shares larger would be for you to own all the property, so that your will can control all the property, not merely half of it. But chances are that your spouse might feel the same way and want all the property in his or her name in case he or she died first. In other words, what is good for one ought to be good for the other.

You might hope to have your property protected from a second spouse by having your surviving spouse enter into an antenuptial agreement before the second marriage. But if you are concerned about the possibility of your spouse's second marriage and what may thereafter be done with your combined property, how can you be certain that your spouse would have the foresight or willingness to enter into such an agreement?

The larger your estate, the better the possibility of salvaging something for your children. If your combined estates exceed the $600,000 federal estate tax exemption, then you and your spouse probably have marital deduction wills. These wills would contain a bypass trust. To the extent your property is in the bypass trust your children could be protected. Your children would be named as contingent beneficiaries of the trust property, receiving the property upon the death of your surviving spouse.

Another way to protect your children is for you and your spouse to split your property, each of you putting all of your individual property in a separate, living trust. Each trust would be similar to a life estate, in that your children would receive the property upon the death of the last spouse. This trust would also have the advantage of avoiding probate. (See Chapter 11 for a detailed discussion of avoiding probate.) But such trusts are normally revocable. While the property in your trust would eventually go to the children, you cannot be sure that the surviving spouse won't revoke his or her individual trust, possibly to the detriment of your children. Trusts also could have other problems. (See Chapter 8 for more about trusts.)

Perhaps now you realize the futility of trying to protect your children by legal maneuvering. But what if your spouse promises to take care of the children upon his or her death? Is that promise enforceable?

The answer is probably "no." Your spouse's promise does not appear to be a contract that could be enforced upon either of your deaths. Promises must have consideration in order to be enforceable. It is doubtful that your spouse would receive anything of value in return for that promise.

What, then, are your possible options, assuming you have some control of your finances and have adequate funds? One, you can begin placing some of your assets into joint tenancy with your children. You would have use of this property during your lifetime. But at the time of your death whatever was so held in joint tenancy would go automatically to your children, regardless of your will. It would also pass to them regardless of the laws of descent and distribution and, of course, regardless of whether your spouse were still living. Of course if you died first, your spouse would have no access to these funds even if he or she needed them for care and support. Certain dangers exist with this type of joint tenancy (see Chapter 3).

The other possibility is that you could set up a living trust, as noted earlier. You could be trustee as well as primary beneficiary of the property placed in the trust. Your spouse could be the first contingent beneficiary, and your children would be the final contingent beneficiaries, receiving the property after the death of both of you. The trust could be funded from the same sources your joint tenancies had. Again, certain problems of a trust might not make it an attractive alternative.

The Pourover Will

For various reasons a testator may wish to create a living, or inter vivos, trust. Often the testator may want the trust to be a repository for his or her property at the time of his or her death. In order for this to be accomplished, some mechanism must be used to ensure that the testator's property enters the trust after his or her death. The mechanism is the pourover will.

A *pourover will* provides for certain designated property, which may constitute all or only a part of the testator's estate, to be transferred—poured over, in other words—from the estate into a trust previously set up by the testator. The trust may have been created by the testator specifically for this purpose.

Why would a testator want to create a living trust when a testamentary trust could serve the same purpose? There may be several advantages in doing so.

Perhaps the favorite reason for creating a living trust is that its terms are normally private, whereas the terms of a probated will become public property and thus subject to the view of the curious. Among the wealthy, at least, privacy often is of great concern.

The terms of a living trust, assuming it to be revocable, may be more easily changed than a will, which requires more statutory formalities. This would be true whether the entire will were redrawn or just a codicil were added later.

If a will that contains a testamentary trust fails, then the whole estate plan may fail, unless a living trust exists. However, if the living trust is unfunded because it is waiting for the influx of estate property, then this argument is meaningless.

Some commentators believe that administration costs are lessened by use of the living trust. This assumes that the trust already contains some of the estate property and thus would be treated as nonprobate property—

property not subject to probate. Nonprobate property often is not considered in determining fees.

The pourover provisions of a will are valid in all states if the living trust is in existence at, or prior to, the date of the will. Almost all states require the trust to be at least nominally funded. Most also allow the trust to be amended subsequent to the date of the will but prior to the testator's death. States vary as to whether the trustee is subject to eligibility rules, such as being required to live in the testator's state of residence. Of course, if the trust is revoked prior to the death of the testator, then the testamentary disposition will fail unless the will provides for an alternate disposition.

Life Estates

A *life estate* has been defined as a dual method of holding title to property. With this method, one party, the life tenant, holds a life interest in the designated property, and another party, the remainderman, holds legal title to the same property but subject to the life interest of the life tenant.

Life estates evolved from the common law and can be quite complicated in design and in terminology. For instance, the remaining interest can be contingent or vested. And the interest held by the life tenant is termed a freeholder interest, that by the remainderman, a fee. For your purposes, think of the tenant as having a right of possession as long as certain conditions are met. Also think of the remainderman as being the titleholder subject to the rights of the life tenant.

Life estates can be created by will, sale, or gift. The following discussion is only concerned with life tenancies created by will. An example of such a life tenancy would be a testator giving a life estate in a residence to his spouse, and the remainder interest to his children. One of the conditions of the life estate could be that the surviving spouse must live in the residence, otherwise the life tenancy fails.

Life estates usually are given only in real property, since life estates in personal property present problems of control and loss. Life estates ordinarily are, but need not be, conditional—that is, they terminate upon the happening of one or more specified events, such as the life tenant's nonpayment of taxes or insurance on the life estate property. The tenancy might also terminate upon the life tenant's failure to maintain the property, although this condition is difficult to prove and enforce. Upon termination of the life estate for whatever reason, possession of the property automatically passes to the remainderman, who already has title.

As trusts have become more popular, life estates have become less common. But life estates, especially in the smaller estates, are considered to have some advantages over trusts. One commentator listed 21 advantages. Here are a few of them:

1. Life estates are easier to understand than trusts. Trusts seem to have a certain mystique about them. They usually are wordier and not as easy to comprehend. As a result, laypersons tend to be leery of trusts.

2. Life estates require no third party, such as a trustee, to be involved. The possible interference and costs of using an outsider thus are eliminated. Should the designated trustee be a family member, disputes and infighting could result.

3. Life estates, unlike trusts, require little or no administration. Trusts require reports, accounting, and possibly tax returns.

4. Life estates are likely to be more flexible and their termination is normally much simpler than that of trusts.

The same commentator also listed some disadvantages:

1. A life estate may tie up property for a long time. This could result in unfortunate loss caused by disrepair and depreciation. The property could end up being unsalable.

2. The life tenant has no one, like a trustee, to look after the tenant. Because of the terms of the life tenancy, the life tenant may be housebound to his or her detriment.

3. Life tenants are often not required to be accountable to the remainderman. For instance, what if, unknown to the remainderman, the tenant fails to keep the property properly insured and a loss occurs?

Remember, advantages and disadvantages should always be compared with the realization that different circumstances may require different conclusions.

Keeping Control After Death

Life estates are one way of keeping control of your property for a period after your death. Trusts are another way. What might be a reason that some testators want to control the devolution of their property? Let's use an example to discover a typical reason.

Suppose that your son has married a woman who has a child by a previous marriage. You want your son to have all of your property upon your death but you want none of this property to end up in the name of his stepson. Because of his wife's possible influence, you are afraid that this might happen. Or you might believe that upon your son's death all of your property will go to his wife and upon her death all of it will go to her son.

This is not an uncommon situation involving second marriages. You wish to favor your own heirs but are fearful that your property will eventually go to persons not of your own blood and not of your own choosing.

If in this example your son had entered into an antenuptial agreement, you might feel more comfortable, but the agreement can always be bypassed by your son by use of joint tenancy, gifts, or a will, any of which could favor his spouse or stepson.

Suppose your son told you that he made a will that would protect your property. His intentions might be admirable, but state statutes might and generally do protect a surviving spouse regardless of the existence of a will.

There is no way to absolutely ensure that your estate will not ultimately end in the hands of your son's spouse or his stepson, unless you are willing that the property not go directly or outright to your son. There are only two ways your son can indirectly use and enjoy your estate property, although neither is necessarily desirable.

One way is by giving your son only a life estate in the property. This would give him, as life tenant, the use and enjoyment of the property during his lifetime, or such shorter period as your will may specify. In this circumstance your son would have no control over where the property goes upon his death, since the remainder would be designated by you.

The second way is by creating a trust in your will. This trust would operate like a life estate in that your son would receive such benefits from the trust during his lifetime as you would stipulate. Upon his death the trust property would go to the parties you specified in the trust. Unless provided in the trust agreement, neither your son's spouse nor her son would be entitled to any portion of the trust property upon your son's death.

In this situation, the trust has many advantages over a life estate. The trust property can easily consist of personal as well as real property. With a trust, you have more flexibility in setting out the terms of the arrangement than would be possible with a life estate. A trust provides management of, and supervision over, estate property whereas the life estate does not. See the discussion of trusts in Chapter 8.

A disadvantage of using the trust is that the trustee would be entitled to an annual fee for services rendered in managing the trust, the fee payable out of the trust property. Although this fee may appear to be a burden to the trust property, a qualified trustee is more likely to conserve the property than would a life tenant, since management of the trust property is one of the responsibilities of the trustee. A life tenant often has little incentive in preserving the life tenancy property beyond his or her death.

Miscellaneous Will Clauses

It was stated earlier that wills tend to look alike, at least at first glance. Perhaps this is because all wills must contain certain specified parts. But, quite obviously, every will must be custom- or tailormade. It must fit the person for whom it is designed. Thus one will may contain a clause that another will does not. Some of these more common clauses are mentioned in the following paragraphs.

Some individuals—Roman Catholics, for example, want masses recited for the repose of their soul and wish to specify a stated amount of money for this purpose. Although the saying of masses probably will be done in any event, such testators feel more comfortable if their will contains a clause providing for them.

Other individuals are concerned about perpetual care for their grave and possibly that of their parents. Rather than arranging for such care during their lifetime, they prefer that it be done upon their death. A clause in their will guarantees that this will be done.

Sometimes testators believe that a certain beneficiary may be dissatisfied with the bequest provided in the will, or may be unhappy about being omitted from the will altogether. In either case, the testators want to make certain, insofar as possible, that such a party won't contest the will, presumably in an attempt to receive more. Such testators thus want a provision, called an *in terrorem clause,* placed in the will.

This clause takes many forms, but generally it states that if any individual contests the will or any of its provisions, then either that individual forfeits any rights thereunder, or any provision in favor of that individual is revoked. Such an individual shall then not be entitled to share in the estate in any manner.

Many states, however, hold that the in terrorem clause goes against public policy and is void if the contestant acted in good faith and for probable cause. And some states invalidate this clause under any circumstances.

Some wills direct that a certain lawyer or law firm be named as attorney for the estate. While this may be deemed proper in some jurisdictions, many states ignore the direction as being improper or hold that such a clause is invalid. The reason is that the estate attorney represents the personal representative, who has the choice of attorney, not the testator. Many lawyers and bar associations are of the opinion that this clause should never be placed in a will, as it gives an appearance of the lawyer maneuvering his own employment by the personal representative.

Perhaps this attorney clause would be more acceptable if it were in terms of being a wish. Such clauses, which are not binding, are known as precatory clauses. Precatory clauses express a hope or a wish. They are not mandates. They must be carefully worded so that the suggested action is clearly discretionary and not deemed mandatory.

Effect of Will on Nonprobate Property

You may be one of those people who believe that all of your property, however and wherever situated, is disposed of as directed by your will. That probably isn't true.

A will affects only probate property, not nonprobate property. You may recall that nonprobate property, at the time of death, is disposed of according to some agreement or arrangement made as to that property outside of the will. It thus is not subject to the provisions of a will or the laws of inheritance. Rather, such property passes according to the provisions of the instrument that created it.

Nonprobate property can take many forms, such as life insurance, but perhaps the most common form is property held in joint tenancy. When a joint tenant dies, the property held by the deceased joint tenant passes on to the remaining joint tenant(s), regardless of the will of the decedent. This is one of the reasons that lawyers are generally insistent on looking at your entire situation when you want a will made. Everything that you do in regard to your estate should be consistent with your overall plan. Otherwise you could be badly misled.

The Alien as a Distributee

Can there be a problem if you bequeath property to a citizen of another country? This question is important because of the great influx of immigrants from foreign countries, both legal and illegal, into the United States. Many of these foreigners who have chosen to live in the United States may want to distribute, upon their death, a part or all of their estate to their heirs who are citizens of another country. For convenience, these nonresident, foreign citizens are referred to as aliens.

As a general rule, aliens have only such right to property located in the United States as is permitted by federal and state law. Federal laws which may be relevant to the ownership of such property by aliens are numerous and tend to be difficult to interpret.

Rights of succession to property, although normally determined by state law, are subject to any treaty that may exist between the United States and the particular alien's country. Any state law conflicting with a federal treaty on the subject of inheritance by an alien would be superseded by the treaty. Unfortunately, treaties, if any, vary from country to country and thus each situation is a separate and new problem.

In addition to treaties, various federal laws may have some bearing on the situation. Portions of the following federal acts could affect the inheritance or ownership of property by an alien: Trading with the Enemy Act of 1917, Securities Act of 1934, Currency and Foreign Transactions Reporting Act of 1976, International Investment Survey Act of 1976, and Agricultural Foreign Investment Disclosure Act of 1978. Even though this may not frighten you, trying to accurately answer a specific question posed by you on this subject probably would terrify your lawyer.

Under some state statutes, whether an alien can inherit real or personal property depends upon the existence of a reciprocal right of United States citizens to inherit similar property from that particular alien's country. In view of certain United States Supreme Court decisions, it might be questionable whether these state statutes are constitutional.

Some state statutes permit the inheritance by an alien of personal property. Some also permit an alien, under certain conditions, to inherit real estate. In some situations, however, if the real estate is suitable for farming, then the alien must dispose of it within two years. Particularly because of the federal involvement with inheritances to aliens, care should be taken in estate planning involving this situation.

Postwill Treatment

Once you have made a will you cannot mark on it in any manner whatsoever. If you are thinking of redoing your will, you may be tempted to scribble your proposed changes on the face of your existing will. But if you do so, you may not have any will at all until you make a new one, or your action may cause a lawsuit.

Don't deface your existing will no matter what your reasons may be. Of course you can revoke it pending the making of a new will (during which period you would have no will at all), but perhaps this should be done only under the guidance of your lawyer. You will need to contact him or her anyway if you are considering a new will.

Some Common Questions Answered

Q. I am not wealthy, so why should I pay out good money now to make a will?

A. Without a will the moment you die your estate will be fixed by statute. With a will, you can determine how your property will be distributed upon your death. Without a will, a statute dictates how your property shall go, regardless of what you might have wanted. With pure luck, the inheritance statutes may pass your property on to your heirs as you would have wanted. But that is uncertain.

Even though it probably isn't true, your question makes it appear that you are mostly concerned about yourself. At the least, you should contact a lawyer to see what will happen to your estate upon your death if you leave no will.

Q. Now that I have my will, what should I do with it?

A. Your will should be located where it can be found upon your death, but in a place free from the dangers of fire, theft, or manipulation. You have several choices, all of which have some good and bad points. You will have to decide which is best for you.

One choice is to leave your will with your attorney. She will then have the best opportunity to administer your estate. But this action has three drawbacks: (1) you and your heirs may be placed in an uncomfortable position in the event that you wish to change attorneys; (2) since it is actually the prerogative of the personal representative to choose its own attorney, some awkwardness in changing lawyers may result; and (3) these wills sometimes cannot be found because the heirs do not know who prepared them.

Another choice is to keep your will at home, in a desk, strongbox or safe. Some testators like this because they feel they then have complete control of their will. But these wills are in danger of being lost, stolen, or destroyed. And it sometimes results in being too easily found and read by some disgruntled heir who may conveniently lose it.

Your safe deposit box is the safest place for your will. It can be easily found, because heirs naturally gravitate toward a box. Unfortunately, state laws and regulations and even rules of many depository banks inhibit the free access to the box after a death. Sometimes another name on the box will help solve this problem. But it is not always a good idea to allow another person (other than your spouse) to have entry to your box.

In order to access the box, a personal representative may have to be appointed, even though no formal administration of your estate is found to be necessary after your box and other assets have been inventoried. But when no sure evidence exists that administration will be necessary, usually some arrangement can be worked out with the bank to obtain the will.

Q. How long is my will good?

A. It lasts forever, in the sense that it does not expire by lapse of time. Of course certain provisions may lapse, become undesirable, or become inoperative by reason of a change of circumstances, such as the death of a beneficiary, unless your will anticipated and prepared for such a possibility.

Q. Should I tell anybody that I made a will?

A. No law exists as to publicizing your will. As a general rule, your will's contents are only a matter between you and your lawyer. One reason for this is that you may wish to change your will. Your new will might omit someone who was named in the prior will. Might not this create an awkward situation for those who survive, if they were aware of what your prior will provided?

A will should never be used for leverage purposes. Might that not be the intent of such disclosure in the first place? No need should exist for you as the testator to explain, or apologize for, your will provisions.

On the other hand, the main beneficiary and perhaps the executor should be told that you made a will and where it is located. They may not remember where it is located, but they will remember that you said you had a will and act accordingly upon your death. If the executor is a bank, you may want to leave the will, sealed, with the bank that oftentimes will have a will file kept for that purpose. In that situation, the bank should be told it is named as executor so that it may then take appropriate action upon your death.

Q. What happens if I lose my will?

A. The will should be redrawn and executed properly, although under some circumstances the original could be proved after you death. But by hoping that it will you are taking an unnecessary risk. Someone who might benefit otherwise might try to prove that the will is missing because you intentionally destroyed it. The burden—and the cost—of trying to prove your will may fall upon the ones you wish to benefit.

Q. What if one of the people named in my will dies before I do?

A. The legal effect of such a death should be considered by you in relation to how your will was prepared. If and when such a death does occur, you should reexamine your will to determine whether you provided for that contingency. For instance, your will might state "to John Doe, providing he is living four months after my death. If he is not then living, then the same shall go to . . ." Your will will thus have provided for that contingency.

If you are uncertain as to the effect of the death, you should consult with your attorney to determine whether any changes in your will are necessary. Oftentimes, you can make this inquiry merely by calling your attorney on the phone.

Q. What if my executor can't or won't serve?

A. Provide for this possibility by naming an alternate. The safest procedure is to name your bank, at least as the final alternate. By doing this, you can be assured that you have designated at least one that can and will serve.

Q. What should I worry about if I move after making my will?

A. You should consider at least three things. One is the continued legality of the will. Will the laws of the new state affect your will? Another is the availability of the personal representative. Is your executor still in a position to handle the responsibilities? And the third is, What is the effect on some of the specific bequests? Suppose, for instance, that you left your home to one of your children but now you and that child no longer live in the same city. Is the gift still what you—and the child—would want?

Q. Can I change or alter my will without returning to my lawyer?

A. Legally you can make your own will or amend it at any time without hiring a lawyer to help you. However, this is not the same thing as saying that you ought to do so, for what you end up with might well be unenforceable. Wills are strictly construed by courts. And wills not executed according to the requirements of your state statute are invalid.

Your word *alter* is bothersome. No markings of any kind can be made on a will after it has been signed and witnessed. Such markings are not valid and raise the question of validity of any part of your will. A new, separate instrument is necessary.

Q. Is one time better than another to have a will?

A. A flippant answer would be yes, just moments before you die. But perhaps in a way that reveals what the answer to your question should be.

It is not really possible to categorically state that one time is better than another. If you believe that your wife is the most important person alive, then you should make a will as soon as you marry. If you believe that your children are important, then you should make a will as soon as the first one is born or adopted. If you have accumulated a small estate and would like to dictate where it goes upon your death, then you should make a will. But if you are the gambling type and believe that you can wait until old age (whenever that is), then wait and take your chances.

Q. Are the expenses of an estate proceeding greater or smaller if I have a will?

A. They usually are smaller, for one particular reason. One of the purposes of a will is to save bonding costs. In naming a trustee or an executor in a will, you usually provide that such fiduciary shall serve without bond. Otherwise, the fiduciary must put up bond, which actually amounts to an annual premium payable to a bonding company.

Some people believe that their having a will will result in greater expenses and problems. Actually the reverse is more likely to be true. Nothing more is required of an estate administration when there is a will than when there is none. The same general probate procedures have to be followed in both instances, and the legal necessity of an administration proceeding is the same regardless of the existence of a will.

Q. Should I have signed copies of my will, and who should get them?

A. The lawyer should retain a copy of your will. You may want an extra copy of your will so that you may refer to it periodically. This way you do not need to disturb the original, signed will, which may be in your safe deposit box and rather inconvenient to get to when the need arises. You may also want your executor to have a copy.

None of these copies should be signed. Only the original should be signed. Otherwise, if you decide to change or destroy your old will, you have to remember who has copies and retrieve them. You would want all copies, whether or not signed, returned to you. Preferably, all copies of a revoked will, except that of your lawyer, should be destroyed. Thus the fewer copies distributed, even though not signed, the better.

No reason should exist for giving any of your beneficiaries a copy of your will. You may never need to change your will, but you might feel yourself "locked in" to terms that you later would like to change. If one or more of your beneficiaries know what is in your present will, this makes subsequent changes rather difficult.

Q. Should I reveal the contents of my will to my children?

A. A few parents like their children to know what they have done in their will. Perhaps these parents are unsure of themselves and want to be assured that their children approve of how the property is to be handled and distributed.

If children are being treated equally, or if the parent is trying to make a fair distribution and wants to try to make certain that all the children are in agreement, then in most cases little harm can result from disclosing the will contents to them. But take care to make sure that family relations are harmonious and will probably remain so after the disclosure.

Q. I have a will but I keep changing my mind about its provisions. Would I be better off without a will?

A. Your question is frightening because it raises other questions. Are you changing your will frequently because others are influencing you? Or are you changing it because you do not have any close heirs and are trying to favor distant heirs? Or are you trying to reward individuals who from time to time are being nice to you? Or are you unwilling to give to charity and thus are "reaching" for someone to give your estate to?

You should try to analyze why you keep changing your mind. What is it that causes you to change your mind? Why are you doing this to yourself? Perhaps you are elderly and now find it difficult to make decisions. If so, you may have additional estate planning decisions to consider, such as whether you should now designate someone to take care of your other affairs.

In direct answer to your question, the laws of inheritance might work more to your ultimate advantage than a "temporary" will apparently made on the spur of the moment. It is quite possible, under the circumstances, that your will changes are ill-conceived, making any will you have probably ill-advised. Perhaps you should listen more to your lawyer.

Q. Could I save myself some expense if I drew up my own will and then let my attorney look it over?

A. It is doubtful. By you taking the will to your lawyer you are really asking only for approval. You might not be happy with any other response. You are putting your attorney on the spot. But let's assume that you want an honest analysis of your will.

First of all, it is difficult for a lawyer to accept another's work product, whether it be yours or another lawyer's. Each lawyer has his or her own methods of doing things. The lawyer understands the language he or she uses and is uncomfortable trying to interpret someone else's wording. Regardless of those feelings, however, your attorney would have to go through the entire estate planning procedure in order to determine whether the will you submitted is the correct one for you.

Your "will" can be beneficial in that it will reveal to your lawyer your desires. Otherwise, this self-drafted document doesn't provide many advantages. It doesn't save in terms of costs. Having your lawyer evaluate your own document will probably cost you about the same amount as having him draft a new will from scratch. And with an attorney-drafted will you would have peace of mind. You might have good cause for worry if what you presented as a "will" were accepted as is by your lawyer.

Q. I want my children to understand why some of them are receiving more than others, but I would rather not discuss it with them now. Should I explain in my will why the shares are unequal?

A. If it is obvious why your gifts are unequal—for example, two went to college and two did not—then it probably would be better not to try to explain. And even if it is not so obvious, problems could arise if one receiving less is unhappy with your reasons.

It is possible that the dissatisfied one could claim that you made your will under a misapprehension—a misunderstanding—and therefore use that as a reason to try to break the will. Explaining could exacerbate the situation, not alleviate it.

Your reluctance to explain your intended actions now to your children seems to indicate that you feel some adverse reaction could result, and you are unwilling to face it. If that is true, then it probably would be better if you omitted any explanation and left well enough alone.

The best way seems to level with your children now. If one or more of them react adversely, that may tell you something too. You can then act accordingly.

Q. May I make a bequest to my daughter but stipulate that she is not entitled to receive the bequest unless she does such and such?

A. You are referring to what is known as a conditional bequest. In general, states allow conditional bequests unless the condition is considered one against public policy. However, states are not in agreement as to which conditions are valid and which are not. And sometimes the same state will have varying degrees of approval or disapproval on the same general subject matter, such as a condition concerning religion.

If you propose a conditional gift, your attorney probably will have to do research before it can be stated with any certainty whether the desired condition is permissible. Conceivably the condition you propose has not yet been decided in your state. In this event, you have several alternatives: state the condition and let the bequest be questionable, forget the condition, or provide an alternative in the event the condition is found to be unenforceable.

Q. My attorney insists that I use a trust in my will to avoid death taxes both when I die and when my spouse dies. Although I want to save taxes, I don't understand all the gobbledygook that he says is necessary. Should I take my attorney's word that the will is OK?

A. Yes, if you have confidence in him. Probably most testators don't fully understand their wills, especially the marital deduction wills that you are talking about. This is rather disconcerting because testators are supposed to know what they are doing. But the Internal Revenue Code, and to some extent the courts, don't allow wills to be stated in plain English.

Q. My wife and I have marital deduction wills, based upon the present federal estate tax exemption, per individual, of $600,000. But what if the exemption goes up or down due to a change in the law? Will our attorney let us know so that we can change our wills accordingly?

A. Since you presently have marital deduction wills, your attorney should do so—one hopes. When Congress first raised the exemption after a long period of not doing so, bar associations advised lawyers that they should notify their clients with marital deduction wills of the law change. Since that time, many lawyers have kept a record of such testators and have notified them of subsequent changes.

But lawyers have no way of knowing which of their clients might now have an estate either larger or smaller than the federal exemption. These two groups must continually be aware of their estate values and of what law changes might have occurred. This is one reason why a periodic review of your estate might be advisable.

Q. In my will I want to give $15,000, which is about 1 percent of my estate, to my nephew. My attorney says the will should describe the gift as a percentage, not in dollars. But 1 percent sounds so paltry. What should I do?

A. Use the percentage, as it remains constant in terms of your total estate. You should never make a will based upon pride or worrying about what people will think. It is your property to do with as you wish. If you let inconsequential matters interfere with your judgment, you may end up with a will that really does not do what you want it to. If you can possibly do so, forget about what other people may think. Otherwise your attorney may throw up her hands and not do the best job for you.

8
Using Trusts Wisely

You probably have heard of trusts. You may have read that trusts are advisable for various purposes. Perhaps you have a trust in your will. But do you really understand what trusts are, and when to use them?

What Is a Trust?

In this discussion, the word *trust* refers to a legal document, a form of contract reduced to writing. It does not here refer to your dependence upon and confidence in someone to do something, even though the two types of trust are often interrelated.

A trust has been defined as "a right of property, real or personal, held by one party for the benefit of another." Legal title to, and possession of, the trust property is held by one party, called a *trustee*, usually for the benefit of another, called a *beneficiary*—technically called a "cestui que trust."

Actually, the trustee and the beneficiary may be the same person. In fact, the one who creates the trust, the grantor, and the trustee and the beneficiary may all be the same person. However, a sole trustee cannot be the only beneficiary, although it may be the primary beneficiary. If it were, the trust would then be deemed to terminate by reason of the equitable and legal interests merging. The trustee holds and manages the property placed in the trust, as instructed by the instrument which created the trust.

A trust may be unfunded (meaning no property is immediately placed in the trust), awaiting, perhaps, a pourover (bequest) from a will. Or it may be fully funded with the grantor's entire estate, as would occur if the trust were formed to avoid probate. Or it may be partially funded with specific assets, as might occur if the trust were created for management purposes.

Reasons for Creating a Trust

Most trusts are formed for one or more of the following reasons: retention of control by the creator, charitable giving, property management and conservation, possible incapacity of the trust creator, protection of beneficiaries from themselves or others, defeat of rights of a spouse or a forced heir, avoidance of probate, consolidation of assets, flexibility, and minority or incompetency of the beneficiary.

Note that tax advantages are not among the reasons to create a trust. Under the Tax Reform Act of 1986, the ability of a trust, almost certainly a revocable trust, to save income taxes may no longer be possible. As to death taxes, all property in a revocable trust is treated as property of the grantor at the time of her or his death. It thus is taxed as if no trust existed. And because of the unified credit, little or no death tax benefit is realized in the event an irrevocable trust is created. (See the comments below concerning the irrevocable life insurance trust.)

Many individuals are also interested in the use of a revocable trust to avoid probate. See Chapter 11 for a discussion of this matter.

Naming a Trustee

If you create a trust, whether by express instrument or by will, you should indicate in the instrument whether you wish the trust to be court-supervised. This may be exactly what you do or do not want. If you want privacy, for example, you may not want a court-supervised trust, since most court records are open to the public.

The trustee has a fiduciary relationship similar to that of a personal representative, an executor, an administrator, a conservator, or even an attorney in fact. He holds legal title to the trust property but cannot use it for his own benefit. The trustee is held to a strict code of conduct, and his powers and limitations are as imposed by the trust instrument and possibly by statute.

As should be surmised, if a family member does not have all the necessary qualifications, then a bank should be seriously considered as trustee. However, sometimes because of the nature of the trust, the initial trustee will be the grantor of the trust. (For further details, see Chapter 11, on trusts to avoid probate.

Two Types of Trusts

Basically, there are two general classifications of trusts: the living, or inter vivos, trust, and the testamentary trust. The former type is created and takes effect during the grantor's lifetime. The latter type is provided for in a person's will and takes effect, if at all, when the will is admitted to probate after the person's death.

Both types of trust have some common provisions. They relate to the following concerns:

How is the trust funded—what property is transferred to the trust and by whom?

What is the identity of the trustee who will administer the trust, and the extent of her or his powers and authority?

Who are the beneficiaries of the trust, the ones for whom the trust is designed to benefit?

What is the trust period?

This last common characteristic has to do with the purpose of the trust, in that the reason for the trust will usually dictate the life of the trust.

With both types of trusts, statutes generally will set out the basic powers of a court-supervised trustee, although the trust instrument should never rely on statutory powers alone. The statutes may also set out certain requirements concerning annual reports and discharge of the trustee. These statutes generally won't apply in the event that the instrument creating the trust contains provisions relating to these concerns.

Each class of trust is discussed separately below. Even though you may be interested in only one of these types of trusts, read both sections. Both types have similar appearances and purposes, and you want to make sure that you use the one that is right for you.

Rules Against Perpetuities

The uses of a trust are only limited by what would be considered a contravention of law or against public policy.

One limitation has to do with the period of a trust. Most states, either by statute or because they follow the common law rule, prohibit a violation of what is called the Rule Against Perpetuities. In brief, this rule, which originated under the common law, holds that no contingent (as opposed to a vested) interest is valid unless it vests not later than 21 years after some life in being at the creation of the trust.

The rule was designed to prevent a trust from lasting forever, that is, from withholding a distribution of the trust property in perpetuity. Hence the name for the rule.

Several states have modernized the rule by statute, nine by adopting the Uniform Statutory Rule Against Perpetuities approved by the National Conference of Commissioners on Uniform State Laws. The Uniform statute adopts a so-called wait-and-see period of 90 years. Under this rule, a contingent interest cannot be struck down until at least 90 years have passed. At that time it is determined whether any then-contingent interest fails to meet the rule. If it does fail, then the interest is voided and a court determines the interests of the parties.

But regardless of any improvements, the rule is still complicated and difficult for many, including lawyers, to understand. Because of the rule, however, trusts have to be formulated with great care. Trusts cannot withhold a distribution of the trust property forever, that is, in perpetuity. Otherwise, a violation of the rule may upset what is otherwise a carefully drawn trust.

Living, or Inter Vivos, Trusts

If you create a living trust, you are referred to as the grantor, settlor, donor, creator, or trustor of the trust. You do so by executing a written document—the trust instrument—which sets out the terms of the trust.

Revocability of the Trust

One term, which appears only in the living trust, provides for the trust to be either revocable or irrevocable. You as grantor may wish to retain the right to revoke or amend the trust at any time. Or you may wish not to retain these options. In the latter event, the trust presumably would be irrevocable.

If the trust were irrevocable, it could not be changed or terminated at will. As grantor of such a trust, you would be locked in forever to the terms of the instrument, even though someday you might like to, or ought to, modify or revoke the trust. Despite these limitations, you might want to create an irrevocable trust because of some anticipated, although probably nominal, tax advantage, or because you want to protect the trust assets and beneficiaries from a possible future dilution of your estate.

The creation of an irrevocable trust subjects the grantor to gift tax consequences if the value of the trust property exceeds the annual exclusion. Each time property is transferred to the trust, a potential gift tax liability exists. Unlike with a revocable trust, with an irrevocable trust upon the death of the grantor no part of the trust property is considered by the IRS as a part of grantor's estate. Trust income may or may not be taxed to the grantor, depending upon whether the grantor is a beneficiary under the trust.

Some Purposes of a Living Trust

A trust can take the place of a conservatorship. Suppose your widowed mother no longer feels capable, because of her physical or mental condition, of caring for her income property. She wants you to do it for her.

Let's assume that the circumstances are such that a power of attorney is not advisable. Your mother could set up a trust, placing her income property in the trust and naming either you, another individual, or a bank as trustee. This might be better than a conservatorship, which always requires court supervision and results in periodic court costs and attorney fees.

Or suppose that you have inherited a considerable amount of property, much of which you wish to retain in the same form as you received it. The property, or some of it, needs constant management attention, but you do not feel capable of handling this. For various reasons, a power of attorney may not be advisable. And you might not want a conservatorship, as that would also affect all of your other property, since a conservator is responsible for all property of a ward.

Again, you have the opportunity of setting up a trust specifically for that property which is beyond your ability to handle. In this situation you would want to be particularly careful in naming a trustee capable of managing the trust property.

Privacy is often cited as a reason for the creation of a trust, since a trust normally is not required to be a matter of public record. Hence the terms, assets, and beneficiaries of the trust are not subject to public scrutiny. With a revocable trust, however, because the trust property is deemed part of the grantor's estate upon his or her death, such privacy is at least partially lost in those states which require the property, or at least the value of it, to be listed in the decedent's probate inventory.

Charitable Remainder Trusts

If you are wealthy, then you probably have thought of setting up an estate plan that includes a *charitable remainder trust.* No doubt you think that by setting one up you can save money for yourself, your family, and your favorite charitable organization. All of that, or maybe just part of it, may be true.

Two Types of Charitable Remainder Trusts. The Internal Revenue Code breaks down charitable remainder trusts into two categories: a charitable remainder *annuity trust* and a charitable remainder *unitrust.*

With both types of trusts the grantor names two or more beneficiaries—designated as "income beneficiaries"—to receive payments from the trust. At least one of the income beneficiaries must be a person who is not defined under the code as a charitable organization. The grantor may—and usually does—name him- or herself as one of these beneficiaries.

Any designated individual beneficiary must be living at the time of the creation of the trust. Upon the death of the last individual beneficiary, the remainder (ultimate) interest passes to the designated charitable organization, such as a college or university.

Both kinds of charitable remainder trusts have some similarities. The following are some of the basic ones:

- Payments to the income beneficiaries may be for life or for a term up to 20 years.
- The payments must be made at least annually.
- The fixed amount of the payment cannot vary.
- The format of the two types of trust are exceedingly restrictive.
- Because of valuation problems, both trusts ordinarily are funded with assets that are easily valued.

The two types of trust also have some dissimilarities. The following are the main ones:

- With the annuity trust the assets are valued only once, at the inception of the trust, but with the unitrust the assets are valued annually.
- Both trusts specify annual payouts based on a percentage of trust assets (not less than 5 percent of the net fair market value), but the annuity trust bases that percentage on the *initial* valuation of all the property placed in the trust while the unitrust bases it on the *annual* revaluation.
- Additional contributions can be made periodically to the unitrust, but they cannot to the annuity trust.

Thus, with an annuity the payments do *not* vary. With a unitrust they do. If you were a beneficiary under a unitrust, this variation could work in your favor in two ways:

1. Should the total income your unitrust receives in a year be less than the fixed amount then a lesser amount may be paid to you (if your trust so provides. However, in subsequent years, should the amount of trust in-

come exceed the fixed amount, any shortfalls must be made up. Thus, you will keep receiving trust income, although in varying amounts, but not at the expense of total trust assets.

2. The annual revaluations of the unitrust allow for some hedge against inflation. Your payments go up and down in relation to the income that your trust receives. With an annuity trust, they do not. Payments are fixed, and are not subject to change.

By now, you may have concluded that a unitrust may be more advantageous for you. That may not be true, however, if you intend to make only one contribution to the trust and want to, or need to, rely on the same distribution year after year.

Charitable Remainder Trusts and Taxes.   Except for unrelated business income, a charitable remainder trust is exempt from income tax. And the gift of the remainder interest can be deducted by the grantor on her income taxes. The gift would be considered a charitable contribution during the year of transfer. Tax regulations detail how the remainder interest should be computed, differing as to the two types of trust.

The amount received by the income beneficiary has the same characteristics it did in the hands of the trust. If the amount paid to the income beneficiary is income, it becomes a part of the gross income of the beneficiary. If it is capital gain, then it is capital gain. And it may also be a distribution of the principal of the trust, the *trust corpus* (as distinguished from its income).

If an individual income beneficiary is other than the grantor or grantor's spouse, then the transfer is subject to gift taxes. But offsetting any liability for gift taxes are the $10,000 annual exclusion and the unified credit.

When the grantor dies, to the extent that an income beneficiary survives, then the trust assets are included in the grantor's estate for federal estate tax purposes. However, the estate tax charitable deduction is available.

Considerations Before Entering a Charitable Remainder Trust.   Should you enter into a charitable remainder trust with your favorite charitable institution—say, your alma mater? It depends upon several considerations. What is your purpose in giving? Is it to benefit yourself or your charity, or both? Do you want to deprive your close heirs, if any, of the property placed in trust, or do they have sufficient assets of their own? Are you sufficiently wealthy so that placing some of your estate in a charitable remainder trust is somewhat immaterial to the welfare of your heirs?

The Charitable Lead Trust

A variation of the charitable remainder trust is the split-interest charitable *income, front-end,* or *lead* trust. It usually is used only by people with large estates.

The lead trust, as it is generally known, operates in a manner directly opposite to that of a charitable remainder trust. Whereas under the charitable remainder trust a specified amount periodically goes first to someone other than the ultimate charity, under the lead trust a specified amount periodically goes first to a charity for a specified period of time. Thereafter, the reversionary or remainder amount in the lead trust goes to the grantor or a designated party other than a charity. You should be aware that if the reversionary or remainder interest passes to someone two generations or more removed from the grantor, the generation skipping transfer tax must be considered. For a detailed discussion of the generation skipping transfer, see Chapter 16.

The Irrevocable Life
Insurance Trust

The Internal Revenue Code provides that the value of a decedent's gross estate includes proceeds received by a personal representative and all other beneficiaries from the decedent's life insurance policies. The decedent at the time of death must possess "incidents of ownership" of the policies in order for the code provisions to take effect.

Because of this statute, individuals whose estates are likely to be subject to a federal estate tax try to plan so that no life insurance on their life falls under the provisions of the code. In other words, if the value of your estate is approaching or exceeding the federal estate tax exemption of $600,000, then it would not be advisable for your estate to include life insurance proceeds upon your death.

Ideally, any deceased's estate should be sufficiently liquid to be able to pay the estate expenses, including the death tax. Life insurance could fulfill this function except that the very fund—the life insurance—that would be set up for this purpose could, itself, be subject to the tax—a no-win situation.

If no death taxes are anticipated, it may be desirable for the estate to become the beneficiary of a life insurance policy. Liquidity could then be available for the payment of obligations. But if state or federal taxes could possibly result, then the decedent's beneficiaries should probably be made the owners of the life insurance policies. The decedent should have made sure, of course, that she had no incidents of ownership. If she didn't, then the insurance does not escape from being considered an asset of the estate.

"Incidents of ownership" is broadly interpreted by the Internal Revenue Code. They are not only the actual ownership of the policy but also any powers or right that the insured has over the policy. Such powers include the right to change the beneficiaries or to deal with the policy in any manner.

The ideal situation would be for the insured never to have owned the policy. But suppose that during the process of estate planning it is determined that John Doe, the insured owner of a large policy, ought to no longer have any incidents of ownership in the policy. Otherwise, he would be subject to federal estate tax consequences. What options does he then have?

One option would be for Doe to give the policy to another party who would then own the policy, make the premium payments, and otherwise assume all incidents of ownership. The gift, however, would be subject to the federal gift tax statute, unless the transfer were made to Doe's spouse. But if the transfer were made within three years of Doe's death, then the life insurance proceeds would be considered part of decedent's estate for federal estate tax purposes.

Whether a gift tax return and a possible gift tax or use of the unified credit is required depends upon the value of the policy at the time of the gift. IRS regulations specify various ways of determining this value, depending upon the nature of the transaction and the status of the policy at the time of the gift. If the calculated value is $10,000 or less, then no gift tax consequences result.

Another possible option, although not as clear-cut as to gift tax consequences, is to create an irrevocable life insurance trust. Such a trust then becomes the owner of the insured's life insurance policies. The intended benefit usually is to reduce or eliminate the federal estate tax by keeping the insurance proceeds out of the estate of the insured. This would not be possible, however, if the trust were revocable.

Other, perhaps lesser, benefits could be gained by such an arrangement. For example, the estate could be guaranteed for the beneficiaries. Or more flexibility in use of the proceeds would be available than would otherwise be possible under a mere life insurance policy.

The difficulty encountered with the irrevocable trust is that the annual $10,000 gift tax exclusion does not apply to gifts that are not of a present interest. As a basic rule, the IRS holds that a gift of a life insurance policy, or of premiums payable for such a policy, to an irrevocable trust is of a future interest. Why? The interest—the life insurance proceeds—is not received by the beneficiary until the death of the insured.

Thus any such transfers by the insured grantor to the trust are deemed to be gifts of future interests. The result is that the insured's unified credit (the $600,000 exemption) is reduced by the value of each of such gifts. To the extent reduced, the credit is not available to the insured's estate at time of death.

No clear agreement exists between estate planners and the IRS as to the method by which a gift of a present interest may be achieved. Some planners believe that a gift of a future interest may be avoided by granting immediate powers of withdrawal to one or more of the trust beneficiaries.

Another method deemed available to avoid the future interest rule is the so-called 5 and 5 power. This exception requires that the beneficiary under the trust have the power to withdraw $5000 or 5 percent of the value of the trust, whichever is greater. By having this power, the beneficiary is thought to have a present interest in the trust. In granting this authority, however, the grantor is taking some risk as to what the beneficiary may do.

You might want to consider using an irrevocable life insurance trust if your estate is large. Otherwise you would not ordinarily want to establish this kind of trust.

Testamentary Trusts

A testamentary trust, which is a trust provided for in your will, can serve in lieu of a conservatorship. Your lawyer probably will advise you to set up this type of trust for any property going to your children while they remain minors. If you fail to set up such a trust and you die while any of your beneficiaries are still minors, then a conservatorship would have to be set up for those minor children before they could receive their share of the inheritance.

An exception might be if the value of the bequest were considered by statute to be a nominal sum, say $4000 or less. In that event, under many statutes the bequest might be paid to the parent or other person entitled to the custody of the minor. Under those circumstances neither a trust nor a conservatorship would be necessary.

A testamentary trust for a minor has other advantages. It can provide for the disposition of the trust property to another beneficiary in the event the minor child dies before reaching legal majority or some specified later age. In this manner you actually retain control of the trust property for a period of time beyond your death.

Your will can also withhold the paying out of the trust property to the child beyond the age of legal majority—because one of the children is incompetent, for instance. The document can also provide for a guardian of the child during minority. The purposes for which the trust property is to be used—for higher education, for example—can be spelled out. And you can designate whom you want to serve as trustee.

Testamentary trusts can be set up for other purposes too. Suppose you have an aged parent or any other beneficiary who is either considered incompetent or likely to be so at some stage of his or her life. As indicated elsewhere, trusts can serve in lieu of a life estate or other vehicle used to manage another person's property. But testamentary trusts under certain circumstances are also a great means to avoid the federal estate tax. The marital deduction trust is one type of testamentary trust that can accomplish this objective.

The Marital Deduction Trust

To understand the marital deduction trust you must first understand the concept of the unlimited marital deduction. Under the federal estate tax law, all property that goes outright to the surviving spouse goes tax-free. This is referred to as the marital deduction. It is further described as the unlimited marital deduction since the amount which may pass tax-free to the surviving spouse is unlimited.

There is no ceiling on the size of an inheritance which may be received by the surviving spouse from the deceased spouse's estate. Because of the unlimited marital deduction, the size of the federal estate tax exemption, which is presently $600,000 per person, is irrelevant insofar as outright, unrestricted transfers between spouses are concerned.

Three prerequisites are required in order for a marital deduction to qualify. First, the property must pass unconditionally to the surviving spouse. Second, although it passes tax-free in the estate of the first spouse to die, whatever remains of it upon the death of the surviving spouse is included in the estate for federal estate tax purposes. Last, the bequest must be an absolute bequest of an absolute interest. If these three conditions are not met, the transfer is deemed to be a terminable interest. In this event the bequest does not qualify for the marital deduction—in other words, it does not go tax-free.

Generally speaking, an interest is deemed terminable if it will end or fail by reason of lapse of time or the occurrence or nonoccurrence of a specified event. A life estate is a good example of a failing interest, as the interest fails (ends) upon the death of the life tenant (the surviving spouse).

Some exceptions exist, one of them being the so-called QTIP trust which is discussed below. Because any size of inheritance goes tax-free to the surviving spouse, you may ask, Why not just leave everything outright to the surviving spouse, since no federal estate tax results from the gift? Why bother with fancy wills or trusts? If you read on, you will understand why this could be an expensive mistake.

The Bypass Trust

Now consider the bypass trust. This type of trust is used for the purpose of saving federal estate taxes upon the death of the testator's chief beneficiary, the surviving spouse. Many variants of the tax savings procedures exist.

Ordinarily the bypass trust would be used by a married couple whose total taxable estate exceeds the federal exemption of $600,000. At this size, the estate of a married couple is usually split between the spouses, not necessarily half the total in each person's estate, although that form often is preferable. Their respective wills should provide that the first $600,000 of each partner's estate be placed in a trust.

The bypass trust is also known as a credit-shelter trust, since the property in this trust is "sheltered," by reason of the $600,000 exemption, from the federal estate tax. The objective of the bypass trust is to maximize the exemption rather than the marital deduction.

Because of the federal exemption, any property placed in this trust and having a total value of $600,000 or less is not taxed when the first spouse dies. The balance of the decedent's estate—the residual—then is bequeathed to the surviving spouse. Because of the unlimited marital deduction, no tax results from the residuary bequest to the surviving spouse either. This arrangement is sometimes referred to as the zero-tax marital deduction formula.

When the second spouse dies, the amount in the bypass trust (which is created in the will of the first spouse) is not considered by the IRS as a part of the second spouse's estate. The reason is because the bequest in trust is considered a terminable interest, so named because the amount in the trust—for the benefit of the surviving spouse—terminates upon the death of such a spouse. Being a terminable interest, it would be subject to tax in the estate of the first spouse to die, except that since the amount in the bypass trust is not more than the exemption of $600,000, the estate of the first spouse to die suffers no tax on that amount either.

In summary, the property placed in the bypass trust is not taxed in the first estate unless its value exceeds the exemption of $600,000. It is not taxed in the second estate because it is not considered to be part of the surviving spouse's estate when she or he dies.

An Alternative to the Bypass Trust.   Instead of establishing a bypass trust, one spouse could bequeath all of the property outright to the other spouse. Because of the unlimited marital deduction, after the death of the spouse no federal tax upon the first death would result from this transfer arrangement. In this respect, the tax consequences are no different than the bypass trust arrangement, which also results in no federal tax upon the first death.

When the second spouse dies, however, the surviving spouse's estate would include the amount that otherwise would be in the trust—a sum up to $600,000. Unlike the bypass trust situation, all of the estate of the first deceased spouse thus becomes a part of the estate of the surviving spouse. This is an undesirable result since all that part of the surviving spouse's estate which exceeds the $600,000 exemption is taxed at a minimum rate of 37 percent.

How a Bypass Trust Works. Let's further examine a bypass trust with a simple example. Assume Hernando and Wanda are husband and wife with a total estate of $1,200,000. Of this amount, each has only a $600,000 estate in his or her own name. Each makes a will which provides that the first $600,000 of that person's estate will be placed in a bypass trust for the benefit of the other spouse. Both wills also provide that any balance of one spouse's estate will go outright to the surviving spouse. Hernando dies first. His total estate of $600,000, less deductions, goes into the bypass trust. Since the federal exemption before any federal estate tax is $600,000, his estate pays no federal estate tax.

Wanda subsequently dies. Her estate remains at $600,000, since no part of the $600,000 placed by Hernando in the bypass trust can be included as part of Wanda's estate. Wanda's estate also pays no federal estate tax, since it is $600,000—the amount of the exemption. In other words, Hernando's estate bypasses Wanda's estate through the device of a bypass trust.

If Hernando had not provided for a bypass trust in his will, then all of his property would have gone to Wanda. Upon Wanda's death her estate would have totaled $1,200,000. The federal estate tax upon that amount is $235,000. This amount is based upon the applicable tax table as furnished by the IRS. From the gross estate tax computed from the table is deducted the unified credit of $192,000. Thus the use of the bypass trust in this example saves $235,000 in federal estate taxes.

Suppose in the above example that both wills provide that upon the death of the second spouse the property in the bypass trust goes to the couple's children and that both wills name these children as residuary beneficiaries. With the bypass trust provision, the children would eventually receive from two separate estates. Upon the death of the second spouse the children would receive a total of $1,200,000, $600,000 from the trust set up in Hernando's will and $600,000 from Wanda's estate.

If no bypass trust had been provided for, upon the death of Wanda the children would receive from one estate only, Wanda's. An estate of $965,000 would remain, which is the original $1,200,000 less the $235,000 federal estate tax. While $965,000 still may seem to be a large sum of money to you, why would anyone purposely pay out $235,000 if taxes could be reasonably avoided?

A bypass trust ordinarily provides that the income from the bypass trust shall go to the surviving spouse, although there is no requirement that it must. In making this provision a surviving spouse is not likely to be left in a precarious or worrisome financial position even though the total of the two estates may be much smaller than in the above example.

Use of Two Trusts.   Sometimes, particularly with very large estates, a will provides for two trusts—one being the bypass trust—for the benefit of the surviving spouse.

Many reasons may exist for setting up the second trust, usually called the *spousal* or marital *trust*. For example, the advanced age or the lack of investing or managerial ability of the other spouse may require her or him to have the estate managed. Or the loyalty of the other spouse to the couple's children may be in question. Or the testator may wish to shield the property in the second trust from the spouse's creditors or partners in remarriage.

Upon the death of the surviving spouse, however, the estate property in the second trust will be subject to federal estate taxes. In other words, a trust per se does not avoid death taxes. Thus, there is no estate tax advantage in setting up the second trust.

The QTIP Trust

Another type of testamentary trust is the QTIP trust. QTIP is the commonly used abbreviation for the Internal Revenue Code's term *qualified terminal interest property.* This type of trust is often used for the marital trust.

The QTIP trust operates much like a life estate, although it is set up in trust form. The surviving spouse is the beneficiary of the trust but has no control over the trust property. He or she, however, may be given a power of appointment over the trust property, which can be exercised only in his or her will. When the surviving spouse dies, the trust property passes as provided in the trust or as designated in the surviving spouse's will. Some testators like the feature of being able to control the disposition of the property following the death of the surviving spouse (assuming no power of appointment was given).

It has been suggested by some people that the QTIP trust remains popular because of the "loophole mentality" of some testators. These testators believe that by setting up a QTIP trust they can get around one of the requirements to qualify the property for the marital deduction—that the interest passing to the surviving spouse not be terminable. That is true, but if the estate were $1,200,000 or less, no federal estate tax would be payable whether the will provided for one or two trusts. Thus use of a second trust, the marital trust, should be for reasons other than saving taxes.

The QTIP form of trust seems to violate one of the rules making a bequest eligible for the marital deduction, that the gift be an outright one. The testamentary gift from one spouse to the other in a QTIP trust is not an outright gift. Since the QTIP trust is a form of life estate (thus being a terminable interest), it does not meet the basic requirement to qualify the bequest under the marital deduction rules. But it qualifies for the marital deduction because of the specific exception in the statute.

The law creating the QTIP trust (The Economic Recovery Tax Act of 1981, usually referred to as ERTA), however, provides that if a trust meets the QTIP requirements, and if the proper procedures are followed, then the trust is treated the same as an outright gift to the surviving spouse. The bequest is then qualified under the marital deduction rules. Because it is, the property in the QTIP trust is not taxed in the estate of the first spouse to die. It is taxed, however, in the estate of the second spouse to die.

In the QTIP trust, except for the possible inclusion of the power of appointment, the surviving spouse has no control over naming the ultimate beneficiaries upon the surviving spouse's death. This is what sometimes appeals to the first spouse in creating the QTIP trust.

ERTA has strict requirements for the trust to be eligible for the marital deduction. For instance, the surviving spouse must be entitled to all of the trust income payable at least annually. And only the surviving spouse is entitled to the trust principal during the trust period. The personal representative must elect at the time of the testator's death to treat the trust property as a QTIP trust. This election must be made on the federal estate tax return and, once made, is irrevocable.

If the personal representative chooses not to elect to treat the trust as a QTIP trust, then the trust property becomes part of the estate. It is then subject to the federal estate tax, since it does not fall under the marital deduction classification. Whether or not a tax results depends upon how much of the $600,000 exemption is still available to offset the value of the trust property.

In case you have not already realized it, many marital deduction trusts are not really for the benefit of the surviving spouse. Instead, many are for the benefit of the next generation of beneficiaries. The benefit is the amount of the federal estate tax saved.

If simplicity is the only concern, then the testator should arrange for the surviving spouse to receive outright all of that testator's property with no strings attached. The cost of the will preparation would be nominal and the administration of the first estate would be simplified. And there would be no possible continuing costs of administering one or more trusts.

Thus if a couple's total estate is considerably less than, say, $700,000, the question arises: Is all the bother worth the costs? Or do other possible benefits exist which should be considered also?

Some Common
Questions Answered

Q. If I want to set up a charitable trust with my alma mater, do I need to contact my attorney to do so or can I deal directly with the university?

A. That depends upon many things. Do you feel competent to handle it yourself? Do you trust the school representative you are dealing with? Will the probable gift in trust be so large that it is likely to upset your estate planning? Will your will have to be reviewed, and perhaps changed, accordingly?

   Qualified charities that promote charitable trusts undoubtedly use their own attorneys to set up trust agreements. Presumably, therefore, the agreements are in proper form to meet IRS requirements. But their attorneys do not, and cannot for ethical reasons, also represent you in the transaction. Thus if you do not engage your own attorney, you are unrepresented. Because of this situation, many charities will recommend that you obtain independent counsel, this being for their protection as well as yours.

   As far as the trust agreement is concerned, in 1990 the IRS made available sample declarations of trust for qualified charitable remainder annuity trusts and unitrusts. No requirement exists for using the forms, and some charities, lawyers, and individuals may not wish to do so. But the IRS will not raise any objection if one of their forms is used and followed.

Q. Can you give me the main reasons for having a trust?

A. A trust is used for management purposes, to avoid having an alternate estate proceeding, to avoid probate, or to reduce or eliminate death taxes. In using a trust for one reason, you may also realize other benefits. In attempting to achieve these goals, however, never lose sight of the possibility that not creating a trust or choosing an alternative may be equally or even more beneficial than doing so.

Q. Can you give me the main reasons for not having a trust?

A. You should not use trusts if you want to avoid (1) having additional costs of creating and managing the trust, (2) getting involved in procedures that may not be readily understood, or (3) losing personal control of your property. By weighing and comparing the benefits with the drawbacks, you should be able to determine whether a trust is worth the trouble and costs. Knowing the main reason for wanting or needing a trust may be helpful in determining its worth.

Q. Is there any rule of thumb that is helpful in determining whether a trust in any particular situation is desirable?

A. Not really. But this doesn't mean that you can't use your own judgment to advantage. Your most important concern should be simplicity. What is the simplest way to accomplish your desires? For example, if your goal is to avoid costs, what is the simplest way to achieve that goal? If it is to avoid probate, what is the simplest way to do that? When making your decision, don't let your prejudice of something (such as probate) affect your good judgment.

Q. I am the ultimate beneficiary of a trust. Do I have any right to receive periodic accountings from the trustee prior to the death of the primary beneficiary?

A. This may depend on many things: the wording of the trust instrument, the controlling statutes, and any controlling court decisions. If none of these are of any help, then asking the trustee for periodic reports may be all that is necessary. If the trustee is not cooperative, then the only way you may be able to determine your rights is by going to court. If the trust is a court-supervised one, this would not be too difficult. If not, then you would be forced to start a suit, a procedure you might not find to your liking.

Q. I would like to set up an irrevocable trust for the benefit of my grandson, but my attorney wants the trust to be revocable. Is there any good reason why my attorney should object to my wishes?

A. He or she might object because very few trusts need to be, or in fact ought to be, irrevocable. An irrevocable trust is so final, so fixed, so far reaching, even, perhaps, so irresponsible that no lawyer wants to be a part of it unless there is absolutely no alternative. Two possible occurrences—a change of mind or a change of circumstances—dictate that a trust should be made revocable. If trusts were not made revocable, it is conceivable that they would soon lose their appeal.

This particular discussion pertains to living trusts, not testamentary trusts. Recall that testamentary trusts are set up conditionally. Such conditions might be "If my son is under 18, . . . " "If my wife is living six months after my death, . . . " They are set up for particular purposes. Once they go into effect, however, they are, in effect, irrevocable. But the testator can always change his or her will, so in that sense the testamentary trusts are also revocable—until death.

Only the subsequent incompetence of the maker of the trust (or will) in effect makes a revocable trust (will) irrevocable.

Q. Which is generally considered better, a charitable remainder annuity trust or a charitable remainder unitrust?

A. That depends on the situation. Presumably all charitable organizations would prefer the unitrust because this gives them an opportunity to receive subsequent additional contributions from the grantor.

You may recall that under the annuity trust the grantor is prohibited from making more than the original contribution.

From the point of view of the grantor, other considerations are more important. Perhaps the grantor wants the amount of the payments to be fixed so that plans can be made accordingly. If so, then the annuity trust would be more appealing, since under the unitrust the amount of the payment is refigured annually.

Or perhaps the grantor has certain stock purchase options. The stock has value but pays only a small dividend. By exercising his or her purchase rights annually, the grantor could contribute such stock to the trust. The trustee would not be required to convert the stock to cash as it was acquired. Instead, she or he could do so at the time the grantor retires, thus increasing the grantor's income at a time when other sources of income may have terminated. With this arrangement, the grantor could receive less income from the trust at a time when it was not needed, and more income when it was. But to enable the grantor to make additional contributions would require a unitrust to be used, since the annuity trust does not allow additional contributions.

Many considerations must be taken into account before the grantor can decide which type of charitable trust is better for him or her. The charitable organization will be happy with either choice, although it would probably prefer the unitrust, despite the extra bookwork.

Q. Won't a personal representative always elect to treat a QTIP trust as such upon the testator's death? Presumably she or he would do so to prevent the trust property from being taxed in the first estate. If so, why does the testator bother with this type of trust, which requires action upon the part of the representative within a prescribed time? Why not just leave the property outright to the spouse or set up the usual spousal trust?

A. Several reasons exist, some valid, some not so valid. Some testators think they know more than their spouses, or maybe they just don't trust their spouses, so they prefer to control the ultimate disposition of the trust property. They can do this with the QTIP trust.

Or a testator may like the idea of the QTIP trust being another post-mortem strategy available to the personal representative. But this actually only adds another burden to the many responsibilities of the personal representative.

9

Providing for
Disability

Many of us will need someone to look after our affairs at some point in the future. This situation may be brought about by either a mental or physical disability, an incapacity serious enough for us to be unable to handle our own affairs. If you think you may be one of these people, you will probably want to do some planning for such a possibility. At the least, you should know what your options are.

One thing is certain and that, of course, is death. But what is usually not so certain is how you approach this inevitability. From a legal point of view, the concern is whether you will travel gracefully toward the end, without difficulty. Or will you encounter a roadblock, such as a mental or physical impairment, that results in a need for help?

In other words, will you need an agent to be responsible for your estate at some stage of your life? Finally, do you want to choose the option, or pathway, or would you rather let someone else make the choice for you?

This discussion concerns the options or choices, referred to herein as *pathways*, you have both prior and subsequent to physical or mental incompetency. The pathways are economic, in effect a legal decision involving management and disposition of your estate. All of these pathways have been tried numerous times by others. Unfortunately, they have often ended unfavorably since the planning for incapacity was either insufficient or unprofessional.

The emphasis in this chapter will not be on death and disease. Instead it will be on life—as it exists, not as you hope it will be. Certainly you should maintain an optimistic attitude, but that doesn't mean you should try to escape realism by burying your head in the sand.

You may wonder what the odds are that you will need help at some point in your life. What, you may ask, are the percentages of people who eventually end their last years in need of help? In asking this, you might believe that the odds are so slight that you need not prepare for the future. If you researched this, your findings probably would be inconclusive. But surely you recognize that a great number of people need someone to look after their affairs, especially as they grow older.

Suppose you have not taken any action and are unprepared for your disability. If it appears without warning—for example, as a result of an accident, stroke, or heart attack—then any action taken on your behalf would have to be involuntary. This situation most likely would not be to your liking, if you were competent enough to realize it.

The means of providing for someone else to handle estate affairs have been discussed before, in different contexts. Much of what has already been said, therefore, will not be addressed again, although you may refer to Chapters 2, 3, 4, 5, and 8 for a detailed review. In a sense, then, this chapter will serve as a practical application of what you learned in those chapters.

As you traverse the legal pathways toward having someone else manage your estate, you should be aware of two things: (1) that you may already have taken one or more of these paths for other reasons, and (2) even under the same set of facts, any two people would probably not agree on what would be the best path to take under those particular circumstances. Consequently, do not be influenced by others or by the order in which the paths are set out.

Before contemplating the pathways, think of the following goals as set out by one commentator:

1. Insofar as possible, retain control over your property.

2. Protect your property from harm, waste, and intrusion.

3. Make sure that all jurisdictions in which you own property are covered.

4. Try to ensure that your property is managed in a single, economical, private, and effective manner.

5. Carefully define the role of your fiduciary.

6. Be certain that your estate plan is left intact.

The Legal Pathways

The following are six common legal means, or pathways, of having someone else assume control over your estate:

1. *Do nothing.* Here some indication of planning might actually exist, even though it was not deliberate and even though it might be mostly wrong. A joint tenancy might fit this category.

2. *Joint tenancy.* With this pathway you may feel that the other joint tenant can take over at such time as you need help.

3. *Power of attorney.* You can designate someone to look after your affairs if you take this path. A bank agency account may serve in this capacity.

4. *Gift.* Here you trust the donee to use your property for your benefit.

5. *Trust.* With this path you can set up a formalized system to take care of your affairs—your estate.

6. *Conservatorship* (guardianship). This is the only court-supervised system to take care of your affairs, although a trust could specify court supervision. Depending upon the type of conservatorship used, this may be the only path available to you—actually to your estate—if incompetency arrives before action is taken.

Other means of having someone else assume control of your estate, such as estate planning, wills, antenuptial agreements, and living wills are not directly applicable to the subject of preparation for disability and thus will not be discussed here.

Doing Nothing

Regardless of what might be said here or elsewhere, or even regardless of what you yourself might believe, doing nothing is bound to be the most popular choice. No one wants to do something believed unnecessary. Until something adverse happens, it is generally believed that doing nothing saves time and money and maybe frustrations.

As a result, you may have a "don't care" attitude, which might in part exist because you have no close heirs. Thus you may feel that what happens to your estate is of no great concern to you. Or maybe you feel that if and when the time for incompetency comes, something can then be done, that you will have plenty of time to take action.

Reasons for Doing Nothing. Many of the reasons for doing nothing seem to be interrelated. What might some of them be? "I have a fatalistic attitude." "There's time enough to plan." "It won't happen to me." "I have no close heirs." "I don't know what to do." "I can't make up my mind." "It's too much trouble." "I don't like lawyers." You might also blame procrastination, indifference, ignorance, or expense. Most of these excuses are not valid.

Possible Condition of Your Estate.   When nothing has been consciously done, what might be the possible condition of your estate? Have you done something, after all, that might serve your estate if you become incapacitated?

It is doubtful. You may be holding some of your estate in joint tenancy with another for other reasons. But the chances that you intended the other tenant to use your property for your welfare in the event you needed help are slim.

You may have made some gifts for various reasons. Here again it is doubtful that the donees were instructed to use those gifts to benefit you if you needed such help.

Because you have designated no one to act as your agent, no one is prepared or authorized to act for you and on your behalf in case of emergency. Whatever action might be required, under these circumstances, would have to be involuntary because of your failure to plan in advance.

You and your heirs may luck out if you die without first experiencing incompetency. But if you do fail to plan and become incapacitated, the involuntary route—the conservatorship—would still be an available option, although not a good one.

Joint Tenancy

The second pathway is created by setting up one or more joint tenancies. You and the other joint tenant would have an understanding that the assets in the tenancies would be used for your support when you needed them. If you choose this pathway, you must have a careful understanding with the other tenant as to when he or she is to take over. You must also have complete faith in the integrity and judgment of the other tenant. And you must take into account how this arrangement will affect the other heirs.

Although legally the other tenant would have equal access to your assets, the joint tenancies would actually be set up for your convenience. That is why these joint tenancies are sometimes referred to as joint tenancies for convenience. They would not be true joint tenancies.

Because such joint tenancies are set up for the express purpose of taking care of you, the assets in such tenancies must be in liquid form, such as funds in a financial institution. You would receive no benefit if the joint tenancies were in real property—real estate, for example—since your cooperation in selling or mortgaging the property would require the joint cooperation of both of you as well as any existing spouses. If you were incapacitated, you might not be able to physically or legally do this at such time as the funds were needed.

The Awkward Position of the Other Tenant.   Consider the position of the other joint tenant in the event you became incompetent to handle your own affairs. Would this tenant feel comfortable in encroaching upon the joint tenancy property even though it was purely for your welfare. And when would he or she do so? The tenant in effect would be judging that you are no longer fit to handle your affairs yourself. Being unfit and not knowing what is happening are two different things. You may in fact be unfit but still know what is going on.

Suppose the tenant is your child. Will that child want to incur your possible anger by "meddling" in your accounts, even though in fact the child is doing what he or she was charged to do by you in your saner moments? Suppose, because of your present condition, you threaten to cut the child out of your will, or actually do so. Or suppose you don't do these things but the other tenant feels that you are eager to do so.

Inherent Problems of a Joint Tenancy.   The tenant may not abide by your mutual understanding. He or she may be afraid to do so. Or the tenant may no longer be able to do so, because of having moved a distance away or also having become incapacitated. Or, even worse perhaps, the tenant may want to save the assets in the tenancies until your death. As a surviving joint tenant, he or she might then end up with all of such joint property regardless of your will. You lose total control of your property.

You may not be able to deal alone with your property without the other tenant's cooperation. Suppose the tenant deals with the property behind your back, contrary to your understanding. Only limited property, intangible personal property, can be used in this manner.

Setting up the joint tenancy could upset your estate planning, particularly if you have more than one child. Suppose, for instance, that one of your two children is named as the other tenant. What happens to the tenancy assets upon your death, even though you have an understanding among your heirs and the joint tenant? Will those states that have an inheritance tax be understanding and accept a situation different than the standard one with joint tenancies?

Income from the jointly held assets is ordinarily split evenly between the tenants. But suppose you think of the joint property as yours and are willing to report the total amount of income therefrom on your tax return. You couldn't do this legally (or at least until proven otherwise) because half of the income is considered as belonging to the other tenant and should be reported on the other tenant's returns.

Any claims against the tenant could affect the safety of the tenancy assets. Suppose one of the other tenant's creditors levies a judgment upon the tenancy assets. Or suppose the spouse or ex-spouse of the other tenant makes a claim to that tenant's share of the assets.

Power of Attorney

You may recall that a power of attorney is a legal document in which an individual, called a *grantor* or *principal*, authorizes another person, called an *attorney in fact*, to act as that grantor's agent with respect to certain of his or her property rights. The written, signed power of grantor defines the powers granted and specifies the property covered by the instrument.

Remember, an attorney in fact is not to be confused with an attorney in law. For convenience the attorney in fact will only be called an attorney.

Unlike the joint tenancy creation, which is usually accomplished without a lawyer (or a lawyer's advice), the power of attorney is prepared by a lawyer, with her or his blessing (one hopes).

The power must contain the durable clause, as otherwise no purpose would be served in creating this particular pathway. Recall that the durable clause allows the power either to continue or to spring into use, whichever is designated, upon the disability of the grantor. Without the benefit of durability, under the common law the power would lapse upon the disability of the grantor.

Timing the Grant of the Power.   As to when the power should be given, the first impulse is to say, "whenever the grantor feels a need for it." But that isn't necessarily true. The power can be given anytime. Often it works out that the sooner it is granted the better.

If all qualifications of the attorney have been met, then no harm is done by you entering into the power long before you feel it may be necessary. Remember, the power does not have to be used. In fact, you would not want it to be used until a need arose. You can always instruct your attorney in this regard. In the meantime you can always revoke the power, as long as you remain competent, in the event the situation changes.

Although not all commentators agree, the power has many advantages over other pathways—if it is appropriate to the particular situation. That last caveat is important.

Qualifications of the Attorney.   Almost never should you think of naming an attorney who is not a close relative, just as you shouldn't think of naming a joint tenant who is not a close relative for the same purpose. Such a relative could be a descendant, ascendant, sibling, or spouse. Rarely would any other relative be considered, although exceptions can exist.

Other than the relationship, what do you look for in an attorney? Like any party in a fiduciary position, the attorney should be physically able to serve. "Physical" here refers to location as well as to health. The attorney must be aware of your wants and comfort and be conveniently located to do something about it. And, similarly, the attorney must have the competency to serve, as well as be trustworthy.

What might not be so evident is the necessity for the attorney to be deemed suitable by your other heirs and to be free of the influence of others, including the attorney's spouse. The attorney has considerable responsibility, something that should not be disrupted by the interference of others.

When Is the Bank Agency Account Advisable?   Although a bank agency account is a form of limited power of attorney, this account would not be appropriate for a pathway unless you wanted the bank to begin using it immediately. It is not something that ordinarily is held in abeyance. Once the account is set up and once assets are placed in it, you lose control over those funds. Unlike the regular power of attorney, you do not have equal control over such transferred assets.

It is doubtful that the bank agency could lay dormant, like a regular power of attorney, until needed. However, if a qualified attorney is not available, you may want to investigate this possibility with your banker. Probably, however, you will find that the bank would prefer that you use a trust. In either event, the bank will be entitled to a fee for its services. With an ordinary power of attorney, you may escape a fee, although not necessarily so.

Gifts

It should be difficult to believe, but parents, for all kinds of reasons, often transfer property to their children without consideration. The usual reasons for such gifts are laudatory.

Sometimes, in transferring assets, parents are convinced that their children will use these gifts to take care of them in the event social security and government social programs are insufficient to do so. In this scenario, the gifts are made with the express intent that the assets will be used, if required, for the parents' comfort and care.

It is reassuring to know that parents have faith in their children and that children fully intend to look out for their parents. But good intentions don't guarantee good performance. For any number of reasons, the gifted property can disappear. A child's spouse may enter the picture to the detriment of the parent. The same things that can happen in the joint tenancy situation can happen in this situation.

If parents transfer property without consideration, they lose control of it, no matter what they otherwise think. And if the value of the gift exceeds $10,000, then a gift tax return is required. If the amount of the gift exceeds the $10,000 annual exclusion plus the lifetime $600,000 federal estate tax exemption, then a federal gift tax liability would result. In a few states, a state gift tax may also result from a gift.

Trusts

A trust, you may recall, is a written instrument that provides for a trustee to hold the property of the grantor. The property is to be administered in accordance with the terms of the trust instrument. Both the beneficiary of the trust and the trustee are designated by the grantor in the agreement.

Trusts are formed for many different reasons. Often the reason for the trust determines who should be the trustee and even who should be the beneficiary. For example, in a trust formed to avoid probate, the trustee is usually the grantor and the beneficiary is always the grantor.

In the situation now being discussed, however, while the beneficiary of the trust will be the grantor, the trustee would not be the grantor, since this trust is formed because of the disability or expected disability of the grantor. It would make no sense for the initial trustee to be the grantor who at some point, at least, would be unable to take care of his or her own affairs.

The trust is funded by whatever property the grantor turns over to it. Since the purpose of this particular trust is to support the grantor for the balance of his or her life, in many cases all of grantor's property would be transferred into the trust. One reason not to do so might be because the blanket transfer would upset the grantor's carefully designed estate plan.

Making Multiple Uses of the Trust. When a trust is formed for one purpose, often it is wise to try to utilize the trust for as many purposes as possible. The primary purpose with a trust here, of course, is to establish an agency of sorts for managing the grantor's property and distributing it for the grantor's benefit for the balance of his or her life. But, once formed, it can serve other purposes as well.

It can serve as a private conduit of the grantor's property to the grantor's heirs upon his or her death. It can be used to avoid probate administration (but probably not all estate proceedings) of the grantor's estate. It can also be used to sidestep family problems, especially if the trustee is a disinterested third party such as a bank.

Conservatorships

Of all the pathways, a conservatorship is the only one which is a formal, court-supervised proceeding. A trust could specify that it be court-supervised, but it rarely does so and then only because a peculiar situation requires it.

The Likelihood of a Conservatorship Being Involuntary. Whether the conservatorship is voluntary or involuntary depends to some extent upon what the proposed ward does or fails to do during his or her competency. If the individual puts off the decision of planning for disability, then the involuntary proceeding eventually will be the only available pathway if he or she becomes incapacitated.

Since a conservatorship normally would be the last choice for serving as a pathway, most likely it will be involuntary. This means that a third party will make the choice of a conservator and the time when such conservatorship should be instigated. As a practical matter, members of the disabled party's family, if any, usually make the decision. This is not a happy time for such family members.

Since an involuntary conservatorship is a court proceeding, a family member is required to petition the court and cause notice of the action to be served upon the proposed ward. The petition usually suggests who is to serve as conservator. If the court agrees that the disabled party is a fit subject for conservatorship, then the disabled party becomes a ward of the conservator. Thereafter he or she normally loses all legal rights, although in some states the ward can continue to act in a limited capacity.

Deciding Which Pathway to Use

As you read through the various alternatives, you probably could not help but compare one to another. You might have wondered if they would be right for you or how they would be for your ailing parent. You might have liked one pathway more than the others but maybe, for one reason or another, it was not appropriate for your situation. Thus you had to make a second choice.

What are some of the factors that might enter into a decision? Costs, formalities, privacy, court interference, management, family situation and concerns, additional benefits, type of disability involved, or any combination of the above might play a part in your consideration.

If you are in good health, your attorney might be reluctant to suggest something that to you seems drastic. And it is doubtful that any lawyer would recommend or even want to be a part of you using joint tenancy or gifts as a pathway for the incapacitated.

If all conditions are right, if the necessary criteria are present, then the power of attorney is superior to any other pathway. It is easy to set up and easy to administer and takes no power away from the principal. For this latter reason especially, it can be—and probably should be—set up long before any need for it is present. But don't consider it if potential problems exist. Wishful thinking that the problems will not materialize is not wise.

Of the two remaining pathways, the trust is ordinarily much better than the conservatorship. The initial costs in setting up each are comparable and so are the continuing fees of the conservator and trustee. But no continuing attorney fees or court costs are usually present with the trust. And no court supervision is usually required of a trust. The trust can be flexible and is not particularly bound by rigid statutes as is the conservatorship.

In a conservatorship, annual fees are usually paid to an attorney for making reports to the court and for meeting with the conservator from time to time. Thus from a monetary point of view it would seem that lawyers should prefer a conservatorship. But generally they do not. If the power of attorney or trust is a possibility, then your attorney probably would suggest a conservatorship only as a last resort.

Both you and your attorney must evaluate and balance the good versus the bad points of each pathway. If you are like most everybody else, you will wait until the last minute to decide which pathway to use. No doubt costs will enter your thinking. But waiting too long may result in your being unable to make the best choice.

What are some of the things you should consider in making a decision?

1. *Independence.* What is likely to interfere the least with your way of life? Are you willing to allow someone else to handle your property and, in this sense, partially control you?

2. *Security.* What gives you the most comfort in knowing that something has been done? What offers your estate the most security? Which procedure best safeguards your property?

3. *Financial.* What are the comparable costs of each pathway? Will these costs be continuing, or will they merely be one-shot expenses? Are costs a primary concern in your decision?

4. *Personal choice.* What can you do to make it your choice and not someone else's? Do you want someone else to make this decision for you?

5. *Management.* Are you willing to let someone else manage your affairs? Do you want this management to be total or merely co-existent with you?

6. *Collateral benefits.* Will the choice possibly result in other benefits for you and your estate, or will it be limited only to its primary purpose? Are these other benefits of any great significance?

It is doubtful that any pathway is perfect. Discussing your situation with your attorney should help you decide which one to use. Perhaps you will have ample opportunity to mull over the various choices. If you do nothing, the result may not totally be to your liking. Your choices, or those of your heirs, could become limited, but at least a choice would exist.

In any event, it is best that you know your options. Do nothing that takes away those options.

The Importance of Looking Ahead

Suppose you are one of the many people that don't plan for the future because you trust your children will help you when you need it. Is this wise?

It is not, for three reasons: (1) if you wait, you and your children's options are limited; (2) the choice, such as it is, becomes your children's and not yours; and (3) by delaying a decision, you are putting your children on the spot. No matter how much you may have discussed this possible situation with them, you are asking them to read your mind at some point in time.

Unfortunately, your mind may be a bit mixed up at the time that your children need to take over. At that point you may resist them. For some reason, the more people need help the more they think that they do not. If you make your plans while healthy, your children understand that that is what you want to do. They will be nervous enough during your incompetency without having to decide what you really intended. Such a situation comes about because you delayed until the last moment or until it was too late. Let's consider an example. Suppose your spouse was killed and you became incapacitated by a sudden accident. As a result of injuries, you are unable to move and speak. Because of this condition, it is difficult for anyone to know whether you know what you are doing. Now someone needs to take over, to pay your bills and handle your affairs. You had done nothing to plan for this eventuality.

Your children call in an attorney to discuss the situation. She tries to talk with you about options, but is unable to understand you. Without your input, the attorney recommends that a power of attorney be used for you. The children agree. Both of them concur that you, the incapacitated, would want this done, as it seems to be the best recourse in the situation. Someone guides your hand when the power is signed, and your estate is thus managed by someone else.

But suppose the attorney refused to comply, thinking that you didn't know what you were doing. What recourse would you have then? Or suppose that after the power went into effect it was challenged legally. What would happen if the courts thought that coercion played a part?

At best, if no legal complications arise, your children and your attorney might feel guilty. They might think that what they did perhaps was not what was best for you. After all, they would have no way of knowing for sure what you would have wanted.

Had you established the power of attorney when you were well, the power would have gone into effect when the accident occurred without any doubts, worry, or legal headaches for others.

Thus, one thing should be clear to you when providing for disability: plan ahead!

Some Common
Questions Answered

Q. Is it recommended that everyone plan ahead for incapacity?

A. As a general rule, yes. Estate lawyers like a neat, complete package, including even such things as a directive for health care. But when planning for your possible incapacity, you may realize that your choices are quite limited, that your only options are not to your liking. Thus you may do nothing, which, in effect, is an option.

Q. Why do some lawyers treat a conservatorship as a last resort?

A. Probably because of their past experiences. Some conservatorships are legally designated as voluntary. But actually a parent might be pressured into signing a "voluntary" petition by her children who believe that she has become senile. The parent may have been a long-time client of the lawyer. It is not a happy time for any of the parties.

Or suppose that the parent refuses to sign a voluntary petition or to take any other action. The children could bring an involuntary petition against their parent. This would be an even more unhappy time. These examples assume that no other pathway is practicable.

Conservatorships are formal proceedings. Being formal, they tend to be impersonal and thus somewhat inflexible. Practically every step requires the services of a lawyer.

Q. You stress that if an individual serves as my agent in some capacity, such as an attorney in fact, he or she should be closely related to me. Is this absolutely necessary? Is there any legal reason for this?

A. No, to both questions. Obviously, some individuals are both competent and trustworthy to serve in any fiduciary capacity. But it is not wise to choose an individual to serve merely because he or she is a good friend, a neighbor, someone recommended to you, or a distant relative. Many lawyers prefer to rely on a professional rather than a nonfamily fiduciary.

Anyone who serves you is entitled to a fee. Sometimes this fee is set by a statute, court rule, or court order. This fee is usually the same, regardless of the identity of the party serving. Why, then, take a chance with someone more or less a legal and financial amateur, if a close family member is not an optional choice? In this situation it seems that a bank is almost always better than an individual.

A close family member no doubt is also a legal and financial amateur, but two things can be said in her or his favor. One is that that individual can provide family love and devotion, something no one else can claim. The other is that often the family member does not want reimbursement for the services rendered.

Q. Why isn't a durable bank agency account just as good as a durable power of attorney?

A. Conceivably it could be, but it usually isn't. The bank agency account differs in two important respects from the power of attorney.

First, the bank agency is, in effect, a limited power of attorney while the power of attorney usually is a general power. The bank agency account only includes that property turned over to it by the grantor. A formal transfer of the property occurs. The bank only deals with that property turned over. In the power of attorney, no transfer of property occurs.

Second, under the bank agency account, the bank has control and possession of the transferred property to the exclusion of the grantor. Under the power of attorney, both the grantor and attorney in fact have joint powers over the same property.

Which method you choose depends on what you are trying to accomplish. But for overall, long-term benefits, the power of attorney is likely to be better. You may not now want to relinquish control of even a portion of your property. And later, if you become incompetent, the bank agency account might not be sufficient for your needs.

As always, other factors enter into the picture. Is the power of attorney even available as an option? Would you want to pay the expense of a bank agency account, or could your estate even afford it? Would the bank agency account seem too impersonal to you? How much personal involvement do you still want with your property? Whether one or the other is best comes down to what you like best and need the most.

Q. Assuming that the proposed attorney in fact meets all prerequisites for serving, what might still be some drawbacks to a power of attorney?

A. For one, the attorney might not be available when you need him because he died or moved away. This problem of inavailability can be avoided if you originally name an alternate attorney or joint attorneys.

Another drawback to the power of attorney is that during the course of the power the principal might become unmanageable, thriftless, or troublesome. The attorney has no legal control over the principal.

If any of these situations develop a conservatorship might have to be created. But in the meantime the power of attorney could have saved the principal's estate considerable expense.

Q. Are there times when a conservatorship could be the best pathway?

A. Absolutely. A particular family situation or the difficulty in dealing with an incapacitated person could easily dictate that no other method would be feasible or even possible. Being in court, the family has a forum to resolve problems, to settle disputes. Maybe the presence and easy access to the lawyer is helpful. Or maybe a bank as a disinterested party to serve as conservator is warranted under the circumstances. All these things should be taken into consideration when choosing a pathway.

10

Choosing the Right Fiduciary

The term *fiduciary* is applied to all persons who occupy a special position of confidence towards others, such as a trustee, executor, administrator, personal representative, guardian, or conservator. These positions of trust are often listed in the various state probate codes. In a broader sense the term can apply to another position of trust as well, such as an attorney in fact or a bank operating as a custodian of funds, but this chapter concerns only the formal, usually court-supervised, fiduciary.

The subject of fiduciaries deserves special consideration. Whatever area of estate management, planning, or administration is being discussed, a fiduciary or someone in a fiduciary capacity is likely to be involved at some point.

In spite of the necessity of having a fiduciary, its importance is frequently ignored. For instance, when you plan your will, you undoubtedly give much thought as to how you want your estate to be distributed but little as to who should administer your estate. Yet the success of your planning could well hinge on whom you choose to represent your estate upon your death.

Consider the personal representative of an estate. By law this fiduciary has many legal responsibilities, some of which are obvious. But some duties are not so obvious—for example, making certain that all estate assets are properly protected by insurance. And what about the fiduciary's ability to serve? Are you willing to let the fiduciary's attorney alone have the responsibility of seeing that your estate is properly served? Or do you

161

want your personal representative to also be capable of handling its responsibilities?

Even though an individual fiduciary may not be a professional, as is a bank or another corporate fiduciary (hereafter referred to merely as a bank), such fiduciary is still legally responsible for all actions which it takes or fails to take. In order to avoid liability, a fiduciary cannot plead ignorance, incompetency, or inexperience. Nor can the fiduciary place blame entirely on its attorney. By accepting the position, the fiduciary assumes the obligations that the job entails.

For example, in an estate administration the personal representative has the duty of filing proper income tax returns for both the decedent and the estate. He or she must also file any required federal and state death tax returns. The same obligation to file tax returns also applies to any other fiduciary, such as a conservator or trustee.

Many articles have been written about the fiduciary's duty to minimize taxes. But whether it is for failure to either file a timely return, pay the required taxes, or minimize taxes, the fiduciary is held personally liable. It makes no difference whether the mistake was the result of an oversight or inadequate knowledge of the law. While relying on their attorneys for guidance, the fiduciaries still are legally liable both to the taxing bodies and to the parties they represent for any mistake. It is ordinarily irrelevant that the fiduciaries may have a cause of action against their attorneys, for, say, malpractice.

In one respect, at least, a fiduciary differs from an individual. If an individual overpays a tax, no one is likely to object, least of all, perhaps, the taxing authority. But if a fiduciary overpays a tax, the parties that fiduciary represents have every legal right to complain and will, if the overpayment comes to their attention and if they can benefit by doing so.

Investment Responsibilities

Fiduciaries are responsible for safekeeping and managing property in a particular estate, whether they are conservators (guardians), personal representatives, or trustees. Their duties include safely investing and reinvesting the estate property. Unfortunately for the fiduciaries, this may mean some duty to diversify the portfolios, unless some instructions exist to the contrary. And diversification, by its very nature, often implies some risk.

For instance, what help does a trustee have to guide its performance in the area of investing? States may have a statute known as the Model Prudent Person Investment Act or another one modeled on this act. To judge the performance of a trustee, courts frequently resort to use of the "prudent man rule," now generally known as the "prudent person rule" or the "prudent investor rule." In effect, this rule answers the question, "What would a prudent person do under the prevailing circumstances?" As you might well imagine, no two courts are likely to reach the same conclusion, even under the same set of facts.

As to investment policy that is not clearly set out in the trust arrangement, a trustee is somewhat caught in a trap. Usually, the safest procedure for the trustee is to be on the conservative side, but the beneficiaries of a trust may then object—especially in times of inflation—that the conservative investment strategy was to their detriment.

But if the trustee were to constantly turn over the assets, the beneficiaries might complain of the costs being incurred. Sometimes, the safest course of even professional fiduciaries is to secure expert advice, a delegation which the courts now tend to look upon with favor. But the expense involved may not be allowed against the estate unless the hiring of the expert has been approved by the court.

For a long list of other responsibilities of the personal representative, see the checklist in Chapter 15. The duties and responsibilities of any fiduciary may be specified in the instrument that creates the position, in various state and federal statutes, or in relevant court rules.

If these obligations are not accomplished or not performed according to applicable law or regulations, the fiduciary and not someone else has to answer to the IRS, the state tax department, the probate court, or the heirs and beneficiaries. While the fiduciary's attorney must do everything possible to protect and guide the fiduciary, the fiduciary ultimately is legally responsible to those parties, not the fiduciary's attorney. In fact, in many instances the fiduciary's attorney is not even aware of the actions of the fiduciary.

But even though a fiduciary may have some consequent claim against its attorney, and to a great extent should rely upon its attorney, are you willing that your representative be totally ignorant of what should be done and how to do it?

The Costs of a Fiduciary

One of the considerations in naming a fiduciary is the expense that will be incurred for using that party. Undoubtedly you realize that if you name a corporate fiduciary, expense will be incurred for its services rendered. On the other hand, you may feel that a member of your family will handle the responsibility without compensation. Possibly to your detriment, the cost looms as a larger factor in your selection than it should.

But you must keep several things in mind. Are you doing your family a favor in naming one of them to serve? Will the one named be willing to serve when the time comes, even though he or she may now indicate a willingness to do so? Can the designated family member be held to a promise not to charge for his or her services? Has the matter of compensation even been discussed, or are you merely assuming that no charge will be made? Or do you even care, even though your other heirs will certainly care?

Does the proposed fiduciary have management abilities? If not, would the cost of hiring support people, such as accountants and property managers, offset any savings by naming a family member? Would the fiduciary have the time or even the inclination to do the job? Is the proposed individual fiduciary a natural peacemaker in the family, or is he or she somewhat of an irritant to the other family members?

You may believe that if your chosen personal representative is also a beneficiary in your will then the bequest will serve as sufficient compensation. In fact, you may specifically state in your will that the bequest is in lieu of such compensation. But the beneficiary may be able to renounce the bequest and take the compensation. Or she or he might receive the bequest plus an additional amount for services rendered. Courts cannot agree as to when the renouncement, if any, must occur.

Some testators name their attorney to serve as their personal representative, perhaps believing that one fee thereby will be saved. This may or may not happen. Some statutes and courts allow only the one fee, while others allow dual compensation. And even though the personal representative may be a lawyer, he or she is frequently allowed to hire another lawyer, perhaps even from the same law firm, to do the legal work.

Some states take a dim view of a lawyer being named in a fiduciary capacity, unless he or she is closely related to the parties. They do so because such action gives the appearance of unethical conduct.

No doubt many individuals accept the job of fiduciary either to help the testator save administration expenses or to secure a fee for themselves. Or, more likely, they do so because they believe they can do a good job and want to abide by the wishes of the party naming them. But if you ever find yourself in a position to serve as a fiduciary, you should make certain that the liability factor is minimal.

Since fiduciaries render a personal service, they are entitled to be compensated. If the form of trust is court-administered, such as an estate administration or a conservatorship, then the amount of compensation is ultimately determined by statute and the courts.

The Uniform Probate Code, for instance, specifies that the fiduciary may set its own fee, subject to review of the court. In the absence of statute, the courts talk in terms of what is reasonable, a nebulous term at best. The factors usually considered are time, value of services rendered, results obtained, responsibilities assumed, labor performed, nature of the estate, and difficulties encountered. An hourly rate may or may not be a controlling factor.

If the proceeding is not court-administered, such as are many trusts, then the fees may be set by agreement of the parties, by custom, or perhaps according to a schedule of fees as set by a corporate trustee.

The Special Liability of the Fiduciary

In considering liability, something new has been added to the concerns of a fiduciary: the environmental factor. For instance, a recent commentary suggests that liability could be asserted against a fiduciary for cleanup costs "without regard to either the assets in the particular trust or estate or the fault of the fiduciary."

You may not be aware of, but you can be held liable under, federal environmental laws for environmental contamination even though you were not the original party responsible for it. Some people believe that if the assets of the estate or trust are insufficient to remedy the situation, the fiduciary may be personally liable for any deficiency. The theory is that the law has nothing to do with fairness, only with enforcement.

Because of this possibility of personal liability, a potential fiduciary may want the estate's real property, especially if it is or has been commercial property, to be evaluated for environmental concerns before he or she accepts the position.

In spite of all that has been said above, if an estate is not large and you are either the spouse or a child of the party owning it, your exposure to liability as a fiduciary probably is nominal. It would be because you already should have some knowledge of the situation. And it is unlikely that any other party will be willing to serve with the same amount of love and diligence.

Otherwise, you should carefully consider your qualifications to serve before accepting the liability and responsibility of the position. And you should also consider whether your acceptance of this position is agreeable with other members of the family. Unfortunately, jealousy or suspicion of family members, or even in-law meddling, often enters into the picture.

Choosing Your Fiduciary

If the person selected as fiduciary is doubtful of his qualifications, or if he doesn't want to accept the risks, or if he thinks that family squabbles will result, then it usually is best to let a corporate entity serve as the fiduciary. Besides acting as an unofficial mediator, the professional fiduciary possesses various skills, such as asset management, which could be beneficial to the estate.

Consider the following scenario. You are a widow with only a modest estate, consisting of a home and various bank accounts. Your children, all of whom are capable and trustworthy, live near you. Is there any reason why you shouldn't name one or more of them in your will to serve as your personal representative?

Probably not. Lawyers have mixed feelings about whom they prefer to act as personal representative, a layperson or a bank. In part it has to do with whether they want to run the show through a personal representative at their own speed—which may be faster or slower than what a bank might do—or be dealing with a professional representative, such as a bank, over whom they may not have much control.

No doubt the size and complexity of the estate and the lawyers' own abilities have a lot to do with their feelings. When lawyers feel competent to handle the estate and have the time to do so, they are more likely to want to run the show through the personal representative, so to speak. But when an individual personal representative fails to perform properly, lawyers probably wish a bank were serving.

When a professional is not involved, the lawyer in effect serves not only as the attorney for the representative but also as the unofficial representative, what some people have referred to as the "de facto executor."

The use of nonprofessionals as fiduciaries is not likely to continue forever, because of the costs involved. Depending upon how the lawyer charges, either the estate pays higher fees to the attorney (because the lawyer is in effect doing two jobs) or the attorney loses money on the arrangement (because the lawyer absorbs the extra time involved). Thus, it is likely that at some time only professionals will be considered as fiduciaries.

The above commentary mainly concerns a personal representative, but a conservator, sometimes still known as a guardian, has similar responsibilities. The word *conservator* itself should be a clue that this particular fiduciary must be careful in handling, managing, and investing—in other words, *conserving*—the assets of the ward. Tax and insurance responsibilities are similar to that of a personal representative. Reports filed by the conservator must be accurate and on time.

If you are asked to serve as a conservator, your attorney will attempt to guide and instruct you. But your lawyer cannot continually follow up on you to make certain that his or her instructions and directives are followed or even understood by you.

Other types of fiduciaries have similar responsibilities. Each person's specific situation should be carefully considered before a fiduciary is selected. And the particular duties of the position should probably also be considered before the fiduciary is chosen.

The Requisite Qualities of a Fiduciary

Some of the qualifications needed for the position of fiduciary are obvious, such as integrity and competence. But other requirements might not be so obvious. Will the party be able to handle the responsibilities in terms of time and availability? And will that party have sufficient physical and mental capacity to do a satisfactory job? Is the prospective fiduciary likely to survive the term of the particular trust? And is there a statute that might prohibit the appointment?

Some statutes limit the position of fiduciary, especially as to conservators and personal representatives, to residents of the state. And some states make a distinction between corporate fiduciaries and individual fiduciaries. For example, a corporation may be allowed to be a nonresident but not an individual, or vice versa. And still other statutes may allow a nonresident to serve as long as a resident serves as a cofiduciary. And, finally, some nonresidents may legally serve in one fiduciary capacity but not in another.

Because of the various residency requirements for a fiduciary, if you own property in more than one state, you should ask your attorney to check the residency laws of each state in which you own property. Or if you are subject to being transferred, or in fact have been notified of a transfer, you should make certain that your designated fiduciary will still be able to serve in the new state of residence. If not, then you have no choice. You must amend the instrument creating the fiduciary relationship.

Because state laws vary so greatly as to the right of a nonresident fiduciary to serve, you should check with your attorney to be sure that the fiduciary you select is acceptable to your state of residence. For example, suppose you were contemplating naming one of your nonresident children to serve as your personal representative. After telling your attorney of the nonresidency, you might find that the appointment would be disallowed by your state. You would then have to keep selecting among your children to find one that would be acceptable.

If no family member qualifies for a particular appointment, consideration should always be given to naming a corporate fiduciary, usually a bank, as fiduciary. Otherwise, the presumed saving of fees and avoidance of impersonal attention through use of a close personal representative might not be justified. As to fees, courts tend to assume that all acting fiduciaries—whether or not professional—are qualified, until proven otherwise. Therefore they have determined that both individual and professional fiduciaries are entitled to the same fee. Thus an individual fiduciary is not necessarily cheaper than a professional fiduciary, although naming a family member may make you feel that you are keeping your money in the family.

If your will or other instrument names an individual to serve as fiduciary, then it is imperative that you name one or more alternates to serve in the event the first chosen party refuses or is unable to serve. In this situation it is wise to name a corporate fiduciary at least as a final alternate, so that you can be certain that you have named at least one party that will always be able to serve.

When you designate a bank to serve, it is wise to conclude by saying "or its successor." Many banks are now being merged or closed out of existence and confusion might result if the bank named no longer exists and you have not given directions for a successor fiduciary.

Use of More Than
One Fiduciary

Which is more advisable to use, a single fiduciary or multiple fiduciaries? In most cases, probably the single fiduciary is the better one to use. Working with one is more practical. Working with two or more is usually a bit more effort. But this is not the same thing as saying that a single fiduciary is always better than cofiduciaries. The circumstances should always be considered.

First, consider the professional fiduciary, such as a bank. A bank does not need any help in proceeding with the legal requirements of the position. What it may need is information from the beneficiary's family, or some physical help, such as cleaning out a decedent's home. The ones cooperating with the bank do not need to be fiduciaries in order to fulfill these requirements.

But some people who are naming a fiduciary prefer someone else to be named as cofiduciary along with the named bank. They feel that there will then be joint control and knowledge of what is going on. With two or more cofiduciaries, the bank usually will want to take control of and be responsible for the assets, since it is equally responsible for them. Otherwise it may not be willing to serve.

Sometimes a cofiduciary is named because the desired fiduciary is a nonresident. In this situation a state statute may not allow the nonresident to serve alone so a resident has to serve as cofiduciary.

Sometimes, if your two children are your sole heirs, it might seem better to name both children as cofiduciaries rather than choose between them. Family harmony can then be preserved, because the one not serving does not feel left out. Sometimes, when individuals are not on the inside, not part of the proceeding, they become suspicious even though they have no justification for feeling so.

Three or more children can legally serve as cofiduciaries. But obviously the more named, the greater the difficulty in securing compliance and agreement among the fiduciaries. Without this cooperation, nothing can be accomplished.

When multiple fiduciaries serve, usually the fee is divided between them in some manner. Each of them are not normally entitled to the full fee.

Considerations in Requiring Bond

The purpose for bonding a fiduciary is to protect the claimants and beneficiaries for whom the fiduciary is acting. This protection only applies to the honesty, not the judgment or competence, of the fiduciary. If a fiduciary embezzles property under his or her care, the bond would cover the loss. If a fiduciary foolishly makes a bad investment, the bond would not cover the loss.

If the wrongful act of a fiduciary is covered by a bond and the fiduciary fails to reimburse the estate for the loss, then the bondsman (the surety) covers the loss and looks to the fiduciary for possible recovery.

If you have chosen your fiduciary carefully, then you should consider making a provision that the fiduciary serve without bond. If you are unable to make this provision, then perhaps you have not made a wise choice. Maybe you should then rethink who should be named as fiduciary.

If the instrument creating the fiduciary does not waive bonding, then the law usually requires the fiduciary to put up bond before it can qualify for the position. The size of the bond is determined either by statute, court rule, or the court itself.

An annual premium, like any insurance policy, is payable in order to maintain the bond. The size of the required bond is usually determined by the amount of assets, especially personal property, which it protects. Thus the annual premium can be substantial in that the cost is usually so many dollars per thousand dollars of such assets.

Good reasons may exist for requiring a fiduciary other than a corporate fiduciary to be bonded. Both the necessity of having a bond and the cost of having it should be considerations in choosing the fiduciary. It is unusual to require a bond of a bank since bank officials are already bonded and the assets of the bank would back up any failure of its officers.

Regardless of the fact that corporate fiduciaries already may be self-bonded, however, many courts still require them to be bonded for a particular position. Sometimes, however, they may be allowed to be bonded at a reduced amount, if the instrument naming them fails to specify that they are to serve without bond.

The Public Administrator

Several states, such as California and New York, have statutory provisions for a public administrator in the event that a decedent has left no will. These administrators serve in a quasi-official capacity. They do not automatically serve. Rather, they serve when an estate has lain dormant for an unusual length of time and no next of kin or other interested party has appeared to assume the responsibility. Statutes specify when the public administrator is to serve. Putting your estate in a position that might require a public administrator is not likely to be a suitable option.

Some Common Questions Answered

Q. Why is a fiduciary required in the administration of an estate? Why can't the heirs or beneficiaries merely do what is required?

A. Someone must be responsible for the estate proceeding. Such a party must be approved by the court. It may have to be bonded. If the fiduciary is also an heir, it wears two different hats, one as an heir and one as the personal representative. Neither can be commingled with the other, nor should any confusion exist as to which hat the party is wearing when any action is taken.

If an heir is unable to separate duties as an heir from duties as a personal representative, then she should refuse the title and decline the position. In fact, if a conflict of interest arises, the heir may have to resign or ask that a special administrator be appointed so that the estate may be properly represented in that particular dispute.

Q. Why is the choice of a fiduciary so important? Aren't fiduciaries guided by their attorney anyway?

A. First of all, it is the fiduciary who represents you or your estate, not the lawyer. It is the fiduciary who is legally responsible to fulfill all legal requirements. Suppose, for instance, that you are depending upon your attorney to see that the fiduciary does the job correctly. But suppose further that the fiduciary ignores the responsibilities of the job or ignores the lawyer or moves away before the job is completed or even embezzles some of your estate. Can the lawyer be held responsible for any of these actions?

It is true that the fiduciary's attorney helps guide the fiduciary. The lawyer directs the fiduciary as to what to do and the fiduciary does it, although it is the attorney who prepares the necessary reports and other papers for the fiduciary's signature.

But if the fiduciary fails to take any required action or does it badly, the lawyer is handicapped in trying to remedy the situation. Since courts often believe that the lawyer represents the fiduciary and not the estate, an ethical question may arise, "Can the lawyer report the failings of the fiduciary to the court or to the beneficiaries?" As a matter of practice, the lawyer usually will, but only after getting permission from the local bar's ethics committee.

One more thing. Not all fiduciary situations require the services of a lawyer. Take, for example, the noncourt trust. Once the trust is set up, the lawyer usually is no longer a part of the proceedings. Thus the trustee is out on its own, free of any guidance or interference. Does this help to convince you that a careful choosing of the fiduciary is important?

Q. Are fiduciaries always chosen by the person whose estate is being affected?

A. Not if the circumstance is an involuntary one. This covers two situations, the involuntary conservatorship and the intestate estate. In both these situations, you don't make the choice, someone else does.

Consider the involuntary conservatorship. If you become unable to handle your own affairs and have failed to designate some agency to represent you, then someone else must assume the responsibility. At this point, the only recourse is the involuntary conservatorship. The party taking responsibility will propose the fiduciary. Certainly you can't because you are incompetent to do so.

The second situation occurs when you die without a will. Since you had no will, someone else must step forward and suggest a party to act as the personal representative. The court or any interested party may do this. Again, you would have no voice in this choosing. In both cases you could have avoided someone else choosing the fiduciary merely by taking appropriate action at the right time.

Q. May a chosen fiduciary refuse to act?

A. Yes, always (one of the few times "always" may mean what it says). No law requires a party, whether an individual or a bank, to serve if it does not want to. It might be a different matter, from a legal point of view, if the position were accepted and reliance placed upon the acceptance. But even then it is doubtful that beneficiaries would want a reluctant fiduciary to represent the particular estate.

Because of this right to decline, it is sometimes wise to secure the consent of the proposed party before naming the party. If your estate is small, for example, it might be wise to secure consent of the proposed bank to serve as executor, before naming it in your will. Some trust departments are reluctant to serve as fiduciaries in situations in which their fees would be small. Fortunately, however, most banks have come to realize that it is bad public relations to refuse to serve because the anticipated fee wouldn't be large.

Q. What happens if the designated fiduciary cannot serve, and no alternate or successor was provided for in the will?

A. In that event an application or petition is made to the probate court for the appointment of a substitute personal representative, sometimes known as an administrator with will annexed. The party applying is presumed to be one of the beneficiaries named in the will. The application or petition usually will suggest the name of the proposed successor.

Q. What relationships do banks have with lawyers? Is the bank named as personal representative obligated to engage the lawyer who drafted the will? And suppose a bank recommends a certain lawyer for drafting a will. Is the lawyer then obligated to recommend the bank as personal representative?

A. From a legal standpoint, the answer to both questions is no. But as a practical matter the result is often otherwise. It may be a courtesy, an "understanding," or even what the testator wanted. Consider the first question.

Courts generally agree that the personal representative has the right to choose its own attorney in administration of an estate. Even if a certain lawyer is named or suggested in a will, such instructions may be ignored by the personal representative. But since the testator engaged a certain lawyer to draw the will, it usually is assumed that the testator would prefer the same lawyer to handle the estate proceeding. Banks usually follow this procedure.

The other question poses more problems, as it often creates a conflict of interest. When a bank recommends a certain lawyer to draw a will, he or she feels some obligation to return the favor by suggesting the bank as personal representative.

Yet when an estate is uncomplicated and when an appropriate family member is available to serve as the personal representative, the lawyer should indicate this to the testator. In this situation the referring bank may be named only as an alternative representative. If that happens, the bank may not be very happy.

Q. Can I name my attorney as the personal representative in my will?

A. Even if you want to, it may not be possible. Some statutes, some bar associations, some courts, and some lawyers feel that this is inappropriate unless the attorney is a relative of the testator. Especially this is deemed a breach of professional standards if a particular lawyer makes a practice of naming herself or one of her relatives as the personal representative. Some courts are able to discourage the practice by allowing the attorney only one fee, not two fees, for serving in both capacities.

Aside from any ethical question, questions arise as to whether a lawyer acting as representative should take time away from his other clients and whether the lawyer should expose other members of his firm to liabilities arising from such representation.

In direct answer to your question, you probably should consider another party to serve. This removes any appearance of impropriety. This same answer could apply to any other fiduciary position.

Q. What if my will names co-executors, each living in a different state than I do? Will this cause any trouble in administering my estate upon my death?

A. Two difficulties might be encountered, one a legal one and one a practical one. First, let's examine the possible legal problem.

States usually specify the necessary qualifications of a fiduciary such as an executor. One of the requirements often is that an individual serving as a fiduciary, more so a personal representative than a trustee, be a resident of the state where the proceeding is taking place. But the same statutes usually permit exceptions to the rule.

For instance, the court may waive the residency requirement or, if not, one of two or more executors may not have to be a resident of the state if the other is. If the court refuses to waive the requirement, then upon your death a resident party would have to be named to act as an additional co-executor. This could be expensive or at least a nuisance to the others. Thus from a legal point of view it is generally advisable that your will name at least one co-executor who is a resident of your state. If a suitable resident individual is not possible, then you should seriously consider using your bank as one of the co-executors.

Now as to the practical difficulties. Let's assume that two nonresident parties are individuals and not a bank or trust company, since some states also prohibit a so-called foreign corporate fiduciary. From a practical viewpoint it may not be wise to have two such widely separated executors. It is difficult enough when the sole executor does not live near the property of the estate. The problem, though by no means an impossible one, is partly one of communication, reporting to each other and consulting with the estate's attorney.

It is also partly one of availability. Who can conveniently perform the necessary labor that might be required? Since the representative runs the necessary errands relative to the estate assets, who will fill this role if neither are available for this purpose? These things should be taken into consideration when you name your personal representative.

11
Avoiding Probate

You may be perplexed to find that avoiding probate is a more complicated subject than you'd thought. Your surprise may be due to the interpretation you give to the phrase "avoiding probate." Perhaps you think of the word *probate* as it originally meant, referring to the proving and administering of a will. But the meaning has been broadened to include intestate (no will) as well as testate (a will) proceedings. Probate, as now commonly used, describes the administration of any form of estate following the death of an estate owner. "Avoiding probate," then, is actually another way of saying "avoiding estate administration."

Administration refers to a formal, court-supervised legal proceeding. This proceeding is commenced in the probate court and administered by a personal representative. If a will exists, it is offered for probate. The statutory procedures, whether testate or intestate, are in accordance with the state probate code.

The misunderstanding goes beyond these definitions. From a layperson's point of view, if administration can be avoided, the belief is that no need exists for engaging a lawyer when death occurs, on the theory that nothing needs to be done. As you will see in Chapter 15, this statement is not likely to be true.

Simply put, avoiding administration (or avoiding probate) is not the same thing as avoiding all estate proceedings. Almost every estate of a decedent requires some legal proceedings following the death. The layperson's hope, of course, is that such proceedings will not necessitate the engagement of a lawyer. But "avoiding probate" is not synonymous with "avoiding lawyers."

If your attorney tells you that a specific trust—a grantor trust, for example—will avoid lawyers and any estate matters at the time of your death, or even during the period of the trust, then ask him or her to give you a letter to that effect. Direct that it be addressed both to you and to your successor beneficiaries under the trust.

For that matter, you should request the same from any company that proposes to sell you a trust form. If either your lawyer or trust company are unwilling to back up their representation to you in writing, then you should consider another procedure or try another source.

If probate is avoided, however, whatever estate proceeding that is required is apt to be somewhat simpler, and thus presumably less costly, than administration. Avoiding probate, therefore, may still be appealing even though not everything anticipated can be accomplished. However, the costs incurred in avoiding probate, both initially and subsequently, may well match or even exceed the costs of actual probate.

Three main reasons are usually advanced for avoiding probate. One is to reduce the time involved in settling an estate at the time of death. Another is to reduce costs. And the third is to avoid lawyers and legal complications. None of these objectives may actually be met. Actually in some (or is it most?) instances, all that is accomplished in trying to avoid probate is the shifting of time, costs, and lawyers to an earlier time, and even this perhaps only to a limited degree.

It has been suggested that by entering into a trust to avoid probate all of the following can also be avoided: court supervision, accountings, court-ordered appraisals, ancillary administration, will contests, and publicity. Again, some of these objectives may not necessarily be met.

The fact remains, however, that the lay public is looking for alternatives to administration procedures. Horror stories—some no doubt valid—abound as to what transpires in an estate proceeding, almost all relating in some way to lawyers and the law. Such vivid exaggerations have inspired many individuals to avoid probate by any means possible.

Laypersons may fail to realize that estate administration involves more than the mere distribution of assets, that it may have some other benefits as well. Estate lawyers are also involved in the payment of the decedent's debts and charges, the handling of the decedent's and the estate's tax problems, the location and identification of assets, the liquidation of assets, the arbitration of family disputes, the closing of the decedent's business affairs, and the passing of proper title. As you will notice later on, many of these functions are not eliminated merely by the use of a trust to avoid probate.

Understanding the Effect of Nonprobate Property

You must have a good understanding of the difference between probate property and nonprobate property.

Probate property is that property of the decedent which at the time of death is subject to administration. The property can be held in the name of the decedent alone. Or it can be held by the decedent and another as co-owners other than as joint tenants or as tenants by the entirety. The property is subject to administration because title passes according to the decedent's will or, if no will exists, according to the laws of descent and distribution (the laws of inheritance).

Nonprobate property is that property of the decedent which at the time of death is not subject to administration. Neither a will nor the laws of inheritance have any effect on how the property is disposed of or distributed at the time of death. This does not mean, however, that nonprobate property is not subject to some kind of estate proceeding.

If all, not just some, of your property is held in one or more nonprobate forms, then your estate normally will not have to be probated (administered). At the most, a shorter form of estate proceeding would have to be done. Stated another way, if all your property is in one or more nonprobate forms, then there would be nothing to probate—hence the popular, descriptive term "avoiding probate."

If you now understand the theory behind nonprobate property, you may recognize certain property interests as constituting nonprobate property. Consider these examples:

Life insurance. Suppose at time of your death your total estate consists of nothing but life insurance, all of which is payable to a third party (not your estate). Since the life insurance proceeds bypass your estate, there would be nothing to probate.

Pay on death (POD) accounts. These accounts are sometimes known as transfer on death (TOD) accounts. Under this arrangement, say with a financial institution, upon the death of the account owner the proceeds in the account are paid to another party. Sometimes U.S. Savings Bonds are held in this manner. In short, the account is set up similar to "John Doe, pod Mary Doe." Note that because of the instruction "pod," the account clearly bypasses the estate. These accounts may not be available in a community property state.

Annuities and pension plans. With these plans, the beneficiary is usually named as a third party, unless your estate is named. Thus upon your death any benefits remaining in these plans would again bypass your estate. If your estate were named as beneficiary, then of course upon your death your estate would end up with probate property—the proceeds from the annuity or pension plan.

Life estate property. Two general forms of life tenancy exist. One is the retained life estate and one is the received life estate. In the former, you transfer property but retain a life interest in the property. In the latter, someone else transfers to you a life estate in their property. In both instances what you have is nonprobate property, since at the time of your death title to the property automatically vests in another party known as the remainderman. Again, your estate has nothing to probate.

Joint tenancy property. When one of the two or more joint tenants dies, title to the jointly held property automatically vests in the remaining joint tenant or tenants, regardless of any will or laws of inheritance to the contrary. Thus, if at the time of your death all of your property were held by you in joint tenancy with another, you would have no property to probate, since all you would have is nonprobate property.

Joint tenancy is sometimes considered to be an anomaly in estate planning because the public embraces joint tenancy as an estate planning technique to avoid probate, whereas lawyers generally do not. An exception to the latter part of that statement would be where joint tenancies pertain solely to husband-and-wife situations.

For example, suppose a happily married couple with a total taxable estate of less than $600,000 and with the same set of children (or no children) make wills leaving everything they own to each other. They could also have made certain that all of their property would remain between them by establishing a joint tenancy.

Why? Because the result would be the same under either circumstance—that of the wills or that of the joint tenancy. Upon the first death, all of their property would end up in the surviving partner's estate, regardless of which situation controls. All of the joint tenancy property, being nonprobate property, would go to the survivor regardless of the will. If all of their property were in joint tenancy, then the will of the first deceased would not have to be used, thus avoiding probate.

This does not mean that spouses should rely solely on their joint tenancies without having reciprocal wills (see Chapter 7). The wills are needed to back up, or guarantee, that the survivor receives everything.

Consider the following situations in which wills would be required, in spite of your joint tenancies: Your estate is entitled to damages resulting from an act of negligence. Or you die while an inheritance is pending, waiting for the closing of an estate. Or you and the other joint tenant die simultaneously, which results in a situation similar to tenancies in common.

Revocable Living Trusts to Avoid Probate

As indicated from the above, for the average, middle-class couple—arbitrarily one that has an estate of less than $600,000—joint tenancy is probably the most frequently used method of creating and holding nonprobate property. But joint tenancy, although a popular vehicle for many purposes, does not seem to have the same appeal as trusts as a method for avoiding probate. Probably three reasons exist for the appeal of trusts, two of which might be for selfish reasons.

1. *Commercial interests tout the use of trust forms for avoiding probate.* This promotion occurs despite the fact that they may be of little value or dangerous to use without legal advice. You won't see these ads for joint tenancy since there is nothing to sell. No universal form exists for the creation of joint tenancy. But if the form existed, it would not be profitable to sell.

2. *Lawyers who champion such trusts also have a vested, financial interest in such promotion.* The legal work involved in a correctly drawn trust is time-consuming, thus entitling the lawyer to a sizeable fee. And the fee comes now, not when you die.

3. *Some trust arrangements may actually achieve their goal, that of avoiding probate and, perhaps, other forms of estate proceedings.* But, as you will hereafter note, a trade-off exists, no matter how well the system otherwise works. Whether this trade-off is always worth it, is another matter. As you read this chapter, you will have to decide for yourself whether you and your estate would benefit by using the trust.

At this point, if you haven't done so already, you might be wise to read Chapter 8, which discusses trusts in greater depth than is done here.

The overwhelming opinion is that revocable trusts are a valid means of passing on property at time of death, even though they serve as a substitute for wills and are not executed in accordance with the Statute of Wills. This has been true at least since 1858 when a Massachusetts court found such trusts to be valid. This does not mean, however, that if you have such a trust, you do not need a will.

Kinds of Trusts

In broad terms, two kinds of trusts exist, the testamentary trust (see Chapters 7 and 8) and the living trust. Testamentary trusts are created by will. Hence they are not important in this discussion.

The other kind, which we are concerned with here, are living trusts, sometimes known as inter vivos trusts. These trusts are either revocable or irrevocable. If they are revocable, the grantor (the creator or trustor) of the trust may amend, change, add to, subtract from, and revoke the trust agreement at any time, at least until or unless he or she becomes incompetent.

If the trust is irrevocable, the grantor has no power to do any of these things. The grantor is locked into the agreement forever, regardless of mistakes, changes of circumstances, changes in the size of the estate, changes in heirs and beneficiaries, changes in laws, changes of mind, and so on. Total inflexibility results from an irrevocable trust.

Because of this rigidity the irrevocable trust is rarely, if at all, considered as a vehicle for avoiding probate. No matter how eager you may be to escape probate, you undoubtedly aren't so certain of yourself and of conditions beyond your control that you would want to lock yourself into the trust agreement for the rest of your life, without hope of change. And even if you think you are, no doubt your lawyer would not agree with you. The escape mechanism, which the revocable trust provides, is deemed too important.

The specific kind of living trust that is being discussed here is variously known as the self-declared trust, the self-declaration trust, or the grantor trust. It operates as a will substitute in that upon the grantor's death the trust property is distributed as specified in the trust. The trust could by its terms continue beyond the death. It is important that you realize, however, that you should have a will as a backup even though you have the trust.

Ideally, but not necessarily, the grantor—the declarant—of the trust is also the trustee. The grantor is also the primary beneficiary of the trust property and of the income therefrom. Upon the grantor's death, a substitute trustee (named as an alternate in the trust agreement) takes over and distributes the trust property to the secondary or alternate beneficiaries, all as provided in the trust.

You must continually be aware that all of grantor's property must be transferred into the trust in order for the decedent to successfully avoid probate of his or her estate. The one exception would be if the remaining property were in some other form of nonprobate property.

Form of the Revocable Trust

A carefully drafted trust agreement can run as long as 16 pages or more. The reason it is so detailed is that later changes cannot be made if the grantor becomes incompetent. In effect, incompetency causes the instrument to become irrevocable. Thus an attempt is made to cover all possible contingencies in the original preparation. The necessary length makes both lawyers and laypersons unhappy, since both groups prefer simple, short documents that are more easily understood.

As with wills, trust forms have many similarities since each trust must contain comparable clauses. Because these provisions look much alike, you may feel that there isn't all that much to a trust, but each trust, like a will, should be customized to fit the particular individual.

As with all endeavors, your lawyer will use certain past experiences and forms—so-called boilerplate clauses—to guide the formation of your particular trust instrument. It would be foolhardy for your attorney not to do so, as otherwise it would be too easy for him or her to miss something.

These boilerplate clauses must be used judiciously and worked over carefully to fit the situation. Do not be fooled into thinking that you can buy a trust form and make up your own trust instrument. Even non-estate lawyers would have difficulty making up these forms with a great deal of success.

The following is a partial list of boilerplate clauses, in no particular order:

1. *Every trust agreement must be in writing.* Oral arrangements won't work. Reference to the agreement may have to be made periodically. Some jurisdictions may require the agreement to be placed of record so that titles to real estate can be properly transferred into and out of the trust.

2. *The trust must have a name and prescribe the conditions under which it operates.* All trust property is held in this name. The trust agreement will spell out the terms of the trust, including the powers and authority of the trustee, and whether the trustee or any alternate is to be bonded. The trustee is instructed, or directed, how to distribute income and principal. The agreement may specify that a periodic accounting shall be made by the trustee to the beneficiaries. And it will state whether the trust is subject to the jurisdiction of the court.

3. *The agreement usually will have a spendthrift clause.* This in effect prohibits a beneficiary from anticipating his or her income from the trust. It will provide that the beneficiaries cannot alienate or encumber their interest in the trust property. It will state that the property is not subject to claims of creditors.

4. *The trust must specify whether it is revocable or irrevocable.* Presumably it will be revocable. As in many of the clauses referred to herein, this provision can be very detailed. For instance, this clause would not only specify that the agreement is revocable, it would also give authority and the means for amending and changing the terms.

5. *The trustee is identified.* Presumably, to save costs and other immediate problems, the grantor of the trust will name him- or herself as primary trustee. But if she or he does so, then an alternate trustee must be named. To ensure continuation of the trust without interruption, a professional (corporate) trustee should always be the final alternate designated.

Since the trust is designed to last the grantor's lifetime—otherwise it would be of little value as a method of avoiding probate—some problems can be expected if the grantor names herself as primary trustee. Because the trustee is handling her own property, carelessness often occurs in designating all property as trust property. And the bother of doing so may sometimes not seem worth the effort.

What if the grantor-trustee becomes, or appears to have become, incompetent? Who will feel that they have the authority, or will want to exercise their authority, to remove the incompetent person from the position of trustee? What if the grantor-trustee resists efforts to be removed? Unfortunately, if you are contemplating naming yourself as trustee, you probably figure that this situation will never happen to you.

Finally, what happens upon your death if you are the trustee? Is the trust agreement clear that the alternate trustee will then take over? That trustee must be able to continue the trust or to make distribution of the trust assets and close the trust, as the case may be.

Final Steps in Preparation of the Trust

When the final draft of the trust instrument has been approved, it is signed by the grantor and the trustee. This means that if the grantor is also the trustee, the document must be signed twice by the same individual, once in each capacity. The trustee signs separately to show its approval of the terms and responsibilities of the fiduciary position.

For the final step, the grantor transfers all of his or her property into the trust. This means that different transfers will take place, depending on the type of property involved. For example, if the property is real estate, appropriate deeds running from the grantor to the trust will be prepared and recorded. If the property is a vehicle, licenses will be transferred. If the property is intangible personal property, stock will be transferred and names and identification numbers on bank accounts will be changed. If it is tangible personal property, a bill of sale will be prepared and possibly recorded. And, as additional property is received, this process will be repeated as long as you live.

All this is done to prepare for your death, so that no property remains in your name to be administered after you die. In effect, what is being done is converting all your probate property into nonprobate property.

Matters to Be Considered

After all that you have read or heard about trusts to avoid probate, you might think that you would like one. If so, you should ask four key questions, and apply the answers to your particular situation, in order to determine whether the trust is advisable for you:

1. What, if any, legal proceedings will the trust eliminate at the time of my death?
2. How will I and my estate benefit from having the trust?
3. Does the trust create any problems for me?
4. Are there any alternatives to the trust that will be as, or more, beneficial to me?

As you ask yourself these questions, try to realize that your concern should be "Will the trust be good for me?" not "Are such trusts good or bad?" The other important thing to keep in mind is that your estate may not realize any financial benefit from the trust, especially if you yourself are unable to serve the entire term as the trustee. If you don't anticipate realizing a substantial financial benefit from the trust, then ask yourself one more question: "Is the trust worth all the hassle?" Or, "Why do I want the trust?"

When trying to find the answers to the four key questions, you and your attorney will want to discuss at least the following matters:

1. *The proceedings that may be eliminated if all property is in trust.* An example would be administration of your estate.

2. *The proceedings that may not be avoided.* Since the trust is revocable, the two taxing bodies—the state and the federal—regard the trust property as yours for purposes of determining liability, if any, for death taxes. A lawyer must be engaged to handle these tax matters, which involve detailed tax returns and discourse with the taxing authorities. Of course, if the total estate per individual is under $600,000, a federal estate tax return is not required. (See Chapter 16 for a discussion of death taxes.) The trust property is subject to possible tax liens until such taxes, if any, are determined and paid.

3. *When an administration of your estate is not avoided even though the trust exists.* If not all of your property is nonprobate property, then an administration may be necessary. In other words, not all of your property need be in the trust, but all of it must be in some form of nonprobate property in order for administration to be avoided.

4. *The problems that might occur if you forget which hat you are wearing.* If you are the trustee, you can never deal with your property in an individual capacity. Your management of the trust property must always be in accordance with the trust agreement. You cannot deviate from this in order to satisfy your convenience. Many commentators and lawyers are skeptical that most grantors can abide by this requirement.

5. *The amount of inconvenience you are willing to put up with.* Everything must be done in the name of the trust, not the grantor. Documents must back up what you have done. All property, no matter how received, must immediately be placed in the trust. All property leaving the trust must leave in the name of the trust.

6. *Your willingness and ability to serve as trustee.* Unless you serve as trustee, the advantage of the trust over probate administration would likely be lost.

Advantages of the Trust

Use of the revocable trust for more than avoiding probate should be considered. This may make the trust more palatable. Suppose you want to give up management of your estate for any number of reasons. This would mean, though, that you would not be acting as your own trustee and that any other acting trustee would be entitled to a fee.

Trusts can be created because good management of one's estate is desired or because one's possible future incapacity is anticipated. But if you name yourself as trustee of the trust, then you are not creating it for one of these reasons. If your primary motive for setting up a trust is to have good estate management, then possibly you should consider other means of accomplishing the same thing, such as a power of attorney or a bank agency account.

Suppose your family is trying to take over your affairs. You are not willing to continually face this pressure, so you think it is time to let an independent trustee handle your estate. Or suppose you want to give your estate some privacy upon your death. A trust could hide both your successes and your failures. For state death tax purposes, however, an inventory may have to be filed of record at the time of your death. While this inventory may not have to identify your trust property specifically, it would have to show the total value of your trust estate.

Avoiding the publicity concerning one's estate is often a heralded, though usually an overemphasized, reason for trusts. This may be a factor with the rich and famous, but not much of an incentive for the ordinary individual. And privacy might inspire more rumors than would routine handling of an estate administration.

If properly created and maintained, a trust will normally avoid probate administration upon your death, but probably not all legal proceedings. And some abnormal situations could arise that would still require administration.

Suppose, for instance, that you died in a car accident as a result of someone else's negligence. An estate administration would then have to be opened in order to have a means by which your estate could sue the negligent party for damages. The trustee would have no right of suit. Any damages received would be considered probate property, not nonprobate property.

Or suppose that you were in the process of inheriting property at the time of your death. Chances are the pending inheritance would be considered probate property.

Many people believe that a trust will involve less delay at the time of your death than would a full administration. This may be somewhat wishful thinking, since many of the proceedings involved in administration may also be involved in a trust before final distribution is made.

For instance, debts and charges against your estate and the trust would need to be handled. Your estate's death tax liabilities would need to be resolved. Liquidation of trust assets might have to be done in order to effect distribution. And any business matters would have to be consummated.

If you own property, especially real property, in more than one state, then you may have additional reasons for setting up the trust. By placing all of your property, wherever located, in the trust, you can normally avoid duplicate administration proceedings—once in your state of residence and once in the other, the ancillary, state. However, if your primary motive in setting up the trust were merely to avoid an ancillary proceeding, then you might want to use it only for the property located in the foreign state.

Disadvantages of the Trust

A trust does not come cheaply. And it may not be inexpensive to maintain. You must consider the initial costs of setting up the trust, the continuing costs of operating the trust, and the costs that might be incurred at the time of your death. You might find that the issue becomes, "Do I pay now or wait and pay later?" In other words, do you gain by prepaying your expenses?

Another kind of cost exists, a psychological one. Are you willing to give up certain freedoms that you now have in handling your affairs? Are you willing to go through, and continue with, the likely nuisance of a trust?

Does setting up the trust make you feel that life is about over for you, that your end is not far off? The inconvenience and hassle of a trust, especially if you are the trustee, and your personal feelings concerning it should not be overlooked.

Before entering into a trust arrangement, your estate situation must be gone over thoroughly with your attorney. Since your principal effort with the trust is to avoid probate, you must be certain that you are willing to place not only all of your present property interests in a trust but also all future accumulations, whether earned or unearned.

Keep reminding yourself that to maintain a nonprobate estate you must be sure that all of your estate resides in the trust (or in some other form of nonprobate property) at all times. You cannot keep some of your property, such as your checking account, outside of the trust because you think it is handier to do so. Every bit of your income, whether from wages or other earnings, must be directly deposited into your trust account. Property passing through your hands first may not be wise.

Many lawyers doubt that individuals can successfully maintain all their property in a trust. Over a period of time, it is believed, the individual will become careless or indifferent as to how title to his property is maintained. Lawyers feel that the individual will relapse to his former status—that of titleholder to his property. If true, such property would regain its former character as probate property. The efforts to establish a nonprobate estate would thus be in vain.

Assuming you believe that you have both the desire and the ability to effectively operate under a trust, what are some of the obstacles that you must face?

Costs of the Trust. First, you must face the initial costs of setting up the trust, attorney fees primarily, although transfer and recording fees will likely also have to be paid. Ideally, you will name yourself as trustee, but at some point a third party may have to take over. Any trustee other than yourself that does serve is entitled to a fee. This fee is payable at least annually, so you must estimate how long a period you could be paying the trustee for his or her services.

The cost of creating a trust can be a deterrent to utilizing the trust concept. The amount could be equivalent to a substantial portion of what an administration at a later time would cost. In addition, these funds would have to be expended now and thus would be unavailable for future use for the rest of your life. You should always weigh the costs of prepaying any kind of expense.

You must also weigh the possible cost of ongoing expenses, if you are not the trustee or if, at some point later in your life, you must relinquish the position of trustee. A third-party trustee could be more expensive than the cost of administration, especially if this type of arrangement exists for any length of time. And with a third-party trustee the advice of professionals might be sought from time to time, which might not be necessary if no trust existed.

Loss of Control.   If you are not the trustee, you must accept the fact that you have lost some control over your own property, although you can revoke the trust (until you become incompetent to do so) if third-party management becomes an irritant.

Alternatives to Using Trust to Avoid Probate

When you are considering the trust, your attorney probably will suggest other possible alternatives for avoiding probate. You should carefully weigh these alternatives, as they may suit you better than the trust.

Precautionary Measures to Take When Using the Trust

If you do decide to proceed with the trust, your attorney will probably recommend certain additional steps for you to take to protect your estate. Some of these, at least, will be deemed precautionary measures.

These are:

1. Prepare a durable power of attorney, if it is feasible (see Chapter 4).
2. Make an updated will (see Chapter 7).
3. Establish a standby conservatorship (see Chapter 5).
4. Make up a living will with power of attorney for health care (see Chapter 12).

Of all these, you may wonder why use a will, since you have a trust. If for no other reason, you should do so in case you don't successfully follow the trust requirements. Some property might escape the trust, in which event it would have to be probated at the time of your death.

You will probably feel that these other legal documents unnecessarily add to the cost of the trust. Actually, the reverse is true. It is the trust that adds to the cost of the other documents, which you should have in any event.

Lost Opportunities for Post-Mortem Estate Planning.   Unlike administration, with the trust you may lose some spousal rights or other opportunities for post-mortem estate planning. Among these are widow's election and choosing where to take certain expenses and income, such as administration and medical costs, allowances, and savings bond interest.

Whether any of these rights are lost depends upon how the trust is treated by a particular jurisdiction. Some bases for claiming these rights are that the trust is illusory, that it is a fraud on the rights of the surviving spouse, or that it is testamentary in character.

Lack of Court Supervision. Although court supervision in an estate administration sometimes may seem to be a hindrance to speedy settlement, at times such supervision may be of value. The trust is not normally under the jurisdiction of the court. Hence if a dispute arises, no ready forum exists for its resolution. In an administration, the parties already are in court. In the normal trust, court jurisdiction would have to be invoked, something that could be more expensive and time-consuming.

Burden of Keeping Records. During the period of the trust, which could be many years, a nongrantor-trustee must keep accounting records, a real burden to the nonprofessional. And even the grantor-trustee should keep some records because of the possibility of being replaced at some point.

Filing of an IRS Return. A separate income tax return, IRS form 1041, is an annual requirement if the trust is irrevocable. If the trust is revocable, as is more likely, the return is required only if the grantor is not the trustee. In such an event, an IRS identification number must be secured and an information return must be filed annually. During the grantor's lifetime, however, the income, deductions, and credits of the trust must be reported on the grantor's return (form 1040). An additional 1041 return would merely provide information.

At the time of the grantor's death, if the grantor is still the trustee, then the successor trustee—who must continue or close up the trust proceedings, as the case may be—will be required to obtain an IRS identification number. A final fiduciary income tax return must then be filed for the trust. Unlike a probate estate, a trust cannot choose a fiscal tax year in order to gain some tax advantage.

Lack of Guidance. Unlike probate administration, trust administration takes place in somewhat of a vacuum. Few laws and court decisions exist to guide the trustee or lawyer who may be advising the trustee. This could be an advantage or a disadvantage, depending upon one's point of view and intentions.

Few trusts to avoid probate have been in existence for any length of time. Therefore most lawyers cannot honestly say that they have had much, if any, experience as to what happens when the grantor dies.

For instance, how is title to real estate affected and cleared? Is the distribution of trust assets hampered by the trust, especially if the grantor were still the trustee at the time of death? What problems do claimants pose in the closing process? Will courts or statutes require that notice to interested parties be given following the death? If so, to whom should it be given? Because some estate proceedings other than administration probably will still be necessary, has the trust actually saved time and expense overall?

And unanswered legal problems may arise during the period of the trust. What if someone is unwilling to deal with the trustee, because, for instance, they doubt his or her authority? Or suppose the grantor, who is acting as trustee, becomes incapacitated. Does the agreement clearly specify procedures under these circumstances? Or what if the agreement were clear but the designated alternate trustee is reluctant to act without court authority or a showing that the trustee is in fact incapacitated?

Under these circumstances, even the lawyer who prepared the trust agreement may be unwilling or unable to interpret the agreement or to satisfy all the interested parties. Or the lawyer may be willing only to express his or her opinion, advising that it may not be upheld in a court of law.

Disinheriting of a Spouse.   Spouses of grantors could have a concern. Laws are not yet clear as to whether a spouse can be disinherited by use of a trust. Suppose that John, who has a large estate, decides to set up a trust, allegedly to avoid probate. His spouse, Mary, joins with him in all the necessary documents transferring John's property to the trust. The trust now thus becomes the titleholder to the property. By signing the documents, Mary presumably has released all rights of dower and homestead in the transferred property. She was willing to sign because the trust agreement names both John and Mary as beneficiaries.

But Mary forgets or does not realize the implication of the trust being revocable, which means that it is also amendable. Thereafter, John, without the knowledge of Mary, amends the trust so that Mary is no longer named as a beneficiary. Subsequently John dies. Mary ends up with nothing, with no rights as a surviving spouse. (See discussion of these rights in Chapter 14.) Or does she? What must she do to salvage whatever rights she has?

Once the spouse joins in the transfer of the property to the trust, title and possession of the property is in the trust. Since the trust is revocable, the grantor, in this example, John, may, without the knowledge of Mary, amend the trust terms, which includes the designation of beneficiaries. Since the trust is ordinarily not a matter of record, neither are any of its amendments. No one other than the grantor and his attorney, who probably would be a different attorney than the one who originally set up the trust, need know what the grantor, John, has done.

The various jurisdictions are not in agreement as to whether a spouse can be disinherited by use of a trust. Probate statutes may or may not apply to the trust. Or a court may find that it is against public policy to allow a trust to disinherit a spouse. Scheming grantors may or may not bypass the rights of a spouse, but it is likely that their efforts to do so will create havoc.

Disinheriting of Other Heirs. What could happen to the surviving spouse could also happen to the couple's children and other heirs. Do the allowance statutes, which protect minor children, apply to a trust as they do to probate? Are afterborn children, that is, children born or adopted after the execution of the trust, protected the same as they are after the execution of a will? And do the antilapse statutes, which are statutes designed to protect the heirs of a designated, predeceased beneficiary in a will, apply to trusts?

A Final Word About Avoiding Probate

Particularly during the last decade, the use of a revocable trust to avoid probate administration has become a popular topic, since anything that may keep the lawyer's fingers out of the estate pie is attractive to laypersons. Unfortunately, revocable trusts in lieu of probate are not always the cure-all some may think they are.

Why might the public be disenchanted with probate proceedings? Perhaps it is because most state statutes provide some measure of payment for services by the legal representative and the representative's attorney based upon a percentage of the decedent's estate. Perhaps because these percentage statutes in effect tend to place a maximum on what can be charged, state legislatures seem to be in no hurry to remove such statutes.

While most laypersons recognize that the lawyer and the personal representative are entitled to a fee for their services, laypersons are generally not happy that the fees are based upon a percentage of their estate rather than upon other factors seemingly more fair, such as the time involved and benefits received. Because of this irritation, the public is looking for alternatives to probate. One of these alternatives, they think, is the revocable trust.

Setting up a trust to avoid probate has some good points, but it has some bad points too. The pros and cons should be thoroughly discussed with your attorney. Approach the subject with an open mind, if you can, as otherwise you may spend your money foolishly, although not necessarily fatally, as you can usually revoke the trust.

Compare the advantages of the trust with the disadvantages, as they apply to you, not to someone else. Be guided by the practicalities, not your prejudices. Compare the expenses and bother of both setting one up and not setting one up. Be aware of alternatives, which may suit you better, such as the durable power of attorney, a bank agency account, or, especially if you are married and your estate is not large, the judicious use of joint tenancy with your spouse.

Recognize your real reason for wanting the trust. Is it to avoid the expense of probate? By using it, would you really be saving or merely prepaying expenses? Remember, too, that the trust is a continuing, possibly long-term, venture, certainly something intended for a lifetime. Probate, on the other hand, is a one-shot affair. Are you willing to go through the hassle of having everything in trust and maintaining it in that manner, if the paramount reason is merely to avoid probate—which it may not do anyway? In short, is the trust worth all the trouble?

If you can honestly answer all those questions in the affirmative, then you probably are a prime candidate for a revocable trust to avoid probate.

Some Common Questions Answered

Q. I have seen several articles and advertisements featuring the desirability of a revocable living trust to avoid probate. The advertiser indicates that I can fill out its forms myself without the necessity of hiring a lawyer. Should I invest in one of these kits?

A. It is doubtful that any practicing lawyer would recommend you doing so. Before you invest in any of the forms, and certainly before you complete any of them, you ought to consult a lawyer so that this subject is thoroughly explored before you take any final action.

Few lawyers are likely to feel comfortable with you taking action on your own. Lawyers themselves disagree as to the advisability of trusts for the sole purpose of avoiding probate. And few lawyers like to accept the work product of another person, especially if that person's expertise is unknown.

Q. Some alleged benefits of the trusts are that they eliminate costs, lengthy procedures, court interference, and the need for a lawyer at time of death. Is that all true?

A. It is doubtful that all of that is true, although such trusts are planned with all those benefits in mind. Court costs—a rather minor item—should be eliminated. Title to the trust property, however, somehow must be transferred from the trustee to the ultimate beneficiaries. Some jurisdictions may say that this is automatic upon a proper showing of the death of the primary beneficiary, but others may require some instrument of transfer signed by an alternate trustee. If so, a lawyer would be required.

Any liability for death taxes must be disposed of. This would require the services of a lawyer. If the estate size exceeds $600,000, then the lengthy federal estate tax procedure would have to be undertaken, as the revocable trust does not eliminate this requirement.

No doubt as these trusts become more common, claimants and creditors will want the same kind of protection they now receive from an estate proceeding. If so, procedures to close a trust will become more like an estate administration. Unless or until that happens, however, these trusts normally will be able to avoid court supervision.

Q. It is alleged that with the living trust I would have control of my estate and would be able to dispose of it as I wish. Is that true?

A. Yes, but that is true without a trust too. In either event you should make a will. Without a trust you have control of your own estate during your lifetime. With a trust your estate is controlled as you directed in the trust agreement. Upon your death the trust property would go according to the trust, which, for purposes of distribution, would contain provisions similar to your will.

Q. It is also alleged that since a living trust is revocable, you can change your mind at any time. Is that true?

A. Not quite. Similar to the will situation, with a trust, if you become incompetent, you no longer have the legal ability to change its terms. Under such circumstances you are prohibited from entering into, or changing, a contract. At that time the trust becomes, in effect, irrevocable. This should make no difference if you had sufficient foresight to anticipate every possible change in your estate and in your heirs or beneficiaries.

Q. If naming myself as trustee could cause some problems, then why not name a bank in the first place to serve as trustee? Wouldn't continuity be assured, while at the same time the problem of failing ability be provided for?

A. That is true, as far as it goes. But aside from the feeling of losing control of your property, the chief problem is that every trustee (other than yourself), like any fiduciary, is entitled to compensation for its services. The fee for serving over a long period of time could be considerable.

You should not object to paying someone for rendering services to you. But if you are paying a fee year after year for this service, are you really saving any money by avoiding probate? The money not spent during your lifetime—a prepaid expense—can be earning income for you until you die.

Q. It is alleged that the trust avoids the dangers of a will contest. Is this true?

A. Not really. Consider the various bases for a will contest—undue influence, incompetence, incapacity, improper execution, forgery, revocation, fraud, material mistake, or ambiguity. Any of these could also be a basis for setting aside a trust. Thus in this respect neither has any advantage over the other. However, if such instruments are prepared and executed by your attorney, they are less likely to be subsequently challenged.

Q. In transferring property to a revocable trust has a grantor created a gift tax liability?

A. No. Since the trust is revocable, no completed gift has been made. The trust beneficiaries may never receive the property, because at some point the trust may be revoked or amended. No gift tax return need be filed since no gift was made. The answer, however, would be just the opposite if the trust were irrevocable.

Q. If no gift tax results from the transfer of the grantor's property to the revocable trust, then I assume the transfer (distribution) at the time of the grantor's death is subject to death taxes. Is that true?

A. Yes. The creation of the revocable trust creates no change in the grantor's possible liability for death taxes at the time of death. The responsibility for reporting the grantor's estate to the taxing bodies remains the same. Whether any death tax is actually due depends upon the same considerations as if no trust existed, the absence or presence of the trust being irrelevant.

Q. I understand that trusts can be used both to avoid probate and for management purposes. Are these two reasons for trusts conflicting in any way?

A. Yes, they can be. Perhaps the chief incentive for avoiding probate is the presumed saving of costs. But this saving can be fully realized only if the grantor serves as trustee. If the prime motive for a trust is management of the grantor's assets, then the grantor should not be serving as trustee or, at the least, would need a cotrustee. If management of assets is the important consideration, then other vehicles for asset management should be explored.

Q. Can you give me a practical example when the trust might be beneficial?

A. Suppose you became recently widowed. Your husband had handled all of your affairs. You are elderly and tired. At this stage of your life you don't want to be bothered with your affairs. You would just as soon have your bank handle your affairs. The trust might be expensive but it would give you management benefits as well. Assuming you had no available alternatives (see Chapter 9), the trust should be worth it to you.

Q. What estate proceedings are required if at the time of my death part of my property is in a trust and part in my name only?

A. Only one estate proceeding would be required, the full administration. This would be no different than most other estates, which usually consist partly of probate property and partly of nonprobate property. The trust property would be reported in your inventory and for tax purposes along with your other nonprobate property and along with your probate property. Having some of your property in the trust may or may not reduce the court costs and the fees of your personal representative and the attorney. Otherwise the existence of the trust is mostly irrelevant to the proceedings.

12

Understanding Living Wills and Health Care Powers of Attorney

Estate lawyers have become increasingly involved with living wills and health care powers of attorney. As clients plan their testamentary wills, their thoughts have turned to these two documents. All three of these documents are concerned with the testator's death.

Living wills and health care powers of attorney are concerned with terminally ill and severely incapacitated individuals who have no hope of recovery. Without some means of terminating health care for these individuals, their lives can be prolonged indefinitely. The costs of futilely extending life jeopardize a patient's estate planning, even to the extent of totally draining the individual's estate. Thus it now seems appropriate in estate planning to include both a living will and a durable power of attorney for health care. By doing so, the estate planner is more likely to preserve the estate.

Because such documents are so closely related to estate planning, a time when you are consciously planning for an orderly transfer of your estate upon your death, you may find yourself considering whether you should have a living will and a health care power of attorney at the same time that you are doing your estate planning.

Living Wills

A *living will* is not a testamentary disposition of your property. Nor is it a trust. It is a direction to your doctor and other health care providers as to how you want to be treated if you become terminally ill without hope for recovery. The direction must be made prior to you reaching an extreme condition in which your competence to consent may become an issue. It may not even be legally effective unless it is made so by legislation.

One main concern of living wills is to what extent an individual should be able to determine when his or her life should no longer be continued. A concurrent concern is protecting those who carry out the individual's wishes. This discussion does not concern suicide, although some mistakenly think that that is the ultimate aim of living wills.

Living wills have several names, such as "advance directive" or "passive euthanasia," and the acts of various states pertaining to this subject have many titles, such as the Natural Death Act, Right to Die Law, Life-Sustaining Procedures Act, or Living Will Law.

State living will statutes concern the discontinuance or withholding of medical care. This type of health care situation is the direct opposite to that in which someone seeks authority to compel medical care. The latter type of situation might involve trying to force medical procedure—a blood transfusion, for example—upon someone who objects to it on religious grounds. Living wills should also be distinguished from active euthanasia, which has to do with inducing the painless death of a person for reasons assumed to be merciful.

The Quinlan Case

The subject of sustaining life received its first impetus from the widely reported 1976 case of 21-year-old Karen Ann Quinlan, who was comatose and kept alive, some believed, by a respirator. Neither her doctor nor her hospital were willing to consent to the removal of the respirator. Karen's father went to court, seeking to become her personal guardian with authority to discontinue the respirator.

The New Jersey court agreed with the father. The opinion stated that after certain safeguards were taken, the removal of the respirator would not result in any civil or criminal liability on the part of any participant, whether a guardian, physician, hospital, or another party. This case, which received wide attention and controversy, became the impetus for the living will statutes passed by the great majority of the states.

One of the difficulties in the Quinlan case was that Karen was not medically considered "brain dead," although she was considered to be in a "chronic persistent vegetative state." She had sleep-awake cycles. When she was awake she blinked and cried out, but was totally unaware of anyone or anything. Under these circumstances, many people would admit to at least some squeamishness in withdrawing or withholding lifesaving equipment. Their discomfort no doubt is based on moral, religious, or ethical grounds.

The Cruzan Case

Many were comfortable with the living will until the Nancy Cruzan case surfaced. Nancy Beth Cruzan, then age 25, suffered brain damage as a result of an automobile accident in 1983. Although in a "persistent vegetative state" with loss of brain function described as "permanent, progressive and ongoing," a Missouri hospital refused to terminate artificial nutrition and hydration.

Nancy's parents went to court to try to force the removal of the sustaining feeding. The trial court found that Nancy was not terminally ill, but they allowed the removal. The case was appealed and all subsequent appellate courts, including the United States Supreme Court in a much-divided decision, found in favor of the hospital.

The Court, however, did give direction as to what is acceptable in that it held that a state may require "clear and convincing evidence" as to what procedure the patient would desire. The Court also confirmed that an individual has the right to refuse medical treatment, a term which includes artificially administered nutrition and hydration. Because of the Court's guidance, the Cruzan matter has since been resolved.

The Power of Attorney

Due, perhaps, to the Cruzan case, the American Medical Association, the American Bar Association, health care providers, and others have been promoting a durable power of attorney for health care, sometimes accompanied with a medical directive. States, through statutory or case law, are responding with their own acts or interpretations.

One of the problems with this response is that the proposed remedies are not uniform, except that general agreement exists that the living will is not enough. The living will may suffice for the terminally ill, as in the Quinlan case, but not for those that are comatose, as in the Cruzan case. Both cases demonstrate, however, that you need not be elderly for these types of difficulties to arise.

Some people believe that the durable power of attorney for health care may be general in nature. Others believe that it should be specific, spelling out the various possibilities for care and indicating what is desired under each circumstance. It is agreed, however, that both the living will and the durable power of attorney should be executed in accordance with statutes, if such exist. In fact, some statutes require them to be. The two documents should be consistent with each other, if not combined into one.

Another problem with the response to these health conditions is that the states are slow in promoting advance directives, which is the name used to describe living wills and health care powers of attorney. Perhaps this is what prompted Congress in 1990 to pass legislation, known as the Patient Self-Determination Act, which applies to health care facilities, agencies, and programs that participate in Medicare and Medicaid.

The act requires the provider or organization, as of December 1, 1991, to give information to adult patients concerning their rights under state law to make decisions about their medical care during a health emergency. Such rights include the right to accept or refuse medical or surgical treatment and the right to formulate advance directives. This would not have helped Nancy Cruzan or Karen Ann Quinlan, neither of whom were in any condition to make decisions.

Other problems with the living will and the power of attorney exist. Because of the lack of a clear law in many cases, many advocates of the power are operating in a vacuum, not really knowing what will be acceptable to the courts or even to the health care providers. And health care providers may refuse to follow the instructions, for whatever reason. The living will and the power should be reviewed every few years, since both the law and medical technology are still in a state of transition.

The good news used to be that living will forms could be obtained free from your local health care provider. They probably still can be. But the bad news is that in view of the Cruzan case the living will forms, in and of themselves, are no longer adequate. You now also need an advance directive naming a surrogate (an attorney in fact for health care) to act on your behalf under similar circumstances.

Further bad news is that less than half of the states provide for a durable medical power of attorney. Without either this statutory or case authority, no one can be certain that the power will solve the problem. But in this case, something should be better than nothing. If your state does not specifically prohibit it, a combined living will and a durable power of attorney for health care, consistent with each other, should be considered. This will constitute "clear and convincing" evidence of your intentions—and that is what the Cruzan case established as the requirement.

Some Common Questions Answered

> Q. Under living will statutes, does "life-sustaining treatment" include any type of nourishment?

A. No, under many of the statutes. However, where the statutes do not define the treatment, a majority of the courts find that it does.

Q. Will a durable general power of attorney suffice as a power for health care as well?

A. States vary as to the effect of a general power that does not specifically address health care. While it would seem that a significant number of them would answer your question in the affirmative, you would be wise not to rely on your general power for health care purposes.

Q. Do I have an absolute right to consent to or refuse medical treatment?

A. No. Public policy and medical ethics may override your right in some instances.

Q. Do I have a right to name anyone I want as my agent in the power for health care?

A. Yes, but you should consider many things. For instance, should you consider only a close family member? Is there a possible conflict of interest that could result in abuse of the power? Would the nominee be able to make the decision when called upon? Should you name a co-agent or an alternate?

Q. Do I need both a living and a durable power of attorney for health care, or will one or the other suffice?

A. You should have both. Most states have living will statutes but few have statutes providing for the health power. A living will may be sufficient for a terminal illness but not for a comatose condition. And many living will statutes do not provide for the removal of sustenance—food and water. On the other hand, the durable power alone may not be deemed sufficient under some circumstances. Alone, the health care power may not present "clear and convincing" evidence of the intent of the individual. Because a conflict may occur between the two documents in some states, you may wish to check with your attorney.

Some authorities suggest a third document, sometimes called a medical directive. This directive attempts to set out instructions for treating various illnesses that are life-threatening. By making these up, however, the individual may inadvertently omit other possibilities or make it appear that the list is all-inclusive, when it may not have been so intended. It is always dangerous to try to list all possibilities, as any omission may be deemed intentional even with a catch-all provision.

Q. Whom should I give my living will and health care power of attorney document to?

A. Signed copies should go to your physician, hospital, and attorney in fact and to a close family member. Also keep at least one signed copy of each document with your other valuable papers.

Q. Can a health care provider such as a hospital or care facility condition admission to that facility on the existence of a living will or power of attorney?

A. No.

Q. Can insurance be conditioned on the existence of such documents?

A. No.

Q. In event of a dispute, who prevails, a family member or the surrogate (the attorney in fact)?

A. The attorney in fact.

PART 2

Guide to Inheritance and Estate Proceedings

13
Dying Without a Will

When you die intestate, that is, without a will, what happens to your estate? Who is entitled to your property? All states have provided for this possibility by enacting laws of descent and distribution—sometimes referred to as the laws of inheritance.

Inheritance is a statutory privilege, not a natural right. Neither state constitutions nor the federal constitution secure your right to control or dispose of your property after your death. Nor is it the right of anyone, whether or not related to you, to take your property by inheritance or otherwise, except as may be provided by statute.

State legislatures can restrict the succession of your estate upon your death in any manner and, if they please, can repeal the statutes of wills, of descent and distribution, and of distributive share. In the exercise of their sovereignty, states can take any or all of your property upon your death and apply it to public uses.

Understanding the Laws of Descent

Although states through their legislative process have the power and authority to eliminate these laws of distribution, they won't. But if you understand the right of the state to take your property, then you will also understand that the laws of descent and distribution—the laws of inheritance—are by the grace of the state.

Inheriting property is not something that you have an inherent right to. Generally, the laws of property distribution are based upon your legislators' idea of what you and others want to happen to your property should you die intestate. Each state is jealous of the property located within its respective borders. Thus, if you own property in more than one state and you die without a will, your property could be subject to more than one set of laws of descent and distribution, since all states provide for intestacy.

In many cases these descent laws provide for distribution of your property not much different, or perhaps not any different, than you would have made had you drafted a will. Remember, however, that this distribution is made according to the laws of descent in existence at the time of your death. Both the laws and circumstances might be considerably different upon your death than at a previous time when you were contemplating making a will. And keep in mind that your heirs are determined when you die, not before. So those who you think will inherit your estate may not necessarily be the same who actually do. If they predecease you, the estate passes to whatever heirs are found according to the laws of descent and distribution.

A particular inheritance statute may not be at all how you would desire it. If so, you can avoid the effect of it and most other similar statutes by making a will. Not *all* such statutes can be avoided, because your spouse, if so desired, can circumvent your will to some extent. And sometimes your children can as well.

For reasons already stated in previous chapters it is not wise to let the state make your will. Your will accomplishes more than mere distribution of your property. And without it, you can never be sure that your property will be distributed, both as to shares and timing, in the manner that you would wish. Descent laws only ineptly provide for the not-so-unusual circumstances, such as the incompetency of an heir or the sale of real property by the estate's personal representative.

Application of the Inheritance Statutes

Most state inheritance laws have some common characteristics, although they do vary among states. First, subject to the rights of a surviving spouse, the decedent's children and more remote descendants are the preferred heirs. Second, in the absence of descendants, parents are the preferred heirs. Finally at some point, when all else fails, the property goes to the state.

As you will discover in Chapter 14, the surviving spouse is entitled to a substantial portion of the deceased spouse's estate, whether or not the decedent left a will to the contrary. But after the surviving spouse receives the statutory share, who is entitled to the balance of the intestate decedent's estate? A relevant question, calling for a similar answer, is, Who is entitled to the decedent's estate if the intestate decedent dies without a spouse?

In a sense, a statute looks for the nearest or most closely related relative, and it specifies the direction in which the search must proceed. The usual order of preference provides that first you go downward, that is, you look for descendants first. Thus the children of the decedent come first.

You don't search beyond the children unless a deceased child leaves living children, in which case such children—your grandchildren—take the share that their parent would have taken. And you continue downward in that manner. All it takes is the finding of one descendant in a particular line of descent in order for the search to stop. What this means is that the children of your living child, your grandchildren, do not inherit because the search in that line stops with your child. But all lines of descent must be searched.

For example, suppose that four children were born to you but by the time of your death three of them had died. Each of your four children had married and all of their spouses are still living. Of the three deceased children, one has no living descendants, one has one living child (your grandchild) and no other descendants, and one has a living grandchild (your great grandchild) and no other descendants.

First of all, none of the spouses of your four children would receive anything since they are not your descendants and thus not considered your heirs. Your estate would be divided into thirds, of which one-third would go to your living child, one-third to your living grandchild, and one-third to your living great grandchild. No share would go to (or through) the deceased child, who had no descendants, because that line ended with that child. That share thus lapses.

Note that inheritances normally follow bloodlines, which explains why the in-laws receive nothing. Note, also, that the descendants only receive the share, or interest, that their ancestor would have received, if living. Thus if there had been two living children of a predeceased child, then each grandchild would have received one-half of the one-third interest (or one-sixth) of the inheritance to which the predeceased child would have been entitled.

What the above indicates is that the heirs take per stirpes and not per capita. *Per stirpes* means "by right of representation." The children take the share which their parent would have taken if the parent had then been living.

Per capita means "per person, by the head or individual." When heirs take per capita, each one, regardless of living parentage or line of descent, receives an equal share. Suppose in the above example that the one predeceased child had left two living children instead of one, so that you had two grandchildren instead of one. If the per capita rule applied, then each of your four heirs—your child, your two grandchildren, and your great-grandchild—would receive one-fourth of your estate. If the per stirpes rule applied, then your estate would divide unequally—one-third for your child, one-third for your great grandchild, and one-sixth to each of your two grandchildren. (In effect, one-third to each bloodline.)

Continuing the search for heirs, if no descendants of the decedent are found, then you first search one step up, which means the parent or parents of the decedent are next in line. If both are living, each receives one-half of the decedent's estate. If only one is living, then that surviving parent normally receives all of the decedent's estate.

If neither parent is living, then the descendants of the parents receive in the same manner or proportion that the descendants of the decedent would have received if living. Thus if a decedent's parents are deceased, but the decedent had a brother and sister (who are the other descendants of the parents), both of whom survive the decedent, then each would receive one-half of the decedent's estate. The children of the living brother or sister would not receive, as the finding of an heir in a line of descent stops the line of search from continuing.

Continuing the search further, if neither parent is then living and the decedent never had any siblings, then the search goes up one more step, to the grandparents of the decedent. The process downward is then repeated. This process of going up one step and then down, going up another step and then down, and so on, is repeated until heirs are found.

The search first looks for "lineal" heirs. This is done by following a direct line, either up or down. If the lineal search does not produce an heir, then a search for "collateral" heirs is made. *Collateral heirs* are relatives who share a common ancestor. The relationship is one of "consanguinity," which imparts blood through some common ancestor, although your dictionary may state that the word refers to any close connection or affinity.

As will be seen later, under most statutes if a search does not produce either lineal or collateral heirs, then a search is made by looking for a relationship by "affinity." This is a tie between one spouse and the blood relation of the other.

The chart in Figure 13-1 can be used to help determine heirship in an intestate situation. Use the per stirpes method. Start with the decedent and work down to and through "child." If no children are found in that line of descent, move to "parent" and if necessary down that line of descent through "brother & sister." If none are found in that line, move to "grandparent" and down that line of descent through "uncle, aunt," and so on.

By working up and then down, in other words through ascending ancestors and their heirs, heirs should be found. But, if no heirs are found, then escheat would result. Note that a reasonable search to locate heirs has

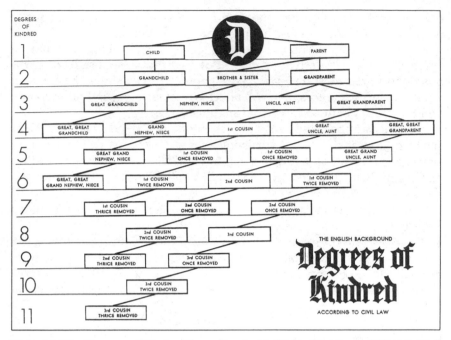

Figure 13-1. Degrees of Kindred According to Civil Law. (*Courtesy of West Publishing Company*)

to be made. Escheat doesn't result because heirs don't exist somewhere at some level. Escheat occurs because no heirs can be found.

Because states are not uniform in determining the intestate shares of heirs, the above description of lines of descent might not apply to your state. Part of the discrepancy may be due to how the spouse is treated under different situations.

Most states are fairly generous with the spouse. To what extent they are generous often depends upon the existence of children of the decedent and upon whether such children are also those of the surviving spouse. And several states, to some extent, specify shares going to the surviving spouse in dollar amounts rather than percentages or fractions.

Note that the word *child* refers only to natural born or legally adopted children. Stepchildren and foster children, unless legally adopted, are never considered as heirs. Except for legally adopted children, heirs must all be of the same bloodline as the decedent. When no lineal or collateral heirs exist it may be necessary to resort to relationship by affinity to determine heirs.

Both the decedent and the heir must each have a common ancestor, except for the situation described below. Contrary to common law, half bloods—those having only one common parent—usually take equally with the whole blood—those having the same (common) parents.

Regardless of what you may believe, legally the word *heir* may not include a decedent's surviving spouse. But a surviving spouse has numerous rights under most state laws (see Chapter 14). You should be aware of what these rights are, as they will affect how your heirs and your spouse will take under both your will and statutes.

Even though the spouse may not legally be described as an heir, he or she often is treated as one. A surviving spouse may receive all of the property either (1) if all of decedent's children are also the surviving spouse's or (2) if no heirs of decedent are found by following the lines of descent and ascent as described above.

If the latter situation applies and the spouse is not then living, then the decedent's estate may pass to the heirs of the spouse in the same manner and according to the same rules of descent and distribution. In this event, the predeceased spouse takes the place of the decedent. Again, the heirs normally take per stirpes and not per capita. If the decedent had more than one spouse, then the estate may pass equally between the spouses or their heirs, as the case may be.

Compare the search for heirs to that of an animal in a maze in a laboratory experiment. The animal travels down one path without success, then retraces its steps and tries another path without success. And it continues doing so until it succeeds. This is similar to the search for heirs.

But suppose, in the search for heirs on the decedent's side of the family, no heirs are found. In this event, the search repeats itself with the spouse's side of the family, assuming there is no spouse then living.

Escheat

What if all searches for heirs end up in blind alleys? What then? Only in this instance—a rare one—does the estate pass, or *escheat*, to the state. Since the total lack of heirs, either of the decedent or the decedent's spouse, if any, is unlikely, you should not be overly concerned with escheat.

But perhaps you know of someone who died without a will and all his property went to the state. How could this happen?

Everyone has heirs, however remote. If no heirs are found, however, after a reasonable search, the property of a decedent escheats to the state.

Escheat is an old English feudal doctrine. If title (originally to lands) failed, usually for "failure of blood" or for a felony, the title reverted back to the original lord. Whatever the cause, it was considered an obstruction of the course of descent. The estate itself which so reverted was called an escheat.

In this country states act in the place of the feudal lord. By virtue of their sovereignty, the states are the original and ultimate owner of all the lands (and other property) within their respective jurisdictions. But states generally do not rely on the common law. Instead, state statutes ensure the right of escheat under certain conditions, the conditions having to do with the lack of heirs.

Escheat only occurs if no heirs are found. Thus the break in the chain of title actually occurs not from a lack of heirs, but because of the failure to locate heirs. Statutes setting forth the rules of descent will invariably end with a statement such as "but if heirs are not thus found." In such a situation the intestate property would escheat to the state.

Of course, you never have to worry about escheat, since you can always make a will whether or not you have any known heirs. Remember, except for certain laws that protect a surviving spouse and afterborn children, you can always will your estate to whomever you wish.

You should never depend upon the laws of descent as a means of transferring your property upon your death. Even if your state inheritance statutes are totally consistent with what has been stated here—an unlikely event—they probably will not remain so forever. Since state inheritance statutes do change from time to time, you should not rely on them in lieu of making a will.

Some Common Questions Answered

Q. Isn't my granddaughter also my heir?

A. It depends. It is assumed that by "heir" you mean the one who will inherit your property in the event you die intestate, that is, without a will. At the least, your granddaughter is your potential heir, potential in the sense that she may become your heir in the event that her parent, your child, has predeceased you.

For example, say you have two children, each of whom has one child. At the time you die one of your children has predeceased you. Thus at the time you die you have one living child, but two living grandchildren, one grandchild by your living child and one grandchild by your deceased child. Your heirs in this instance are your living child and the one grandchild by your predeceased child. The other grandchild, the one by your living child, is not considered an heir under the laws of descent and distribution.

From a legal standpoint, the word *heirs* must be distinguished from the common use of the word in other contexts. When a person dies, most of us wonder who survived, who was left behind. We refer to such surviving persons as survivors, next of kin, or merely as heirs. But statutes think of heirs in the sense of who will inherit the decedent's property.

Q. If I have no will when I die, do the inheritance laws of my state consider the respective needs of my heirs before passing out my property to them?

A. No. The laws of inheritance are rigid and make no exceptions as to need or other criteria. Circumstances of the various parties who will inherit under the state laws of descent and distribution are not taken into account. This fact applies whether or not the inheritance could work a hardship on one or more of the heirs. An incompetent heir, for example, is treated no differently than a competent heir.

Q. If I die without a will, does a will of one of my predeceased sons have any effect on how his share goes?

A. No, as your heirs are determined by statute and not by someone else's will. No one, whether or not in your line of descent, can control who inherits from you. You alone have that control, but only if you leave a will. If you leave no will, then the laws of inheritance would control who inherits from you. The fact that your son may leave a will contrary to the laws of inheritance as applied to you is irrelevant.

Of course if your son had died subsequent to you, then his will would control any inheritance that he had received from you. At the time of his subsequent death his inheritance from you would actually have been his property, not yours. And since he would have inherited your property and thus owned it at the time of his death, he could do anything he wanted to with it.

Q. My father had a will prepared by his lawyer, but he died before he had a chance to sign it. Does the unsigned will now have any effect, or does his property now go intestate?

A. The will must be executed according to the statute before it is considered valid. Thus his property will go according to the laws of descent and distribution. However, if his heirs all agree and certain other parties are taken into account (see Chapter 17), they could enter into a family settlement that could be consistent with the terms of the will.

Q. Which statute would control, the one in existence at the time of my death or the one in existence at the time of the distribution of my estate?

A. The laws in existence at time of death would control, since an inheritance vests at the time of death. A subsequent law change cannot divest your heirs of their vested interest in the property, even though distribution of your estate had not yet been made.

14

Salvaging the Rights of the Surviving Spouse

Although the word *heir* does not normally include a decedent's surviving spouse, all states provide a surviving spouse with certain rights to all or a portion of the deceased spouse's property. Usually these rights are substantial, but in a few instances such rights are limited to allowances or homestead rights.

In certain situations the spouse is actually treated as an heir. And since a surviving spouse is entitled to certain benefits and distributions from the estate of the deceased spouse, it should make little difference to you how a surviving spouse is identified.

Some of these rights exist regardless whether the decedent left a will. But some of them exist only when the decedent left a will and some only when the decedent left no will. And some of these rights are similar to the rights of the decedent's minor children.

The Common Law Dower

Historically under the English common law, a surviving wife had a minimum one-third life interest in her deceased husband's lands, a right referred to as *dower*. The husband, in turn, might have a life interest in the lands of his deceased wife under a right of *curtesy*, but only under certain conditions.

Common law dower and curtesy have been abolished in most states. Statutes have taken their place, which vary from state to state. The substitutes for dower and curtesy are part of the laws of descent and distribution. Unfortunately, some states still do not treat the surviving husband and the surviving wife in the same manner, although they are more likely to do so as time goes by.

Because of tradition, lawyers and laypersons alike still frequently refer to the statutory share of the surviving spouse, whether man or woman, as a dower or curtesy interest, although generally the former.

But the words *dower* and *curtesy* no longer appear in many state probate codes. And the interest that a surviving spouse has in the deceased spouse's estate now may be much different, depending upon the circumstances, the location of the property, and the place of the decedent's death.

Surviving Spouse's Rights When the Decedent Dies Testate

What right to the decedent's estate does a surviving spouse have if the decedent dies testate, that is, with a will? The discussion that follows applies to the great majority of states that give the surviving spouse either a right to take against the decedent's will or at least some elective rights to the decedent's property.

Spousal Election

Upon the death of a spouse, the surviving spouse is obligated to make a decision. Does the surviving spouse want to take the share, if any, provided for in the will? Or does that spouse prefer to take the share provided for by statute in lieu of the bequest? The share which the surviving spouse has a right to take, instead of that provided by the will, is variously called the *statutory share*, the *elective share*, or the *forced share*. For convenience, the proceeding is hereafter referred to as an election.

If your spouse dies leaving a will, then you as the surviving spouse are required to elect to take or not to take under the provisions of your spouse's will. It is your option. No one can dictate your choice or make it for you, unless you are incompetent to do so on your own. Sometimes a statute will do it for you if you fail or are unable to take any action on your own.

Should you elect not to accept the bequests, if any, of your deceased spouse's will, you may instead elect to take the distributive share provided for you by statute. This choice may be made regardless whether, by doing so, you receive more or less than that set out in the will. Your decision could depend upon factors involved in post-mortem estate planning.

Whether you are willing, or even want, to accept what the will bequeaths to you depends upon many considerations. You might be concerned about the size of your bequest as compared to the statutory amount that you would receive if you elected not to take under the will. Or you might be influenced by the comparative size of each of your estates or your particular needs. Or you might think that a disclaimer would be more appropriate if it affected how the other beneficiaries in the will would receive.

The election procedure is set by statute, the provisions varying from state to state. Either the surviving spouse or the executor may initiate the procedure. A time limit usually is imposed upon the spouse to make a choice. A special procedure may be specified if the surviving spouse is incompetent to make the election. Death of the surviving spouse prior to making an election may or may not terminate the right to an election. If it does, the terms of the will would prevail.

Some statutes provide that if the surviving spouse is also the executor and no election has been made, it is assumed that the spouse automatically elects to take under the will. As a precaution, if the spouse wants to take under the will, he or she should make the election to take. By doing so, no doubt could later exist as to that spouse's intention.

Under the statutes, the time limit for making the election varies anywhere from 30 days to 3 years. Sometimes a statute may only specify that the election must be made within a reasonable time. Obviously an estate proceeding cannot be closed and distribution of the estate assets made until the matter of the election has been determined. Thus the spouse's election should be made as quickly as possible.

If you as the surviving spouse elect not to take under the will, then you receive—in lieu of any bequest—that portion of your spouse's estate which is provided for by the will election statute. This portion may or may not be roughly one-third of the entire estate. If it is, then it would seem that the statute is still influenced by the old common law dower interest of one-third. Again, the one-third share may be more or less than what you would have received under the will.

Most states, however, even common law ones, no longer appear to be influenced by the old dower interest. If they allow for election, their statutes vary widely as to what interest the electing spouse is entitled to receive in lieu of the bequest. The following may have a bearing on what the surviving spouse is entitled to receive: the value of the surviving spouse's separate estate, the existence and even the number of descendants of the deceased, and the existence of community property. The interest passing from the decedent's estate to the surviving spouse may vary all the way from a life estate to one-half of the decedent's estate.

To illustrate the election, suppose your deceased spouse's will gives nothing to you, the surviving spouse. If you elect to take under the will, then you receive nothing—since that is what the will provided. But if you elect not to take under the will, then you receive that portion of the decedent's estate provided for you by statute rather than nothing.

Now suppose your deceased spouse's will gives all of the estate to you as surviving spouse. If you elect to take under the will, then you receive the entire estate, since that is what the will provides. But if you elect not to take under the will, then you receive only that portion of the decedent's estate provided for by statute. You do not receive the whole estate as provided in the will.

Using the last illustration, what happens to the balance of your bequest if you elect not to take under the will and thus receive less than what the will gives you? Who receives the part not "claimed" by you? If the will is drawn, as it should be, to provide for an alternate residuary beneficiary, then that alternate would receive the remaining part of the bequest.

But if the will does not provide for an alternate, then the remaining portion of the estate is said to go intestate, as if no will existed. In that case, the heirs of the decedent would receive the balance of the estate in accordance with the laws of descent and distribution, since no alternate or residuary beneficiaries are designated.

By now you should realize that if your deceased spouse's will attempts to disinherit you, your state, like most others, should protect you at least to some extent under its will election statute. Public policy does not favor a disinherited spouse. In effect, you are guaranteed, through the election process, at least a portion of a decedent's estate. You are not compelled to go penniless, although some forced-share statutes are not very generous.

On the other hand, by making a will leaving you no more (or less) than what the forced-share statute provides, your spouse can make certain that you will receive the minimum amount provided for by statute.

In most states, the amount of the forced share is less than the amount statutes provide to a surviving spouse of an intestate decedent. Thus by making a will and leaving you only an amount equal to the forced share, your spouse could see to it that beneficiaries other than you receive more of the estate. Under such circumstances, you would have been better off if your spouse had made no will at all.

What is the effect of an election to take against the will insofar as the following property is concerned: (1) nonprobate property, (2) out-of-state real estate, or (3) local real estate owned by a nonresident decedent?

Spousal Election and Nonprobate Property. In most states an election to take against the will would have no effect on nonprobate property. Upon a death, title to or benefits from any nonprobate property passes according to the terms of the nonprobate document (such as a bank account or an insurance policy) and is not affected by any election. For example, any joint tenancy property, being nonprobate property, would go to the surviving joint tenant, and any life insurance proceeds, also being nonprobate property, would go to the beneficiary named in the policy. Both would be exclusive of any election.

In a few states, particularly those that have adopted the Uniform Probate Code, property that appears to be nonprobate property may actually be treated as a form of probate property known as the *augmented estate.* Such property can be used to determine the elective share.

The Uniform Probate Code, adopted in whole or in part by 15 states, describes the augmented estate as the "value of property transferred by decedent during marriage and for which did not receive adequate and full consideration." It further provides that the property must comprise one of the following categories: a retained life estate, a revocable trust, a joint tenancy, or a defined transfer made within two years of death.

Augmented property may include a lifetime transfer by the testator to the surviving spouse without full consideration. If this situation exists, then transferred property is credited against the share the surviving spouse would otherwise receive.

In a few states, if during the marriage the testator conveyed real property without the consent of the spouse, then such property is brought back into the decedent's estate for the purpose of determining the elective share. Such lack of consent normally is referred to as a failure of the spouse to release the dower interest.

As a general rule, however, the election process can be circumvented by a lifetime transfer—a testator giving away his or her property prior to death. Some states, however, particularly those which have adopted the Uniform Probate Code, have imposed some restrictions on these types of transfers. One restriction, for example, may apply as to those transfers deemed in contemplation of death such as a gift made within a prescribed period prior to the event. A statute may assume that it was made in contemplation of death.

A somewhat similar result occurs in the community property states when one spouse makes a lifetime transfer of community property without the consent of the other spouse. In some instances personal as well as real property is included in the restriction. And in some situations the effectiveness of the transfer may depend upon whether or not full consideration was received by the transferring spouse.

Spousal Election and Out-of-State Real Estate.   Most states make no provision for an election as to out-of-state real estate. Of those that do, some provide that the election is governed by the law of the state in which the property is located. The others provide that the property is subject to the election if it is part of the augmented estate.

Spousal Election and Local Real Estate Owned by a Nonresident.   As to the effect of an election on local real estate owned by a nonresident decedent, states vary. Some make no provision for this occurrence. Some provide that the election can be made as if the nonresident were a resident of the state where the property is located. The remaining states provide that the election is determined by the law of decedent's place of residence.

Spousal Election in Community Property States.   In the community property states, a surviving spouse is deemed to own one-half of the community property. But suppose a testator attempts to make a testamentary disposition of the surviving spouse's half interest. In some community property states, the surviving spouse must elect not to take under the will in order to retain that half interest. In the others, the election would apply only as to the testator's half share and his or her separate property.

When the Election May Not Be Available.   Under some circumstances, the election is not available to the surviving spouse. This usually results from a poor marriage relationship. For instance, if the surviving spouse had abandoned or deserted the deceased spouse, he or she might not be able to elect. However, the other spouse's consent to such abandonment or desertion or reconciliation following the abandonment or desertion might remove the bar of making an election. The same situation could exist if the surviving spouse had refused or neglected to support the deceased spouse. And legal separation may bar the election.

When You May Not Receive the Entire Elected Share.   Even though you as a surviving spouse elect to take under your deceased spouse's will, you may not receive the entire amount provided for therein. This might happen if the will were made prior to the birth or legal adoption of your spouse's child for whom no provision was made. These children, known as afterborn children, have the same rights that they would have had if the decedent had made no will. Thus their rights are possibly paramount to your rights as surviving spouse.

Considerations in Making Election

What factors should be considered in making the decision to take or not to take? Let's assume that you are the surviving spouse trying to decide what to do. If your goal isn't just to receive all that you can get, then your decision should be based on three considerations: (1) What is best for you? (2) What is best for the decedent's estate? (3) How does the election affect third parties? In part, at least, these questions concern post-mortem estate planning.

Best, for you, does not necessarily mean getting the most out of the decedent's estate. Your estate may already be large—more than adequate to take care of you for the balance of your life. Would any reason exist for loading up your estate some more? Would it be better for the property to bypass your estate insofar as possible so that your estate would be subject to the lowest possible overall taxes?

Best, for the decedent's estate, might mean whatever would lessen taxes. Would there be any income or death tax advantage in placing the maximum amount of the decedent's property in your estate? Or would this merely increase the overall liability for taxes?

The two estates should be compared to determine the effect of property being in one or the other of the estates. Which heirs would ultimately benefit the most? If the heirs would have different benefits under different estates, does this pose a problem?

Suppose that you are incompetent to make the election, or that someone else, as provided by statute, must do so on your behalf. That person needs to consider the same factors as the surviving spouse when making a decision. Whoever represents the incompetent spouse must be careful and probably would want to set out the reasons for a particular election with the court when seeking its approval.

Surviving Spouse's Rights When the Decedent Dies Intestate

What right to a decedent's estate does a surviving spouse have if the decedent dies intestate, that is, without a will?

What the surviving spouse receives in an intestate estate usually depends upon the existence and identity of the decedent's heirs, the existence of community property, and the size of the decedent's estate.

According to the Uniform Probate Code, if your spouse dies intestate, and if all his or her descendants are also your descendants, then you are entitled to the first $50,000 plus one-half of the balance of that spouse's estate.

Apparently, states having a statute similar to this theorize that if your spouse's descendants are also yours, then upon your subsequent death you will want to protect the inheritances of these mutual descendants.

But this statute seems to disregard the possibility that you may have other descendants (who are not your spouse's) with whom you may also want to share your estate. If so, then any inheritance received from your spouse could be spread not only among his or her descendants but also among your other descendants. The amount received by your spouse's descendants thus could be quite diluted, or even lost entirely, at the time of your subsequent death—this, because you presumably would want to treat all of your descendants (some of whom were not your spouse's) equally. Or you may even want to give preferential treatment to your own descendants to the disadvantage of your joint descendants.

But in these same states what if some of your spouse's descendants are not also your descendants? In other words, what if your spouse had children by virtue of another, earlier marriage? Are you still entitled to the same proportion of your deceased spouse's entire estate?

You are not entitled to the same proportion if your state follows the Uniform Probate Code. You are then entitled to one-half of the estate. In some other states, the size of your deceased spouse's estate may be controlling under these circumstances. In these states you may be entitled to receive a minimum amount that is no less than one-half of your spouse's estate. For example, say the minimum amount is $50,000. If the whole estate is less than $50,000, then you may receive the entire estate. If the entire estate is more than $50,000 but less than $100,000, you still might receive only $50,000. But if the entire estate is more than $100,000, you may be entitled only to one-half of that estate.

In other words, under this latter situation your inheritance would be one-half of his estate or $50,000, whichever is more. The balance of the estate, if any, would go to the heirs of your deceased spouse according to the laws of descent and distribution.

The Uniform Probate Code treats community property somewhat differently. The one-half of the community property that belongs to the decedent passes to the surviving spouse. That part that does not pass in this manner, because no spouse survives or for another reason, goes as follows. First it would pass to the decedent's issue—that is, children or their lineal descendants—per stirpes. If no issue exists, it would pass to parents. If no issue or parents exist, then it would pass to siblings per stirpes. If none of the above exist, then one-half would go to paternal grandparents per stirpes and the other one-half would go to maternal grandparents per stirpes, or would go to grandparents on one side if none were found on other side.

State statutes vary considerably as to the rights of a surviving spouse to share in the real and personal probate estate of the spouse who died intestate. To determine the surviving spouse's rights to share in the deceased spouse's estate, the following questions should be answered.

If the decedent died intestate, did she or he leave issue? If the decedent died testate, what are the elective rights of the surviving spouse to take against the will? Did the decedent die while a resident in a community property state?

And how are these rights affected by the rights of dower or curtesy, or the homestead rights, or the rights of the surviving spouse and family to allowances? In other words, if these particular statutory rights exist, do they reduce the amount that the surviving spouse is entitled to under the laws of inheritance?

Finally, are the rights of the surviving spouse affected, perhaps eliminated or forfeited, by such things as antenuptial or postnuptial agreements, inter vivos (lifetime) transfers, or certain predeath actions of the surviving spouse, such as murder or abandonment of the spouse?

Because inheritance statutes are complicated and seem to change—although infrequently—from time to time, you and your spouse should not depend upon them to protect each other. Rather, for your mutual protection you should rely on your wills to distribute your estate.

Interim Support Before the Estate Proceeding Is Closed

You may be one of the many individuals who is concerned about how you and your dependent children will survive during the period of administration of your deceased spouse's estate. You may know just enough about estate administration to realize that often no distribution of an estate is made to the distributees until the estate proceeding is ready for closing.

You may have heard that the estate property is "locked up" or frozen during the period of administration, that no estate assets are distributed to the distributees until all other estate matters have been disposed of. If it is true that no portion of the probate estate is available to you during the estate proceeding, you may wonder how you will be able to survive in the meantime.

You probably have access to some forms of interim support, such as your own property or nonprobate property. Like most married couples, you probably keep at least some of your property together with your spouse in joint tenancy. As a surviving joint tenant spouse, you normally would have immediate access to the joint tenancy property, regardless of any estate proceeding which may be required upon the death of your spouse.

The reason for this is that joint tenancy property is considered nonprobate property and thus is not subject to estate administration. This does not mean that such property is not subject to death taxes. Rather, it means that your joint tenancy property is not subject to the terms of your spouse's will or the laws of inheritance.

If you and your spouse do not hold your property in joint tenancy, then it is probable that each of you have your own separate estates. If so, you again do not need to be concerned about lack of available living expenses, at least in the short run. In this situation, as surviving spouse you would have your own assets to use for your support during the period of your spouse's estate administration as well as thereafter.

Another possibility exists for your interim support. You may live in a community property state. Either your separate, community, or joint tenancy property could be sufficient for your support during the period of administration.

The Statutory Allowance.   Your best protection during this period, however, would be an interim arrangement known as the *statutory allowance*. All states afford this protection except Pennsylvania, South Carolina, and West Virginia, which only have limited protection. Let's consider this allowance available to the surviving spouse, regardless of how title to the estate property is held. Since this type of family allowance was not known under the common law, it is purely statutory. Thus states vary as to the extent of the allowance. Because some statutes provide only for a fixed amount, not taking into account changing times, the adequacy of these allowances may be questionable.

Other statutes are not so rigid. When your spouse dies, you as the surviving spouse are entitled to a reasonable support allowance for the statutory period. In some states this period is up to 12 months or more following the death of your spouse. The allowance may be granted by the court for the statutory period even though the estate proceeding may be completed and closed—as many estates are—within a shorter period. The allowance approved by the court may be paid in lump sum or over the period of the estate proceeding.

The amount of the allowance is sometimes based upon the station in life enjoyed by you prior to your spouse's death as well as upon the assets and condition of the decedent's estate. The size of the award also takes into consideration whether dependents or minor children of the decedent reside with you, since the allowance is for their benefit as well as yours.

The size of the allowance often is within the court's discretion, although courts tend to liberally construe the statute for the benefit of the surviving spouse and dependent family members. The size of your own estate and your ability to support yourself during the administration period frequently are deemed irrelevant.

The allowance is considered a debt of the estate, preferred over creditors and subordinated only to the costs of administration and funeral expenses. Being so, it can be deducted from the estate of the decedent to determine the net taxable estate for inheritance and estate tax purposes. Because of this deduction, which in effect reduces the amount of the death taxes, it would seem that the allowance should always be sought.

However, a portion or all of the allowance received may have to be reported by the surviving spouse as income on his or her individual income tax return. So the effect on the two taxes perhaps should be considered before an allowance is sought.

Only a lawful surviving spouse and one not the cause of the death is entitled to the allowance. Other prior conduct of the survivor may also be a factor in whether he or she receives the allowance. Some states do make a distinction between a widow and a widower, such states disagreeing as to whether such distinction is constitutional.

Minor children are usually included in the family allowance statutes. "Children" may include stepchildren. The marriage of the minor child or the child's illegitimacy may or may not affect the right to allowance.

Salvaging the Estate of an Unscrupulous Spouse

You may still be wondering whether your spouse could entirely disinherit you. What, you may ask, could my spouse do to prevent me from receiving part of his estate upon his death? This question assumes that you do not presently share in any part of his estate, as, for example, a co-owner of some of his property.

Before detailing the answer, it should quickly be said that even those states which never had or have since eliminated dower or curtesy have some plan protecting the surviving spouse.

Consider first the community property states. All property, with certain exceptions such as gifts and inheritances, acquired by the husband and wife during their marriage and while they are living in one of the community property states is community property. This property is shared equally between them even though, say, it may all have been accumulated by the efforts of only one spouse.

A will by one spouse leaving nothing to the surviving spouse cannot take away the survivor's share of the community property. However, most community property states do not provide for a widow's election except possibly as to augmented or quasi-community property. In brief, quasi-community property consists of *all* personal property, no matter where situated, and all real property situated in a community property state acquired by the decedent while he or she was living outside of that state.

The community property states do allow for some benefits, referred to as rights and allowances, for the surviving spouse. These may consist of the family dwelling (homestead), certain (exempt) personal property, or statutory amounts, as well as allowances for maintenance of the spouse and the decedent's children during the period of estate administration.

All states, including the community property states, give the surviving spouse at least a portion of the decedent's estate in the event that that decedent died intestate. And all the non–community property states (the common law states) give the surviving spouse the right to elect to take against the will and to take the distributive share. Such election can be used, for instance, in the event the decedent attempted to disinherit the surviving spouse.

Precluding the Spouse From Inheriting. So far we have been reviewing the rights of the surviving spouse at the time of the decedent's death. But what can one spouse—say, the husband—do during his lifetime that might preclude the surviving spouse from receiving any part of his estate?

In about half the states he could do nothing that would be successful unless the surviving spouse consented to and joined in the procedure. In many others he could do three things. Two of the methods involve creating nonprobate property so that neither a will nor laws of inheritance would apply. None of the ways contemplate that the other spouse consents to or joins in the transaction.

The following are three means of disinheriting the spouse:

1. *The one spouse can place his property in joint tenancy with someone other than his other spouse.* Upon the first spouse's death such jointly held property goes to the surviving joint tenant, to the exclusion of the surviving spouse. This would happen despite any will or laws of descent and distribution to the contrary.

2. *The one spouse can transfer his property into a trust which excludes his other spouse as a beneficiary.* Upon his death the trust property goes to those beneficiaries named in the trust. Again, this would happen despite any will or laws of descent and distribution to the contrary.

3. *The one spouse can transfer his property outright to a third party.* In other words, he can make a gift. The gifted property presumably is no part of his estate upon his death.

But these methods, since they do not involve the other spouse as a participant, will not be totally successful in many states. In these states, transfers of property by one spouse, without joinder or consent of the other spouse and especially if not for full consideration, are ineffective as to the statutory interest—often referred to as the dower interest—of the other spouse. In these situations the word *property* always covers real property, but in some states it also includes personal property.

If such nonjoinder transfers are made, the other spouse retains an interest in the property, which is recoverable by the nontransferring spouse at the time of death of the transferring spouse. Thus in these states it is impossible for one spouse to dispose of his or her property, and be totally successful at doing so, without the knowledge and consent of the other spouse.

Of course the transferring spouse could obtain the other spouse's consent and joinder through falsehoods and fraud but, if this fact were proven, such transactions would not stand up if challenged.

The Augmented Estate.   Normally, as indicated earlier, it is only probate property that is subject to the terms of the decedent's will or, if there is no will, the laws of inheritance. Nonprobate property, such as the decedent's property held in joint tenancy or in trust, is not subject to either.

But the property that has been disposed of by the decedent during his lifetime without such consent or joinder is for some purposes treated as probate property, at least to a limited extent. Some states label this property as the *augmented estate,* but all states that recognize this type of estate property tend to treat it somewhat the same insofar as protecting the interests of the surviving spouse.

If your husband made these transfers in an attempt to disinherit you, and if he lived in one of those states which protected your (dower) interest, then you would have the right to claim that portion of the transferred property given to you by statute under these circumstances. In most instances this share would be similar to or the same as the share you would receive if you elected to take against his will.

Some Common
Questions Answered

Q. Are my rights as a surviving spouse affected in any way if I have minor children?

A. Your concern seems to be whether the laws of descent and distribution give you a larger portion of your deceased spouse's estate under two circumstances: if your deceased spouse died intestate or if you elected not to take under the will. The answer is "no," since no state law distributing a decedent's estate after all debts and charges have been paid takes into consideration the wants or needs of an heir or a surviving spouse.

The above statement, however, applies only after the charges against the estate have been taken care of. One of the charges may be any allowance which you as surviving spouse may be entitled to. Many states provide for an allowance to the surviving spouse. The amount of the allowance may be fixed by statute or it may be discretionary with the court, based upon reasonableness.

The existence of dependents or minor children may or may not have a bearing on the allowance. It could make a difference, however, depending on whose children they are. It is not a question as to whether they are your children but, rather, whether they are children born to or legally adopted by the decedent. Stepchildren would not qualify. For those states that provide for family allowances and allow some discretion in the court to so provide, then you would be "affected" if your spouse left such minor children surviving.

Q. If I make an election either to take or not to take under my husband's will, can I subsequently change my mind?

A. It is doubtful. State statutes provide for the procedures involved in a will election. These procedures do not provide for revoking the election. Thus any attempt to do so would be a matter for the probate court to decide. What the court's decision would be could depend upon several things.

If the probate administration were completed and closed or if distribution were already started, it would be difficult for the court to permit an undoing of the proceedings. On the other hand, if the surviving spouse could show a misunderstanding or some other equitable reason for permitting a revoking of the election, such as fraud or duress, then the court might look favorably upon the request.

Q. Is the widow's allowance affected by the widow's election to take or not to take under the will?

A. No, the two are not normally connected in any manner. Regardless of how the widow(er) elects, the widow's allowance is a statutory right which is not based on whether the widow elects to take or not to take under the will.

In most states, the allowance only indirectly affects the widow's share of the estate by reducing the divisible estate. This doesn't apply to those few states that have no provision for a widow's or family allowance or that provide for a deduction of the widow's elective share based upon the allowance. This means that because the allowance has some priority and is treated as a court cost, the larger the allowance, the less estate assets remain for distribution to the widow and others.

Q. Is it possible, by use of the will election process, to select what portion of the bequest is desired?

A. No. If you elect to take under the will, you take exactly what the will provides. If you elect against the will, you take exactly what the statute provides. However by use of your state disclaimer statute, if any, you may be able to disclaim a portion of the bequest.

Q. If I elect against my husband's will, is it possible for me to receive a portion of his property which he holds in joint tenancy with another party?

A. You may, depending upon whether you consented to join or actually joined in the transfer of the property into the joint tenancy. If you did join in or consent to the transfer into joint tenancy, then at that point you gave up your rights, if any, to the property. Thus upon your husband's death you can make no claim to the property.

Otherwise it depends upon what state your husband resides in at the time of his death. The general rule is that the rights of election only apply against probate property. Joint tenancy property is considered nonprobate property and thus would not normally be included.

However a number of states specifically include, in addition to probate property, the augmented estate and quasi–community property. Gifts (such as joint tenancy) in fraud of marital rights are sometimes specifically included, and fraudulent gifts of any sort probably would be included in many other states as well, even though not specifically included in their statutes.

Q. Why isn't there conformity among the states as to the rights of a surviving spouse to share in the deceased spouse's estate?

A. Perhaps there is no conformity because each state has the sovereign right to control—actually to own—the property located within its borders. The federal government has no voice in the matter. Any right to inheritance and right to property given to individuals is by the grace of the state. Thus the possibility exists that there could be 50 different versions as to any particular property matter.

Fortunately, there is some similarity among the states' laws due to their ancestry either in the English common law or in the French and Spanish laws. Similarity has also come about because of the efforts of the National Conference of Commissioners on Uniform State Laws. This conference proposes uniform and model acts which are then available to the states for passage. Some states enact the proposals intact, some pass acts substantially similar to the proposed ones, some ignore these suggested acts and devise their own statutes, and some take no action whatsoever. But until, if ever, agreement is reached among the various states, no hope for conformity exists.

Q. If I am considered legally married to my wife at the time of her death, are there any circumstances which could preclude me from any rights to her estate?

A. Yes. All but a handful of states provide that certain predeath actions of the surviving spouse preclude him from exercising rights otherwise available under the law. Murder, or participation in such action, of one spouse by the other is the most common of these actions.

But other actions of the surviving spouse may also be grounds for loss of rights. These are (1) obtaining a divorce or an annulment or consenting to do so in another state even though the action may not be valid in the state of residence, (2) participating in a proceeding to terminate all marital rights, (3) unintentionally causing the death of the other spouse, (4) abandoning, deserting, or failing to support the other spouse, or living apart from her, without sufficient cause, or (5) living in adultery or in a bigamous relationship with another person. Also a loss of rights could occur if the marriage is determined to have been incestuous, bigamous, or prohibited by law, and thus void, or if a valid decree of separation existed between the two parties.

Q. If during our marriage my spouse conveys away to a third party, including a trust, all of his real property without my consent and joinder and thereafter dies, do I have any claim to such property?

A. An inadequate but correct answer is "possibly, but probably not." Most states no longer protect a spouse from inter vivos—that is, lifetime—real estate transfers made by the other spouse, unless the transfer (1) was deemed fraudulent, (2) was not made in good faith, (3) consisted of part of the augmented estate, (4) consisted of community property, (5) was made for the purpose of defeating the spouse's marital rights, or (6) was made to an inter vivos trust over which the decedent retained substantial control.

Unless the transfer is seen to have occurred under one or more of the above conditions, the rights of the surviving spouse usually, but not always, apply only to the probate estate assets of the deceased spouse. The old common law concept of protecting the surviving spouse with dower or curtesy has to a great extent disappeared. The community property states do not have any consistent pattern as to the spouse's rights. Some have determined that the living spouse's rights only apply to the decedent's probate assets, and some have not. And in a few states whether the transferred property by the deceased spouse is free from any claim of the surviving spouse depends on when the transfer occurred.

15

Minimizing
Estate Proceedings

When a person dies owning property of any kind, usually an estate proceeding of some kind is required. This proceeding sometimes is known as a probate proceeding, although the term *estate proceeding* is used here because the proceeding may take many different forms. Some of these proceedings are informal and held out of court and thus should not be labeled as probate proceedings. Thus the word *estate* is used in lieu of the word *probate*, which tends to have a limited meaning.

Avoiding probate is a desirable objective, but it is one difficult to achieve since some form of estate proceeding is usually necessary upon a death, regardless of whatever steps you might have taken to avoid it.

Whether the decedent leaves a will is irrelevant. The statutory laws relating to the necessity and form of proceeding are governed by the extent and kind of property left by the decedent and how title to it was held. They are not governed by whether the decedent died testate (with a will) or intestate (without a will).

As noted, the term *estate proceeding* denotes any kind of proceeding legally required or deemed necessary after the death of an owner of real or personal property. Perhaps the only necessary estate proceedings would be tax procedures required to relieve the property of any possible tax liens. Or perhaps the only required procedure would be to effect the transfer of title out of the decedent's name into that of another. In either event only the most minimum proceeding would be utilized to accomplish what needs to be done.

Obviously, no estate proceeding of any kind is necessary if upon death a decedent had no interest in any property whatsoever, either inter alia, as a titleholder, co-owner, reserved life tenant, or beneficiary under a self-created revocable trust. Unless you are unusual, however, most likely you cannot claim that you have no property interests of any kind and no property rights whatsoever. Only if you actually did could you avoid an estate proceeding.

There can be many reasons for having an estate proceeding, such as for payment of a decedent's debts and handling of claims against the estate, for supervising and managing the estate property, for collecting and distributing estate assets, for establishing marketable title to real estate, for securing title changes and transfers, for reporting and paying death taxes, and for carrying out the provisions of the decedent's will or the laws of inheritance.

Many things determine what type of estate proceeding is required after the death of a property owner, such as the nature and extent of the decedent's property, how title to the property was held by the decedent, the terms of a will, family relationships, the age and competency of heirs or beneficiaries, the existing creditors, and even the amount of cooperation given to the surviving heirs by third parties.

Preliminary Procedures

Before any estate proceeding is begun, a lawyer must analyze the situation with the help of the surviving spouse and heirs. Technically, the word *heirs* refers to an intestate situation and the word *beneficiaries* to a testate situation, but for convenience both groups will hereafter be referred to as heirs or distributees.

The lawyer analyzes the situation to determine what type of estate proceeding needs to be undertaken. This step is an important one because a full estate proceeding—variously called an administration of the estate, a formal probate, or a supervised administration—should not be instigated unless it is found to be necessary. In this regard, what probably dictates the need for administration is the existence of probate property, not the mere existence of a will.

The initial inquiry requires an examination of the decedent's assets to determine their nature and how title to such property is held. The assets might include bank accounts, certificates of deposit, title certificates, abstracts of title or deeds representative of real property, stocks, bonds, life insurance, and so on. As you can imagine, evidence of such assets may be found almost anywhere, which sometimes makes the search for it frustrating. But, with luck, most of the assets will be found in the decedent's safe-deposit box.

The lawyer's first order of business, therefore, is to locate and assemble, with the help of the heirs, all of the decedent's property in which she or he had an interest. At this early stage, however, it may not be possible to complete the inquiry because some information may be missing. And it may not be available until or unless a personal representative has been appointed.

This property is then listed and categorized according to how title was held by the decedent. And the will, if any, of the decedent is read either formally or informally to determine the wishes of the testator. By doing these things the lawyer is able to advise the heirs as to what is required.

A delay in immediately taking steps toward an estate proceeding following a death has been advocated. This delay, it is thought, will prevent the heirs from doing something that upon reflection would be found to be unnecessary. For instance, suppose an administration is opened and thereafter it is determined that all of the decedent's property was held in joint tenancy with the right of survivorship. Since the decedent's jointly held property would be considered nonprobate property, no reason would exist for administration.

The delay may also enable the heirs to experience less stress. By waiting, they may be better able to act conscientiously.

With this suggestion, though, one thing not considered is what needs to be done by the heirs following a death. By carefully assembling all of the assets and determining how the decedent held title to each, as well as reading the decedent's will, a lawyer can easily determine the required form of probate proceeding. Mere delay cannot change the kind of proceeding that will be required. Of course, choosing the procedure should be delayed until enough relevant information has been obtained to determine the route that must be taken.

Be aware that when estate procedures are delayed, the decedent's personal assets, whether tangible or intangible, have a way of disappearing or at least of becoming more difficult to identify. This, unfortunately, is a result of human nature.

Delay may never be an option if the decedent is a businessperson, such as a farmer, and the business is a part of the estate. In many business situations the parties involved cannot wait for "things to calm down." Often, decisions involving the estate must be made expeditiously, and they can only be made by someone with authority. Possibly the only one having such authority under these circumstances is a personal representative.

Remember, a distinction should be made between an estate proceeding and an administration of an estate. As has been pointed out, an administration is only one kind of estate proceeding. Other kinds of estate proceedings exist, and any one of them may be sufficient at the time of a person's death.

For example, real property of the decedent held in joint tenancy—called *nonprobate property*—is not subject to administration. But such property upon the death of its owner must be reported in some form of estate proceeding, however minor. The death of the first tenant must be noted of record and such property must be cleared from the possibility of any death tax liens. The latter requirement is necessary because joint tenancy property, like other nonprobate property, is subject to death taxes, the same as probate property.

The sections that follow discuss some of the various estate requirements that may arise upon the death of a property owner. While reading them, keep in mind that upon a death the circumstances of the situation will dictate what minimum procedures are required.

The following general discussion of procedural law should enable you to be better informed about the various legal requirements in an estate proceeding. Specific procedures in any particular situation should be left to your attorney to determine and apply.

Probate Procedure Versus Administration

Confusion apparently exists because of the inability of many laypersons to distinguish between the terms "estate (or probate) proceeding" and "administration of an estate." Perhaps this difficulty is caused by lawyers themselves who in everyday language tend to use the various terms interchangeably without regard to which is technically correct.

An administration of an estate is only one of several kinds of possible estate proceedings. It occurs when a court is petitioned to appoint a personal representative, sometimes called an *administrator* if no will exists and an *executor* if one does, to administer the estate (property) of a decedent.

Probate Property Versus Nonprobate Property

What determines whether or not an estate will be administered is not the existence or nonexistence of a will but whether the decedent owned probate property. Such property is subject to formal probate administration. It is to be distinguished from nonprobate property, which is not subject to probate administration. With certain exceptions, probate property can be dealt with only by a personal representative who handles or manages the administration proceeding.

Nonprobate property is not subject to a decedent's will or to the laws of inheritance. Such property might be held in joint tenancy, trust, or life insurance. Life insurance might also become probate property, but only if the beneficiary named in the policy were the decedent's estate.

The decedent's probate property is disposed of according to his or her will or, if no will exists, according to the laws of inheritance. Nonprobate property is disposed of according to the instrument that created it. For example, joint tenancy property goes to the surviving joint tenant and proceeds from a life insurance policy go to the designated beneficiary, all regardless of other considerations.

Not being subject to administration does not mean that the nonprobate property escapes being subject to death taxes. For this reason nonprobate property must be listed and included in any estate proceeding that is used to determine death taxes.

Determining the Right Estate Proceeding to Use

If the decedent's probate property is not administered, possible results for the decedent's estate could be title to probate property not being rendered marketable, debts not being paid, personal property not being correctly distributed, and income and death tax returns not being filed (which could result in a penalty).

On the other hand, if the decedent owned nothing but nonprobate property at the time of death, or if the size and nature of the decedent's property fell within certain statutory exceptions, then the proceeding might be something less than a formal, court-supervised administration of an estate.

The term *estate proceeding* may also refer to other kinds of legal proceedings not necessarily related to death, such as a conservatorship or a court-administered trust. Or it may refer to a legal proceeding within an estate proceeding, such as a contested will or a sale of real estate.

Good estate planning takes into account the type of proceeding that may be required at the time of a person's death. But avoidance of administration is only one of the factors considered by a lawyer in planning an estate. This may be difficult for most of us to understand, especially since we no doubt would like to avoid any kind of legal proceeding.

Determining the right estate procedure to use is a difficult situation for lawyers, too. Their motives may be misconstrued. They could be regarded as having a conflict of interest. For example, suppose your lawyer advises against joint tenancy. You may perceive her motive to be to perpetuate estate administration, to promote her self-interest.

So that both you and your lawyer are comfortable about deciding which procedure to use, you should openly discuss the pros and cons of using a particular procedure. You should also discuss what type of attorney's fees could be charged.

Four Types of Proceedings

At least four different estate proceedings exist upon a death: (1) affidavit or notice type of proceeding, (2) death tax proceeding, sometimes referred to as short form of estate proceeding, (3) informal or small estate administration, and (4) formal administration, sometimes referred to as full, regular, or solemn administration. The first two and sometimes the third are unsupervised proceedings whereas the last one is a supervised proceeding.

Three things should be mentioned before the types of proceedings are discussed. One is that states vary in their interpretation of what constitutes a probate asset. For instance, most states refer to real property as a probate asset. But some consider it a nonprobate asset. For those that call it nonprobate property, however, the real property can still be deemed available for the payment of debts and claims against the decedent's estate. It can be when other assets are found to be insufficient for the payment.

The second thing is that in some instances time alone may do away with the requirement of certain estate proceedings. This may be the result of a statute of limitation, other statutory authority, or merely a particular local custom.

Few lawyers are willing to advise their clients to wait for the passage of any extended time, however. Too many events can occur in the meantime that would require an estate proceeding of some sort. And clients tend to forget what they promised to do or not to do in order to avoid the particular estate proceeding.

The third thing is that you do not have to know every detail about every possible variance. You should just be aware in general terms of the most customary forms of proceedings. Which specific procedures to use should be left to your attorney to decide.

If you feel that your attorney is requiring more elaborate proceedings than deemed necessary, then you should seek a second opinion or change lawyers.

The Affidavit

An affidavit might not ordinarily be considered an estate proceeding, but in estates with total assets having little or minimum value an affidavit may accomplish all that is necessary after a death. Possibly all that is required is the filing of a certified copy of a death certificate.

An affidavit may also be all that is required when the decedent owns nothing other than nonprobate property at the time of death. This would especially apply if such property were jointly held with a person exempt from death taxes.

For example, suppose a decedent dies while individually owning nothing but a small bank account. Ordinarily upon an account owner's death, a financial institution will release the monies in that account only to the personal representative of the decedent's estate.

But what if the account owner were trying to avoid formal administration, in which case no personal representative would be appointed? Assuming no controlling statute dictated otherwise, if the financial institution could be convinced that no probate proceedings would be opened, that the account was the only property owned by the decedent, and that the institution would not incur any liability in doing so, it might be willing to release the account without a formalized estate proceeding.

Often this release of account monies can be accomplished by use of an affidavit, sometimes accompanied by an indemnity agreement. The affidavit serves as notice to the interested party. To be acceptable to a financial institution, the document may have to accomplish several things. It must identify the decedent with the account, identify the heirs and spouse, if any, of the decedent, recite that no other estate proceeding will be instigated, state what other assets are owned by the deceased, show that no death taxes are due or payable, and prove that all debts and expenses of the decedent have been paid. The heirs may also be required to agree to indemnify and hold harmless the financial institution from any and all claims that could result from the release of the monies in the account to someone other than the decedent's personal representative.

An affidavit must be signed before a notary—sworn to, in other words—by all the heirs and the surviving spouse, if any. Even then the institution may be reluctant to release the funds unless, as an added precaution, it could issue a check made payable to all of the heirs and surviving spouse—all as identified in the affidavit—and to the mortuary that handled the decedent's funeral. The latter is included because a funeral home normally has statutory priority to the funds. By including the funeral home in the check the institution could further protect itself from claims by third parties.

The above affidavit procedure is not necessarily based upon any statute. Sometimes it is based upon custom developed over a period of years. However several states, primarily those that have adopted the Uniform Probate Code (UPC), have enacted an affidavit procedure that allows personal property of limited value to be transferred without court involvement. A short waiting period, say 30 to 40 days, may be required before the procedure can be utilized.

The affidavit is signed by one or more successors in interest who may be heirs or beneficiaries. A will may have to be admitted to probate or otherwise filed and made a matter of record. Because the affiant, the one who signs the affidavit, may be subject at some time to perjury charges, he or she may be required to enter into an indemnity agreement or put up bond.

The value of the entire estate, less liens and encumbrances, cannot exceed the statutory limit. Among the states the limit varies anywhere from $5000 to $60,000. Any party responding to the affidavit is held free from liability and need not inquire into the truth of the affidavit.

If an estate is liable for death taxes, then additional or substitute procedures may be required. And if for any reason an administration proceeding is opened, then the affidavit procedure either will not be available or will be nullified.

Because of the small dollar limit involved and because many people die owning valuable real property not held in joint tenancy or some other nonprobate form, the affidavit procedure has somewhat restricted availability.

The Short Form of Estate Proceeding

The short form of estate proceeding is primarily concerned with those estates containing only nonprobate property. The main purposes of the proceeding are to establish merchantable title in real estate (see below) and to remove any possibility of death taxes.

Establishing Title.   As is the case whenever a titleholder of real estate dies, the record must show an unbroken chain of title. If nothing whatsoever were done upon the death of a titleholder, a break in the chain of title would occur since the record would be silent as to what happened to the deceased titleholder.

Suppose, for instance, that land records show that Carl and Anne hold title to certain real estate as joint tenants with right of survivorship. Subsequently, the title record shows a deed from Anne to a third party. Nothing appears in the record as to what happened to Carl. Do you believe that anyone, a lawyer or layperson alike, would accept title as the record stands without demanding to know what happened to Carl? Without this showing, the title would be deemed *unmerchantable*, meaning that no one would be willing to purchase the property.

In this example, the record thus must show that the titleholder died. The mere absence of a titleholder in the chain—referred to as a break in the chain or a missing link—does not legally give rise to a supposition or presumption that the missing titleholder is dead. The record title must show or prove this to be the case.

When a titleholder to real estate at the time of death owns property alone or with others as tenants in common, so that each tenant owns an undivided interest in the property, then the only way to avoid a break in the chain is by a formal administration. The administration proceeding, which is a matter of record, itself is the link in the chain, thus preventing a break.

When a titleholder owns property with a spouse as tenants by the entirety or as joint tenants with right of survivorship, then, upon the titleholder's death, title to the property automatically vests in the surviving spouse. Whether the titleholder died testate (with a will) or intestate (no will) or also owned other property is immaterial. Title to that particular jointly held property vests in the spouse as surviving tenant.

Although the title vests automatically, the fact of death must be proven of record as stated above. States vary as to how this is to be accomplished. Sometimes the mere filing of a death certificate is sufficient. Sometimes a filing of an affidavit by a knowledgeable person is all that is necessary. Sometimes the filing of an inventory or other more formalized document is required. Information contained in the inventory would show the fact of death, the same as would an affidavit.

These estate proceedings, such as they are, all have one thing in common. They reveal and prove the fact of death. By operation of the law of survivorship the rest is automatic.

Removing the Possibility of a Death Tax Lien.   What about the second need, to show that the death of the first tenant did not create a liability—and hence a possible lien on the property—for death taxes? These so-called death taxes are the federal estate tax and any state estate or inheritance tax. If liability for death taxes was incurred by the death, then the goal would be to show that such taxes were paid and any possible lien therefore released and satisfied.

Until these taxes are paid and the lien released or until it is proven that no liability for the taxes exists, then the title to the decedent's real estate would again be deemed unmerchantable. No one would be willing to buy the property because a lien might exist for the payment of these taxes.

As noted in Chapter 16, in tenancies by the entirety, and in joint tenancies where the sole surviving tenant is the spouse of the deceased, then no showing need be made as to the federal estate tax. Since the surviving spouse has an unlimited marital deduction, meaning a 100 percent exemption, any property passing outright to him or her in any manner is free of any claim for federal estate taxes. A state death tax may not exist either.

That fact may not be true with joint tenancies between persons other than spouses. Spouses generally have the most generous tax exemptions. Exemptions for others decrease and eventually disappear entirely as the relationship of the joint survivor to the decedent becomes farther removed.

When the joint tenants are not spouses, or when the joint tenants include a third party in addition to the two spouses, then tax proceedings will usually be required. They will be because the surviving joint tenant will either have no federal or state exemption or will have an exemption limited in value. Tax proceedings will then have to be undertaken to determine the tax, if any, and to have it paid. These tax proceedings may be nominal if only a state tax is involved, but extensive if a federal tax is involved.

If the total gross estate, as defined by the IRS, exceeds $600,000, then a federal estate tax return, known as form 706, must be filed. As you might expect, a 35-page form is not simple to complete. Many attachments (exhibits) are required and some decisions (called elections) must be made. Any mistakes in judgment and preparation can be extremely costly.

State death tax returns may be simple or also quite extensive. For uniformity, presumably, some state tax forms tend to follow the federal form, regardless of the size of the estate. Others have managed to keep their forms more simple. When required, returns must be filed to determine liability and to avoid possible liens against the property.

The end result of both the federal and state tax procedures is that an official document is filed of record to show that the particular tax proceeding has been accomplished.

Additional Requirements.　Even after the two goals—preserving the chain of title and clearing the title from possible death taxes—are accomplished, other things not a matter of public record should also be done.

The deceased tenant's name and social security number must be removed from all joint accounts, stocks, bonds (except E or EE bonds), and similar assets. The decedent's name must also be removed from all insurance policies, whether casualty, medical, life, or otherwise. It might not have to be on a life insurance policy if alternate names were shown as beneficiaries. But as to a casualty policy, the name's removal precludes a later claim check from being made out to the deceased tenant in the event of a loss.

You must also remove the decedent's name from any licensed vehicle registration. You should check with the tax assessor and be sure that you do not need to reapply for homestead or veteran's exemptions, if these are available. Otherwise subsequent property tax bills may be higher than they need to be.

Finally, if your will names the deceased tenant as a beneficiary, you and your attorney should review the will to be certain that the tenant's death does not necessitate any changes. Ordinarily no change should be necessary, since a will should always provide for alternate beneficiaries. But it would be foolish for you to merely assume so. The possibility always exists that the death creates a new situation that requires your will to be redrawn. And you may want to provide for another alternate.

One more thing should be considered. If the deceased tenant was your spouse, presumably you were named in the decedent's will as primary beneficiary. Under these circumstances many lawyers take one more precautionary step.

Many state statutes place a time limit on when a will may be admitted to probate after the testator's death. Thus very cautious lawyers prefer that the decedent's will be admitted to probate without administration in order to preserve it. This is considered a safeguard in case other assets of the decedent turn up in the future, assets which were not held by the both of you as joint tenants. Assuming the will bequeaths all property to you, you are thus certain to receive all of decedent's property, whether by reason of the tenancies or by reason of the admitted will.

Administration Proceedings

Upon your death the above procedures may not be adequate to fulfill the requirements of the law. Your estate may then have to be formally administered by a personal representative appointed by the court. The personal representative serves in a fiduciary capacity, the same as does a conservator or trustee.

The court oversees the administration proceedings. Thus the process is sometimes called a supervised or formal legal proceeding.

All states have a probate code of some sort. These codes specify what a personal representative can or cannot do. Generally he or she oversees the management and disposal of an estate.

The person who administers an intestate estate is called an administrator and the person who administers a testate estate is called an executor. To avoid having to make this distinction, this book will hereafter refer to such a person as the "personal representative."

Only a few distinctions can be made between administration of a testate estate and administration of an intestate estate. Generally, the differences are procedural rather than substantive in nature and thus they should concern only your attorney.

During the estate proceedings, the probate court, through one of its officials, supervises the proceedings. The official may be variously known as the probate referee, the probate clerk, the Registrar, or the Register of Wills. Whether the court itself does more than merely oversee the estate proceeding depends upon what the particular situation may be. A contested or adversarial proceeding directly involves the court, rather than one of the court's agents.

The administration of an estate has many purposes, but in a sense it allows for the completion and termination of the decedent's legal and financial affairs. It determines who are the successors in interest to the decedent's property. And, of course, it is the vehicle for handling all tax matters, including both income and death taxes. Other purposes perhaps will become obvious as you read through this section.

General Procedure. To open an estate proceeding, a petition is filed in the appropriate state court asking that the decedent's will, if any, be admitted to probate, and that the party named in the will be appointed as executor. If there is no will, then the petition asks for the appointment of a specific party as administrator.

Notice of this action then is published in an approved newspaper, generally in the county in which the estate is pending. Some deadlines for taking various types of required probate actions run from the date of death and some run from the date of this publication.

Missing a deadline of any kind can be cause for the removal of either the lawyer or the personal representative, or both. Or, possibly even worse, a missed deadline, such as in tax matters, can result in personal liability of the personal representative or possibly a malpractice claim against the representative's attorney.

After the estate is opened, the first duty of the fiduciary is to marshal all of the decedent's assets, that is, to secure information concerning all of the property interests of the decedent, whether owned in his or her name alone or jointly with others. Such assets must also include such things as unpaid wages, life estates, property located in another state, trust property, growing crops, livestock, business property, pensions and profit-sharing plans, and life insurance. The existence and correctness of the assets must be verified before the next step is undertaken.

This asset information is then reported on an inventory form and filed with the county official, hereafter referred to as the probate clerk, handling probate matters. Presumably much or all of the information required for the inventory is secured before the estate proceeding is opened.

A copy of the filed inventory is sent to each heir or residuary beneficiary. Beneficiaries who receive only a specified bequest in a will normally are omitted, since the inventory of total estate assets ought not be their concern. The same would apply to a surviving joint tenant who is otherwise not a residuary beneficiary. The inventory will reflect the market values of all of the estate property, including accrued interest to date of death as to those assets bearing interest.

Ordinarily the state probate code will specify the time limit as to when this inventory is to be filed. Sometimes, however, there can be delays in filing the inventory. These can happen for any number of valid reasons. For example, if estate property is to be sold, the estate lawyer may wish to delay the filing of the inventory until a sale, so that the purchase price may be used as the value of the property inventoried. Courts have discretionary powers in granting extensions of time to file.

The values shown on the inventory determine whether a federal estate tax return is due upon the death. The values also indicate whether any state death taxes are due.

If you are appointed as the personal representative, the court will give you a document perhaps entitled "Letters of Administration" or "Letters of Appointment." This document shows your authority to take charge of the assets of the decedent. As may be required by a holder of a particular asset, such as a financial institution, the letters are presented to show the authority of the personal representative to take over the asset.

If the decedent owned stock in a publicly held corporation, then the process of transferring the stock may be more difficult. Corporations of publicly held securities designate a transfer agent, usually a bank, to handle transfers of their stock. Although similarities exist among the transfers, each transfer agent has its own requirements for transferring the stock out of the name of the decedent. No standardized procedure for such transfers exist.

Keeping Books of Account. The personal representative has the responsibility of keeping books of account of all financial transactions occurring during the period of the estate. This is done for two purposes.

One is to be able to account to the distributees at the close of the proceeding as to all financial transactions that occurred during the period of the estate. The books must balance and every item must be accounted for. This itemized accounting is given to all distributees sharing in the residue of the estate. They are given it at the time they are asked to approve the proceedings and consent to the closing of the estate. Each heir or beneficiary has the right to determine that the proceedings have been carried out properly. In many instances this can be determined only by examining the accounting records.

The other purpose in having a record of the financial activity is so that the state and federal income tax returns can be prepared and filed for the estate. Normally, the estate cannot be closed until an income tax release or acquittance is received from the state. This release is obtainable only after the required returns are filed and taxes paid. A similar release is seldom requested of the federal government because of burdensome requirements imposed by the IRS.

Unfortunately, many individuals serving as personal representatives fail to understand the importance of keeping accurate books. Probably they do so because they lack training or experience in keeping financial records. As a result, their accounting records are often incomplete or indecipherable.

Miscellaneous Procedures.   Many situations occur during the administration of an estate, some of which may be peculiar only to that estate. Because many are not common to all estates, only mention of some of them will be made: sale proceedings, proceedings to surrender possession of estate assets prior to closing, proceedings to retain possession of estate assets beyond the statutory period, proceedings to determine heirship, proceedings regarding claims against the estate, proceedings involving will construction, proceedings to set off share to surviving spouse, and proceedings relative to a small bequest to a minor.

Closing of the Proceeding.   When all statutory and estate requirements have been met, then the personal representative gives a copy of the accounting and final report to each residuary distributee. If the distributee approves of the actions of the personal representative, then the distributee is asked to sign a waiver of any further notice and to consent to the closing of the estate proceeding. When all distributees do this, then the papers are filed with the probate clerk. If the court or appropriate official approves of the proceedings and finds all matters completed, then the estate proceeding is ordered closed.

If for some reason a distributee objects to any part of the proceedings or accounting, a court hearing is held on the final report and accounting. A determination is then made by the court as to the objections. Then the court, upon such objections being satisfied, enters an order closing the estate, discharging the personal representative, and releasing the bond, if any.

How Is Title Transferred?   Sometimes people who inherit real estate worry because they have nothing in hand, such as a deed, to show that they are now the owners of such inherited property. This situation does not present any legal problem at all.

Recall the expression "link in the chain of title." Each time a transfer of title to real property occurs, a link in the chain of title is established. Each time a warranty deed is given by a seller to a buyer, the deed constitutes a link in the chain.

If the record shows a deed from A to B and then a deed from C to D, there is said to be a break in the chain of title since no deed appears from B to C. But the chain is not broken if title passed from B to C in some other manner. One way of title passing other than by deed is by inheritance.

If a parent dies and the child inherits the property, either by will or by the laws of inheritance, the deceased parent's administration proceeding constitutes a link in the chain of title. This estate proceeding is a matter of record the same as the deed is a matter of record. Because of the estate record, there is no missing link.

Unlike the usual deed transfer, however, in an estate administration normally no document passes from, or is issued by, the personal representative to a distributee who inherits the property. In this situation the estate record is deemed sufficient to show change of title. This sometimes makes the heir or beneficiary uncomfortable, because he or she has nothing in hand to prove or show title.

But the public record of the estate proceeding exists. The estate record will show up on the record title to the inherited property the next time it is checked because of a pending sale transaction or mortgage loan.

What About Estate Costs?   Not surprisingly, laypersons worry about the costs of administering an estate. These expenses consist of court costs and fees payable for services rendered by the personal representative and the representative's attorney. Other expenses may consist of charges for the fiduciary's bond and for appraisal fees and sometimes sales expenses.

Some jurisdictions require all property to be appraised. Others may require an appraisal only of that property that is to be sold by the representative. In the latter event the appraisal will guide both the representative and the court in determining that a fair price is being obtained for the sale property. And sometimes a state taxing body or the IRS wants certain property, such as real estate, to be appraised in order to be reassured that it is properly valued for death tax purposes.

As to bond costs, if a decedent dies testate, then chances are that the decedent's will provides that the personal representative is to serve without bond. But if the will does not so state, or if the decedent dies intestate, then most jurisdictions require that the representative put up a bond. The cost of the bond is generally based upon the size of the bond. The size, in turn, may depend upon the amount of personal property in the estate, or the court may set the amount of bond based upon some other criteria.

No doubt you are concerned about administration costs. Because of this concern you probably have thought about trying to avoid probate. That topic is covered in Chapter 11.

All states but Connecticut and New Hampshire make some provision in their statutes for fees payable to the personal representative. Fees in those two states generally are based upon what the probate court believes is reasonable, although, through usage, fees tend to be somewhat uniform. Such fees tend to be based upon a percentage of the estate, although all property, whether considered probate or nonprobate property, is not necessarily included in the computation.

Other state statutes provide that the fees either shall be reasonable—as determined by the court—or shall be as set out in a percentage table. As the value of the chargeable estate goes up, the percent chargeable goes down. Mostly the tables are intended to show the maximum percent that may be charged and rarely the minimum. Usually the so-called statutory fee may exceed the amounts set by the table if extraordinary services are performed by the representative.

Some states seem to provide for a high percentage rate. However, it is difficult to compare rates, since what is included in the chargeable estate varies considerably from state to state. For instance, the value of the probate real estate may not be included in the chargeable estate unless it is sold. Or the chargeable estate may or may not include the value of receipts and disbursements passing through the hands of the representative. Or the chargeable estate may be based only upon the value of the probate assets, excluding nonprobate property such as life insurance.

No matter how fees are determined, the probate courts or one of their designated officials ultimately determine and approve the reasonableness of the charges and whether extraordinary fees are justified. Extraordinary services are often deemed warranted for services rendered in connection with real estate sales, taxes, and litigation.

The Attorney's Representation.   In some states, the lawyer handling the legal work for the estate proceeding is deemed to be the attorney only for the personal representative. In other states, the lawyer is deemed to also represent the estate and the distributees.

If a possible conflict of interest appears, the estate lawyer must be certain that all interested parties are aware who he or she represents. In such instances the lawyer normally recommends that opposing parties engage their own lawyer to personally represent them.

As to fees for services rendered, many state statutes treat the attorney in much the same manner as the personal representative. If a statute provides for reasonable fees for the representative, then the same goes for the attorney. And if a statute provides for a percentage fee for the representative, then the same applies to the attorney.

The application for attorney fees is usually, but not always, made by the fiduciary. But it is the attorney that prepares the application for the representative's signature, as would normally be true of any document filed with the court.

Attorney and representative fees are figured in much the same way whether the proceeding is testate or intestate, since both the administrator of an intestate estate and the executor of a testate estate and their respective attorneys have similar duties and responsibilities.

The closeness of the family relationship of the personal representative to the decedent has no bearing on the representative's right to be paid, since the fees are for services rendered and for the time spent by the representative in handling the affairs of the estate.

This does not mean that the representative, even though entitled to a fee, necessarily takes or even wants one. Nor does it necessarily mean that different parties who might represent the same estate are entitled to the same fee. Many estates, for one reason or another, may require a more professional fiduciary, such as a bank, to be used. Under such circumstances the more-experienced representative may well be entitled to a larger fee than the novice fiduciary.

Probate Procedure Checklist.   Many of the more important estate procedures required upon the death of a property owner have been discussed in this chapter. But a checklist of possible estate procedures may be of some help to you, even though this list is by no means exhaustive. It only covers the more typical situations. Because some of this list applies whether or not a full administration is required, you may want to use the list for the informal, unsupervised estate proceedings as well.

By perusing the list you may be able to anticipate what type of proceeding might be required upon your death or that of a family member. And if you are now or will become a personal representative, you may wish to determine what actions you may be required to take in order to accomplish your obligations. As you examine the list, assume that a death has just occurred and that the decedent died testate. If the decedent died intestate, most of the procedures would still be similar, however. The list is somewhat in chronological order, but the order in any estate proceeding will vary to suit its own needs.

It is the personal representative who is legally responsible for performing the listed tasks. Thus the list is prepared from the point of view of the representative. If the representative is a bank, many of these duties would be performed without the help of the lawyer. But if an individual is serving as the representative, then the lawyer actually does much of the work.

When you are told to do something, do not be alarmed if you cannot do it without help. In one sense, the lawyer is your assistant, guiding you along. In another sense, the lawyer is your boss, telling you what must be done and how to do it. In almost all cases, if a document needs to be prepared and filed or mailed, the lawyer will do it for you. In such instances, perhaps all you need do is sign your name.

Now suppose a testator has died. His or her will names you as the personal representative. What must now be done?

1. Immediately notify the lawyer. He or she may possess the deceased's instructions as to organ donations and funeral arrangements. Such instructions may be contained in the decedent's will, although their primary location should be independent of the will.

2. Arrange for a meeting with the lawyer. It should occur before heirs leave town after the funeral for their own places of residence. All parties will benefit if they hear the initial comments from the lawyer. This first interview is probably the most important consultation in the proceeding. The lawyer has an opportunity to advise the spouse and heirs what to expect in the way of procedure, time frames, and costs. At the same time the survivors have a chance to ask questions.

3. Conduct a reading of the will and determine the estate's assets. A preliminary inventory of the decedent's assets may have to be made to ascertain the extent of the assets and how title was held by the decedent. Included in the inventory should be the contents of the safe deposit box, if any. When these preliminaries are completed, the attorney should be able to determine the kind of probate proceeding required.

Note: In this sample list the decedent is assumed to have left a substantial estate so that full administration of the estate would be necessary. However some of the following steps would also apply even if the decedent only held nonprobate property, such as joint tenancy property, or had a living trust to avoid probate.

4. Secure your qualification as the personal representative. This involves filing a petition with the probate court, asking that the will be admitted to probate and that you as the personal representative named in the will be appointed. The procedure for proving the will depends upon whether the will is self-proved. If it is not, one or both witnesses to the will must be produced to testify as to its authenticity. If the will fails to waive bond, then you must secure either a bond or a waiver of bond. You must sign an oath of office.

5. Make certain that the clerk has entered an order opening the estate, admitting the will to probate, and appointing the personal representative. Obtain your Letters of Administration (Letters Testamentary) from the clerk. These show your authority to act for and on behalf of the estate.

6. Give a photocopy of the will to all beneficiaries named in the will (except possibly minors or incompetents). Include an explanation of the estate process and the expected time before completion and distribution.

7. File a designation of the attorney so that the court (clerk) will know with whom to deal in the proceeding.

8. File with the court a declination to take a fee, if you intend not to take a fee for serving as representative. This will prevent the IRS from later imputing a fee to you for serving as such fiduciary.

9. Mail IRS form SS-4 to the IRS, applying for an employer identification number. Since the estate is considered a taxable entity, an identification number must be obtained. This number is used on all subsequent communications with the IRS.

10. Mail IRS form 56 to the IRS when the number is obtained. This gives the IRS its initial notice concerning your fiduciary relationship.

11. Safeguard all assets of the decedent, since you are responsible for their safety and must account for them at all times. This means not only storing them safely but also making certain that all estate property is adequately insured against all possible hazards. The estate should be substituted as the insured on any existing policy.

12. Give statutory notice of the probate of the will and of your appointment as the representative to all possible heirs, beneficiaries, creditors, and claimants of the decedent. Until such notice is given, some time periods do not begin to run and the estate cannot be closed.

13. Obtain correct names, addresses, and social security numbers of spouse and all heirs for use on inventories and subsequent communications.

14. Secure information concerning reportable gifts and copies of the decedent's gift tax returns, if any. Also locate any copies of the decedent's previous year's income tax returns for future use.

15. Verify title to the decedent's real estate through a title (abstract) company. The will may bequeath the real estate to certain beneficiaries or it may direct that the real estate be sold. Or, regardless of the will, you may be required to sell the real estate in order to satisfy the bequests or to pay claims. In the event of sale, you may engage an agent or attempt to sell the real property on your own. Statutory procedures for sale of real estate must be followed, unless the will provides otherwise.

16. Complete collection and verification of the decedent's assets. This procedure could involve contacting every financial institution in the area as to accounts the decedent may have, contacting the Bureau of Public Debt as to possible government securities owned by the decedent, examining the local real estate records, and contacting the decedent's broker as to registered and unregistered securities.

All property of the decedent then must be valued as of the date of death, or, if an alternate valuation date is used for federal estate tax purposes, six months thereafter. Some property not having a ready market value, such as real estate, artwork, and antiques, may have to be appraised. As to assets bearing interest, the valuation must include interest figured to date of death. Special rules apply as to valuation of closely held corporate stock.

The inventory and the federal estate tax return ordinarily list the same value for the property. That figure, with minor exceptions, becomes the basis to determine gain or loss upon a subsequent sale by either the estate or the ultimate distributee of the property.

The probate inventory is then prepared and filed. A copy of the inventory is mailed to all residuary beneficiaries. Each party receiving a copy should be asked to examine all the information and to immediately notify your attorney if any mistakes are found in it.

Recipients of nonprobate property, such as surviving joint tenants and life insurance beneficiaries, as well as specific beneficiaries under a will, are not believed to be entitled to a copy of the inventory, even though the proceedings are public. The contents of the inventory should be of no concern to them.

17. Ask the spouse to file an election to take or not to take under the will.

18. Make certain that any beneficiary who wants to decline part or all of a bequest file a disclaimer within the required statutory time limit.

19. Determine whether the spouse desires to file an application for a widow(er)'s allowance. Such application may also be desirable as to other dependents, such as minor children. The allowance may be based on need or on some presumed tax advantage.

20. Make a claim of all life insurance companies that have insured the decedent's life by sending to them a certified copy of the death certificate. Ask each company to complete IRS form 712, the Life Insurance Statement, in triplicate for each policy and return it to your attorney. A copy of each of these forms must accompany the federal estate return and sometimes any state death tax return. Much delay is encountered unless this form is requested at this time.

21. Notify the postmaster as to the forwarding of decedent's mail, if no other member of the family lives in decedent's home.

22. Notify all financial institutions having the decedent's accounts of her or his death. At the same time, substitute the estate identification number for that of the decedent. One or more accounts may immediately be transferred into an estate checking account set up for that purpose. This new account becomes an operating account so that funds can be available for estate expenses. Under no circumstances would these funds be commingled with your personal funds. All receipts, including liquidated assets, and all disbursements should flow through this account.

23. Set up books of account. All receipts and disbursements of the estate are noted in this record, as well as run through the newly opened operating account. This ensures a double check of all financial transactions handled by the representative.

24. Liquidate the securities, assuming that they have not been specifically bequeathed. An exception may be if a beneficiary prefers to take such stock in payment of his or her bequest. A stockbroker must be engaged to sell the stock. The timing for selling the stock may be critical because of market conditions and income tax considerations. To satisfy the requirements of the various stock transfer agents, consents or waivers of death tax liens may have to be obtained from the state tax authority.

25. Pay out specific legacies, when the estate contains adequate funds to do so, upon receiving (1) proper receipts and waivers from such beneficiaries and (2) their share, if any, of the death taxes.

26. If appropriate, provide for perpetual care of the grave and for any monuments or headstone.

27. Continue various business matters of the decedent, such as collecting rents or subletting leased property. Also collect any unpaid wages, pensions, and fringe benefits owing to the decedent. Generally you have power to compromise, abandon, or sue for collection of amounts owed to the decedent, although sometimes only after court approval.

28. Determine and pay all legitimate claims against the estate. Any contested claims may be heard by the probate court for determination.

29. Collect any veteran's benefits and social security benefits. If the decedent was collecting social security, notify the social security office of his or her death. Possibly any payments that were received after the death will have to be returned. Arrangements should be made for new benefits to be paid to a surviving spouse or to minor children of the decedent.

30. At some point convert all personal property of the estate into cash, unless specifically bequeathed. Depending upon the circumstances, this may be done through public or private sale. An alternative would be for the heirs to agree among themselves as to a division of this property.

31. Cancel all credit cards, charge accounts, and newspaper and magazine subscriptions and obtain refunds.

32. Terminate insurance coverage on property as it is disposed of, and obtain refunds.

33. Prepare and file death tax returns. Where necessary, make protective elections on the returns. The short power of attorney form on the face of the federal estate tax form 706 should be executed, as otherwise the IRS

will not deal directly with your attorney. If this is not done, completion of the process is hindered, since almost all 706s are audited.

All other necessary enclosures should be added, such as a certified copy (not a photocopy) of the death certificate and a certified copy of the will. Payment of the computed death tax should also be included. Because of time limitations and to secure proof of mailing, the package should be sent by certified mail, return receipt requested.

34. Immediately after filing the federal 706 return, request the IRS to make a determination of the estate tax due (even though already paid) and for discharge of the personal representative from personal liability. Doing this ordinarily reduces the time the IRS has for the audit from 3 years to 9 months following the request. In lieu of this request, a request for prompt assessment can be made, but this ordinarily reduces the time period from 3 years to 18 months, rather than 9 months.

These requests should also be sent certified, return receipt requested. The aim of either procedure is to obtain what is called a closing letter from the IRS. Upon receipt of the letter the federal estate tax matter is closed unless some fraud in the proceedings is subsequently found.

35. Follow through with any special proceedings necessitated by the situation, such as early surrender of certain estate property, or retention of estate property, or (in an intestate situation) a determination of heirship.

36. File the decedent's final federal and state income tax returns. This usually is done jointly and in cooperation with a surviving spouse. The process may involve making certain elections as to income and deductions.

37. File the estate's federal (form 1041) and state income tax returns. This involves making choices as to fiscal year, number of returns, and timing of income and deductions so as to minimize the overall taxes. It also involves making certain elections as to where to take certain deductions— on the federal estate tax return or on the income tax return.

A federal K-1 form, and probably something similar for the state return, must accompany the final returns. A copy of the K-1 is given to the residuary beneficiaries. The K-1 informs them as to what estate income and deductions are required or allowed to be reported on their individual 1040 and state income tax returns for that calendar year.

38. Obtain court approval of your fees and those of your attorney for the services rendered the estate.

39. Prepare the final report and accounting, sending copies to the residuary beneficiaries for their approval. If approval is not obtained, then the matter must be set down for hearing and notice given to all interested parties.

40. Obtain a court order approving final report and accounting and your discharge and release of your bond, if any.

41. Distribute remaining assets to residuary beneficiaries.

42. File change of title of real property notices with appropriate county officials for property tax assessment purposes.

43. If you are bonded, notify the bonding company agent of your discharge.

44. Send notice of your termination as personal representative to the IRS on form 56.

45. Set up testamentary trusts, if any.

If deadlines exist as to any of the above listed items, then a tickler should be set up for each such deadline immediately upon the opening of the estate proceeding. A *tickler* is a calendar notation as to when something is to be done. It notifies you of a deadline or alerts you that a deadline is approaching. For instance, ticklers should be set up for the filing of income tax returns, for both the decedent and the estate, and for the filing of death tax returns. And many statutes or court rules impose deadlines on the filing of an inventory or other reports, including the final report.

Informal, Small-Estate Administration

Beginning mostly in the 1970s, a few states started to experiment with optional forms of probate administration. These states set up statutes intended to expedite probate proceedings, to decrease the costs of administration, to avoid court-supervised proceedings, to make informal the procedure, or to avoid the need of legal counsel.

Some of these statutes limit their applicability to probate estates under a certain size. Others limit it to those situations in which the heirs or beneficiaries are related to the decedent within a certain degree of consanguinity. Whether the decedent died testate or intestate is of no consequence. If the procedure is allowed under the one situation, it is also allowed under the other.

Some state statutes are silent as to the degree of cooperation desired between the probate clerk or other designated official and a nonlawyer. Other statutes encourage or even mandate that their clerks, within their competence, shall aid laypersons with the legal requirements of the probate code.

But use of these statutes vary not only from state to state but also from county to county and even from lawyer to lawyer. Some probate officials refuse to help laypersons for fear of personal liability. Others feel incompetent to give legal advice or feel they lack the time to counsel a layperson who may be trying to avoid hiring a lawyer.

Lawyers themselves often are reluctant to use these statutes because of the uncertainty of their acceptance or because the ending of the statutory proceeding does not necessarily close the case at that time. Even though the legal proceedings may have been completed, some statutes allow a stated amount of time thereafter for interested parties to reopen the proceeding. And in some cases lawyers feel that the objective of a shortened proceeding cannot be met without some jeopardy both to the personal representative and to the title to the decedent's property.

States that follow the Uniform Probate Code, at least to some extent, provide for what is called an informal probate and appointment proceeding. This may occur in either a testate or intestate situation. The heirs are entitled to their share of the estate in accordance with the will or laws of intestate succession, as the case may be. The proceedings are similar to regular administration proceedings, but they are not normally supervised by a court. The personal representative, however, may invoke the jurisdiction of the court. The proceeding is closed by the personal representative filing a sworn statement with the court.

Another proceeding under the Uniform Probate Code can be used, one similar to the informal one. This is sometimes known as the small-estate or summary administrative procedure. If it appears that all of the debts and charges of the estate exceed the value of the entire estate, then the personal representative may immediately disburse and distribute the estate to the parties entitled to it and file a closing statement with the court, without giving notice to creditors.

Real Estate in Probate Administration

This section discusses how real estate owned by the decedent alone or in common with another person is treated at the time of the decedent's death. It does not concern real property owned by the decedent and another person as joint tenants or as tenants by the entirety.

Real property held in survivorship tenancies is clearly nonprobate property. As such, it is not subject to administration. That is, title to such property, upon the death of the first tenant, vests in the surviving tenant(s) to the exclusion of heirs or beneficiaries. This occurs regardless of the laws of descent and distribution or of any existing will.

For the purposes of administration, several states consider real property as a nonprobate asset, even though such property is not held in a survivorship situation. Because of this viewpoint, several things can result:

The real property might not be considered as a chargeable asset when the personal representative's or the representative's attorney's fees are computed.

Upon the opening of the administration proceedings the personal representative might not be able to take control of the real property, as is done with the personal property. If this situation exists, then those heirs inheriting the property have the responsibility to take it over upon the owner's death.

Or the real property might not be subject to estate expenses. This means that the personal property bears the costs of the creditors' claims and administration expenses, at least until it is exhausted.

From your point of view you may not be able to detect how your state treats real property. Even in those states which consider real property as a nonprobate asset, at some point the personal representative may be required to take charge of the real property.

This may occur because the personalty—property other than real property—is inadequate to pay the expenses of the estate, in which event the real property may be subject to such expenses. Or it may be because the decedent's will authorized or directed the personal representative to sell the real property and convert it into cash. Or, for various reasons, the probate court may direct or authorize the representative to take steps to preserve (maintain) the property and pay the property taxes.

Regardless of how the real property is treated under state law, title to such property by operation of law is deemed vested in the heirs immediately upon the death of the titleholder or at such time as the will is admitted to probate, as the case may be. But the distributee's title is always subject to divestment if the real property involved is needed to pay claims and expenses. It would also be divested if the property were sold pursuant to court order or under the terms of the decedent's will.

Even though a state may treat real property as nonprobate property, no matter how title is held, that property may still be subject to administration proceedings. At least one state, however, (Missouri) has enacted comprehensive transfer-on-death legislation, which under certain circumstances provides for the avoidance of administration by providing for nonprobate transfers of real estate.

The Safe Deposit Box

Although the safety of a safe deposit box is seldom challenged, rumors persist as to its accessibility upon the death of a box holder. The supposition is that upon the death the box is frozen and no one can enter it until a personal representative is appointed. Thus, it is said, you are required to have a full administration proceeding even though you otherwise would not need one. Is this necessarily true?

No, it isn't, although you should check with your own depository to determine what their policy is in this regard. Two reasons may exist as to why entry to the box is initially prohibited.

First, the institution holding the box must be certain that whoever has access to that box is authorized to enter it. A personal representative who has letters of administration of your estate obviously is authorized to enter it and remove its contents. But heirs, or those claiming to be your heirs, might not.

If you consider the matter rationally, you will realize that you don't want just anybody, possibly even some of your heirs, to have unauthorized entry to your box. You want the institution to protect you in this regard. And it will want to do so.

The problem of entry sometimes occurs, at least momentarily, when your estate consists entirely of nonprobate property and thus no personal representative is appointed for your estate. The institution must be convinced that this situation actually exists before allowing entry to the box holder's successors in interest. Usually little difficulty is experienced if such parties first contact a lawyer who then accompanies them to the box.

A second reason may exist as to why the box is temporarily locked. Some states prohibit entry to the box following the death of a holder, or one of the holders, until its contents have been inventoried by a representative of the state tax department. This representative may be a bank official or actually an employee of the state.

A copy of the inventory is given to the state tax department so that it may follow up if no proper death tax return is subsequently filed with the department. This is one way that the department ensures that the required death taxes are paid to the state.

Some Common
Questions Answered

Q. Although my spouse died about a month ago, my life seems to go on as before. I am able to write checks and deposit monies received. Why should I have to see a lawyer about his estate?

A. Many reasons immediately come to mind, such as title and tax problems, insurance questions, social security notification, and correction of records. These cannot be ignored just because, for the moment at least, no one has questioned your lack of action.

For instance, taxing bodies have various ways of finding out about a death and about assets held by a decedent. You may believe that you have gotten by because no one has contacted you. But a year from now you may receive a letter from your state tax department or from the IRS requesting you to file a death tax return. If such return shows a tax due, you could be assessed interest and penalties for late filing.

And what about insurance, both life and casualty? Has his name been removed from such policies? Suppose his name remained on the policy to the family car and you later have an accident. The insurance company might not be willing to issue a claim check in your name only, since the policy named your spouse as an additional insured. Do you realize that at that time you may have difficulty in cashing the check?

What about personal property assets? Have your spouse's name and possibly his social security number been removed from these assets, assuming they were jointly held with you? If not, at some point you may have difficulty in cashing the income checks therefrom or liquidating them in the future. And of course if they were not jointly held with you, you may not be the owner of such assets, which could give you no right to them or the profits therefrom.

For peace of mind and perhaps a savings of money in the long run, you should contact a lawyer now and not wait for something to happen.

Q. After my wife died, I was told by my neighbor that her will would have to be probated. Is that true?

A. Not necessarily, but that can be determined only after a thorough investigation is made of your wife's assets.

State statutes generally provide that upon a death the decedent's will is to be filed with the appropriate county official, usually the probate clerk. The purpose of this statute, obviously, is to prevent someone from secreting a will for personal advantage. But filing it and probating it are not the same thing. The mere filing, without a petition asking that it be probated, does not constitute the opening of a probate proceeding nor does it constitute a probating of the will. Until the will is properly admitted to probate, it has no legal effect.

Q. I am a widower. When I die, will my children have to go to a lawyer or can they handle my affairs without a lawyer?

A. It is assumed you own some property, perhaps your home, at least.

No law exists anywhere that requires your heirs to consult a lawyer upon your death. This is different than saying, however, that they need not consult one, or that they can get by without consulting one. If you are sick, would you be foolish enough not to consult a doctor, even though no law requires you to do so?

States are trying to simplify estate proceedings upon a death, but usually these efforts are directed toward what they consider to be a small estate. In many instances, these state statutes provide for informal proceedings generally not requiring the services of the probate court.

Even if you have a large or complicated estate, your children are not required to hire a lawyer. But this does not mean that they should take this route. Various laws set out requirements that cannot be ignored, such as filing death tax returns and final income tax returns. Your children could luck out, but without proper legal advice they could experience many a headache.

Q. During my lifetime, is there anything that I can do so that my heirs are not required to have a formal, court-supervised administration of my estate upon my death?

A. Yes, but you should keep in mind that taking actions to avoid formal administration may not be in your best interest, nor may it be in the best interests of your heirs.

To best ensure that your heirs can avoid formal administration, you must create an estate that contains no probate property. Whether this would be advantageous for you should be decided only after consulting your lawyer.

Q. If when I die I own both probate and nonprobate property, would my heirs be required to go through two different estate procedures?

A. No. When a situation which you describe exists—one that is quite common—only the more elaborate, or formal, administration procedure is required. The procedures required for the nonprobate property would be included in the formal procedure. No duplication would occur, as the procedures required for the nonprobate property are always part of a formal procedure.

Q. Why is it necessary to remove my deceased spouse's name from our jointly held HH bonds but not from our jointly held EE bonds?

A. You must keep in mind the basic difference between the two types of bonds. The HH bonds pay out interest semiannually, whereas interest accumulates on EE bonds and is only paid out at the time the bonds are redeemed. Thus your spouse's name becomes an issue almost immediately as to the HH bonds, but perhaps not for a long time as to the EE bonds.

The interest checks on the HH bonds will always include all the record owners thereof. Thus immediately you would want to establish that you are now the sole remaining owner of such bonds. Otherwise, you might have difficulty in cashing (depositing) the checks. And, of course, at some time you will be redeeming the matured bonds, thus again not wanting your spouse's name on the check.

Only at the time that the EE bonds are redeemed is it important to establish that your spouse is deceased. To make it easier for you or someone at that time, you should place at least one certified copy of his or her death certificate with the EE bonds, more than one if you contemplate redeeming such bonds at different times.

Q. Suppose that upon examining the final report and accounting of the personal representative in an administration proceeding, I believe that some action of the representative was improper. What can I do?

A. You have a choice of taking informal action or formal action or, if necessary, both. Formal action would constitute filing a resistance in the probate court proceeding.

Ordinarily, but depending on the circumstances, you should first try resolving your doubts by directly contacting the representative or the representative's attorney handling the estate. Your inquiry may be easily resolved either by determining that you were mistaken or by the representative making some adjustments in the proceedings. Be careful, however. In taking this route, you dare not let pass any time limitations in resisting the report and accounting.

If a formal protest is deemed necessary, you will have to engage your own counsel, again in the time period allotted to you. The representative's attorney cannot represent you also, as this would constitute a conflict of interest.

Q. As executor of an estate, I am now ready for closing and distribution of the assets, but one of the distributees has just died. Who do I give her property to?

A. You give it to her estate. If an estate has not yet been opened for her, then it now must be so that you, in turn, may close your estate. Since her inheritance is considered probate property, the proceeding must be a full administration. Once it is opened, then the personal representative of her estate shall be in a position to accept and receipt for the inheritance from your estate.

Q. Should a beneficiary under a will hire a lawyer to protect his or her interests?

A. No, unless you have some particular reason for doing so. Some reasons may be distrust of the personal representative or the representative's attorney. Or you may not be receiving information that you are entitled to, such as a copy of the will or inventory. Or you may not be receiving answers to your inquiries. Or you may wish to contest some part of the proceedings or even the will itself.

Just keep in mind that the estate attorney often legally represents only the personal representative, not the distributees. Regardless, if the attorney feels that a conflict of interest exists, he or she should tell you so.

16
Understanding Death Taxes

The term "death taxes" refers to those taxes assessed by the state and federal governments as the result of a death of an individual. The assessment may be based upon the amount of an inheritance received by an heir or beneficiary of the decedent or upon the size of the decedent's estate. Or, in the case of a state death tax, the assessment may be based upon the size of the federal credit for state taxes.

The tax is referred to as an inheritance tax if the inheritance determines the tax. This tax is assessed by about 18 states, some of which seem to be in the process of doing away with it or substituting a different kind of death tax.

The tax is referred to as an estate tax if the size of the estate determines the tax. The federal government and a few of the states use this tax. A third form of tax, used by many of the states, is the so-called pick-up tax, described later.

All states now impose some form of death tax, even though the trend among the states has been to minimize the tax. The state tax may be an inheritance tax, sometimes called a succession tax, an estate tax, a combination of both, or merely the pick-up tax.

The federal government has only the estate tax. Both the states and the federal government have exemptions to some extent and have some similarities.

State Death Taxes

An estate may be subject to the imposition of a state death tax if the decedent either resided in that state at the time of death or did not reside but left property, primarily real estate, located therein.

Real property can be taxed only by the state in which it is located. Generally, tangible personal property is taxed in the same manner by all the states, but intangible personal property, wherever located, is taxed according to the laws of the state where the decedent resided.

Usually no problem exists unless a dispute arises between states as to the nature of the property. Is it real or personal? If personal, is it tangible or intangible? If a dispute does arise, the same property can possibly and legally be taxed twice (in addition to a possible federal tax), once by the state where the owner resided and once by the state where the property is located.

Death taxes are feared and disliked by laypersons. Unlike the federal estate tax, however, state death taxes are generally not a great burden to the distributees. This fact especially applies if the distributee is closely related to the decedent, because of exemptions and low rates.

Kinds of Property Interests Taxed

Various state statutes describe numerous kinds of property interests that are subject to the death tax. Many of these interests are similar to those taxed for federal estate tax purposes and hence may not be referred to again when the federal estate tax is discussed. Some interests are obvious, such as property that passes by will or inheritance. Some are too technical or rare to discuss here. But some kinds of taxable property may surprise you.

For instance, one taxable interest includes all transfers, whether by deed, sale, or gift, made by the decedent within a stated period immediately prior to death, except bona fide sales for adequate and full consideration. Statutes sometimes describe these taxable transfers as transfers in contemplation of death, even though in fact they may not have been.

Another taxable interest may be individual gifts exceeding $10,000 in value in any one year. Presumably, the $10,000 figure is tied in with the federal gift statute. Suppose, for example, your parent gave you an automobile worth $15,000 and then within the period set by statute died. Part of that gift, $5000 ($15,000 minus the $10,000 maximum), would be considered a taxable transfer. It should be reported on your parent's tax return filed in his or her estate proceeding.

Another taxable interest might be property transferred at any time by the decedent prior to death in which she or he retained a life estate. For example, suppose your widowed mother deeded her farm to you 20 years ago but retained a life estate in it so that she would have a place to live and on which to draw income for the balance of her life. At her death, the farm would be considered a taxable interest. Its total value at the time of her death would have to be reported on her estate's tax return.

For taxing purposes, a distinction normally is made between a "retained" life estate, described above, and a "received" life estate. To illustrate the latter, suppose that your mother had deeded the farm to you outright, without any life estate reservation. Subsequently you deeded back to her a life interest (life estate), you retaining what is referred to as a remainder interest in the farm. Upon your mother's death, the property in which she had a life estate interest (which was received, not retained) would not be subject to tax in her estate.

Another possible taxable interest is property held by the decedent in joint tenancy with another. How much of the joint tenancy property is subject to being taxed—in other words, how much is considered part of the gross taxable estate? The answer might depend partly upon the identity of the surviving joint tenant. It also might depend partly upon the extent that each tenant contributed toward the purchase of the property.

Almost all joint tenancy property is subject to tax. Only that part that can be proved to have been contributed by the surviving joint tenant is not. The taxing bodies assume that the deceased joint tenant contributed the entire value of the property. But this presumption is rebuttable. It may be overcome to the extent that the surviving joint tenant can show contribution, in other words the amount contributed for the acquisition of the jointly held property. The procedure showing contribution is sometimes referred to as the tracing rule. The consideration paid by each joint tenant is traced.

If the only surviving joint tenant is the spouse of the decedent, then under the federal rule only one-half of the joint tenancy property is subject to the tax. The tracing rule is not applicable. But because of the unlimited marital deduction rule, which provides that all property going outright to the surviving spouse passes tax-free, the amount that can be included is irrelevant. States that follow the federal rule of one-half may reach a different result, if they do not have the unlimited marital deduction.

Whether a liability for payment of a tax arises may depend upon two things: the relationship of the recipient to the decedent and the net value of the estate property. The closer the relationship of the distributee to the decedent, the more likely the distributee will have a large exemption and low tax rates. It makes no difference whether the recipient is an heir of the decedent or a beneficiary under the decedent's will. The tax, if any, is computed in the same manner.

Deductions Allowable to Determine Taxable Estate

Only the net value of a decedent's estate is taxable. "Net value" is the gross value of the estate less many categories of deductible debts. Some of the more common deductions follow:

1. Debts incurred during the decedent's lifetime and owing at time of his or her death

2. Three kinds of taxes owing by the decedent at time of death or resulting from the decedent's death: property taxes, federal and state income taxes, and the federal estate tax

3. Reasonable funeral expenses, which are quite inclusive, but usually do not include such items as long-distance costs for notification of kin or for a meal following the funeral

4. Support allowances for the surviving spouse and minor children

5. All items considered as administrative expenses, such as court costs, appraisal fees, fiduciary and attorney fees, bond costs, and selling costs

Since only a few states have an estate tax and since such taxes are patterned after the federal estate tax, no separate discussion of such taxes will be made under this section.

For purposes of their inheritance tax, many states place heirs and beneficiaries in categories, depending on their relationship to the decedent. They do this because exemptions, if any, vary from group to group, and because the rate of tax may also vary from group to group. An exemption applies only to the extent that a particular distributee receives a part of the decedent's estate.

Often the decedent's surviving spouse, regardless of the quality of the spouses' marital relationship, is in a preferred position. The spouse, like under the federal estate tax, may have an unlimited marital exemption, meaning that no state tax is assessed regardless of the size of the inheritance. Children of a decedent usually are the next-preferred group. A third preferred group may be the decedent's parents, grandchildren, and other lineal descendants.

The Pick-Up Tax

Slightly less than half the states impose only a pick-up tax, sometimes called a "sponge" or "slack" tax. To understand this type of tax, you need to understand the credit for state death taxes under the federal estate tax law.

After the gross federal estate tax is computed, certain credits therefrom are allowed so that the net federal estate tax due can be determined. One of these credits is the credit for state death taxes.

At least a portion of the state death tax, if it is actually imposed and paid, may be used to reduce the amount of the federal estate tax. The amount used for the deduction is called a credit. The federal statute, however, after adjustment is made, limits the amount of the credit to the actual amount of the state tax paid or to an amount determined from a tax credit table, whichever is less. Almost invariably, it seems, the amount computed by use of the table is the maximum amount available for the credit.

For those states imposing only the pick-up tax as their death tax, the amount computed by use of the federal table constitutes their death tax. In other words these states do not want to lose the amount of the federal credit so they "soak up" or "pick up" the credit and make it their death tax. Actually, because of this arrangement, no overall tax savings is realized. It merely affects which governmental entity receives the tax (the amount of the credit).

Federal Estate Tax

The federal estate tax is based upon the total value of a decedent's estate, wherever it is situated and in whatever form. It is not based upon what any particular individual, other than a spouse, receives. Thus it is called an estate tax rather than an inheritance or a succession tax.

State death taxes generally apply only to a decedent's property located in the decedent's state of residence. They may sometimes apply to his or her intangible personal property located elsewhere. But the federal death tax includes all property interests of the decedent regardless of where they are located. And oftentimes more kinds of property interests are covered under the federal statute than under state death statutes.

Except as to the surviving spouse, the identity of the recipient of the decedent's property is irrelevant. All property in which the decedent had an interest at the time of death and which passes to any party other than the surviving spouse is subject to the federal estate tax. It is irrelevant whether the decedent died with or without a will.

For each decedent who is a citizen or resident of the United States or its possessions, if his or her total gross estate—as defined by statute—exceeds $600,000, then it is subject to the federal estate tax. This is not the same as saying, however, that all such estates actually pay a tax.

The Spouse's Deduction

To the extent that a surviving spouse who is a citizen of the United States "receives" (as defined by law and the IRS) the decedent's property, such property is exempt from the tax. For example, if all of the decedent's estate is bequeathed to the surviving spouse, regardless of the size of the estate, then there is no federal estate tax.

Since the enactment of the Technical and Miscellaneous Revenue Act of 1988 (TAMRA) a different result occurs, however, if the surviving spouse is not a United States citizen at time of the decedent's death. Subject to certain exceptions, in this situation no marital deduction is allowed unless the decedent's property passes to or is placed in what the statute describes as a "qualified domestic trust" (QDOT). Among the statutory requirements, at least one trustee of the trust must be a United States citizen or domestic corporation.

The effect of this trust is to make the trust property available for taxation. A federal estate tax is imposed upon any distribution from the trust and upon the value of the property remaining at time of the surviving spouse's death. However, no tax is imposed on any distribution of income to the surviving spouse or in event of hardship.

TAMRA was passed because Congress believed that it was unlikely that the inherited property of a noncitizen spouse would be available for taxation upon the death of such a spouse. Congress did not want such property to escape taxation in both estates because of the marital deduction otherwise available in the estate of the first to die. TAMRA, as subsequently amended, provides for certain exceptions in the event the surviving spouse thereafter becomes a United States citizen.

If a surviving joint tenant spouse is not a United States citizen, then all of the decedent's property is subject to the tax except for that portion for which consideration was furnished by the surviving spouse. Thus, in respect to joint tenancy property, if the spouse is a noncitizen, then the tracing rule is exercised.

In order for the spouse's exemption to apply, the property passing to the spouse must have no conditions attached to it, with two important exceptions: the QTIP trust and the power-of-appointment trust. Both types of trusts are discussed later in this chapter.

The general rule, as stated by the statute, is "Where, on the lapse of time, on the occurrence of an event or contingency, or on the failure of an event or contingency to occur, an interest passing to the surviving spouse will terminate or fail, no deduction shall be allowed . . . with respect to such interest. . . . " This is known as the terminable interest rule. Everything turns on this rule, which is often difficult to decipher.

The property that passes to the spouse and that qualifies for the marital deduction, if not consumed or given away, must be reported in the spouse's estate at the time of the spouse's death.

The property so passing to the surviving spouse is termed *marital deduction property.* Since all property passes tax-free, the circumstance is referred to as the *unlimited marital deduction,* a situation which has existed since 1982. There is no limit on the amount of marital deduction property that can pass to the surviving spouse tax-free.

The Estate's Exemption

All property passing to a party other than a surviving spouse is subject to the tax. Whatever part of the estate assets exceeds the $600,000 exemption is taxed.

But if the total taxable estate, as adjusted for allowable deductions and credits, is below the $600,000 exemption, then there is no tax, regardless of who the distributees are. However, a federal estate tax return may have to be filed to prove it. In fact, a return, regardless of the possibility of a tax, is always required if the gross, not net, estate exceeds $600,000. In other words, the IRS wants the opportunity to determine that no tax is due. Your opinion, or that of your attorney, is more or less irrelevant, at least at this stage of the proceedings.

If your total gross estate is less than $600,000, then no federal estate tax return (form 706) need be filed. When you die, if your gross estate exceeds this amount, then the federal estate tax return must be filed for your estate. This filing requirement exists even though your will leaves your entire estate outright to your surviving spouse. Despite the fact that no tax will be due because of the unlimited marital deduction, you must submit a return.

It has already been stated that state death tax rates are relatively low. But if a federal estate tax is payable, the rate starts at 37 percent and goes as high as 55 percent. On January 1, 1993, the top rate reduces to 50 percent, unless Congress decides otherwise.

This possible taking of your property upon your death is one of the reasons that estate planning, with properly drawn wills, for married couples having a combined gross estate exceeding $600,000 is so important. Of course, even if you have an estate considerably smaller, many other reasons may exist for estate planning.

Even without predeath estate planning, however, certain actions that will tend to minimize or at least reduce death taxes are sometimes available. These actions, collectively referred to as post-mortem estate planning, are discussed in Chapter 17.

Determining the Gross Estate

Since your estate might be liable for a federal estate tax upon your death, you should be aware of a few additional things about this type of tax.

Under the federal gift tax law, each year you may give gifts totaling not more than $10,000 in value to any number of persons without incurring a gift tax liability. And if your spouse consents to the gift, then the amount is doubled to $20,000. Any gifts to any one individual in any one year exceeding these amounts must be reported to the IRS, even though no gift tax is actually payable.

The reporting is required so that the IRS may maintain a record of such gifts exceeding the limits. The accumulated total of such excessive gifts is used to determine whether a federal estate tax return must be filed upon an individual's death. In effect, such excessive gifts are added back into the estate for the purpose of determining tax liability.

Thus a return is required if the sum of your total gross estate (which may be substantially under $600,000) and your accumulated excess gifts is $600,000 or more.

In other words, you cannot escape the filing requirement by making excess gifts—gifts exceeding the $10,000 (or $20,000) exemption—in order to maintain your total gross estate under $600,000. The making of excess lifetime gifts is not a tax loophole, because such excess gifts are brought back into your estate at the time of your death.

You may wonder what the term *gross estate* includes. The general description is that it includes all property in which the decedent had an interest. What may some of these be? The following is a short list of some of them:

Certain transfers made during the decedent's life without adequate and full consideration, which includes property transferred into a revocable trust

Annuities

Joint tenancy property

Tenancies by the entirety

Life insurance proceeds as to policies owned or considered owned by the decedent

Property over which the decedent possessed a general power of appointment

Community property

The Importance of Elections

In filing the federal estate tax return, your estate must make certain so-called elections. These are options to take or not to take certain actions. Unfortunately, these elections must sometimes be made early in the taxing process, usually before the preferable choice can be determined. Fortunately, however, in some cases your representative may make what is termed a "protective election." This allows the representative more time to determine whether or not to proceed under the election.

Making the wrong decision or failing to file an election can be extremely costly. It may even subject the representative and the representative's attorney to a claim for personal liability or malpractice. For this reason, some of these elections ought to be mentioned.

The Alternate Valuation Date

Property of the decedent generally is valued as of the time of his or her death. However, the representative may elect—in effect, choose—to value the property as of the date six months following the death, adjusted as to any property sold prior to the end of the six-month period.

Such an election is not available unless it would decrease both the value of the gross estate and the total net taxes after application of all allowable credits. Presumably this would prevent the representative from choosing an alternate date in order to establish a higher basis of certain capital items for income tax purposes.

All capital items owned by the decedent at the time of death have as their new basis for income tax purposes the value at either the date of death or the alternate valuation date, whichever is chosen. This is referred to as the "stepped-up" basis. The theory behind this name is that inflation will cause the market value of the property to be higher at the time of death than when it was acquired by the decedent. Being higher, the basis has "stepped up" in value.

The person who inherits property naturally likes the inherited property to have as high a basis as possible. But if, in choosing the alternate valuation date, the effect is to increase the value of the total gross estate, then the alternate valuation date would not be an available option.

Special Use

Another possible election is the special use valuation. This valuation is available only for those estates that contain certain farm, ranch, or other closely held business real property. The purpose of choosing this valuation method is to reduce the value of the property qualifying for special use below what otherwise would be considered its fair market value.

But election of this valuation method may be neither available nor advisable because of the strict statutory prerequisites and postrequisites for special use. Failure to abide by the rules can disqualify the special use, resulting in severe penalties. Requirements of the special use statute are too numerous and complex to be enumerated here. But if a taxable estate consists in part of closely held business real property, then special use should always be considered.

The QTIP Trust and the
Power-of-Appointment Trust

One more election that should be mentioned is the QTIP election. QTIP stands for Qualified Terminable Interest Property. QTIP passes from the decedent and is that property in which the surviving spouse has a qualifying income interest for life. This interest is similar to a life estate interest in the qualified property. (See Chapter 8 for a more detailed explanation of the QTIP.)

If the decedent's personal representative makes the QTIP election, then the property is treated as marital deduction property, even though it otherwise would not seem to qualify. When the election is made, the property escapes being taxed in the estate of the first spouse to die—by reason of the unlimited marital deduction. But it is subsequently subject to tax in the estate of the second spouse to die.

The QTIP trust is the first of the two major exceptions to the terminable interest rule mentioned previously. You may recall that, under the rule, in order for the property to qualify as marital deduction property the interest passing to the spouse must not be subject to termination.

Under a QTIP trust, the spouse is entitled to the income generated by the trust property for the rest of his or her life. In fact, under the statute he or she *must* receive it. But upon the death of the receiving spouse the property must go as specified in the trust. In other words, the property is not subject to a will of the receiving spouse, since the spouse in effect only has a life estate interest in the property. The interest of the receiving spouse in the trust property terminates at that spouse's death. Thus the QTIP trust would come under the terminable interest rule if it were not for the statutory exception to the rule.

The second major exception to the rule is the power-of-appointment trust. Basically, the statute states that if the spouse is entitled to all of the trust income and is given the power to appoint the property interest, either during lifetime or by will, then the trust is not considered a terminable interest. Note that here "to appoint" actually means to select or to designate.

Under either the QTIP trust or the power-of-appointment trust the trust property passes to the surviving spouse tax-free. So why does a testator bother with either of the trusts? Why not just give the property to the spouse outright, since the results are the same?

The answer is partly one of control. In setting up the QTIP trust, the testator controls to whom the trust property passes upon the death of the receiving spouse. And if under the power-of-appointment trust the power is not exercised by the surviving spouse, then again the testator controls where the property goes upon the death of the spouse.

Sophisticated estate planners, however, will claim that these trusts are established for many reasons other than mere postdeath control. For example, they allow for additional post-mortem estate planning, and management opportunities. If you have a very large estate, you may find that using them will be to your advantage.

Both the federal estate tax return and the tax payment are due within nine months after the date of the decedent's death unless extensions of time are granted. These nine-month deadlines can create difficulties. An accurate valuation sometimes cannot be determined until the property is sold, which may not happen until long after the nine-month period. And sometimes money is not available to pay the tax until some property is converted into cash.

Extensions are normally granted by the IRS if the requests are reasonable. But interest on the amount due is charged from and after the nine-month period. No extension for filing the return may be granted beyond six months from the due date. But extensions for payment of the tax (and interest) may be granted for up to ten years from the due date.

Generation Skipping Transfer Tax

Your estate may be large. You may be concerned about the large federal estate tax that you and your equally wealthy children will have to pay upon your respective deaths. Therefore, you may think, it might be a good idea to give, now or at the time of your death, some of your estate directly to your grandchildren and bypass your children. This may not be feasible to any great extent. In fact, the tax result could be disastrous.

The 1976 Tax Reform Act introduced a new tax concept, a tax on so-called generation skipping transfers (GSTs). This act was repealed retroactively and superseded by the Tax Reform Act of 1986. The latter act is the one that will be referred to hereafter. The purpose of the act is to prevent the transmission of wealth by lifetime or testamentary gifts, thus avoiding or "skipping" one or more generations. The IRS likes the idea of taxing every generation, not allowing one generation to "get by" without being taxed.

Under the act, if you try to escape the payment of the federal estate tax on certain property by skipping over one generation, then your estate may be subject to the GST tax. Whether your estate actually has to pay the tax depends upon the value of the property bypassing your next succeeding generation.

The Skip Person.   The donee or distributee is deemed by the statute to be a skip person if he or she falls two or more generations below that of the transferor. If an individual is not a lineal descendant of the transferor's grandparent or the transferor's spouse's grandparent, then the statute arbitrarily assumes that anyone more than 37½ years younger than the transferor is a skip person.

Generally, a skip person is a grandchild, grandnephew, or grandniece or a more remote descendant of the transferor's grandparents. Under some circumstances a skip person may be a trust. A spouse, or former spouse, is always of the same generation as the transferor or skip person, as the case may be.

However, a grandchild is deemed to be a "direct skip" (a nonskip person) and not a "skip person" if, at the time of the transfer (not date of distribution), the parent of the grandchild is dead. The same rule applies to a great grandchild if the parent and grandparent of the great grandchild are dead.

Types of Taxable GSTs.   Three types of GSTs are subject to the tax: the taxable termination, the taxable distribution, and the direct skip. The first results from a termination of a trust. At this time a skip person receives the property. In this situation the tax, if any, is payable by the trustee.

The second results from any distribution from a trust directly to a skip person. In this situation the tax, if any, is again payable by the trustee. The last refers to any other transfer directly to a skip person. In this situation the tax, if any, is payable by the transferor.

How the GST Is Taxed.   When the tax comes into play—for example, when a transfer (gift) made to a skip person exceeds the sum of the lifetime exemption—then it is imposed on the amount of excess at the highest federal rate, currently 55 percent. This tax is imposed in addition to any other federal estate tax normally due. Thus when the GST comes into play, the estate in effect is taxed twice.

As noted earlier, the maximum federal estate tax rate of 55 percent under the present law is scheduled to lower to 50 percent beginning January 1, 1993. Thus a flat GST tax rate of 50 percent is scheduled likewise. However, because of the government's fiscal problems, it is problematical whether this prospective rate deduction will remain the same by that date.

In this respect, the GST tax differs from the federal gift tax and the federal estate tax in that the latter two are taxed at graduated rates. Another distinction exists in that the various tax credits, particularly the unified credit (the $600,000 exemption), which are available for the other two taxes, are not available for the GST. The credits only apply to the transferor and not to each succeeding generation skipped.

The GST Lifetime Exemption.   The act presently grants to each transferor—not to each transferee—a GST lifetime exemption of $1 million. (For transfers occurring prior to 1990 each grandchild had a $2 million exemption under certain circumstances.) For married couples who wish to generation-skip and have extremely large estates, each spouse should have a sufficient estate so that both spouses may take advantage of the $1 million exemption. This is important because the exemption is not transferable from one to the other.

That portion of a gift to a skip person which exceeds the annual $10,000 gift tax (or GST) exclusion is deemed a GST. However, gift splitting between the spouses is allowed, the same as with gifts for gift tax purposes, in which event the exclusion becomes $20,000.

Each year that a taxable distribution or termination or a lifetime gift in excess of the exclusion is made, then a GST return (Form 709, United States Gift Tax Return) must be made to the IRS. The IRS uses these to keep track of the donor's remaining lifetime exemption of $1 million.

The amounts in excess of the $10,000 (or $20,000, if gift splitting occurs) are cumulative until the transferor has used up his or her lifetime exemption. That part of the GST exemption that the transferor has not used during his or her lifetime may be used by the transferor's personal representative in the event a GST occurs at that time.

The allocation of the $1 million exemption is automatically applied to the GSTs as they occur, unless the transferor chooses to do otherwise. The act allows the transferor to allocate or not to allocate, as desired. But an allocation, once made, is irrevocable.

Since the GST is taxed at the highest rate, little tax advantage exists for skipping a generation or, at least, for bringing the tax into play. Some advantage may be gained, if the value of the skip is limited, so that each individual can take advantage of his or her lifetime exemption of $1 million. But, in skipping a generation, the possibility exists that the skipped generation could lose its unified credit ($600,000 exemption) as well as its annual gift tax exclusions of $10,000 ($20,000 if gift splitting).

On the other hand, the Revenue Act of 1987 imposes a surcharge of 5 percent on amounts transferred in excess of $10,000,000 but not exceeding $21,040,000 ($18,340,000 after 1992). Since the GST tax flat rate is not affected by the surcharge, in rare situations the GST rate could be less than the federal estate tax rate. And because of some state transfer taxes, in a few instances the GST tax could be lower than the combined state and federal taxes.

The GST Act over the years has not only been changed from time to time, it has also been difficult to administer and to plan for. Obviously, it is directed toward, and only affects, the most wealthy individuals. These individuals must determine what is best for all parties: the federal estate tax, the gift tax, or the GST tax. The act should not trouble other, less wealthy individuals, even if they make gifts to skip persons.

Apportionment of Death Taxes

A decedent's will may specify how death taxes are to be apportioned among the beneficiaries. It may specify that all death taxes are to be treated as a cost of administration, stipulate which beneficiaries are to bear the taxes, or be silent as to death taxes.

If the will makes no provision for the payment of death taxes or if the decedent died intestate, then states vary as to who is liable for the death taxes. The great majority of states provide for apportionment of death taxes among the distributees. In the remaining states, the tax may be assessed against those who benefit, the residuary estate, or a combination of both.

In relation to the apportionment of estate taxes, the Uniform Probate Code states as follows:

> Unless the will provides otherwise, the tax shall be apportioned among all persons interested in the estate. The apportionment is to be made in the proportion that the value of the interest of each person interested in the estate bears to the total value of the interests of all persons interested in the estate.

But no uniformity exists among the various states as to such apportionment, perhaps because no uniformity exists among the states as to their death taxes. Some states charge only the probate property with the death taxes. Others charge both the probate property and the nonprobate property. And some states charge the residue with the taxes before any specific legacies are touched.

If a state has an inheritance tax, it may impose the tax directly on the transferee or it may apportion it among the distributees proportionately in accordance with a formula. Or it may burden the residuary estate with the tax.

In many instances, a testator providing for a specific bequest might want a designated beneficiary to receive exactly what was bequeathed, free of any tax burden. This would especially apply if the bequest were a small gift of money or tangible personal property. In such a case the testator, in making his or her will, should then provide who should bear the burden of the tax: the specific legatees, the residuary legatees, or some combination of both.

For example, suppose a will provides that the car owned by the testator is to go to a granddaughter. And suppose that no tax provision has been made. The testator dies. Under the applicable state statute all beneficiaries are to share in the death taxes. Before the granddaughter can claim the car, she must pay her proportionate share of the death taxes. Is this what the testator intended? It is doubtful, but under this example that is the result, since the will failed to contain a tax clause.

Perhaps because so many wills leave everything to one beneficiary or equally to many beneficiaries, the issue of who is to pay the death taxes is not discussed between the lawyer and his client. In these situations, such taxes are shared equally regardless of any apportionment rule. As a result, the issue is irrelevant and not important.

But in some wills the matter of who is to bear the burden of the taxes could be important. Unfortunately, perhaps, many lawyers suggest using the standard will clause that provides that all death taxes shall be paid out of the residue. In effect, this means that the amount of inheritance to the residuary beneficiaries is reduced accordingly. In some cases this may be exactly what the testator intended. But in others the testator might have wanted something different had the matter been thoroughly explained to him or her.

Probably the testator in making his or her will is thinking only in terms of the probate property. But nonprobate property may also be subject to death taxes. If a large amount of such nonprobate property exists, then the death taxes could be substantial. If the residuary death tax clause is used, the residuary beneficiaries may not receive what was intended by the testator.

Some Common Questions Answered

Q. Why may it be beneficial to delay filing an inventory until property is sold?

A. It is because the selling price, if the sale is fairly entered into, truly represents the market value of the property. Waiting until the market value is determined results in all interested parties being treated the most fairly. It also prevents either an overvaluation, which could increase death taxes and administration costs, or an undervaluation, which could result in a capital gains tax.

   No better way exists to determine true market value than to sell the property on the open market. And no one ever disputes the value of property when sold on the open market.

Q. By making a will, can I reduce the amount of death taxes payable by my estate?

A. Yes, in many cases. In and of itself, however, whether you die testate or intestate has no effect on your estate's liability for death taxes or the amount thereof. But this does not mean that you cannot reduce or eliminate death taxes by making a will. Use of the marital deduction and the bypass trust are two good examples.

   Other members of your family may also have some exemptions

from state death taxes. By coordinating your bequests with these exemptions, you may achieve some additional reductions. But this should be done only if such action fits in with your giving plans. Except in the large estates, your will should be used primarily to achieve your giving goals, not to avoid taxes.

Q. With an estate less than $600,000, should I worry about death taxes?

A. Since your estate is less than the federal exemption, your concern is only as to state death taxes. Whether your estate would be liable for any state death tax could depend upon who your beneficiaries are.

Since about half of the states have enacted only the pick-up tax—a tax which takes effect only if you have a federal estate tax liability—you may have no death tax to worry about at all. The other states have some form of inheritance or succession tax, but generally their exemptions are generous as to close relatives and their rates are not considered confiscatory.

Q. By placing all of my property in a trust, can I avoid death taxes?

A. No, unless your trust is an irrevocable trust, which would be unlikely. But if it were an irrevocable trust, you could be liable for federal gift taxes. If so, you would be paying your (death) taxes upfront, rather than at the time of your death.

Many individuals are enchanted with the idea of avoiding probate by placing their property in a revocable living trust. They sometimes confuse "avoiding probate" with "avoiding death taxes." The two terms are not synonymous as far as the federal estate tax is concerned and may not be true as to state death taxes either.

A few states have gift taxes. And many states tax transfers made without full and adequate consideration if they occurred within a certain period prior to death. A revocable trust is one of those transfers covered by these statutes.

Q. Which is preferable, the federal gift tax or the federal estate tax?

A. Because of the unified credit, you are in effect discussing the same tax, although the timing of each is different. Because of this timing, you are normally better off to pay the tax upon your death.

You would have use of the property during your lifetime. And, if the lifetime transfer was so large as to cause a gift tax—because the value of the gift exceeds your lifetime exemption—then your estate would lose the use of the monies paid for taxes during your lifetime. In effect, you would be prepaying your taxes.

Q. What if choosing the alternate valuation date on the federal estate tax return benefits one beneficiary over another? Who makes the decision whether to use the later valuation date?

A. The personal representative is responsible for filing the federal estate tax return. He or she thus is responsible for making all decisions relative to valuations, elections, time of filing, and so on.

If the estate consists of several pieces of property, possibly some properties will benefit by the election and some will not. The benefit might arise for those properties that end up with the highest valuation, or basis. Of course, some beneficiaries may not want a higher valuation because it could mean liability for higher death taxes.

If the personal representative determines this to be a problem and the parties cannot agree among themselves, he or she may want to go to probate court. The court can then make the determination as to what date to use. However, the problem would have to be resolved quickly because of the time limitations in filing the return and paying the tax.

Q. What if a distributee refuses to pay his or her share of the death tax?

A. Normally, any taxes owing by the various distributees in an estate are advanced by the personal representative out of estate assets. At the time of distribution the amounts so advanced are deducted from the distributees' respective shares. This saves time and usually eliminates many difficulties.

But if this cannot be done for any reason, the personal representative should make an application of the court for instructions, giving notice to the nonpaying distributee. Presumably, the court would not be in sympathy with that distributee.

Q. If a personal representative makes an election to use the alternate valuation date on the federal estate tax return, can the election later be rescinded if it is found to be a mistake?

A. No. Once made, the election cannot be revoked.

The federal estate tax return also asks for other elections. Making the wrong decision on some of these can be avoided by making a protective election. In doing so, the personal representative is in effect saying, "I don't know whether to make the election, but I want the right to do so later if I find it to be advisable." But this hedging is not available as to the alternate valuation date.

Q. With a combined estate of husband and wife exceeding $1,200,000, should an arrangement be made for both estates to bear some tax? Or should only the estate of the last one to die be taxed? Is there any rule of thumb that would apply?

A. No, although some lawyers may have their own rule, which their clients may or may not agree with.

One argument is that if both estates pay some tax, the rates will be kept lower. But reasons may suggest a contrary plan. One may be that if no tax is paid in the first estate, more monies will be available for use by the surviving spouse. This is sometimes referred to as giving the spouse a greater security blanket.

You may be aware of the "rule of 72." This rule states that if your money earns 7.2 percent compounded annually, then it doubles in 10 years. Or if it earns 10 percent, it doubles in 7.2 years. To determine the answer, you divide 72 by the interest rate. Knowing this, you may conclude that the money saved by not paying the tax upon the first death will earn more than what the increased tax will be upon the second death, even though computed at a higher rate.

Commentators often say "do the numbers." But many factors have to be taken into consideration, such as your ages, your respective healths, the prospect of inflation, and the likelihood of a growing estate of the survivor. If you do the numbers, the answer still might be, psychologically yes, financially no, as to deferral.

17
Post-Mortem
Estate Planning

Many times, following a death, the decedent's personal representative or his or her survivors, whether heirs or beneficiaries, have an opportunity to benefit the estate or themselves by taking certain actions. These actions generally are referred to as post-mortem estate planning.

The actions actually constitute options or elections that may be available following the death of a deceased estate owner. Every such available option is considered an estate planning tool which, like any other tool, may or may not be used, depending upon what benefits are gained by doing so.

Some people think of post-mortem planning only in terms of saving death and income taxes, probably because of the importance of these costs, particularly in the larger estates. But with this type of planning other choices may be made, activities that may have little or no relation to taxes. These nontax actions may benefit any number of individuals, whereas any federal estate tax saving—and possibly a state tax saving—will benefit only the residuary distributees, except in those states providing for tax apportionment or unless the will provides otherwise.

Whether tax or nontax benefits result, each planning decision must be made with care. The overall effect of each action must be considered. Otherwise, difficulties may arise. For example, a determination may shift economic benefits or burdens from one distributee to another.

Three distinct parties may benefit from, or be harmed by, post-mortem planning: the decedent, the decedent's estate, and those who inherit. Because benefiting one party may harm another, the parties may experience a conflict of interest. Sometimes this conflict places the personal representative in the uncomfortable position of making choices between individuals. Usually, though, the action chosen is the one that will result in an overall tax saving or benefit. Some jurisdictions may require an equitable adjustment to be made between the distributees should this action result in unequal benefits.

Post-mortem "planning" has been referred to as post-mortem "opportunities"—a term deemed more accurate in defining what should be considered upon the death of an estate owner. Such opportunities could be subdivided into "planned" post-mortem opportunities and "natural," or "unplanned," opportunities.

The planned opportunities would be those anticipated or designed by the decedent prior to his or her death. The natural, or unplanned, opportunities would be those that become available to the personal representative and distributees following the decedent's death, regardless of his or her wishes or planning. The following sections will make this distinction.

As you proceed, you should be aware of two things. First, if a decedent has failed to make a will, it is doubtful that any premortem estate planning has taken place or even could have taken place. Second, it is unlikely that post-mortem estate planning is relevant to a decedent who dies owning no probate property.

As you will soon determine, the opportunities of a testator in planning for post-mortem actions, although important, are quite limited.

Decedent's Planned Post-Mortem Opportunities

Disclaimers

Just because you have inherited property, either by will or by descent or even by joint tenancy—an occurrence known as a *deemed transfer*—does not mean that you are required to accept the inheritance. Under federal law and many state laws you are allowed to disclaim all or a portion of your inheritance, as long as you follow the detailed procedures prescribed in the applicable statutes.

Disclaim means "to renounce" or "to refuse." It is not the same as "to relinquish" or "to release." The latter terms have some element of acceptance upon the part of the recipient, an act which is totally prohibited under the disclaimer statutes.

A disclaimer is normally considered as a post-mortem estate planning technique. Although the disclaimer statutes normally apply to lifetime transfers by gift as well, this discussion will be limited to the usual post-mortem situation.

In order to be able to make a partial disclaimer, the property must be severable. However, if real estate is involved, a fractional interest or an undivided portion of the property may be disclaimed.

A qualified disclaimer does not constitute a gift from the disclaimant to the party receiving the property as a result of the disclaimer. The rationale is that if the disclaimant never received the property, he or she never had anything to give. This is the reason that the disclaimant cannot first accept the property and thereafter disclaim it. Since the disclaimer does not constitute a gift, neither the federal gift tax statute nor any state gift tax statute comes into play.

The federal disclaimer statute and regulations have many procedural requirements, none of which can be violated. For instance, the disclaimer must be in writing. It must be received by the transferor of the interest, the legal representative, or the holder of the legal title to the property not later than nine months after the date of transfer (upon a death, for example) or the day on which the person making the disclaimer attained age 21, whichever is later.

State disclaimer statutes may vary somewhat from the federal statute. If a variance does exist, then the higher standard—the more strict—of the two laws will normally apply. For instance, the federal statute provides that the disclaimer shall be made within nine months, but if a state statute provides that it shall be made within six months, then the six-month time period (being the higher standard) will apply. Of course if the federal statute does not apply, because the gross estate does not exceed the amount of the federal exemption of $600,000, then only the state disclaimer statute applies, regardless of the higher standard rule.

Individuals who plan their estates are the only ones who are likely to plan for possible disclaimers. Since very few testators expect a bequest to be disclaimed, however, most testators make no provision in their wills for such a possibility. Those testators that do provide for a possible disclaimer are likely to be wealthy and consequently require more complicated wills.

Although disclaimers generally may occur in either the testate or intestate situation, they are most likely to be used in the testate situation, which would be a planned post-mortem opportunity.

As indicated above, no part of the property disclaimed nor any of its benefits can have been accepted by the disclaimant. This includes the requirement that the disclaimant must allow the interest to pass according to the statute.

This also means that there can be no express or implied agreement as to the disclaimed property. Nor can the disclaimant receive any consideration in return for making the disclaimer. Nor can any of the burdens or liabilities of the property be assumed by the disclaimant subsequent to the death.

The disclaimer must be unqualified and, once made, is irrevocable. The disclaimer must be effective under state law in order to be effective under the federal act.

Disclaimers may be made for any reason. You may disclaim because your estate is as large as you want it to be or, possibly, because you prefer that someone other than you inherit the disclaimed property. Or you may disclaim because of tax considerations, since no law prohibits a party from trying to avoid (not evade) taxes. Whatever the motive for disclaiming, it should not be made an issue.

If you make a disclaimer, what happens to the property which, in effect, you have refused to accept? State laws, if any, may differ somewhat, so this discussion is directed primarily toward the federal disclaimer act.

If a testator anticipates that you might disclaim, then he or she probably will provide in his or her will for an alternate disposition of the disclaimed property. Otherwise, the property descends or is distributed as if you had died prior to the date of the decedent's death. This means, if the will does not provide otherwise, that if you are the disclaiming party, the property will go to your heirs as of the date of testator's death according to your state laws of descent and distribution. This also is true if the decedent dies intestate.

As indicated earlier, state disclaimer laws, if any, may not conform to the federal law. This can cause problems, especially if the time limits for disclaiming are not similar. Although the National Conference of Commissioners on Uniform State Laws adopted uniform disclaimer acts in 1973 and 1978, only 19 states have enacted one or more of the uniform disclaimer acts or an amended or substantially similar version thereof.

The QTIP Trust

One other situation that is planned by a testator is the QTIP trust. QTIP is the commonly used abbreviation for "qualified terminal interest property," a form of testamentary trust discussed in Chapters 7 and 8.

This trust is set up in a testator's will with the intent that the personal representative will eventually elect to use it. The representative is not bound to do so, however. Or, more rarely, it could be the other way around in that the testator did not want the election to be made, but the representative did so anyway.

To qualify as a QTIP trust, all of the trust income must go to the spouse, payable at least annually. And, under any power of appointment, interest in the property may pass only to the surviving spouse during her or his lifetime.

Post-mortem planning is involved in that the representative must determine, presumably with the help of the surviving spouse, whether any federal estate tax advantage is gained by electing to treat the trust as a QTIP trust. When this evaluation is made, the probable estate tax in both estates is taken into consideration. Thus, the matter considered is, What will be the total of the two taxes if one course or another is taken? It is not solely, What will be the tax in the estate of the first to die?

If the election is not made, then the trust property is subject to the federal estate tax upon the first spouse's death. This happens because in this form of trust the property is not going outright to the surviving spouse. Only the income from the trust is going to the spouse. Thus the testamentary gift under the trust is considered terminal. And, ordinarily, gifts to a spouse must not be considered terminal in order to qualify for the marital deduction.

If a representative elects to treat an existing trust as a QTIP trust, then the trust property is not subject to the federal estate tax upon the first spouse's death. But the property is subject to the tax upon the second spouse's death. This is true even though the trust gift is terminal, because the QTIP election creates an exception to the terminal interest rule.

Decedent's Unplanned Post-Mortem Opportunities

Surprisingly, some of the things that a testator provides for can be undone by his heirs and beneficiaries. But even if a decedent leaves no will, whether intentionally or not, the heirs and personal representative have several opportunities to make choices. Presumably the choices are made to benefit one or more parties. You can determine this for yourself as you read through the following discussion.

Income Tax Strategies

If a final federal individual income tax return (form 1040) of the decedent is due, it is the responsibility of the personal representative to file it on behalf of the decedent. In doing so, the representative may have three options, any one of which may benefit the overall tax situation:

1. *Decide whether to join with the surviving spouse in the decedent's final return.* Although a joint return ordinarily is most beneficial for both parties, it is not necessarily so. And because of possible exposure to additional liability, the representative may not be anxious to join in the same return with the surviving spouse. The option of a joint return with the widow(er)

is not available if the surviving spouse remarries before the end of the tax year in which the death occurred.

The surviving spouse may elect to file the joint return if no fiduciary has been appointed before the due date of the return. In this event the surviving spouse signs the return in her own capacity and also on behalf of the deceased spouse. However, under certain circumstances, a subsequently appointed personal representative may disaffirm the return and file a new, separate return.

2. *Elect whether to take the decedent's medical expenses as a deduction on either the income tax return or on the federal estate tax return.* It cannot be taken on both. Because of the limited availability of the income tax deduction for medical expenses and because most estates do not require a federal estate tax return, this option usually is unavailable in either case.

However, if the medical deduction is to be taken on the income tax return, such medical expenses either must have incurred during the year or must be paid within one year of death. And if these expenses are deducted, a statement must accompany the return, showing that they are not also being taken as a deduction for federal estate tax purposes, that the federal deduction is being waived.

3. *Assuming the decedent died owning E or EE bonds, elect on which income tax return, the decedent's individual return or the estate return, the accrued bond interest should be reported.* This election affects only the federal income tax return since the interest is exempt from state income taxes.

E or EE bond interest normally is accrued by an owner and not reported for income tax purposes until the bonds are redeemed. When the owner of the bonds dies and the bonds are redeemed, the estate can elect to take all the then-accrued interest on the decedent's final federal income tax return (form 1040) or report such interest on the estate's federal income tax return (form 1041).

Oftentimes, the decedent has little income in the year of death. Thus reporting all of the accrued bond interest on the decedent's final federal income tax return can result in good post-mortem estate planning. In any event, by making a proper choice substantial overall income tax savings result.

Unfortunately, the total redemption value of the E or EE bonds at time of death, including all accrued interest regardless whether such interest was previously reported by the decedent, must be included on both the federal and state death tax returns. This results in double taxation of the interest—once on the federal income tax return and once on the death tax returns. Although such interest is exempt from the state income tax, it is not exempt from a state death tax since the total value of the bonds at time of death constitute the date of death value of the asset.

All of what has been said above applies to federal income tax returns. But it could apply to state returns if the statute were similar to the federal one. Thus all the options might be equally beneficial for the state return.

Administration Expenses

Somewhat similar elections are also available as to administration expenses. These consist mainly of fiduciary fees, bond costs, attorney fees, court costs, appraisal fees, accounting fees, and sales expenses. Such expenses may be taken as a deduction on the federal estate tax return (form 706), if any, or on the estate fiduciary income tax return (form 1041). Or such deductions may be split between the two returns in any manner.

If any part of the deductions are taken on the income tax return, a written election must accompany the return. But before making the election the personal representative must take into consideration the comparative benefits to the two returns.

Those expenses not used on the federal estate tax return are sometimes allowed to be used on the state death tax return, even though they were also used on the state income tax return. And if no federal estate tax return is filed, then the total of such expenses may be used on the federal fiduciary income tax return and are often allowed on both the state death tax return and the state fiduciary income tax return.

Fiduciary Fees

If you serve as the personal representative of an estate, you are entitled to receive a fee, sometimes referred to as a commission, for such services. For income tax purposes, this fee is treated the same as any of your other earnings. The income you receive for serving is taxable and reportable on your individual income tax returns.

You may wish to waive the fee for either of two reason. If you are the residuary beneficiary or sole heir, then you should waive the fee, since any property you inherit is free from income tax except income earned off that property. Thus you would be extremely foolish to take a fee and pay income tax on it, when you will be receiving (inheriting) the property anyway.

And for goodwill purposes you may want to waive your right to a fee. Suppose, for example, that you and your sibling are inheriting all of your parent's property. You may not want to take a fee under such circumstances. In this example, you are actually giving up only one-half of the fee, since you would be inheriting the other half of the fee in any event.

Sometimes in goodwill situations you may have difficulty in deciding whether to waive your fee. You may want to delay a decision until first determining how much work is entailed in serving as the personal representative. Or you may delay until you find out what the attitude of the other distributees is toward you.

The IRS requires you to make a formal waiver of any right to compensation within six months after your appointment. Sometimes, however, your conduct is deemed to imply a waiver. Otherwise, the fee may be imputed to you even though the compensation was not taken. If it is imputed, you are taxed on the amount that you are deemed to have earned, even though you did not actually receive it.

Alternate Valuation Date

Federal estate tax law allows the personal representative to elect to report the value of the estate property either as of the date of death or, alternately, six months thereafter, as was discussed in Chapter 16. Some states also follow this rule, although they require the two death tax returns to be consistent if a federal estate tax return is filed. For both returns, the date chosen—the date of death or the date six months after the death—must be used for all property. If that property, however, had been sold within the six-month period, then the date of sale is the date used and the value shown is the sales price.

However, the alternate valuation date is available for federal purposes only if using it will decrease both the value of the gross estate and the net federal estate tax due after application of all allowable credits. In other words, the alternate valuation date is not allowed to be used for increasing the basis of property for income tax purposes. For some individual properties, though, that may in fact occur.

The income tax basis of inherited property is the market value of the property used for death tax purposes. For example, suppose you inherit a farm that is valued on the death tax return (using either date) at $100,000, and this amount is agreed to by the taxing body. Then $100,000 is deemed to be the basis (or purchase price) for determining gain or loss when you sell the farm. If you thereafter sell the farm for $120,000, then, ignoring adjustments for cost of sale, depreciation, and capital improvements, you have a gain of $20,000 (sales price of $120,000 less the basis of $100,000).

Widow's or Widower's Allowance

A request for a surviving spouse's allowance (see Chapter 14) oftentimes is made because a possible state death tax advantage can be gained in doing so.

Suppose that you are a surviving spouse. You have ample assets of your own on which to live during the estate period, but you have little taxable income during this period. By asking for a widow's or widower's allowance, as the case may be, you may secure an additional deduction on the estate's state death tax return. Perhaps you will also incur little or no adverse income tax consequences to yourself.

Usually the allowance is to be taken from estate income first. To the extent that the allowance does represent income, then it must be reported by the surviving spouse on his or her income tax return. This is the reason that the surviving spouse's income must be considered before seeking the allowance. Otherwise, adverse income tax consequences could result.

Choosing the Taxable Year

When an estate administration proceeding is opened, then the estate is considered a taxable entity for income tax purposes, the same as you are. The first taxable year begins from the date of death, even though the estate proceeding may not be opened until some time thereafter.

But what is considered the end of the first taxable year? Like most new income tax payers, the personal representative has a choice of choosing either a calendar year or a fiscal year. The choice depends upon the comparable tax advantage to the estate and, perhaps, to the distributees.

Thus if the decedent died on September 3, 1992, but the estate was not opened until several days thereafter, the taxable year still begins on September 3, 1992. It may end either on December 31, 1992, in which case it is considered a calendar year, or on the last day of any other month up through August 31, 1993, in which case it is considered a fiscal year.

If the first return is also the final return—because the estate is being closed in that time frame—then the ending date may be any day of the month not more than 12 months after the date of death. If the first return is not the final return, then the ending date of the first return must be on the last day of a month, not more than 12 months after death. But ending the period on December 31 in effect creates a calendar year. Any subsequent return that is not the final return must be for the full period of 12 months, the period ending on the last day of the month.

The final return need not be for a full period of 12 months. This is true whether it is also the first return or a subsequent return. And even if it is not also the first return, the ending date may be any day of the month. But of course the final return must start as of the date of death or the day following the previous return, as the case may be.

All net income and excess deductions shown on a final return must be passed on (distributed) to the heirs or beneficiaries. Hence no tax is ever paid with the final return, which actually serves only as an informational return.

Because of the requirement that the final return must pass through all allowable deductions and all income to the residuary distributees, often it is not advisable for the first return to also be the final return. If income is received during the period, it is usually beneficial to split up the period with an initial return and a final return. The initial return can offset deductions from income and can also take advantage of the estate's $600 annual exemption, which is deductible from the estate's adjusted total income. The $600 exemption is not available on a final return, even though the final return is also the first return.

Because of the Tax Reform Act of 1986 there is less incentive to pass on the allowable deductions to the distributees. Both prior and subsequent to the act, the passed-through deductions can be taken as miscellaneous deductions on the individual returns of the distributees (Schedule A, form 1040).

Under the act, however, the miscellaneous itemized deductions on the individual return are allowed only to the extent that the aggregate of such deductions exceeds 2 percent of adjusted gross income. Since the 2 percent floor is seldom exceeded, passing the deductions on to the distributees rarely has any tax advantage. Thus such deductions usually are lost because they cannot be taken. Thus the personal representative should usually endeavor to use the deductions on the estate income tax return (form 1041).

Having a choice of time periods, the personal representative can choose time frames most likely to produce the smallest overall income tax. He or she thus takes advantage of the income tax exemptions and keeps the income in the lowest possible tax brackets.

The following example still may have some merit, but because the 1986 Act has tended to blend tax rates, less benefits may result from taking such action. Whether such action will be beneficial in the future depends upon the ongoing tax changes passed by the federal government.

Suppose, for example, that a decedent dies on January 8, 1992. The administration of his estate is opened January 20, 1992. The relevant state law requires the estate proceeding to be open for a period of four months. At the end of the four months, or on May 20, 1992, the personal representative is ready to close the estate proceeding. But on April 15, 1992, the estate receives a large interest payment on a Treasury note. The sole beneficiary does not want this interest income to be passed on to him, as his own income will be large enough for the year 1992.

If the personal representative made only one income tax return for the estate, for the period from January 8, 1992, to May 20, 1992, then such income would have to be passed on to the beneficiary, who would then be required to report this income on his individual return for the year 1992 (the year the estate is closed).

To avoid the passing of the income, the representative makes an initial return for the period from January 8, 1992, to April 30, 1992. In this return the income received April 15, 1992, is reported. Then immediately the representative makes a final return for the period from May 1, 1992, to May 20, 1992. This last return shows no income and so nothing is passed on to the beneficiary.

In the above example, note that the date the period starts is the date of death, as required, not the date the administration was opened. Note, also, that the ending date of the first return is the end of a month, as required. Again, note that the ending date of the final return need not be the end of a month, as allowed. Finally, note that neither period is for 12 months.

A first-time taxpayer has the right to choose either a fiscal year or a calendar year. In the example above, the taxpayer (the personal representative) chose a fiscal year ending April 30. And the final return need not be for a full 12-month period since the taxpaying entity (the estate) ceased to exist for all practical purposes as of May 20.

For the same reason, the final individual income tax return of the decedent ended on January 8, 1992, the date the deceased taxpayer ceased to exist. Thus the final return of the decedent, who is assumed to have been filing returns on a calendar-year basis—as most taxpayers do—would be for the short period of January 1, 1992, to January 8, 1992. This return may be filed shortly after death or not later than April 15, 1993. But the personal representative must file the return, and so the return actually would be filed before the estate is closed.

If large amounts of income are received on a regular basis by the estate, an heir or residuary beneficiary (to whom the unreported income is distributed on the final return) might not be anxious for the estate to be closed at an early date. If the estate were large in the above example, the beneficiary might want it to remain open at least into the year 1993. This would then allow the beneficiary another year (1993) in which to report the passed-through income on his or her individual income tax return.

Thus timing in closing the estate may be important. But the IRS allows only a reasonable time for the personal representative to perform the duties of administration. If the administration is deemed unduly prolonged, the IRS will impute the estate income to the distributees as if they in fact had received it.

Widow's or Widower's Election

Testator's plans can also be changed if you, as surviving spouse, elect not to take under your deceased spouse's will (see Chapter 14). If you elect not to take under the will, then you do not receive what the will gave you, if anything. Rather, you receive the statutory share as provided by your state statute. The amount varies from state to state, but frequently the amount is about one-third of your spouse's entire estate.

State statutes generally set out the procedures for making the election. Usually time limits are set for making the election.

Will Contest

You may have a fear of a will contest, although you probably haven't actually known of one personally. Yet a will contest or settlement can occur on a friendly basis. For example, it can be used to clarify an ambiguity or to rectify some term of a will believed unfair to one or more parties. This type of contest, if it can be called that, is more like a family agreement.

Family Agreement

A will does not have to be admitted to probate when a family agreement is entered into. For various reasons, such as to benefit a child disinherited under the will, the beneficiaries named in a will may decide not to offer the will for probate. Instead, they may agree to a distribution different from that provided in the will. Such an agreement is generally upheld by the courts as long as (1) all beneficiaries agree to a different arrangement, or are compensated to the extent that the will provides, (2) all of the decedent's heirs who are not distributees agree, and (3) all of the decedent's creditors are provided for. The personal representative named in the will is not a necessary party.

When there is no will, a family agreement also may be used to avoid the consequences of the laws of inheritance. This may be done, for instance, to benefit a stepchild who otherwise would not have been entitled to a share of decedent's estate.

Failure of Probate Property

Of course, a will is not admitted to probate if there is no estate to probate. Possibly the decedent actually has no estate whatsoever, so there is no reason to have the will admitted to probate. But most likely not having an estate to probate means that all of the decedent's property consists of nonprobate property. One of the most likely nonprobate situations is that the decedent held all of his or her property in joint tenancy with another. If so, the surviving joint tenant will receive the property regardless of the terms of the decedent's will. Thus nothing exists to probate.

But even in these situations, the will often is admitted to probate in order to preserve its terms. This is done to avoid a disinheritance in the event probate property is later found to exist. Otherwise, because of various statutes of limitations, it might be too late to probate the will if and when such property is found.

Special Use Valuation

Another possible post-mortem vehicle is special use under Section 2032A of the Internal Revenue Code (see Chapter 16). Because of the potential significant savings in death taxes, the prospect of electing special use cannot be ignored.

Special use has to do with valuing a farm, ranch, or other real property used in a trade or business at "its value for the use under which it qualifies." This means that the property is valued at its actual use. The net effect is that the value of the property for death tax purposes is substantially less than if the property were valued at market value, as is normally the case for property of a decedent. Reducing the value of the property results in lowering or even eliminating the federal estate tax.

Why wouldn't all decedents' estates want to utilize special use if the result is a federal estate tax saving? Unfortunately, the statute sets up numerous prerequisites before special use can qualify. In a particular estate, some of these many threshold requirements may not exist. If not, the election is unavailable.

The statute also provides for numerous postrequisites. The parties inheriting the property, even assuming they and the property qualify, may not be willing to abide by such requirements, or at least they may be fearful that they cannot. Failure to abide by these conditions could result in recapture of all death tax savings. And a sale of the property by the owners before the end of the required holding period could result in disastrous income tax consequences. It would because the basis for determining gain or loss would be the special use value, not the market value at time of death.

For all these reasons, special use should be chosen only after careful consideration and consultation with your attorney.

Whether or not special use is deemed at that time a desirable option and whether or not the estate appears qualified for special use, the personal representative should file a protective election when filing the return. Otherwise, an election cannot be made after the due date of the return. Filing of the protective election does not require the estate to thereafter proceed with the special use if it is later deemed not to be a good idea.

Estate Tax Payment Deferral

Generally, the federal estate tax return is due nine months after death and the tax shown due on the return must be paid with the return. But two exceptions to the payment rule exist.

Section 6166 of the Internal Revenue Code provides, under certain circumstances, for the deferred payment of the federal estate tax in installments. As under special use, certain prerequisites and postrequisites are required. But the worst that can happen if any of the requirements are violated is that the unpaid balance of the tax and all accrued interest is accelerated.

The main requirement is that at least 35 percent of the decedent's adjusted gross estate must consist of a closely held business, such as a farm or ranch operated by the decedent. If the requirement is met, the personal representative may elect to pay part or all of the tax in 2 or more, but not exceeding 10, equal installments.

The attraction of the election is twofold. Interest on the unpaid portion of the federal estate tax is payable at an annual rate of 4 percent (regardless of market interest rates), beginning from the due date nine months after the decedent's death. Second, the first principal installment of the tax is not due until the fifth year following the normal due date of the tax.

For example, suppose the decedent dies January 1, 1992, and Section 6166 is available because all qualifying conditions have been met. Normally the estate tax is due nine months after death, or in this case October 1, 1992. But the personal representative has made an election under Section 6166 to pay the tax in 10 equal installments, beginning with the fifth year (the latest that the principal payments can begin).

Under this set of facts, the computed tax is not paid on October 1, 1992. Beginning October 1, 1993, interest at 4 percent from October 1, 1992 on the amount of tax due is paid. The same applies for the years 1994, 1995, and 1996. Beginning October 1, 1997 (the fifth year), accrued interest on all unpaid balance plus the first of 10 equal installments is paid. And payments are made on each succeeding October 1 until the year 2006 when the last payment is made. Although the Section 6166 grace period is generally referred to as 15 years, the maximum time frame is actually 14 years and 9 months from the date of death.

At the time the federal estate tax return is filed deferment of the tax under Section 6166 may not be desired. Or perhaps the estate does not seem as if it would qualify for the deferment. Even so, it is usually preferable for the personal representative to file a protective election under Section 6166. Then if an election under Section 6166 is later found to be desirable, the right to election is not lost. Like special use, without the protective election an election cannot be filed after the due date of the return.

The second exception to the rule that payment must be made within nine months of death occurs if a request for an extension of time has been granted.

The general rule is that an extension of time for payment of the estate tax may be granted by the IRS for an additional period of 12 months (21 months from the date of death). Under a special rule, for reasonable cause shown and approved, this period may be extended for a total period of 10 years from the due date of the tax (10 years and 9 months from the date of death). Interest, however, from the due date must be paid on all tax amounts outstanding, regardless of the granting of any extension.

Some Common Questions Answered

Q. Can you give me an example of when a testator may plan for a possible disclaimer?

A. Yes. Suppose that at the time a testator is making his will he has a net estate of $600,000. He wants his wife, who has no property in her name, to receive all of his property, or at least all the benefit of his property during her lifetime. His problem is that he believes that by the time he dies his estate could well be worth more than $600,000, perhaps as much as $800,000.

He realizes that if his estate did in fact amount to $800,000 and if his wife died subsequent to him, then upon her death her estate would be subject to a large federal estate tax. But he is reluctant to freeze his property in a "built-in" testamentary trust in the event his calculations are wrong and upon his death his estate amounted only to around $600,000.

Thus in his will he leaves all of his property to his wife but provides that if she disclaims part or all of his estate, that part disclaimed shall go into a bypass trust. Although his wife would receive the benefits from the trust during the remainder of her life, the amount disclaimed and passing into the bypass trust would then be isolated from her estate and not be subject to federal estate taxes in her estate.

This is a good example of a planned post-mortem opportunity. The testator has left the door open for some post-mortem activity which would not harm his estate but could possibly be of great benefit to his spouse and her estate. By doing it in this manner, the testator has relieved himself of the necessity of having to frequently change his will to meet changing circumstances. And perhaps at some point he would be unable to change his will because of some disability.

Q. Is post-mortem planning available if all of the decedent's property consists of nonprobate property?

A. No, with one or two possible exceptions. When the decedent has placed, perhaps unintentionally, all of his or her property out of the reach of a personal representative and heirs, then they have nothing to control, no choices to make.

The exceptions may be the use of disclaimers and family agreements. A surviving joint tenant, for instance, may be able to disclaim the joint tenancy property, if that were desired. And possibly the benefited parties could readjust their inheritances received through the nonprobate route by means of a family agreement.

Q. Before a distributee decides to disclaim, can she or he legally talk to an attorney to determine the effect of such disclaimer?

A. Yes, because determining the effect of the disclaimer is not tantamount to acceptance. All that the distributee is doing is determining whether or not to renounce or refuse the gift.

Q. May the personal representative split some of the decedent's accrued E or EE bond interest between the decedent's final return and the estate's fiduciary return?

A. No. The interest accrued to the time of death must all be reported on one or the other return, assuming the bonds are redeemed during the period of the estate. The personal representative cannot report some of the interest on the decedent's final return and the balance on the fiduciary return.

Once a decision is made to accrue or not to accrue the interest, then it must be followed by the taxpayer as to all similar bonds whether then owned or thereafter acquired. And when the taxpayer decides to report the interest, then for all subsequent years the interest must continue to be reported.

However, each subsequent owner of the bonds has a choice of accruing or reporting the interest as it is earned until such time as the bonds are cashed. In theory, therefore, although such accrued interest has been reported on the decedent's final return, the representative, being a new taxpayer, could begin letting the interest accrue thereafter. It probably wouldn't happen that way for long, since the bonds presumably will be cashed before the estate is closed.

Q. Our father's will seemed unfair, so we children, as sole heirs, entered into a family agreement. We don't want to probate his will, but someone told us that the will must be filed with the probate clerk. Do we have to do so?

A. Your information may be right but your conclusion is wrong. Some statutes do require anyone in possession of a will to file it with the appropriate county official upon the death of its maker. But filing it and offering it for probate are two different things. When filed, it is merely placed with the court official for safekeeping. Until someone asks that it be admitted to probate it lies dormant and unused.

If all interested parties named in the will and any other heirs are part of the agreement, it would not appear necessary to file the will with the court official. No one is hurt and no other party has the right to object. But filing it should do no harm.

Q. When an estate passes income and deductions on to the beneficiaries for reporting on their individual income tax returns, how do the beneficiaries know what to do?

A. It is really quite simple. Attached to the estate's fiduciary return (form 1041) filed by the personal representative with the IRS is a form known as a K-1. This form, a copy of which is given to each residuary beneficiary, shows exactly on which line of their personal federal income tax return the listed items are to be placed.

18

Working With
an Estate Attorney

By now you should have arrived at two conclusions: (1) you will benefit by knowing all the details about estate planning revealed in this book, and (2) you should not try to be your own lawyer.

Let's consider the first conclusion, How can you benefit by carefully reading this book? Two things can be gained:

1. *You will quite likely end up with a better estate plan than you would have had without this background.* This is perhaps the most important outcome. Without knowing the details of estate planning revealed in this book, you would waste a great deal of time with your attorney in estate planning sessions. Your attorney would have to explain many details of estate law to you. And he or she would have to wrangle the correct information from you. Despite this, you might still omit a crucial piece of information.

Knowing what you know, however, you are able to supply your attorney with all relevant information he or she needs to make up your estate plan. You are also able to evaluate his or her work and determine if it is the best plan for you.

2. *The attorney fees can be kept in line.* Without having to devote most of your sessions to explanations of estate planning, you and your attorney can spend your time on more productive matters: determining what is best for you. And more efficient use of time will result in lower costs. In other words, you will get good results for a good fee.

Concerning the second conclusion, Why shouldn't you be your own lawyer? As has been stated before, without knowing all of the intricacies of estate law, you, acting as your attorney, might commit a costly error—one which you might be "locked into" for life.

Instead of using this book as a "how to" book for practicing law yourself, use it as a guide for determining when to see a lawyer and how to prepare for consultations with him or her. Also use it to help you understand your estate.

Choosing Your Estate Attorney

How does one go about selecting a good lawyer, that is, one with years of experience, continuing legal education, and specialization?

Selecting an estate lawyer merely by picking a name out of the telephone book might not result in the best method, despite that individual's accreditation. What are other ways, then, to find an estate lawyer?

One is by hearsay. Who do other people recommend? This has its limitations because the experience of another party may have been in an entirely different field of law.

Another is by lawyer advertising. The best advertisement is one that states that the lawyer's practice is "limited to" estate (or probate) matters. The second-best ad is one that states that the lawyer "specializes in" such work. But any lawyer can now legally advertise. A lawyer is not supposed to misrepresent, but no good system exists for monitoring the ads. Check the ad carefully. Perhaps what the lawyer is really saying is that he or she merely hopes to do estate work.

Another way to find a lawyer is through lawyer referral lists. By calling the state or local bar you can receive names of lawyers who handle (or hope to handle) estate work. Any lawyer can add his or her name to the list. It is not monitored by the bar, nor does the list constitute a recommendation by the bar.

The most reliable, but by no means all-inclusive, group are the Fellows in the American College of Trust and Estate Counsel, formerly known as the American College of Probate Counsel. But finding them may be difficult as they rarely, if ever, advertise their membership.

If a lawyer is not a member of the American Bar Association and hence cannot be a member of its Real Property, Probate and Trust Law Section, then he or she is unlikely to be a serious practitioner of estate law. This is probably the best test of who is, or wants to be, a good estate lawyer. How do you find out if the lawyer is a member of this section? Ask the lawyer.

No method is foolproof, however. If you are unhappy with your first choice, change lawyers. You are never bound to keep the same lawyer. But be sure that you have good reason to change, as moving from lawyer to lawyer can be expensive.

Potential Conflicts
of Interest

In estate matters, the problem of the professional responsibilities of the lawyer arises from time to time. Do some potential conflicts of interest exist that you should be aware of? Lawyers themselves may not always be aware of possible conflicts, but you may be. Thus you yourself should be on the watch and, if necessary, choose a different attorney.

Conflicts With the Married Couple

Consider one of the most common occurrences, that of the husband and wife being counseled by their mutual attorney as to their wills. Then think of the more extreme situation, one where it is a second marriage for both and each have their own set of children by previous marriages. Might not the couple have differing goals?

Yet suppose, too, that their present marriage is harmonious and they both trust each other as well as their mutual attorney. In spite of these trusts, should they each retain their own lawyer? Should they make their respective wills independently of each other? Or should each spouse of the couple retain his or her own attorneys and later try to reach agreement on mutually satisfying wills?

But think also of the difficulty if their estates are nominal and they want to make reciprocal wills. Think, too, of the added expense if each had to consult his or her own attorney who, in turn, would have to consult with the other attorney so that the wills would, in fact, be reciprocal. If the situation is harmonious, it is doubtful that either of you would want separate attorneys. But both you and your mutual attorney should try to be as open and frank about the situation as possible.

Consider, now, another situation. Suppose that you and your spouse had made reciprocal wills, apparently satisfying to both of you. Now you want to remake your will without your spouse knowing about it. Is it proper for you to go back to your original attorney or should you seek another lawyer?

The question may well be, Is it proper for your first lawyer to represent you under these circumstances? Does the lawyer have a conflict of interest that precludes representing you in this new situation?

Bar ethics would consider that it does. Joint representation is not yet seen as a problem until your and your spouse's interests are no longer in agreement. Regardless of bar ethics, however, many lawyers would not want to be a part of this situation and would send you elsewhere. An unusual exception might be if you actually wanted to give your spouse more than the original will and wanted it to be a pleasant surprise.

Two other situations involving a married couple call for separate representation. One is the antenuptial or postnuptial agreement and the other is the dissolution of the marriage. Although years ago lawyers often represented both parties in these two situations, at least until the circumstance got out of hand, that is no longer true. The double representation is now considered a conflict of interest and thus unethical.

Conflicts With the Estate Administration

As a practical matter and usually legally, the so-called estate attorney is the attorney for the personal representative. It is the representative who chooses the lawyer and who may discharge the lawyer. Beneficiaries and other interested parties seldom have legal rights in the matter, although certainly they could complain to the probate court under some circumstances.

Obviously, the attorney must try to treat all parties fairly and determine that the representative follows statutory procedures. But if a disagreement arises as between the representative and the beneficiaries, the beneficiaries in effect are unrepresented. It is up to them to hire their own attorney to see that their rights are protected. If the attorney tries to represent both sides, it is deemed a conflict of interest.

Conflicts With the Conservatorship

In a conservatorship, the attorney also represents the fiduciary (the conservator), not the ward. Yet the ward may be the very one who asked his or her attorney to open up a voluntary conservatorship. In the voluntary petition the ward nominates (suggests) the conservator. But once the conservator is approved and appointed by the court, the lawyer in effect changes allegiance from the ward to the conservator.

This is not what the lawyer wants and in most instances the lawyer will try to protect the ward also. But if a conflict of some sort arises as between the conservator and the ward, the lawyer is bound to represent only the conservator or, alternately, remove him- or herself from the situation entirely. Many states have recognized this vulnerability of the ward and have adopted or modified their laws accordingly.

Whatever the circumstances, however, laypersons should be alert to possible conflicts of interest and alert the acting attorney who may not be aware of the circumstances. The lawyer should be thankful if the potential problem is called to his or her attention before it gets out of hand.

Glossary

Abatement: The process of establishing an order for distribution of bequests in a will and setting aside or reducing some of them when the net assets of a testate estate are insufficient to pay for all of them.

Ademption: Literally, "a taking away." A situation in which a bequeathed item is not in existence at the time of the testator's death. Whether any substitute will be made for that item depends upon the wording of the will and the law of the state where the will is probated.

Administration: A formal, court-supervised probate proceeding of a deceased's estate in which an administrator or executor (personal representative) is appointed. This type of estate proceeding is to be distinguished from some lesser one, following the death of a property owner, that does not require the appointment of a personal representative. The term may also apply to a small-estate proceeding. See also *Administrator, Executor,* and *Small-estate proceeding.*

Administrator: A party appointed by the court to represent and administer the estate of a decedent who left no will. The administrator is a fiduciary who is referred to as the personal representative of the estate proceeding. An administrator may be either an individual or an entity, such as a bank, authorized to serve in a trust or fiduciary capacity. See also *Administration* and *Letters of appointment.* Compare *Executor.*

Affidavit: A written, sworn statement by an individual, setting forth information (in an estate situation) as to the decedent's heirs and as to property owned by the decedent at the time of death. The statement must be signed before a Notary Public or some other official authorized to take sworn statements.

Ancillary proceeding: An administration proceeding that is subordinate or auxiliary to the principal proceeding being administered in another state. The state where the decedent lived is usually where the principal proceeding is situated. An ancillary proceeding is usually required because the decedent owned property in more than one state.

Antenuptial agreement: A contract, ordinarily in writing, made between a man and woman contemplating marriage. The agreement, made before the marriage, provides how title to each party's property is to be maintained to the exclusion of the other party both upon the marriage and upon its termination. See also *Postnuptial agreement.*

Attorney in fact: The party named in a power of attorney to act as agent for the grantor, or principal. The attorney, acting in a fiduciary capacity, has those powers enumerated in the power of attorney. See also *Grantor* and *Power of attorney.*

Augmented estate: Property interests held by a decedent at the time of death that are considered as neither probate nor nonprobate property. Augmented property usually consists of property transferred during the marriage (other than to a bona fide purchaser or a spouse). It generally has the appearance of nonprobate property except it excludes insurance, annuities, and pensions.

Beneficiary: One who is named as a recipient of property in a decedent's will. Or one designated in a trust to receive benefits provided in the trust agreement. In a will, the beneficiary may also be described as a legatee, devisee, or distributee. The beneficiary in a will is to be distinguished from an heir at law, who inherits when there is no will. See also *Devisee, Distributee, Legatee, Trust,* and *Will.* Compare *Heir.*

Bequeath: To give or devise property, either real or personal, although some states still limit the giving to personal property alone. See also *Bequest* and *Devise.*

Bequest: A gift of property, either real or personal, bequeathed to and received by a beneficiary in a will. See also *Bequeath* and *Devise.*

Bond: See *Fiduciary bond.*

Cestui que trust: Beneficiary of a trust. The beneficiary is said to hold the equitable title to the trust property, whereas the trustee is said to hold the legal title. See also *Beneficiary, Trust,* and *Trustee.*

Charitable lead trust: A trust provided for by Sections 673-677 of the Internal Revenue Code in which a charitable organization first benefits from trust income for a specified period of time. The reversionary or remainder interest then passes to the grantor or the grantor's designated beneficiaries at the termination of the period. See also *Charitable remainder trusts.*

Charitable remainder trusts: Two trusts, the charitable remainder annuity trust and the charitable remainder unitrust, provided for by Section 664 of the Internal Revenue Code. These trusts provide for a contribution of property to a charitable organization as defined by the code. A specified amount is paid out of the trust at least annually to a designated authorized person(s) either for a specified term, not to exceed 20 years, or for the life or lives of such individual(s). The remainder interest is in the charitable organization.

In the annuity trust, only one contribution to the charitable organization is made. And the amount of the payment made by the charitable organization is fixed and never varies. In the unitrust, additional contributions by the grantor may be made at any time and the amount of the payment is refigured each year. Compare with *Charitable lead trust*.

Codicil: A written document amending a will by adding, striking, or otherwise changing the terms or provisions of that will previously drawn by the same individual. It must be executed in the same statutory manner as a will, but need not be witnessed by the same witnesses who witnessed the execution of the prior will. See also *Self-proved will* and *Will*.

Common law: One of the two major systems of law, the other being the civil, or Roman, law. The common law, also known as the English law, grew from that law formulated by the English courts from the thirteenth to the nineteenth centuries. It is the basis of the law in the United States, except for Louisiana. It is usually deemed to be the law except as it has been changed or overridden by statutes or constitutions.

Community property: A form of co-ownership of property in nine states. Such property is acquired by either spouse during their marriage, with numerous exceptions and variations, and it is owned equally by husband and wife. Compare with *Joint tenancy, Tenancy by the entirety*, and *Tenancy in Common*.

Conservator: A party appointed by the court to represent and administer the estate of a living person. The conservator, who is a fiduciary, takes possession (custody and control) of, but not title to, the property of the individual (ward) who is under conservatorship. A conservator sometimes is known as a guardian. The conservator may be an individual or an entity, such as a bank, which has trust powers. See also *Conservatorship* and *Ward*.

Conservatorship: Sometimes known as a guardianship. A statutory estate proceeding, subject to and under the control of the court, for the purpose of a party (conservator) managing the property of an individual (ward) who may or may not be able to handle his or her own property because of mental, physical, or other incapacity. The proceeding may be voluntary or involuntary. See also *Conservator* and *Ward*.

Consideration: A necessary element of a contract in order for the contract to be deemed binding and enforceable. It is something of value that serves as an inducement for the other party to enter into the particular contract. It may be either tangible, such as money, or intangible, such as a promise. It may be stated or it may be implied. Lack thereof may be offered as a defense in a suit to enforce the contract.

Creator: The individual, also known as a grantor, settlor, trustor, or donor, who creates a living trust for the benefit of himself or herself or for the benefit of another. See also *Beneficiary, Cestui que trust,* and *Living trust.*

Curtesy: See *Dower.*

Death taxes: The taxes due or possibly due a state or the federal government as the result of the death of an owner of real or personal property. See also *Estate tax, Federal estate tax,* and *Inheritance tax.*

Decedent: A deceased person. One who has died.

Descent and distribution: The statutory order for the succession of heirs to the estate of a decedent who died intestate (without a will). If a person dies intestate, the decedent's heirs are said to take the decedent's property according to the laws of descent and distribution. See also *Heir* and *Intestate.* Compare *Testate* and *Will.*

Devise: (*n.*) A testamentary gift of property (a legacy)—that is, a gift made by will. (*v.*) The act of giving in a will; synonymous with *give* and *bequeath.* At one time, *devise* referred only to real property, but now it often refers to personal property as well. See also *Bequeath, Bequest,* and *Devisee.*

Devisee: One who is bequeathed or devised property in a will. A beneficiary under a will. Originally, the term was applied only to real property, but now it often applies to personal property as well. See also *Beneficiary, Devise, Distributee,* and *Legatee.*

Disclaimer: A device used by a beneficiary, an heir, or a surviving joint tenant, whereby the recipient refuses to accept either a portion or all of the estate to which he or she is entitled.

Distributee: A party entitled to receive real or personal property from a decedent's estate, either through the decedent's will or as a result of the laws of inheritance. A distributee may be either an heir, a beneficiary, or a surviving spouse. See also *Beneficiary, Devisee,* and *Legatee.*

Donee: One who receives a gift of property from another (donor) during both parties' lifetime. See also *Donor.*

Donor: One who makes a gift of property to another (donee) during both parties' lifetime. Also one who forms or creates a living trust. See also *Creator* and *Donee.*

Dower: Normally that portion of a decedent's estate (property) that the law gives to a surviving spouse. The word *dower* is falling into disuse and may not be used in a particular statute. Originally the term referred only to the interest to which the surviving wife was entitled. The term *curtesy* referred to the interest of the surviving husband. This distinction generally no longer exists. The word dower usually now refers to either situation.

Elective share: Also known as the forced share or statutory share. The share that a surviving spouse has a right to take in lieu of the share bequeathed in the deceased spouse's will. The option is exercised by the surviving spouse in accordance with procedures set out in the statute.

Escheat: The reversion of property to the state. Escheat occurs when heirs of one who died intestate cannot be found.

Estate: The real and personal property of an individual, a decedent, a ward, or a trust. It includes all interests in such property, whether of a part or the whole, owned by the individual during lifetime or at the time of death. See also *Administration, Conservatorship, Trust,* and *Ward.*

Estate planning: A conscious and systematic effort to organize one's legal affairs (the estate) to protect the estate property from loss or shrinkage due to waste or taxes, either during lifetime or at, or subsequent to, time of death. Estate planning is primarily concerned with the preservation and disposition of wealth, not with its accumulation except as may result from proper planning. See also *Estate* and *Post-mortem estate planning.*

Estate proceeding: Usually, an administration of an estate following the death of a property owner. However, it can properly refer to any legal proceeding over which the probate court has jurisdiction. See also *Administration, Conservatorship, Estate, Probate,* and *Trust.*

Estate tax: A tax assessed against the estate of a decedent, rather than against the share of one who has inherited property. See also *Death taxes.* Compare *Inheritance tax.*

Executor: The party who represents and administers the estate of a decedent who left a will. The executor, who is named in the will and who is approved by the court, is a fiduciary who is sometimes referred to as the personal representative of the estate proceeding. An executor may be an individual or an entity, such as a bank, which has trust powers. See also *Administration* and *Letters of appointment.* Compare *Administrator.*

Federal estate tax: The death tax that may be assessed by the federal government against an estate of a decedent at the time of his or her death. A decedent's estate is not subject to the tax unless the taxable estate (roughly equivalent to the net estate) exceeds the federal estate tax exemption of $600,000. See also *Death taxes, Estate tax, Federal estate tax exemption, Inheritance tax, Marital deduction, Unified Credit,* and *Unlimited marital deduction.*

Federal estate tax exemption: The amount in a decedent's estate, either during his or her lifetime or at the time of death, which is exempt from the federal estate tax. The present exemption (since 1987) is $600,000, although Congress may change this amount from time to time. See also *Federal estate tax* and *Unified credit*.

Federal gift tax: The tax assessed by the federal government for gifts of property—cash or otherwise—made by one person (the donor) to another person (the donee) during the donor's lifetime. No tax is assessed as to gifts made to the donor's spouse due to the unlimited marital deduction. No tax is assessed nor is a gift tax return required, regardless of the identity of the donee and the number of gifts and the number of donees, if the total of the gifts made to any one donee in any one year does not exceed $10,000. See also *Federal estate tax exemption, Marital deduction, Unified credit,* and *Unlimited marital deduction.*

Fiduciary: Someone who holds property in trust for another, such as an executor, administrator, personal representative, conservator, or trustee, rather than one who merely holds a position of trust, such as an attorney in fact. See also *Administrator, Conservator, Executor,* and *Trustee.* Compare *Attorney in fact.*

Fiduciary bond: A written promise or obligation signed by the fiduciary and a third party known as the surety. It is required unless exempted by statute, a court, or the instrument that created the fiduciary position. It ensures the faithful discharge of all the duties of the fiduciary's office according to law, including the duty to account. If the fiduciary fails to so perform, then the interested parties may look to the surety for redress. The amount of the bond is ordinarily set by the court and is usually based upon the value of the personal property plus the estimated gross annual income. See also *Fiduciary.*

Forced share: See *Elective share.*

Generation skipping transfer (GST): Concept, originally created by the Tax Reform Act of 1976, designed to tax both lifetime and testamentary gifts (transfers) that skip one generation. The theory of the GST is that each generation should be liable for its share of the federal estate tax. Thus if a generation is skipped, the transfer should be taxed. The generation skipping transfer is sometimes referred to as the *generation skipping trust* or the *generation skipping tax.*

Gift splitting: A gift to a third party made by one spouse with the consent of the other spouse. By reason of such consent, the amount of the gift going tax-free can be doubled. See also *Federal estate tax exemption, Federal gift tax,* and *Unified credit.*

Grantor: An individual who either creates a trust or executes a power of attorney. If the latter, the grantor is also referred to as a principal. See also *Creator* and *Power of attorney.*

Guardian: See *Conservator.*

Guardianship: See *Conservatorship.*

Heir: One who inherits property from a decedent who died intestate (without a will). An heir is determined by the statutory laws of descent and distribution in the decedent's state of residence. A surviving spouse, although possibly having certain statutory rights to the property of the deceased spouse, may not be considered as an heir for all purposes. See also *Descent and distribution.* Compare with *Beneficiary.*

Holographic will: A will wholly in the handwriting of, and signed by, the testator. See also *Will.*

Homestead: Literally, "the home place," the place where a person makes his or her home. It ordinarily consists of one or more contiguous lots or tracts of land, together with the building (home) and other improvements on it. If a person owns more than one home, only one of them can be designated as the homestead.

Inheritance: See *Descent and distribution.*

Inheritance tax: A state death tax assessed against one who inherits property from another who died either with or without a will. The amount of tax, if any, is determined by the relationship of the parties and the size of the inheritance. Unlike an estate tax, which is assessed against the estate, the inheritance tax is assessed against, and paid out of, the share that is inherited, unless a decedent's will or statute provides otherwise. See also *Death taxes* and *Estate tax.* Compare *Federal estate tax.*

Intangible personal property: See *Personal property.*

Internal Revenue Code (IRC): That portion of the laws of the United States, known as Title 26, that pertains to its internal revenue laws. The latest IRC is known as Internal Revenue Code of 1986 as amended.

Inter vivos trust: See *Living trust.*

Intestate: The estate of a person who dies without a will. Since no will exists, the so-called intestate property is distributed according to the statutory laws of inheritance (the laws of descent and distribution). Or that portion of a decedent's estate that is not bequeathed in her or his will. That property is treated as intestate property under the laws of inheritance, rather than under the terms of the will. See also *Descent and distribution.* Compare *Testate.*

Joint tenancy: A form of holding title to property by two or more persons who are known as joint tenants. The result of holding property in this manner is that upon the death of the first joint tenant the decedent's title to the property passes automatically to the surviving joint tenant(s), despite the decedent's will or the laws of inheritance to the contrary. Compare *Community property, Tenancy by the entirety,* and *Tenancy in common.*

Legacy: A gift of property bequeathed to someone by will. See also *Bequest* and *Devise.*

Legatee: Technically, one who is entitled to receive personal property under a will. Commonly understood to mean any distributee under a will, including a distributee of real property. See also *Beneficiary, Devisee,* and *Distributee.*

Letters of administration: See *Letters of appointment.*

Letters of appointment: A short, usually one-page document issued under seal by the clerk or officer of the court showing the appointment and qualification of a fiduciary to act as executor, administrator, conservator, guardian, personal representative, or trustee of an estate proceeding. The document is used by the fiduciary to present to third parties to show its authority to act on behalf of the particular estate. Sometimes referred to as letters of administration or letters testamentary, if a probate matter.

Letters testamentary: See *Letters of appointment.*

Life estate: An interest in property, usually real property, either retained by or received from the owner at the time of transfer. The party retaining or receiving the life interest is called the life tenant. The life tenant has use, possession, enjoyment, or income (such as rentals) from the property until he or she dies. At that time life interest terminates and title to the property vests in a party known as the remainderman.

Life tenant: See *Life estate.*

Living trust: Also known as an inter vivos trust. It is created by an individual to go into effect during the individual's lifetime, as opposed to a testamentary trust which is provided for in a person's will and becomes effective at the time of his or her death and admission of the will to probate. See also *Trust.* Compare *Testamentary trust.*

Marital deduction: That portion of a married person's property that may be received by that person's surviving spouse without being subject to either the federal gift tax or the federal estate tax. Certain prerequisites must be met in order for the transfer to qualify for the deduction. In effect, states that allow property of a deceased spouse to pass death tax-free to the surviving spouse also have a marital deduction, although it may not be labeled as such. See also *Federal estate tax, Federal gift tax, Inheritance tax,* and *Unlimited marital deduction.*

Merchantable title: Title to real property that is able to be sold. An unbroken chain of title must exist and the real property must be free and clear of all liens and encumbrances. When a titleholder to real property dies, for instance, action must be taken to show the successor in interest (to furnish the missing link) and to show that the property is not subject to death taxes or other claims (liens and encumbrances) resulting from the death.

Nonprobate property: Property from either a testate or intestate estate that, although it may be subject to death taxes, is normally not subject to probate administration. Such property, therefore, is unaffected by either the terms of decedent's will or the laws of inheritance. Upon the death of the holder thereof, such property, such as property held in joint tenancy, passes according to the terms of the instrument that created the title. Compare *Probate property.*

Nuncupative will: An oral will that may or may not be witnessed. See also *Will.*

Per capita: Literally, "per person," "by the head or individual." The manner in which a person inherits. If all persons inherit per capita, then their shares are equal, regardless of their degree of kinship. Compare *Per stirpes.*

Per stirpes: By right of representation. The manner in which a person inherits. When descendants take by representation, they are said to take per stirpes, that is, the children take the share that their parent would have taken if the parent had then been living. Compare *Per capita.*

Personal property: That property that is movable or separable from land or realty, although some property attached to or growing on land may be considered either real or personal property. Personal property may be either tangible or intangible. If tangible, it is thought of as something having substance or being capable of being touched, such as furniture. If intangible, it is thought of as something that cannot be perceived (although evidence of it might exist), such as a bank account. Compare *Real property.*

Personal representative: An administrator or executor of an estate administration proceeding. See also *Administrator* and *Executor.*

Post-mortem estate planning: Procedures taken by the personal representative and heirs or beneficiaries upon the death of an individual whose estate is being administered. These steps usually are directed toward a saving of death and income taxes, or they may be directed toward a redistribution of the decedent's estate according to the wishes of the surviving spouse and heirs or beneficiaries. Compare *Estate planning.*

Postnuptial agreement: A contract made between husband and wife as to the ownership and disposition of their respective property interests subsequent to their marriage to each other. Unlike antenuptial agreements, a few states consider postnuptial agreements to be invalid for lack of consideration and thus unenforceable. See also *Antenuptial agreement.*

Pourover will: A will that provides for certain property to transfer (pourover) from the decedent's estate into a trust previously established by the testator. See also *Will.*

Power of attorney: A document executed by a grantor (principal) and which grants either broad or limited powers and authority to an agent (attorney in fact) as to some or all of the property of the grantor. The power is not necessarily exclusive to the attorney and usually may be revoked at any time by the principal. See also *Attorney in fact* and *Grantor.*

Power of appointment: A power given by one party to another party, either in a will or a trust, authorizing the second party to dispose of the first party's property. The theory is that the power creates flexibility in an estate plan, in that the second party is able to make decisions on the basis of future events that may not be readily ascertainable by the first party at the time of creating the power.

Prenuptial agreement: A term sometimes used in lieu of the term antenuptial agreement. See *Antenuptial agreement.*

Pretermitted child: A child born to or adopted by a testator subsequent to the testator's will.

Principal: See *Grantor* and *Power of attorney.*

Probate: Originally, the proving of a will. Now it often designates any proceeding or matter relating to estates of persons living or dead, or any legal proceeding over which probate courts have jurisdiction, such as conservatorships, estates, and trusts. See also *Estate proceeding.*

Probate clerk: The state or county official who, as an officer of the court, is responsible for certain probate procedures and the keeping of probate records. Sometimes referred to as the register or registrar of wills.

Probate Code: Refers to that portion of a state code that contains the various probate laws. Usually a series of statutes gathered together under one or more sections, sometimes referred to as chapters, in the state code.

Probate property: Property from a testate or intestate estate that is subject not only to death taxes but also to probate administration. Such property, therefore, is affected by either the terms of the decedent's will or, if the decedent left no will, the laws of inheritance. Sometimes known as the probate estate. Compare *Nonprobate property.*

Quasi-community property: A term used by the states of California and Idaho to describe property acquired by a married couple while living elsewhere but which would have been considered community property if they had lived in the community property state. By designating the property as such, a form of forced share applies to the deceased spouse's quasi-community property.

Real property: Land or realty, or interests in such land or realty. The term includes improvements made on land, such as a building. The term may also include whatever is growing on or affixed to the land. Compare *Personal property*.

Register or registrar of wills: See *Probate clerk*.

Remainderman: See *Life estate*.

Residuary beneficiary: See *Residuary clause*.

Residuary clause: The clause in a will that disposes of all property remaining after previous (specific) bequests, if any, have been satisfied. That property goes to the residuary beneficiary(ies).

Self-proved will: A will that is proved, that is, verified as the testator's actual will, at the time of execution rather than at the time of death. The execution and witnessing of the will must be done before a notary public, all according to procedures prescribed by statute. When a will is self-proved, the witnesses do not have to be produced and the will does not have to be proved at the time of the maker's death. See also *Codicil* and *Will*.

Settlor: See *Creator*.

Small-estate proceeding: An informal, court-supervised probate proceeding. It is usually limited by statute to decedents' estates not exceeding a certain size and to decedents having heirs or beneficiaries within a specified degree of kinship. See also *Administration*.

Statutory share: See *Elective share*.

Survivorship: See *Joint tenancy* and *Tenancy by the entirety*.

Tangible personal property: See *Personal property*.

Tenancy by the entirety: A form of holding title to real property by husband and wife, recognized in about half the states. Upon the death of the first tenant, title to the property automatically passes to the surviving spouse to the exclusion of other heirs or beneficiaries. Similar to a joint tenancy in that the element of survivorship exists. But the effect of tenancy by the entirety is not quite the same during the lives of the husband and wife in that they are considered as one owner. Compare *Community property*, *Joint tenancy*, and *Tenancy in common*.

Tenancy in common: A form of holding title to property by two or more persons who are known as tenants in common. Upon the death of the first tenant, title to the property passes, not to the surviving tenant as in joint tenancy or tenancy by the entirety, but to the heirs or beneficiaries of the deceased tenant. Title passes according to the laws of descent and distribution or according to the decedent's will, as the case may be. All states, except a few of the community property states, recognize this form of holding title. Compare *Community property, Joint tenancy,* and *Tenancy by the entirety.*

Testament: A will. Often used in combination, such as last will and testament. See also *Will.*

Testamentary trust: A trust created and provided for in a will. It becomes effective, if at all, only when the will is admitted to probate. See also *Trust.* Compare *Living trust.*

Testate: The estate of a person who dies leaving a will. In such a case the person is said to have died testate. See also *Testator.* Compare *Intestate.*

Testator: One who makes a will or one who dies leaving a will. See also *Testate.*

Trust: A right of property, real or personal, held (possessed) by one party (the trustee) for the benefit of another party (the beneficiary). It is a written document that details the conditions under which the trust property is administered. See also *Beneficiary, Living trust, Trustee,* and *Testamentary trust.*

Trustee: One who administers a trust, either living or testamentary. The creator of the trust normally names and designates the trustee, who may be the creator. See also *Creator, Living trust, Testamentary trust,* and *Trust.*

Trustor: See *Creator.*

Unified credit: One of the items (credits) deductible from the gross federal estate tax in order to arrive at the net federal estate tax. The unified credit for the year 1987 and thereafter (unless the law is hereafter changed) is $192,800. This sum is equivalent to the federal estate tax exemption of $600,000. The credit is normally discussed in terms of the exemption which determines liability for filing a federal estate tax return. The term "unified credit" originated when the federal tax law tied (unified) the credit for federal gift taxes with the credit for federal estates taxes. To the extent the credit (exemption) has not been used to reduce or eliminate the taxpayer's gift tax liability it is available to reduce the taxpayer's estate taxes. See also *Federal estate tax exemption.*

Uniform Probate Code (UPC): One of many uniform acts proposed by the National Conference of Commissioners on Uniform State Laws, originally in 1969, most recently in 1989. At least 28 states have adopted the UPC or parts of it. The purpose of the various uniform acts is to achieve necessary and desirable uniformity among the states, as well as to minimize diversity and improve the law.

Unlimited marital deduction: The amount of property that may be transferred free of federal gift taxes and federal estate taxes by one spouse to the other, either during his or her lifetime or at the time of death. If the lifetime gift or testamentary gift transfer meets the prerequisites of the law, then the tax liability is zero, regardless of the size of the transfer. See also *Marital deduction.*

Ward: An individual under conservatorship or guardianship. See also *Conservatorship.*

Will: A written legal declaration by an individual, called a testator, as to how his or her property is to be disposed of at time of death. The document, sometimes called a testament or a last will and testament, and all amendments (codicils) thereto, must be executed and witnessed strictly according to statute. The term *will* includes all codicils attached to it. See also *Codicil, Holographic will, Nuncupative will, Pourover will, Self-proved will, Testament, Testate,* and *Testator.* Compare *Descent and distribution* and *Intestate.*

Index

Abatement, 99–100
  definition of, 297
Ademption, 98
  definition of, 98, 297
  explained, 98
  general rule, 98
  "identity" theory of, 98
  "modified identity" theory of, 98
  reason for, 98
Administration, 237–249
  accounting in, 239–240
  appraisals in, 241
  asset determination in, 238, 245, 246
  asset liquidation in, 247
  asset security in, 245
  attorney representation in, 242–244
    of heir, 255–256
  avoidance of, 175
    (See also Avoiding probate)
  benefits of, 176
  bond required in (see Bond; Fiduciaries,
      bond of; Fiduciary bond)
  books of account in, 239–240
  change of title in, 249
  checklist in, 243–249
  claims in, 247
  closing of, 240
  compared with other proceedings, 230
  conflicts of interest in, 296
  costs of, 241–242
  court supervision of, 237
  death of heir in, 255
  death tax returns in, 247–248
  deed to heirs or beneficiaries in, 240–241
  definition of, 297
  description of, 230, 237–239
  designation of attorney in, 244
  disclaimer in, 246
  disenchantment with, 190
  distinguished from other estate
      proceedings, 230–232

Administration (Cont.):
  distributees in, 238
  explanation of, 175
  family allowance in, 246
  fees in, 242–243
  fiduciary in (see Fiduciaries)
  final report in, 248–249
    objections to, 255
  general procedure in, 238–239
  heir in, subsequent death of, 255
  income tax returns in, 248
  inventory in, 238–239, 244–246
  letters of administration in, 239
  letters of appointment in, 239
  as link in chain of title, 234–235, 240–241
  liquidation of assets in, 247
  miscellaneous procedures in, 240
  nonprobate property in, 177–178, 232, 250
    real estate as, 250–251
  notice of, 245
  notification to IRS in, 245, 249
  opening of, 238, 244
  personal representatives (see Personal
      representatives)
  probate clerk in, 237–238
  probate property in, 177, 232
  probate referee in, 237–238
  procedure in, 237–249
    (See also Estate proceedings)
  purposes of, 238, 252, 253
  real estate in, 250–251
  register of wills in, 237–238
  registrar in, 237–238
  short form of, 234–237
  of small estate (see Small-estate
      administration)
  social security benefits in, 247
  spousal election in, 246
    (See also Will election)
  stock transfer procedures in, 239
  support during, 219–221

Administration (*Cont.*):
  tax returns in, 247–248
    (*See also* Death taxes)
  tickler use in, 249
  title to real estate in, 240–241
    transfers of, 240–241
    verification of, 245
  trusts to avoid, 179–191
    (*See also* Trusts to avoid probate)
  veteran's benefits in, 247
  will existence in, 84
  will procedure, 244
    (*See also* Estate proceedings)
Administrator, 82
  checklist of procedures for, 243–249
  definition of, 237, 297
  fiduciary relationship of, 161
  position of trust, 161
  public, 170
Advance directive, 196, 198
  (*See also* Living wills)
Affidavit in lieu of administration, 232–234
  definition of, 297
Afteradopted children, 97–98
Afterborn children, 97–98
Agency accounts, 52–54
Agent, 45
  (*See also* Power of attorney)
Agricultural Foreign Investment Disclosure
    Act of 1978, 121
Allowance to surviving spouse, 220–221
Alternate valuation date, 265
Ancillary proceeding:
  avoidance through trust, 185
  definition of, 297
Antenuptial agreements, 71–80
  abandonment of rights in, 74–76
    allowances, 74–75
    dower, 74
    elective rights, 74
    homestead, 74, 76
    inheritance, 74
    statutory, 74
  allowances affected by, 74–75
  asset disclosure in, 72, 73
  attorney representation of parties in, 73,
    77–78, 80
  capacity of parties in, 73
  claims subsequent to, 74
  cohabitation agreement compared to, 77
  competency of parties in, 73

Antenuptial agreements (*Cont.*):
  concealment by parties to, 72, 73
  conflict of interest by attorney drawing,
    80, 295–296
  consideration in, 73, 76–77
  contemplation of marriage by parties to,
    71
  contents of, 73–74
  as contract, 72–73, 73
  definition of, 72, 297
  disclosure by parties to, 72, 73
  dissolution of marriage of parties to,
    75–76
  dower of parties to, 74–75
  duress of party to, 72
  effect of, 74, 74–76
  enforceability of, 72–73
  evading, 79
  fairness of, 72, 79
  family allowance upon death of party to,
    74–75
  form of, 73–74
  fraud of party to, 73
  good faith of parties to, 72
  homestead rights of parties to, 76
  inheritance by parties to, 74–75
  legal representation of parties to, 73,
    77–78, 80
  legality of, 72–73
  limitations of, 74–76
  minor's rights affected by, 75, 76
  misrepresentation by parties to, 72
  nonmarital agreements compared with,
    77
  oral agreement for, 78
  persons wanting, 71–72
  postnuptial agreement compared with,
    76–77
  practical difficulties with, 72
  protections under, 71–72
  provisions of, 73–74
  purpose of, 71–72
  reasonableness of, 72
  reasons for, 71–72
  recording of, 72, 73, 78
  statutory rights of parties to, 219
  terms of, 73–74
  undue influence upon parties to, 72
  unequal terms in, 79
  Uniform Premarital Agreement Act, 72,
    75, 77

Antenuptial agreements (*Cont.*):
  validity of, 78
  valuation of assets by parties to, 73
  waiver of rights under, 74
  widow's allowance under, 74–75
  by written agreement, 72, 78
Antilapse statute, 96–97
Attorneys at law, 163, 166, 170–171
  and avoiding probate, 175–176
  banks' relationship with, 172–173
  boilerplate clauses used by, 181–182
  choosing, 294
  conflicts of interest of, 242, 295–296
  "deputy" as alternate name for, 45
  fees of, 242–243, 293
  necessity of hiring, 252–254
  and probate avoidance, 175–176
  relationship to banks, 172–173
  working with, 176, 293–296
Attorney in fact, 45, 47–48
  ability to serve as, 47–48, 159–160
  accounting by, 48–49
  agent as alternate name for, 45
  attorney at law distinguished from,
    45
  authority of, 46, 47, 56–57
  bank as, 46, 52–54
  caveats as to, 47–48
  child as, 47–48
  choice of, 46–48, 55–56
  choosing the, 47–48
  commingling of property by, 47
  compensation of, 46
  death of grantor, effect on, 51
  definition of, 45, 298, 306
  delegation of powers to, 46
  fiduciary relationship of, 47, 161
  gifts by, 46
  for health care, 197–198
  joint, 46, 54–55
  limitations on, 46–49, 159–160
  possession of property by, 46
  powers of, 46–49
  qualifications of, 152–153, 158–159
  records of, 46, 48–49
  relationship to principal, 158–159
  responsibility of, 47–48
  restrictions on, 46
  standby provisions of, 50–51
  trust position of, 161
  will preparation by, 46

Augmented property:
  definition of, 298
  explained, 223
Avoiding probate:
  administration compared to, 175
  as alternative to probate administration,
    176
  costs savings in, 176, 192–193
  estate proceedings compared to, 175–176
  explanation of term, 175
  lawyers involvement with, 175–176
  misunderstanding of, 175
  nonprobate property use in, 177–178,
    254
  probate property use in, 177–178
  proceedings eliminated by, 175–176, 183
  reasons for, 176, 190–191
  representations made as to, 176
  spouse disinheritance by, 189–190
  with trusts (*see* Trusts to avoid probate)

Banks:
  as agent, 52–54
  as alternate fiduciary, 168
  bond of, 169–170
  as cofiduciary, 168
  as conservator, 64, 160, 165–166
  as custodian, 159
  as fiduciary, 162, 167–168
  as joint fiduciary, 168
  and lawyers, 172–173
  as personal representative, 87, 103,
    165–166
  as successor fiduciary, 168
  trust position of, 161
  as trustee, 130, 165–166, 182, 192–193
  (*See also* Custodial or agency accounts;
    Professionals)
Beneficiary:
  heir distinguished from, 81–82, 86–87,
    228
  definition of, 81–82, 298
  under trust, 129
  under will, 81–82
  (*See also* Trusts; Wills)
Bequeath, definition of, 298
Bequest, 82, 101–102
  definition of, 298
Blockbuster power of attorney, 50, 56
  (*See also* Power of attorney)

Bond:
  avoidance of, 87
  considerations for, 169–170
  costs of, 87, 241
  definition of, 87
  of fiduciary, 169–170
  premium for, 169
  reasons for, 169–170
Burial arrangements in will, 84
Bypass trusts:
  alternatives to, 140–141
  benefit of, 139–142
  example of, 141–142
  explanation of, 108, 139–142
  life estates compared with, 116–117
  protecting the children with, 114
  purpose of, 108, 139–140
  spousal trust compared with, 142
  taxability of, 140
  terminable interests relationship to, 140
  two-trust will used with, 142,
  zero-tax marital deduction formula with, 140
  (See also Trusts)

Capital assets, 18
Capital gain or loss:
  basis for, 18
  gifts affecting, 18
Cestui que trust:
  definition of, 129, 298
  explained, 129
Change of title, 249
Charitable gifts, 24
  (See also Charitable lead trusts; Charitable remainder trusts)
Charitable lead trusts, 136
  definition of, 298
Charitable remainder trusts, 133–135
  annuity trust as one form of, 134–135
  comparisons of, 133–135, 145–146
  definition of, 298–299
  distinctions between, 134–135
  lawyer involvement in, 144
  tax consequences of, 135
  unitrust as one form of, 134–135
Cheap will, 37, 82
Checklist in estate administration, 243–249

Children:
  bypass trust effect on, 114
  "convenience" joint tenancies with, 40
  disability of parent of, 157–158
  effect of intestacy on, 223
  estate planning for, 112–115, 138
  testamentary trust for, 138–139
  will protection of, 112–115, 117–118
Codicils, 82
  definition of, 82, 299
  necessity for lawyer for, 124
  (See also Wills)
Cohabitation agreements, 77
Common law:
  curtesy under, 211–212
  definition of, 299
  dower under, 211–212
  principal and agent rule under, 47
  Rule Against Perpetuities under, 131–132
Community property, 34–35
  definition of, 299
Competence of minors, 25–26
Conflicts of interest, 295–296
  in administration of estates, 296
  in antenuptial agreement preparation, 80
  in conservatorships, 296
  between married couple, 80, 295–296
Conservators:
  attorney assistance to, 166
  bank as, 64, 160, 165–166
  bond of, 64, 65
  choosing the, 171
  conflicts of interest of, 296
  definition of, 59, 299
  duties of, 64–66
  fees of, 64
  fiduciary position of, 64
  gifts by, 64
  guardian as, 59, 166
  limitations of, 64–66
  named in petition, 60
  position of trust of, 161
  powers of, 64–66
  qualifications of, 64–66
  reports by, 65
  responsibilities of, 166
  termination as, 65, 67, 68
  (See also Banks; Conservatorships; Fiduciaries)

Conservatorships, 59–69
    advantages of, 160
    alternatives to (*see* Disability)
    capacity of ward under, 63–64
    charitable gifts in, 64
    closing of, 65
    compared with power of attorney and
        trust, 59, 66
    competency of ward under,
        63–64
    conflicts of interest in, 296
    Congressional action as to, 66–67
    conservator of (*see* Conservators)
    costs of, 59, 68–69
    court supervision of, 59, 60
    definition of, 59, 299
    disability planned with,
        147–158
    estate plan of ward under, 65
    fiduciary in, 64–66, 161
    as final choice, 158
    flexibility of, 59
    form of, 61–62
    gifts from, 64
    as guardianship, 59
    inventory of, 65
    involuntary, 60, 61
    jury trial in, 61
    as last resort, 158
    lawyer involvement in, 60, 61
    limitations of, 64–66
    minor under:
        choice by, 63
        incompetency of, 63, 67–68
        parent of, 63
        upon reaching majority, 66, 68
    necessity of, 59, 62–63, 67–69
    notices of, 61
    opening of, 65
    petition for, 65
    possession of property in, 65
    preferable form of, 61–62
    procedures in, 65
    reasons for, 154–155
    service of notice of, 61
    spendthrifts under, 68
    standby, 62–63
    statutory control over, 60
    termination of, 65, 67, 68
    title to property in, 65
    trust alternative to, 133

Conservatorships (*Cont.*):
    types of, 61–62
    Uniform Veterans' Guardianship Act, 67
    veterans under, 67
    voluntary, 60
        standby compared to, 62–63
    ward under (*see* Ward under
        conservatorship)
Consideration:
    in antenuptial agreements, 76–77
    definition of, 76, 299–300
    enforceability of contracts based upon,
        114
    in postnuptial agreements, 76–77, 114
Contracts, necessity of consideration in, 114
"Convenience" joint tenancies, 40
Co-ownership, forms of, 29–35
    (*See also* Joint tenancy)
Corporate fiduciaries (*see* Banks;
        Fiduciaries; Professionals)
Creator, definition of, 300
Credit shelter trusts, 108, 140
    (*See also* Bypass trusts)
Cruzan case, Nancy, 197
Curator, 59
Curatorship, 59
Currency and Foreign Transactions
        Reporting Act of 1976, 121
Curtesy, 211–212
    definition of, 300–301
    (*See also* Dower)
Custodial or agency accounts, 52–54, 159

Death taxes, 257–274
    apportionment of, 270–271
    deductions allowable in computing,
        259–260
    definition of, 257, 300
    in estate planning, 9, 271–272
    explained, 9, 257
    federal estate, 261–269
    gift taxes compared with, 19, 23–24, 258,
        263–264, 272
    joint tenancy property subject to, 259
        payable by, 273
    lien of, 228, 230, 235–236, 247–248
    life estate property subject to, 259
    lifetime transfers subject to, 258
    net estate determination for, 259–260
    parties in preferred position as to, 260

Death taxes (*Cont.*):
  pick-up tax as one form of, 257,
    260–261
  state, 257–261
    burden of, 258, 272
    kinds of property with, 258–259
    location of property with, 257–258
    residence of decedent with, 257
    type of property with, 258–259
  understanding, 257–274
  use of trust to avoid, 272
  use of will to avoid, 84
  (*See also* Death tax proceedings; Federal
    estate tax; Inheritance tax)
Death tax proceedings:
  assets reportable in, 258–259
  compared with administration,
    230–231
  federal estate tax return in, 247–248
  life insurance in, 264
  marketable title effect of, 235–236
  purpose of, 235–236
  short form use in, 234–236
  (*See also* Death taxes)
Decedent, definition of, 300
Descent and distribution:
  definition of, 203, 300
  laws of, 203
  (*See also* Dying intestate; Inheritance)
Devise, 82
  definition of, 300
Devisee, 81–82
  definition of, 300
Disability, 147–158
  choice of the pathway to, 155–157
    conservatorship as, 154–155, 158
    doing nothing as, 149–150
    gift as, 153–154
    joint tenancy as, 150–152
    power of attorney as, 152–153
    trust as, 154
  description of pathways to, 149
  goals in anticipating, 148
  of minors, 25–26
  options available for, 148–149
  planning for, 157–158
  providing for, 147–158
  (*See also* Incompetency; Minors)
Disclaimer, 246
  definition of, 276, 300
  (*See also* Post-mortem estate planning)

Distributee, 81–82
  alien as, 120–121
  definition of, 300
Donee, 17
  basis of gift to, 18–19
  definition of, 300
  (*See also* Gifts)
Donor, 17
  definition of, 300
  (*See also* Gifts; Trusts)
Dower, 211–212
  definition of, 300–301
  (*See also* Curtesy)
Durable power of attorney, 49–51, 56
  (*See also* Powers of attorney)
Dying intestate, 203–210
  chart showing kinship, 206–207
  definition of, 203, 303
  escheat possibility if, 208–209
  laws of descent and distribution if, 203
  laws of inheritance if, 203
  state control if, 203
  statutes' effect if, 204–208

E and EE bonds, 42, 280, 290
Economic Recovery Tax Act of 1981 (ERTA),
  143
  and QTIP, 142–143
Elective share, 212–217
  definition of, 301
Escheat, 208–209
  avoidance of, by will, 83
  definition of, 83, 301
  explanation of, 208–209
  occurrence of, 83, 209
Estate:
  administration of (*see* Administration)
  code description of, 3
  definition of, 3, 301
  extent of, 1
Estate planning, 3–15
  age of planner in, 5
  assets involved in, 6–8
  beginning, 5–8
  benefits of, 9, 12–13
  changing conditions affecting, 14
  for children, 10
  conflicts of interest in, 295–296
  considerations in, 4–5, 187
  constancy of, 9

Estate planning (*Cont.*):
  control of property in, 12
  costs of, 14, 15
  definition of, 4, 301
  description of, 4
  development of, 5, 9
  disability incentive for, 147–158
  division of property in, 273–274
  explanation of, 4–5
  factors affecting, 4–5, 10
  family involved in, 6
  federal estate tax affecting, 9
  gifts as part of, 17, 19
  goals of, 6, 12–13
  importance of, 5, 14
  information needed for, 4–5
  insurance in, 11, 13
  inventory as prerequisite for, 6–8
    identity of property, 6, 7
    title to property, 7, 8
    value of property, 6–8
  lawyer involvement in, 5–8, 10, 14, 15
  with life insurance trust, 136–138
  life insurance used in, 11, 13, 136–137
  management of estate in, 12
  marriage significance in, 9
  mistakes in, 5
  nontax considerations in, 10
  objectives of, 5, 6
  process of developing, 5
  professionals in, 12
  reasons for, 5
  residency affecting, 13
  review of:
    as to family status, 13
    as to financial situation, 13
    goals in, 12–13
    time period for, 13–15,
    will in, 13
  satisfaction in, 12
  single persons in, 10–12
  spouse in, 10
    division of property with, 273–274
  updating plan, 9
  will connection to, 9
Estate proceedings, 227–256
  administration as one form of, 229
    (*See also* Administration)
  affidavit as one form of, 232–234
  appraisers in, 241
  attorney's representation in, 242–243

Estate proceedings (*Cont.*):
  checklist for, 243–249
  choosing the correct, 231–232
  closing of (*see* Administration)
  comparison of testate and intestate costs
    in, 125
  continuing decedent's business in, 247
  costs of, 241–242
  death of joint tenant affecting, 36–37
  death tax liens in, 228, 230, 235–236,
    247–248
  definition of, 301
  delaying of, 229
  determining factors in, 227–228
  determination of the, 231–232
  duplicating the procedures in, 254
  explained, 227, 231
  following death, 227–256
  indemnity agreement in, 233
  inventory determination in, 228–229
    effect of sale on, 271,
  with joint tenancy, 36
  lien of taxes, removal of, 228, 230,
    235–236, 247–248
  as link in chain of title, 234–235,
    240–241
  minimization of, 227–256
  necessity of property in, 227–228
  preliminary procedures in, 228–230
  probate versus nonprobate property in,
    230–231
  real property in, 250–251
  reasons for, 228, 234–237, 252–253
  safe deposit box entry in, 251–252
  savings bonds in, 254–255
  short form of, 234–237
    to remove death tax liens, 235–236
    to establish title, 234–235
  tickler use in, 249
  title to real estate in, 240–241
    transfers of, 240–241
    verification of, 245
  types of, 232
    determining, 228, 231–232
  will existence affecting, 125
  (*See also* Administration)
Estate tax:
  definition of, 257, 301
  pick-up, 260–261
  (*See also* Death taxes; Federal estate tax)
Euthanasia (*see* Living wills)

Executor:
  checklist for, 243–249
  definition of, 82, 237, 301
  fiduciary relationship of, 161
  position of trust of, 161
  (*See also* Administration; Personal
    representatives; Wills)
Exemptions (*see* Federal estate tax; Gifts;
  Inheritance tax; Unified credit)

Federal estate tax, 261–269
  alternate valuation under, 265
    distributees affected by, 272–273
    revocability of election of, 273
    selecting date for, 282
  applicability of, 261
  avoidance of, by surviving spouse,
    261–262
  compared with inheritance tax, 257
  definition of, 301
  elections under, 264–265
    alternate valuation date, 265, 273
    QTIP trust, 266–267
    special use, 265
  estate planning involving, 9
  exemption from, 9, 263
    definition of, 302
    gifts in connection with, 19, 23–24,
      263–264
  explained, 261
  generation skipping transfers (GSTs) (*see*
    Generation skipping transfers)
  gifts to save, 19
  gross estate determination for, 263–264
  inheritance tax compared to, 257
  life insurance trust to avoid, 136–138
  marital deduction under, 108
    terminable interest rule as to, 262
    unlimited deduction with, 108
  marital status as affected by, 261
  nonprobate property subject to, 264
  payment deferral of, 287–289
  planning for, 263
  power of appointment affected by,
    266–267
  property affected by, 263–264
  QTIP trust affecting, 266–267
  rates of, 108, 263
  return required for, 263
  special use affecting, 265

Federal estate tax (*Cont.*):
  tax return for elections under, 264–267
  unified credit under (*see* Unified credit)
  unlimited marital deduction exception to,
    108
  will effect on, 84
  (*See also* Death taxes)
Federal gift tax, 20–22
  definition of, 20–21, 302
  exemption under, 19, 20–24
  future interest under, 20–21
  gift splitting under, 22–23
  between married persons, 19, 21
  power of appointment as affecting, 27
  present interest under, 20–21
  relationship to federal estate tax, 20–21
  return for, 19, 263–264
  (*See also* Federal estate tax; Gifts; Unified
    credit)
Fee property interest (*see* Life estates)
Fiduciaries:
  ability to act, 172
  acceptance by, 171–172
  alternate designations of, 168
  asset management of, 162–163
  attorneys as, 164, 173
  attorneys for, 163, 166, 170–173
  banks as, 167–168
    (*See also* Banks)
  bond of, 87, 169–170
    definition of, 302
  choosing your, 165–167
  co-fiduciaries, 168–169
  competence of, 167–168
  considerations in naming, 161–170
  corporate, 167–168
    (*See also* Banks)
  costs of, 163–165
    factors in determining, 164–165
  definition of, 161, 302
  duties of, 161–165
  environmental liability factor of, 165
  examples of, 161
  expense of, 163–165
    factors in determining, 164–165
  explained, 161
  family members as, 167
  importance of, 161
  inability to act, 172
  investment responsibilities of, 162–163
  involvement in estates, 161

Fiduciaries (*Cont.*):
  joint fiduciaries, 168–169
  liability of, 165
  multiple, 168–169
  necessity for, 170
  professionals as, 165–166
  public administrators as, 170
  qualifications of, 167–168
  reasons for serving as, 170
  refusal to act, 171–172
  representation as, 161
  residency requirement of, 103, 167
  responsibilities of, 162–163
  spouses as, 165
  successors to, 168
  in wills, 87–88
Fiduciary bond, 87, 169–170
  definition of, 302
Forced share, 212
  definition of, 302
  (*See also* Will election)
Funeral arrangements in wills, 91

Generation skipping transfers (GSTs),
    267–268
  definition of, 302
  explained, 267–269
  gifts, 27, 269
  lifetime exemption of, 268–269
  skip person under, 267–268
  tax results of, 268
  tax return required by, 269
  types of, 268
Gift splitting, 22–23
  definition of, 302
Gifts, 17–28
  annual exclusion of, 20–22
  of appreciated property, 18
  basis of, 18–19
  of capital asset, 18
  caveats as to, 18
  to charities, 24
  citizenship requirement as to, 21, 27
  comparison of lifetime gift with
      testamentary gift, 18
  consent of spouse to, 22–23
  considerations in making, 17–20, 27, 28
  deathbed transfers by, 21
  death tax savings by, 21
  disability as reason for, 147–158

Gifts (*Cont.*):
  donee of, 17
    basis of gift to, 18–19
  donor of, 17
  for estate planning purposes, 17, 19
  excess, 21
  for federal estate tax savings, 19, 23–24
  federal gift tax of (*see* Federal gift tax)
  of future interest, 20–21
  income tax purposes of, 17–19
  Internal Revenue Code concerning, 20,
      24, 27, 28
  inter vivos, 17
  joint tenancy as, 17, 29
  life estate as, 27
  lifetime, 17–28
  lifetime compared to testamentary, 18
  to minors, 25–26
  Mortmain statutes' relationship to, 24
  notification to IRS of, 19, 21–23, 28
  to parents, 26
  power of appointment as, 27
  precautions in making, 20
  of present interest, 20–21
  of property located in United States, 27
  reasons for, 17, 19–20, 153–154
  relationship with federal estate tax, 19
  splitting of, 22–23
  to spouse, 21
  spouse's consent to, 22–23
  stepped-up basis importance to, 18
  tax liability of, 132–133, 263–264
  tax reasons for, 18–19
  taxation by states of, 26
  testamentary, 17
    compared to lifetime gift, 18
    death tax liability for, 95
    (*See also* Wills)
  testamentary compared to lifetime, 18
  timing of, 27
  trusts as, 17
  unified credit applied to, 23–24
    (*See also* Unified credit)
  Uniform Gifts to Minors Act (UGMA), 25
  Uniform Transfers to Minors Act
      (UTMA), 25
Grantor, definition of, 129, 303
  (*See also* Powers of attorney; Trusts)
Grantor trust, 180
Guardians (*see* Conservators)
Guardianships (*see* Conservatorships)

Health care powers of attorney (*see* Living wills)

Heirs:
  distinguished from beneficiaries, 81–82, 86–87, 228
  definition of, 81–82, 303
  dependency test of, 210
  descendants as, 209–210
  disputes among, 87
  spouses as, 208, 211
  will effect on, 210
  (*See also* Beneficiary; Descent and distribution; Dying intestate; Inheritance)
Heirship (*see* Dying intestate; Inheritance)
Holographic wills, 105
  definition of, 303
Homestead, definition of, 303

Income tax:
  basis of gift for:
    if living, 18
    if testamentary, 18
  in estate proceedings, 248
  returns for trusts, 188
  strategies in post-mortem planning, 279–281
  use of gift to reduce, 18
Incompetency:
  minors, 25
  options, 147–149
  providing for, 147–158
  (*See also* Conservatorships; Disability)
Indemnity agreement, 233
Inheritance, 203–210
  by aliens, 120–121
  application of statutes, 204–208
  ascent method of, 206
  avoidance of, 204
  by bloodlines, 205
  by child, 207
  definition of, 303
    chart showing, 207
  descent method of, 204–205
  determination of, 203–208
  effect of will on, 86–87, 204, 209, 210
  escheat as final step for, 83, 208–209
  examples of, 205–206
  by grace of state, 203
  by half bloods, 207–208

Inheritance (*Cont.*):
  by heirs, 208
    descendants, 209–210
  kinship, chart, 206–207
  per capita method of, 205–206
    (*See also* Per capita)
  per stirpes method of, 205
    (*See also* Per stirpes)
  right of, 203
  by spouse, 204, 207
    as heir, 208
  by state, 204, 208–209
  state similarities in, 204
  statute that controls, 210
  statutory privilege in, 203
  statutory provisions in, 203–205
    controlling, 210
  test for common ancestors, 207–208
  will effect on, 86–87, 204, 209, 210
    if unsigned, 210
  (*See also* Dying intestate; Descent and distribution; Heirs)
Inheritance tax, 257–259
  compared with federal estate tax, 257
  compared with pick-up tax, 260–261
  "convenience" joint tenancies, 40
  death tax as:
    definition of, 257, 300
  deductible debts in determining, 259–260
  definition of, 257, 303
  explained, 257
  factors that control, 257
  interests subject to:
    gifts exceeding stated value, 258
    joint tenancy property, 259
    retained life estates, 258
    transfers within stated period, 258
  property interests subject to tax, 258–259
  real property subject to, 258
  succession tax as alternate name for, 257
  (*See also* Death taxes)
"In terrorem" clause, 119
Insurance:
  agents selling, 13
  of decedents, 246
  (*See also* Life insurance)
Intangible personal property, 305

Inter vivos gifts, definition of, 17
  (*See also* Gifts)
Inter vivos trust (*see* Living trusts; Trusts)
Internal Revenue Code:
  capital asset under, 18
  definition of, 303
  gifts under, 18, 20, 24, 27, 28
Internal Revenue Service (IRS):
  death tax returns requirement of,
    247–248, 263
  extensions of time by, 267
  fiduciary responsibilities to, 163
  form 56 requirements of, 245, 249
  form SS–4 requirement of, 245
  notification of gifts to, 19, 21–23, 28,
    263–264
  social security number required by, 42
  tax returns required for trusts by, 188
International Investment Survey Act of
  1976, 121
Intestate:
  definition of, 81, 303
  effect on children, 223–224
  (*See also* Inheritance; Wills)
Inventory, 5–8
Irrevocable life insurance trust, 136–138
Irrevocable trusts (*see* Trusts)
IRS (*see* Internal Revenue Service)

Joint ownership (*see* Community property;
  Joint tenancy; Tenancy by the entirety;
  Tenancy in common)
Joint tenancy, 29–43
  administration avoidance with, 36, 112
  advantages of, 37–38
  adverse consequences of, 36, 151–152
    examples of, 38–40
  alternatives to, 43
  avoidance of administration with, 36,
    230–231
  bank account in, 42
  as cheap will, 37, 82
  with child, 38–40, 43, 114–115
  common accident among tenants in, 96
  community property compared with, 31,
    34–35
  compared to other forms of tenancies,
    29–35
  conflict with will provisions, 43
  confusions concerning, 36

Joint tenancy (*Cont.*):
  control of property loss with, 39
  for convenience, 40
  co-ownership with, 29–31
  creation of, 30–31, 36
  creditors affected by, 37, 39
  death of joint tenant under, 30–32, 36–38
  debts affected by, 37
  definition of, 303–304
  disability as reason for, 147–158
  disadvantages of, 38–40, 151–152
  EE bonds held in, 42
  effect on heirs and spouse, 30–31, 40
  estate proceedings required by, 36–37, 112
  examples of difficulties with, 38–40,
    151–152
  explanation of, 29–32
  "for convenience," 40
  fragmented ownership with, 38
  as gift, 39–40
  heirs affected by, 30–31, 40
  income from, 39
  inflexibility of, 38–40, 151–152
  inheritance tax effect on, 38–39
  joint control with, 39, 40
  legal advice as to, 43
  with married persons, 38
  and minority of surviving joint tenant, 39
  misconceptions as to, 36, 37
  as nonprobate property, 120, 178
  "or" used to create, 35
  payable on death (POD) accounts
    compared with, 43
  between persons other than spouse, 38–40
  popularity of, 35–36, 179
  power of attorney as alternative to,
    148–149
  reasons for, 37–38, 150–151
  severance of, 40–41
  social security number with, 42
  with spouse, 31, 178
  taxability of, 259
  tenancy in common compared with,
    31–32
  tenancy by the entirety compared with,
    31, 33–34
  Uniform Simultaneous Death Statute
    effect on, 41–42, 83
  will election effect on, 225
  and wills, 43, 82–83, 107
  wording for, 29–31

Karen Ann Quinlan case, 196–197
Kinship chart, 207

Laws of descent and distribution (*see* Dying
    intestate; Inheritance)
Laws of inheritance (*see* Dying intestate;
    Inheritance)
Lawyers (*see* Attorneys at law)
Legacy, definition of, 304
Legatee, 81–82
    definition of, 304
Letters of administration (*see* Letters of
    appointment)
Letters of appointment, definition of, 304
Life estates:
    advantages of, 117
    compared with trust, 116–117
    how created, 116
    definition of, 116, 304
    disadvantages of, 117
    example of, 116
    explanation of, 116
    fee interest in, 116
    freeholder interest in, 116
    gifts of, 27
    life tenant's interest in, 116
    as nonprobate property, 178
    to protect children, 117–118
    received, 178, 259
    remainderman's interest in, 116
    retained, 178, 259
    taxability of, 259
    in wills, 116–117
Life insurance:
    of decedents, 246
    in estate planning, 11, 107, 136–137
    irrevocable trust, 136–138
Life insurance trust, 136–138
Life-Sustaining Procedures Act, 196
Lifetime gift (*see* Gifts)
Link in the chain of title, 234–235,
    240–241
List separate from will, 88–89
Living trusts:
    for avoidance of probate (*see* Avoiding
        probate)
    definition of, 131, 304
    provisions for, 131
    purpose of, 133
Living will law, 196

Living wills, 195–200
    as advance directive, 196, 198
    compulsory medical care distinguished
        from, 196
    conditioning insurance on, 200
    conditioning medical treatment on,
        200
    Cruzan case, Nancy, 197
    definition of, 196
    disputes under, 200
    euthanasia compared, 196
    explained, 195, 196
    forms for, 198, 200
    insurance and, 200
    Life-Sustaining Procedures Act, 196
    Living Will Law, 196
    medical directive compared with, 199
    medical treatment and, 200
    Natural Death Act and, 196
    nourishment under, 197–199
    as passive euthanasia, 196
    power of attorney compared with,
        197–199
    problems with, 196–198
    Quinlan case, Karen Ann, 196–197
    reasons for, 195
    refusal to comply with, 198
    Right to Die Law, 196
    right to refuse treatment under, 199
    statutes providing for, 196
    statutory authority for, 196, 198
    validity of, 198

Management of estate, by single persons, 12
Marital deduction, 107–109
    definition of, 107–108, 304
    life estate compared with, 139
    limits on, 262
    power of appointment with, 262, 266–267
    prerequisites to, 139
    property requirements for, 262
    QTIP trust exception to, 139, 142–143,
        262, 266–267
        (*See also* Qualified terminable interest
            property)
    terminable interest rule under, 139, 262
    trusts, 139–143
    unlimited, 139
        definition of, 309
    in wills, 107–109

Marital deduction trusts, 139–143
Married couple:
  community property held by, 34–35
  conflicts of interest between, 295–296
  estate planning between, 9
  gift splitting by, 22–23
  gifts between, 19, 21
  joint tenancy between, 29–30, 36, 38
  marital deduction between (see Marital
    deduction)
  tenancy by the entirety between, 33–34
  will of:
    children protected under, 112–115
    effect of marriage and divorce on, 106
    joint, reciprocal, and mutual, 109–112
    marital deduction, 107–109
Mental disability, providing for, 147–158
Merchantable title:
  definition of, 305
  effect of death on, 234–235
Minors:
  competence of, 25–26
  conservatorship for, 63
  definition of, 25
  gifts to, 25–26
  incapacity of, 25
  Uniform Gifts to Minors Act (UGMA), 25
  Uniform Transfer to Minors Act (UTMA),
    25
Model Prudent Person Investment Act,
  162
Mortmain statutes, 24

National Conference of Commissioners on
  Uniform State Laws, 132, 278
Natural Death Act, 196
Net assets, 99
Nonmarital agreements, 77
Nonmarital trusts, 108
Nonprobate property, 230–231
  annuities and pensions as, 177–178
  definition of, 177, 305
  estate proceeding with (see Estate
    proceedings)
  explained, 177–178
  joint tenancies as, 178, 250
  life estates as, 178
  life insurance as, 177
  payable on death (POD) accounts as, 177
  will effect on, 120

Nontax considerations in estate planning,
  10–11
Nuncupative will, 105–106
  definition of, 305

One-dollar bequests, 97–98
"Or" in joint tenancy, 35
Order of abatement, 99–100
Organ donation, 91

Parents, gifts to, 26
Passive euthanasia, 196
Patient Self-Determination Act, 198
Payable on death (POD) accounts, 43, 177
Per capita, 205–206
  definition of, 205, 305
Per stirpes, 205–207
  chart showing, 206–207
  definition of, 205, 305
Perpetual care, 119, 247
Personal property, definition of, 305
Personal representatives:
  ability to serve, 103, 161–162
  attorney reliance by, 162
  checklist of duties of, 243–249
  co-executors as, 173–174
  declination of fee by, 245
  "de facto" executors as, 166
  definition of, 82, 305
  duties of, 161–162, 239–249
  family members as, 243
  fees of, 242–243
  lawyers as, 173
  obligations of, 162–163
    checklist of duties of, 243–249
  personal liability of, 162
  position of trust of, 161
  qualifying as, 244
  reliance on attorneys by, 162
  residency requirement of, 167
  responsibilities of, 162–163
  in will, 87–88
  (See also Fiduciaries)
Physical disability, providing for, 147–158
Pick-up tax, 260–261
  (See also Death taxes)
Plain English, 90
POD accounts (see Payable on death
  accounts)

Post-mortem estate planning, 275–291
  administration expenses as, 281
  allowance to spouse as, 282–283
  alternate valuation date as, 265, 282
  basis for income tax purposes in, 18
  conflicts of interest in, 275–276, 296
  deferral of estate tax payment as, 287–289
  definition of, 305
  disclaimers as, 276–278
    attorney counseling as to, 290
    deemed transfer in, 276
    effect of, 278
    example of, 289
    gift consequence of, 277
    irrevocability of, 278
    reasons for, 278
    requirements for, 277
  E and EE bonds, 280, 290
  effect of trust on, 187–188
  election under will as, 285–286
  estate tax payment deferral as, 287–289
  explained, 275
  family agreement as, 286, 290–291
  fiduciary fees in, 281–282
  generally, 275–291
  imputation of fees to, 281–282
  income tax basis in, 18
  income tax returns in:
    of decedent, 279–280
    of estate, 283–285, 291
    strategies for, 279–281
  interest on E and EE bonds as, 280
  medical expenses as, 280
  nonprobate property in, 289–290
  parties benefitted by, 275–276
  planned opportunities in, 276–279
  QTIP trust as, 142–143, 278–279
    (See also Qualified terminable interest
      property)
  special use valuation as, 287
    (See also Federal estate tax)
  spouse's allowance as, 282–283
  tax savings in, 279–285, 287
  trust effect on, 187–188
  unplanned opportunities in, 279–289
  valuation of estate in, 265
  widow's or widower's allowance as,
    282–283
  will contest as, 286
  will election as, 285–286
  will not probated as, 275–276

Postnuptial agreements, 76–77
  compared with antenuptial agreements,
    76–77
  consideration in, 76–77
  definition of, 76, 306
  validity of, 76–77
Pourover will, 115–116
  definition of, 115, 306
  purpose of, 115
  relationship to trust, 129
  validity of, 116
Power of appointment, 266–267
  definition of, 306
  gifts, 27
Power-of-appointment trust, 266–267
Powers of attorney, 45–57
  as agency, 47
  agency account compared with, 159
  agent in, 45, 47
  alternatives to (see Disability)
  attorney in fact under (see Attorney in
    fact)
  blockbuster power as, 50, 56
  caveats as to, 47–48
  commingling property in, 47
  common law rule of, 47, 50
  comparison with conservatorship and
    trust (see Disability)
  competency of grantor of, 49–50
  conditions and restrictions in, 46
  conservatorship effect on, 64
  court participation in, 47
  custodial or agency accounts compared
    with, 52–54
    bank as agent of, 52–54
  definition of, 45
  disability as reason for, 147–158
  durable, 49–51, 56, 187
    standby provision in, 50–51
  family considerations in, 47–49
  forms of, 49
  gifts authority under, 46, 56–57
  grantor of:
    death of, 51
    definition of, 45
    retained powers of, 46
  for health care, 197–198
  jurisdiction of court of, 46, 47
  legal advice as to, 47
  limited, 49, 55
  living wills with, 197–198

Powers of attorney (*Cont.*):
  period of, 56
  plenary, 49
  possession of property in, 46
  principal of, 45
    death of, 51
    definition of, 45
    powers of, 46
  reasons for, 45, 152–153
  requirements of, 46
  revocation of, 55
  short form of, 49
  special types of, 49, 55
  standby provisions of, 50–51
  substitute for, 45
  title to property of grantor, 46
  trust comparison to, 46
  use of, 46, 48
Prenuptial agreements, 71–80
  definition of, 72, 306
  (*See also* Antenuptial agreements)
Pretermitted children:
  definition of, 97, 306
  explained, 97–98
  provision for, 97–98
Principal (*see* Power of attorney, principal of)
Privacy, 123, 133, 184
Probate:
  avoiding (*see* Avoiding probate)
  definition of, 175, 306
Probate clerk, definition of, 306
Probate code, definition of, 306
Probate procedure checklist, 243–249
Probate proceedings (*see* Estate proceedings)
Probate property, 230–231
  definition of, 177, 306
  estate proceeding with (*see* Estate proceedings)
Proceedings following death (*see* Estate proceedings)
Professionals, 166
  attorneys participation with, 166
  estate planning by, 9, 12
  as fiduciaries, 162, 163
  (*See also* Banks)
Prudent investor rule, 162–163
Prudent person rule, 162–163
Public administrator, 170

Qualified terminable interest property (QTIP), 142–143
  benefit of, 143
  election of, 146, 264
  explained, 142–143, 266–267
  life estate compared with, 142
  post-mortem planning with, 278–279
  requirements of, 142–143, 278
  terminable interest requirement with, 142–143, 279
Quasi-community property, definition of, 307
Quinlan case, Karen Ann, 196–197

Real property, definition of, 307
Reciprocity between countries, 121
Remainderman (*see* Life estates)
Residency in estate planning, 13
Residuary clause, 92–93
  definition of, 92, 307
Revenue Act of 1987, 269
Revocable trusts (*see* Trusts; Trusts to avoid probate)
Right to Die Law, 196
Rule Against Perpetuities, 131–132
Rule of 72, 274

Safe deposit box, 251–252
  right of entry to, 251–252
Sales provisions in will, 89–90
Securities Act of 1934, 121
Self-declaration trust, 180
Self-declared trust, 180
Self-proved will, definition of, 307
  (*See also* Wills)
Settlor (*see* Creator)
Short form of estate proceeding, 234–237
  (*See also* Administration)
"Simple" will, 106–107
Single persons, estate planning by, 11–12
Small-estate administration, 249–250
  definition of, 307
  limitations of, 249–250
  (*See also* Administration)
Social security number with joint accounts, 42
Special use, 265, 287

Spouse:
actions that affect rights of, 225–226
allowance to, 220–221
augmented estate of, 223
children of, 223–224
curtesy of, 211–212
disinheritance by trust of, 189–190
disinheriting of, 221–223
dower of, 211–212
election by, 212–217
(*See also* Will election)
forced share under will by, 212
gift splitting with, 22–23
as heir, 211
of intestate decedent, 217–219
interim support of, 219–221
loss of rights by, 225–226
nonjoinders in transfers by, 226
relevance of will to, 211
rights of, in intestate situation,
217–221
as to heirs, 217–219
statutes controlling rights of, 211, 225
statutory share of, 212
support of, 219–221
surviving, rights of, 211–226
of testate decedent, 212–217
trust effect on, 189–190
unscrupulousness of, 189–190,
221–223
will effect on, 211, 212–217
will election by, 212–217
(*See also* Will election)
Standby conservatorship, 62–63
(*See also* Conservatorships)
State gift taxes, 26
Statutory allowance, 220–221
Statutory share under will, 212
(*See also* Will election)
Stepped-up basis, 18
Substitute, 45
(*See also* Powers of attorney)
Succession tax (*see* Inheritance tax)
Surviving spouse, rights of, 211–226

TAMRA (*see* Technical and Miscellaneous
Revenue Act of 1988)
Tangible personal property (*see* Personal
property)
Tax Reform Act of 1986, 130, 267

Tax returns:
for estates, 248
for trusts, 188
Technical and Miscellaneous Revenue Act
of 1988 (TAMRA), 262
Tenancy in common, 31–32
definition of, 308
effect of, 32
explained, 31–32
Tenancy by the entirety, 33–34
definition of, 307
effect of, 33
explained, 33–34
Terminable interest rule, 262
Testament, definition of, 81, 308
(*See also* Wills)
Testamentary gifts, 17
(*See also* Wills)
Testamentary trusts, 89, 138–139
definition of, 131, 138, 308
provisions of, 131
purposes for, 138–139
(*See also* Trusts)
Testate, definition of, 81, 308
(*See also* Wills)
Testator, definition of, 81, 308
(*See also* Wills)
Trading with the Enemy Act of 1917, 121
Treaties with United States as affecting
inheritance, 120–121
Trustees:
code of conduct of, 130
definition of, 129, 308
duties of, 129
fiduciary relationship of, 130, 161
naming of, 130
position of trust of, 161
powers of, 131
(*See also* Avoiding probate; Fiduciaries;
Trusts)
Trustor (*see* Creator)
Trusts, 129–146
advantages of, 184–185
alternatives to, 187
to avoid probate (*see* Avoiding probate)
beneficiaries of:
accounting to, 145
definition of, 129
bypass (*see* Bypass trusts)
cestui que trust, definition of, 129
charitable lead, 136

Trusts (*Cont.*):
 charitable remainder (*see* Charitable
   remainder trusts)
 child protection with, 114, 115, 117–118
 compared with conservatorship and
   power of attorney (*see* Disability)
 costs of, 185–187
 court supervision of, 130, 131, 188
 creator of, definition of, 300
 credit shelter, 108, 140
   (*See also* Bypass trusts)
 death taxes resulting from, 130
 definition of, 129, 308
 description of, 129–130
 disability as reason for, 147–158
 disadvantages of, 185–187
 disinheritance by use of, 189–190
 donor of, definition of, 300
 expense of, 185–187
 funded, 129
 grantor of, definition of, 129, 303
 inheritance under, 189–190
 inter vivos (*see* Living trusts)
 irrevocability of, 132–133
   death tax treatment of, 130
   difficulties with, 145
 legal title to property of, 129, 130
 life estate compared with, 116–117
 life insurance, 136–138
 limitation of period for, 131–132
 living, 132–138
   purposes of, 133
   (*See also* Living trusts)
 marital deduction, 139–143
 multiple uses of, 184–185
 nonmarital, 108
 possession of property of, 129
 powers of trustee, 130
 privacy of, 133, 184
 for probate avoidance (*see* Avoiding
   probate)
 QTIP (*see* Qualified terminable interest
   property)
 reasons for, 130, 144, 145, 154
 recordkeeping of, 188
 relationship to pourover will, 129
 revocability of, 132–133, 179–182
   death tax treatment of, 130
   probate avoidance of, 130
 Rule Against Perpetuities, 131–132
 rule of thumb for, 144–145

Trusts (*Cont.*):
 settlor of (*see* Creator)
 spouse disinheritance by, 189–190
 supervision of, 188–189
 tax advantages of, 130
 tax returns of, 188
 testamentary, 89
   bypass (*see* Bypass trusts)
   credit shelter, 108, 140
   definition of, 138
   QTIP, 142–143
   (*See also* Qualified terminable interest
     property)
   spousal, 142
 title to property of, 129, 130
 trustee of (*see* Trustees)
 trustor (*see* Creator)
 types of, 131
 unfunded, 129
 use in disinheriting spouse, 189–190
 (*See also* Avoiding probate; Trusts to
   avoid probate)
Trusts to avoid probate, 179–191
 as alternative to probate administration,
   176
 alternatives to, 187
 for administration avoidance, 179–191
 advantages of, 184–185
 amending, 192
 benefits of, 183–184, 191–192, 194
 boilerplate clauses in, 181–182
 conflicting goals in, 193–194
 considerations in creating, 183–187
 contesting, 193
 control by grantor in, 192
 costs of, 185–187
 court supervision of, 188
 as cure-all, 190–191
 death of grantor of, 194
 death taxes, effect on, 183
 disadvantages of, 185–187
 drafting of, 180–182
   forms for, 191
   signatures required in, 182
 expense of, 179, 185–187
 form of, 180–182, 191
 gift tax consequences of, 193
 guidance lack in, 188–189
 identification of trustee in, 182
 inconvenience of, 184
 inheritance under, 189–190

Trusts to avoid probate (*Cont.*):
irrevocable, 179–180
kinds of, 179–180
lifetime, 182
matters to be considered in, 183–184
naming the, 181
obstacles to, 186–187
period of, 182
post-mortem planning affected by,
187–188
preparation of, 180–182
reasons for use of, 179, 190–191
recordkeeping in, 188
representations as to, 176
requirements of, 181–182
revocability of, 179–181
savings by use of, 192–193
spendthrift clause in, 181
spouse disinheritance by, 189–190
as substitute for wills, 179
supervision of, 188–189
tax effects of, 192, 193
tax returns of, 188
title transfers into, 182
trustee of, 192–193
bank as, 192–193
death of, 182
grantor as, 182
incompetency of, 182
naming of, 192–193
(*See also* Trustees)
uses of, 184–185
writing requirement of, 181
(*See also* Trusts)

UGMA (*see* Unified Gifts to Minors Act)
Unified credit, 23–24
definition of, 23, 308
as exemption, 23
as gift deterrence, 23
relationship between federal estate and
gift taxes, 23
Uniform Anatomical Gift Law, 91
Uniform Gifts to Minors Act (UGMA), 25
Uniform Premarital Agreement Act, 72, 75,
77
Uniform Probate Code, 111
affidavit under, 233–234
apportionment of death taxes under, 270
definition of, 308–309

Uniform Probate Code (*Cont.*):
fiduciary under, 164
small-estate administration under, 250
spouse dying intestate under, 217, 218
Uniform Simultaneous Death Statute,
41–42, 83
Uniform Statutory Rule Against
Perpetuities, 132
Uniform Transfers to Minors Act (UTMA),
25
Uniform Veterans' Guardianship Act, 67
United States citizen:
gift splitting with, 22
lifetime gifts of, 21, 27
Unlimited marital deduction:
definition of, 309
explained, 139
UTMA (*see* Uniform Transfers to Minors
Act)

Veterans' Administration, 67

Ward under conservatorship, 60
competency of, 63–64
death of, 65
definition of, 309
estate plan of, 65
legal capacity of, 63–64
mental capacity of, 60, 63–64
minor as, 63, 67–68
notice served on proposed, 61
will of:
capacity to make, 64
complying with terms of, 65
disposition of, 65
(*See also* Conservatorships)
Wealth, measurement of, 3
Will election, 212–217
alternate names for, 212
availability of, 216
considerations in making, 212–214,
216–217
determining, 212–214
dower influence on, 213
effect of, 212–216
effect:
on allowance, 224
on community property, 216
on joint tenancy property, 225

Will election (*Cont.*):
  on local real estate owned by
    nonresident, 216
  on nonprobate property, 214–215
  on out-of-state property, 215
  on parties, 217
  illustrations of, 214
  property selection under, 224
  revoking, 224
  statutory procedure for, 212–214
  time limits for, 213
Will substitute, 82–83, 107, 180
Wills, 81–128
  abatement under:
    definition of, 99, 297
    explained, 99–100
  absence of (*see* Inheritance)
  ademption (*see* Ademption)
  advantages of, 85–90
    avoiding bond costs, 87
    avoiding disputes, 87
    avoiding laws of inheritance, 86–87
    choice of beneficiaries, 88
    choice of personal representative, 87–88
    listing small bequests, 88–89
    sales provisions, 89–90
    tax savings, 90
    testamentary trusts, 89
  advocacy of, 81
  and afteradopted children, 97–98
  and afterborn children, 97–98
  aliens as beneficiaries under, 120–121
  amendments to, 82
  anticipating the future in, 92
  antilapse statute affecting, 96–97
  attorney designation in, 119
  attorney-in-fact power to make, 46
  attorney preparation of, 124, 128
  beneficiary under, 94–96
    alien (foreigner) as, 120–121
    alternate, 94, 95
    anticipating prior death of, 94
    choice of, 88
    common accident with, 96
    conditional gift to, 95
    contingent, 94, 95
    definition of, 81–82, 298
    explaining will terms to, 127
    grouping of, 94
    heir distinguished from, 81–82, 86–87,
      228

Wills (*Cont.*):
  identification of, 94
  incompetent as, 94
  minor as, 94
  omission of, 97–98
  prior death of, 123–124
  successor to, 94, 95
  survival period of, 95
  time period for, 95–96
  trust for, 94
  bequests in:
    cash, 93, 128
    conditional, 127
    of money, 93, 128
    of one dollar, 97–98
    residuary, 92
    specific, 92
    suggestions for, 93
    under will, 82
    validity of, 127
  bond of fiduciary in, 87
  burial arrangements in, 84
  capacity to make, 85
  cash bequests in, 93, 128
  changes in (*see* Codicils)
  changing circumstances as affecting, 92
  changing mind subsequent to, 82, 126
  changing residence subsequent to, 124
  "cheap," 37, 82
  child omitted in, 97–98
  choice of form of, 109–112
  codicil to (*see* Codicils)
  common accident clause in, 96
  compared to insurance, 14, 86
  concerns about:
    aliens (foreigners) as beneficiaries,
      120–121
    availability of personal representative,
      124
    change of residency, 124
    disinheriting, 97–98
  conditional bequest in, 127
  conflicts of interest with, 295–296
  conservatorship effect on, 63–64
  considerations in making, 91–92
  consistency of language in, 91
  contents of:
    disclosing for leverage purposes,
      123
    privacy of, 125–126
    revealing, 125–126

Wills (*Cont.*):
  contest of, 85
  control over parties by use of, 117–118
  copies of, 125
    distribution of, 125, 244
  cost of, 125
  counter wills, 109
  death taxes in connection with, 84
  defacing of, 121
  definition of, 81, 309
  devisee in, 82
  disappearance of, 123
  disclosure of, 123, 125–126
  disinheriting in:
    of the child, 97–98
    of the spouse, 221–222
  disposition of, 122
  disputes involving, 87
  distributee in, 82
  divorce effect on, 106
  donation of body, eyes, or organs in, 91
  double wills, 109
  election by surviving spouse, 212–217
    (*See also* Will election)
  and estate planning, 9, 86
  execution of, 103
  executor:
    administrator compared to, 82
    definition of, 82, 301
    refusal or inability to serve as, 124
    (*See also* Personal representatives)
  forced share under, 212
  foreigners as beneficiaries under, 120–121
  form and wording of, 90–91
    the word *child*, 90
    consistency, 91
    effect of statutes and court decisions, 90
    elimination of surplus language, 91
    fractions use in, 93
    funeral arrangements, 91
    the word *heir*, 90
    the word *issue*, 90
    percentage use in, 93
    plain English, 90
    redundancy, 91
    risks in drafting, 90–91
    terminology, 91

Wills (*Cont.*):
  four-month clause, 95
  fraction use in, 93
  funeral arrangements in, 91
  future events, 92
  heirs omitted in, 97–98
  holographic wills, 105
  and household effects, 101
  identification of maker of, 100–101
  "in terrorem" clause in, 119
  information needed for, 107
  informing others of, 123
  inheritance purposes of, 86–87
  intangible personal property in, 88
  intestate comparison to, 81
  introduction to, 81–82
  joint wills, 109–112
    definition of, 110
    distinguished from reciprocal and
      mutual wills, 109–112
    explained, 110, 111
    double and counter wills as alternate
      names for, 109
    undesirability of, 111
  joint tenancy property unaffected by,
    82–83
  language of, 90–91
  lapse of time after making,
    122–123
  legatees in, 82
  life estate in, 116–117
    (*See also* Life estates)
  list separate from, 88–89
    alternatives to, 88–89
  living will (*see* Living wills)
  lost, 123
  marital deduction wills (*see* Marital
    deduction)
  marriage subsequent to making of,
    106
  and married persons:
    effect of marriage, 106
    joint, reciprocal, and mutual wills,
      109–112
    marital deduction (*see* Marital
      deduction)
  and masses, 119
  miscellaneous clauses in, 119–120
  misconceptions concerning, 83–85
  money bequests in, 93
  moving residency as affecting, 124

Wills (*Cont.*):
  mutual wills, 109–112
    as contract, 110, 111
    definition of, 110
    distinguished from joint and reciprocal
      wills, 109–112
    explained, 110–111
    revocation of, 111–112
    tax consequences of, 112
    third-party rights in, 112
    undesirability of, 111, 112
  necessity of probating, 253
  need for, 82–83
  nonprobate property unaffected by, 120,
    178
  nonresident personal representative,
    167
  nontestamentary clauses, 119–120
  notification of, 245
  nuncupative wills, 105–106
  olographic wills, 105
  omitted heirs in, 97–98
  one-dollar bequest in, 97–98
  organ donation in, 91
  parties omitted in, 97–98
  parts of, 100–103
    bequests, 101–102
    debt clause, 101
    introductory clause, 100–101
    personal representative (executor),
      102–103
    procedural clauses, 103
    residuary clause, 102
    revocation clause, 101
    sale clause, 102
    self-proving clause, 103–105
    specific bequests, 101–102
    witnesses, 103–105
  percentages use in, 93
  perpetual care in, 119
  personal effects in, 101
  personal representative in, 87–88,
    102–103
    definition of, 82
    residence requirement of, 167
    refusal or inability to serve as, 124
    (*See also* Personal representatives)
  photocopies of, 125
    signing of, 125
  pick-up clause, 102
  plain English, 90

Wills (*Cont.*):
  postwill treatment:
    copying document, 125
    disposing of property, 122
    locating document, 122
    marking on (defacing) document, 121
  pourover wills, 115–116
  power of attorney authority to make, 46
  predeath of beneficiary, 123–124
  preparation of, 124, 128
  pretermitted children as affected by, 97–98
  privacy of, 123, 133, 184
  probate proceedings (*see* Administration)
  probate property, 120
    definition of, 306
  property of testator of:
    abatement, 99
    ademption, 98
    affected by will, 91–92
    owned at death, 92
    owned at making, 91–92
  protecting the children, 112–115
  proving up, 237, 244
  publicizing contents of, 123
  reasons for, 82–83, 85–90, 121–122
    avoiding bond costs, 87
    avoiding death taxes, 90
    avoiding disputes, 87
    avoiding laws of inheritance, 86–87
    choosing beneficiaries, 88
    choosing personal representative, 87–88
    listing of small bequests, 88
    protecting others, 121–122
    sales provisions, 89–90
    trust provisions, 89
  reciprocal wills, 109–112
    definition of, 110
    distinguished from joint and mutual
      wills, 109–112
    explained, 110, 111
    double and counter wills as alternate
      names for, 109
  residency effect on, 124
    of beneficiary, 120–121, 124
    of personal representative, 103, 167
    of testator, 124
  residuary clause in, 92–93
    definition of, 92
    explanation of, 102
    lack of, 102
    as a pick-up clause, 102

Wills (*Cont.*):
  by Roman Catholics, 119
  sales authorization in, 89–90
    mandatory or discretionary clause in,
      102
  self-preparation of, 126–127
  self-proved wills, 103–105
  "simple" wills, 106–107
  special clauses in, 119–120
    designation of attorney, 119
    "in terrorem," 119
    masses, 119
    perpetual care, 119
  specific bequests, 92
  spouse election under, 212–217
  statutory share under, 212
  substitute wills, 37
  surplus language in, 91
  tangible personal property bequeathed
    in, 88, 89

Wills (*Cont.*):
  testator of:
    capacity of, 85
    definition of, 81
    incompetence of, 85
    understanding terms, 128
    undue influence on, 85
    use of lawyer by, 124
  time to make, 124–125
  titles of parties named in, 101
  two-trust, 142
  trusts in (*see* Bypass trusts; Trusts)
  trusts as substitute for, 179
  undue influence on testator of, 85
  unlimited marital deduction use in, 139
  various forms of, 109–112
  witnesses to, 103–105
  wording of, 90–91

Zero-tax marital deduction formula, 140

About the Author

Theodore L. Kubicek has spent the past 40 years as an attorney specializing in property and probate law. He is a member of the Iowa State Bar Association and of the Real Property, Probate and Trust Law Section of the American Bar Association. A former Fellow of the American College of Probate Counsel and past president of the Linn County Bar Association, Mr. Kubicek is a frequent speaker at legal seminars. His articles have appeared in many legal publications and newspapers.